Readings in English History

Readings in
English History

EDITED BY ARVEL B. ERICKSON
Western Reserve University

AND MARTIN J. HAVRAN
Kent State University

WITH A FOREWORD BY A. L. ROWSE

Charles Scribner's Sons · New York

Printed in the United States of America
Library of Congress Catalog Card Number 67-21338

PERMISSIONS

We wish to make grateful acknowledgment for permission granted by the following to include the selections listed below. Grantors are in alphabetical order, and are also identified in the Source References following each chapter of this book.

Pages v–vi constitute an extension of the copyright page.

D. Appleton & Company, New York: for *Queen Alexandra, A Study of Royalty,* by W. R. H. Trowbridge, 1921.

G. Bell & Sons, Ltd., London: for *The Geography of Strabo,* translated by H. C. Hamilton and W. Falconer, 1906–1913.

The Bodley Head, Ltd., London, and Dodd, Mead & Company, New York: for *The Sayings of Queen Elizabeth,* by Frederick Chamberlin, 1923.

Cambridge University Press, Cambridge: for Sir Thomas Smith, *De Republica; A Discourse on the Commonwealth of England,* edited by Leonard Alston, 1906; and *A Discourse of the Commonweal of this Realm of England,* edited by Elizabeth Lamond, 1929.

Cassell and Company, Ltd., London: for *The Life, Letters and Friendships of Richard Monckton Milnes First Lord Houghton* by Sir T. Wemyss Reid, 1891.

Chatto & Windus, Ltd., London: for *The Paston Letters, A. D. 1422–1509,* edited by James Gairdner, 1904.

The Clarendon Press, Oxford: for *Holinshed's Chronicles of Richard II, 1398–1400, Henry IV and Henry V,* revised by R. S. Wallace and A. Hansen, 1923; for *Voyages of Elizabethan Seamen, Select Narratives from the 'Principle Navigations' of Hakluyt,* edited by Edward J. Payne, 1907; for *Select Statutes and Other Constitutional Documents Illustrative of the Reigns of Elizabeth and James I,* edited by G. W. Prothero, 1894; and for *The Memoirs of Edmund Ludlow, Lieutenant-General of the Horse in* the *Army of the Commonwealth of England, 1625–1672*, edited by C. H. Firth, 1894.

Columbia University Press, New York: for *The Leveller Tracts 1647–1653*, edited by William Haller and Godfrey Davies, 1944.

Peter Davies, Ltd., London: for *Rural Rides in the Southern, Western, and Eastern Counties of England, Together with Tours in Scotland . . . and Letters from Ireland*, edited by G. D. H. Cole and Margaret Cole, 1930.

J. M. Dent & Sons, Ltd., London: for *The Story of Oxford*, by Cecil Headlam, 1907; J. M. Dent & Sons, Ltd. and E. P. Dutton & Company, Inc., New York, and Everyman's Library, New York: for Julius Caesar, *The Gallic War*, translated by John Warrington, 1954.

Doubleday & Company, Inc., New York: for *The Greville Diary Including Passages Hitherto Withheld from Publication*, edited by Philip Whitwell Wilson. Copyright 1927 by Doubleday & Company, Inc. Reprinted by permission of the publisher. Doubleday & Company, Inc. New York; Constable & Company, Ltd., London; David Higham Associates, London: for *An Elizabethan Journal; Being a Record of Those Things Most Talked About During the Years 1591–1594*, edited by George B. Harrison. Copyright 1965 by G. B. Harrison. Reprinted by permission of Doubleday & Company, Inc.

E. P. Dutton & Company, Inc., New York, and John Murray, London: for *Letters of the Prince Consort, 1831–1861*, edited by Kurt Jagow, 1938. Published by E. P. Dutton & Company, Inc., and reprinted with their permission, and by permission of John Murray (Publishers), Ltd., London. For *Parliamentary Reminiscences and Reflections*, by Lord George Hamilton, 1917. Published by E. P. Dutton & Company, Inc., New York, and reprinted with their permission, and by permission of John Murray (Publishers) Ltd., London.

The Economist, London: for *The Economist* (September 4, 1948).

Anne Fremantle: for *This Little Band of Prophets, the British Fabians*, published by New American Library, New York, 1960.

Ginn and Company, Boston: for eight quotations from *Readings in English History* by Edward P. Cheyney.

Harper & Row, New York: for "John: Charter to Ipswich (1200)," from *Gild Merchant*, II, 115f, by C. Gross, in *Sources of English Constitutional History*, edited by Carl Stephenson and Frederick Marcham. Copyright 1937 by Harper & Brothers, New York. Reprinted by permission of Harper & Row, Publishers.

Harvard University Press, Cambridge, Massachusetts: for *The Clubs of Augustan London*, by Robert J. Allen, 1933; and for *The Political Works of James I, With An Introduction by Charles H. McIlwain*, 1918.

Hodder and Stoughton, Ltd., London: for *Letters of John Wesley, A Selection of Important and New Letters with Introduction and Biographical Notes*, by George Eayrs, 1915; for *The Life of Robert Marquis of Salisbury*, by Lady Gwendolyn Cecil, 1924; and Hodder and Stoughton and A. P. Watt & Son, Ltd., London, and Houghton Mifflin Company, Boston, publishers of the American edition: for *The Life of the Right Hon. Sir Henry Campbell-Bannerman*, by J. A. Spender, 1923. Reprinted by permission of Marjorie, Lady Pentland, and the publishers.

Holt, Rinehart and Winston, Inc., New York, and Brown University Press, Providence, Rhode Island: for *The Rise of Universities*, by Charles H. Haskins, 1923. Published by Henry Holt & Company for Brown University Press. Permission granted by Holt, Rinehart and Winston, Inc., New York, and Brown University Press, Providence, Rhode Island.

Keesing's Publications Ltd., London: for reprint from *Keesing's Contemporary Archives*, vol. VI, pp. 7859–7860.

J. B. Lippincott Company, Philadelphia, Pennsylvania: for *Twenty-Five Years, 1892–1916*, by Viscount Grey of Fallodon, 1925.

Longmans, Green & Company, Ltd., London: for *The Annual Register, Or a View of the History, Politics, and Literature for the Year* (1916, 1926 and previous years); for *The Later Correspondence of Lord John Russell*, edited by G. P. Gooch, 1925; and

Longmans, Green & Company, Ltd., London, and Barnes & Noble, Inc., New York: for *Tudor Economic Documents; Being Select Documents Illustrating the Economic and Social History of Tudor England*, edited by R. H. Tawney and Eileen Power, 1924.

Macmillan & Company, Ltd., London: for *Documents Illustrative of English Church History*, edited by Henry Gee and William Hardy, 1896; *Memoirs of Archbishop Temple by Seven Friends*, edited by E. G. Sandford, 1906; and for *The Life of William Ewart Gladstone*, by John Morley.

Manchester University Press, Manchester: for *The Coal Industry of the Eighteenth Century*, by Thomas S. Ashton and Joseph Sykes, 1929.

Methuen & Company, Ltd., London: for *English Diaries. A Review of English Diaries from the Sixteenth Century to the Twentieth Century*, by Arthur Ponsonby, 1923.

John Murray (Publishers) Ltd., London: for *Elizabeth Montague the Queen of the Blue-Stockings Her Correspondence from 1720–1761*, by Emily J. Climenson, 1906; and for *The Autobiography of Edward Gibbon*, edited by John Murray, 1896.

New Statesman, London: for "Advice to Aggressors," in *New Statesman and Nation* (24 September 1938).

Oxford University Press, New York: for *Short Journey*, by E. L. Woodward, 1946.

Putnam's & Coward-McCann, New York, and Raymond Savage, Ltd., Polperro, Cornwall, England: for *Failure of A Mission, Berlin 1937–1939*, by Sir Neville Henderson, 1940. Copyright 1940 by Sir Neville Henderson.

The Royal Society, London: for *The Record of the Royal Society of London for the Promotion of Natural Knowledge*, 1940. Copyright of these passages remains the property of The Royal Society.

Charles Scribner's Sons, New York, and Odhams Books, Ltd., London, publishers of the British edition and proprietors of the copyright: for *My Early Life: A Roving Commission*, by Winston S. Churchill, 1930.

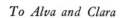

To Alva and Clara

Foreword

Why should Americans study English history?

In the first place, because the roots of representative self-government are to be found in the story of our people in England, and representative self-government is the distinctive characteristic of the English-speaking peoples' development everywhere, the most precious possession they have to contribute to the world. Politically speaking, most countries in the world are very immature and have a lot to learn. Something of what they may learn in constitutional development and social responsibility is exposed, and well illustrated, in this book. It has been a long process of trial and error, and the only way to understand it is historically. That is one of the purposes this book will serve.

It may seem paradoxical, but one reason why self-government developed early in the island-kingdom was because of the strength of a national monarchy in a country small enough to achieve integration. In the bigger continental countries the great independent lords and feudatories had things very much their own way, and there was not much protection or justice for the small man. Not so in England where the king's writ ran and everyone had his rights under the king's law.

All this development was generated and adumbrated in England before ever the colonists crossed the Atlantic. They brought it and its rich potentialities for a self-governing society with them. The Common Law of the English-speaking peoples is part of this development, and another distinguishing characteristic. That is to say, it is not a law imposed from on top—like Roman Civil Law or the Code Napoléon—but coming up from the wellsprings of the people's common life, and part of the same self-governing process.

It all goes back to the Middle Ages, like many other of our institutions—universities, for example—and to the life in the old island. So that the editors of this book are right to cover the medieval period fully, to illustrate the importance of kingship and government, even the personalities of rulers—as important then as they are today—the development of Parliament, the functioning of justice, social institutions.

There are many other reasons for studying English history that we need not go into—there is the sheer interest and variety of the subject. Let us concentrate, rather, on what this book does for us.

It is not only illuminating to have a volume of documents to illustrate the processes of history, it is also indispensable. What are the tests of a good volume of historical documents?

In the first place it should be representative—illustrative of as many aspects of historical development as possible, drawn from a wide span of sources, an extensive reading. Secondly, these sources should be authentic, giving us as close a picture of the event or process under view as possible, as just a view of the person. Thirdly, there should be variety, enabling us to look at the development of the society—the essence of history—from many aspects, constitutional, political, economic, as also social, religious, educational; nor must we neglect the biographical and personal, the individual traits and quirks of character that enter into the story.

This book, in my opinion, passes all these tests not only satisfactorily but admirably. We have to do our homework upon the solid foundation of the laws and statutes, Magna Carta and the Petition of Right, the local regulations concerning wages and prices, health and sanitation. Even in this field we come upon details to spice our interest: it is rather touching to find our Anglo-Saxon forefathers, well over a thousand years ago, rating the loss of front teeth at somebody else's hand at six shillings a tooth, back teeth at just a shilling.

In addition there are all sorts of vivid telling detail. We learn from a contemporary description that the protuberance of William the Conqueror's belly detracted from the majesty of his person; that Elizabeth I was somewhat short-sighted, while her nose rose in the middle. These touches help to bring them before us. There is a wonderful letter of consolation to a father whose son has been killed in battle, written by Oliver Cromwell, which brings *him* before us and presents the stern Puritan in a much more sympathetic and revealing light.

Many of the excerpts are famous in themselves, such as the reception of Augustine and his monks who converted the Old English to Christianity, or Samuel Pepys's description of the Fire of London, Wat Tyler's confrontation of the boy-king Richard II in the Peasants' Revolt, Richard III's murder of the princes in the Tower. Or there are the abdications of kings, from Edward II in the fourteenth century, to Edward VIII in the twentieth century. It is brought home to us how continuous it all is.

There are a good many things that I have come upon for the first time myself—such as Waldegrave's penetrating summing-up of the character of the elder Pitt (after whom Pittsburgh is named, and there is a contemporary statue of him at Charleston, South Carolina). Or there are the statements of English statesmen favourable to the American cause, George III's against; or again, Lord Salisbury's fine tribute to his great opponent, Gladstone.

I end with what was a surprise to me: I have never seen the private song, from the seventeenth century, which the Fellows of All Souls College at Oxford sing at their gaudies, brought into the light of day before. If this book contains surprises and things from which I have learned, I hope it will engage the interest and reward the attention of students in American universities and schools, as well as attract readers in the English-speaking world beyond.

A. L. ROWSE

All Souls College
Oxford University

Preface

This volume is designed primarily for use with any of the existing texts in the college survey course in English history. It is intended, therefore, to serve the undergraduate, not the specialist. We hope that it will be a helpful tool of ready reference to original sources and a few outstanding secondary works as well as a collection of readings for those who might relish an excursion through the rich heritage of British life from the earliest times to the present.

At the moment there is no up-to-date general collection of readings in English history, the last one having been published a generation ago. While these earlier books are excellent, they are no longer adequate because they are largely collections of legal and constitutional documents. The more recent readings books in English history generally include lengthy readings from secondary works and virtually ignore documents. Most students of English history today are not pre-law majors; majors in literature, political science, sociology, marketing and the like are as common in English history classes as budding historians and lawyers. Partly on that account, and partly because we believe the tradition of Great Britain encompasses far more than Parliaments and statutes, we have selected items illustrating the principal economic, social, religious, educational, political, and foreign developments as well as passages describing the leading sovereigns and statesmen. Convinced that the student would enjoy some variety in his intellectual diet, we have often omitted readings on persons, places, and events that are ordinarily described in survey texts. For this reason, readings have been drawn as frequently from diaries, letters, memoirs, and essays as from treaties, laws, and court proceedings.

We have included brief introductory notes to most readings, or to a section of readings. These were kept short because we have assumed that readers will be using survey texts along with this book, and will, therefore, already know the broad background of the periods and issues covered herein. We are convinced, moreover, that most students balk at reading long, unedited passages. Accordingly, we have striven to keep them short and to the point.

The readings have been organized topically, rather than chronologically, within each chapter. Hence, we have grouped them into units dealing with personalities, politics, religion, and economic, military, foreign, and social affairs. In some cases we have modernized spelling, altered punctuation and capitalization, and ignored italics in the sources from which these readings are drawn. In general, however, we have faithfully reproduced the readings as we found them in the sources. If some items should give readers difficulty initially, a good desk dictionary and our glossary should clarify any question. Ellipses indicate the omission of parts of passages and are signified in the usual way by three periods. The information supplied within brackets is either a summary of omitted parts of passages or explanatory material to clarify meaning. The source references to the readings in each chapter will be found at the conclusion to that chapter.

The publishers, Charles Scribner's Sons, have been kind and patient with us. To the members of the College Department, to Professor A. L. Rowse, and to Professor Goldwin Smith we owe thanks for help and advice. We alone, of course, are responsible for any errors which may appear in this book.

A. B. E.

M. J. H.

Contents

xv

CHAPTER THREE

THE LATER MIDDLE AGES (1307–1485)   *43*

CHAPTER EIGHT
THE TWENTIETH CENTURY   *362*

Readings in English History

CHAPTER ONE

Pre-Norman Britain

I. EARLY ACCOUNTS *

A. *Herodotus* (*484–408 B.C.?*) *and* *Aristotle* (*384–322 B.C.?*)

Herodotus and Aristotle were among the first writers to mention specifically the British Isles. The former merely said he knew nothing of the "tin island" (England) except that its metal was brought to the eastern Mediterranean. The latter may have been the first to refer to the islands by name, *if* he was the actual author of *The Universe*, which contains the following description:

In this area [beyond the Straits of Gibraltar] are situated two very large islands, the so-called British Isles, Albion and Ierne, which are greater than any which we have yet mentioned and lie beyond the land of the Celts. . . . There is a large number of small islands round the British Isles and Iberia [Spain], forming a belt round the inhabited world. . . .

B. *Polybius* (*205–123 B.C.?*)

A little over a century later, Polybius, a Greek historian living in Rome, evidences the increasing interest in and knowledge of the British Isles in his

* This book contains readings illustrative of the main developments of English history from early times to the present. The readings have been organized into eight chapters, each chapter covering a major division of English history. While we have followed a chronological sequence in the broad organizational pattern of this book, the readings within each chapter have been grouped topically rather than chronologically. We have grouped the readings topically because we believe this method of organization to be wiser and simpler, and because we wished to assist the student, who will be using this book as a supplement to a survey text in English history, in forming concepts of major trends and developments. Hence the readings have been arranged into units dealing with personalities, politics, religion, and economic, social, foreign, and military affairs. In Chapter Four, "The Tudor Period (1485–1603)," for example, the readings relating to economic affairs of the sixteenth century have been grouped beginning with reading number 113 through number 117, while, in the same chapter, readings illustrative of religious developments have been placed together from number 86 through number 106. To cite another example of the organization of this book, foreign and colonial affairs since 1901 have been grouped in Chapter Eight, "The Twentieth Century," from reading number 353 through number 366.

famous *History*. While chiefly devoted to a discussion of Greek affairs, it contains this reference to the British Isles:

Perhaps indeed some will enquire why, having made so long a discourse concerning places in Lybia and Iberia, we have not spoken more fully of the outlet at the Pillars of Hercules, nor of the exterior sea, and of the peculiarities which occur therein, nor yet indeed of the Bretannic Isles, and the working of tin; nor again, of the gold and silver mines of Iberia; concerning which writers, controverting each other, have discoursed very largely.

2. THE BRITONS AND THEIR WAY OF LIFE

The following description is from the Fourth Book of the *Geography of Strabo,* written by a Greek in the fourth century B.C. who obtained his information from a wide variety of sources, including those from which we have already quoted, and from his own astute observations.

The greatest portion of the island is level and woody, although many tracts are hilly. It produces corn, cattle, gold, silver, and iron, which things are brought thence, and also skins, and slaves, and dogs sagacious in hunting; the Kelts use these, as well as their native dogs, for the purpose of war. The men are taller than the Kelts, with hair less yellow; they are slighter in their persons. As an instance of their height, we ourselves saw at Rome some youths who are taller than the tallest there by as much as half a foot, but their legs were bowed, and in other respects they were not symmetrical in conformation. Their manners are in part like those of the Kelts, though in part more simple and barbarous; insomuch that some of them, though possessing plenty of milk, have not skill enough to make cheese, and are totally unacquainted with horticulture and other matters of husbandry. There are several states amongst them. In their wars they make use of chariots for the most part, as do some of the Kelts. Forests are their cities; for having enclosed an ample space with felled trees, they make themselves huts therein, and lodge their cattle, though not for any long continuance. Their atmosphere is more subject to rain than to snow; even in their clear days the mist continues for a considerable time, insomuch that throughout the whole day the sun is only visible for three or four hours about noon; and this must be the case also . . . among all the neighboring people.

3. ROMAN INVASION OF BRITAIN

Perhaps to satisfy his curiosity about the island across the Channel, and to punish the Celts of Britain for having aided their brethren in Gaul, Julius

Caesar made armed incursions against them in 55 and 54 B.C. In *The Gallic War,* Caesar describes his invasions of Britain in which he successfully penetrated a great part of Kent. He was particularly impressed by the native charioteers:

They begin by driving all over the field, hurling javelins; and the terror inspired by the horses and the noise of the wheels is usually enough to throw the enemy ranks into disorder. Then they work their way between their own cavalry units, where the warriors jump down and fight on foot. Meanwhile the drivers retire a short distance from the fighting and station the cars in such a way that their masters, if outnumbered, have an easy means of retreat to their own lines. In action, therefore, they combine the mobility of mounted troops with the steadiness of infantry. Their skill, which is derived from ceaseless training and practice, may be judged by the fact that they can control their horses at full gallop on the steepest incline, check and turn them in a moment, run along the pole, stand on the yoke, and get back again into the chariot as quick as lightning.

4. THE ROMAN WITHDRAWAL

The Roman occupation of Britain lasted for approximately four hundred years. Then, early in the fifth century, Roman legions withdrew from England to Rome to help protect the Eternal City from invasion by the Goths. More than a century later, a native monk by the name of Gildas wrote a treatise discussing the consequences of the Roman withdrawal.

The Romans, therefore, left the country. . . . No sooner were they gone, than the Picts and Scots, like worms which in the heat of mid-day come forth from their holes, hastily land again from their canoes, in which they had been carried beyond the Cichican valley, differing one from another in manners, but inspired with the same avidity for blood, and all more eager to shroud their villainous faces in bushy hair than to cover with decent clothes those parts of the body which required it. Moreover, having heard of the departure of our friends, and their resolution never to return, they seized with greater boldness than before on all the country towards the extreme north as far as the wall [Hadrian's Wall, begun probably in 122]. To oppose them there was placed on the heights a garrison equally slow to fight and ill-adapted to run away, a useless and panic-struck company, who slumbered away days and nights on their unprofitable watch. Meanwhile the hooked weapons of their enemies were not idle, and our wretched countrymen were dragged from the wall and dashed against the ground. . . . They left their cities, abandoned the protection of the wall, and dispersed themselves in flight, more desperately than before. The enemy, on the other hand, pursued them with more unrelenting cruelty than before, and butchered our countrymen like sheep, so that their habitations were like those of savage beasts; for they turned their arms upon each other, and for the sake of a little sustenance, imbrued their hands in the blood of their fellow-countrymen. Thus foreign calamities were augmented by domestic feuds; so that the whole country was entirely destitute of provisions, save such as could be procured in the chase.

5. THE COMING OF CHRISTIANITY

The principles introduced by Christian missionaries and their converts, the first of whom adopted the new religion probably in the early third century, helped to stabilize the turmoil and moderate the barbarity caused by the Roman withdrawal and the invasions by Picts, Scots, and Anglo-Saxons. Roman Christianity prospered particularly under the inspired leadership of Augustine (d. 604) and his Benedictine companions, as Bede's account in the *Ecclesiastical History of England* reveals.

Augustine, thus strengthened by the confirmation of the blessed Father Gregory, returned to the work of the word of God, with the servants of Christ, and arrived in Britain. The powerful Ethelbert was at that time King of Kent; he had extended his dominions as far as the great river Humber, by which the Southern Saxons are divided from the Northern. On the east of Kent is the large Isle of Thanet containing according to the English way of reckoning, 600 families, divided from the other land by the river Wantsum, which is about three furlongs over, and fordable only in two places, for both ends of it run into the sea. In this island landed the servant of our Lord, Augustine, and his companions, being, as is reported, nearly forty men. They had, by order of the blessed Pope Gregory, taken interpreters of the nation of the Franks, and sending to Ethelbert, signified that they had come from Rome, and brought a joyful message, which most undoubtedly assured to all that took advantage of it everlasting joys in heaven, and a kingdom that would never end, with the living and true God. The king having heard this, ordered them to stay in that island where they had landed, and that they should be furnished with all necessaries, till he should consider what to do with them. For he had before heard of the Christian religion, having a Christian wife of the royal family of the Franks, called Bertha; whom he had received from her parents, upon condition that she should be permitted to practice her religion with the Bishop Luidhard, who was sent with her to preserve her faith. Some days after, the king came into the island, and sitting in the open air, ordered Augustine and his companions to be brought into his presence. For he had taken precaution that they should not come to him in any house, lest, according to an ancient superstition, if they practiced any magical arts, they might impose upon him, and so get the better of him. But they came furnished with Divine, not with magic virtue, bearing a silver cross for their banner, and the image of our Lord and Saviour painted on a board; and singing the litany, they offered up their prayers to the Lord for the eternal salvation both of themselves and of those to whom they were come. When he had sat down, pursuant to the king's commands, and preached to him and his attendants there present, the word of life, the king answered thus:-'Your words and promises are very fair, but as they are new to us, and of uncertain import, I cannot approve of them so far as to forsake that which I have so long followed with the whole English nation. But because you have come from far into my kingdom, and as I conceive, you are desirous to impart to us those things which you believe to be true, and most beneficial, we will not molest you, but give you favourable entertainment, and take care to supply you with your necessary sustenance, nor do we forbid you to preach and gain as many as you can to your religion.' Accordingly he permitted them to reside in the city of Canterbury, which was the metropolis of all his dominions, and, pursuant to his promise, besides allowing them sustenance, did not refuse them liberty to preach. It is reported that, as they drew near the city, after their manner, with the holy cross, and the image of our sovereign Lord and King, Jesus Christ, they, in concert, sung this litany: 'We beseech thee, O Lord, in all thy mercy, that thy anger and wrath be turned away from this city, and from thy holy house, because we have sinned, Hallelujah.'

6. EARLY ANGLO-SAXON LAWS

Early Anglo-Saxon laws were Germanic, not Roman, in origin. Laws and legal procedures were not uniform throughout the land and changed substantially as centuries passed. The procedure followed in the local courts was complex. The plaintiff had to make a formal accusation, the defendant a formal denial of guilt. In general, once a person's guilt was determined by the judgment of his neighbors, he was punished for injuries less than death by being compelled to make a money payment to the family of the injured party (called a "bot"), and by a fine to the state (called a "wite"). Every person of freeman status had a money valuation known as the "wergeld," and if he was killed the guilty party had to pay to his family the wergeld stipulated by law. The amounts were based on one's rank in society. Hence, a king's wergeld was 30,000 shillings, an archbishop's and an atheling's, 15,000, a bishop's and an earldorman's, 8,000. In all trials a very important role was assigned to oath-taking. The Anglo-Saxons put great stress on the oath, for a person spoke it in the presence of his neighbors who knew him well, and in the presence of the omniscient God who took vengeance on all sinners.

Once plaintiff and defendant were before the local court, the plaintiff swore to the truth of his charges; the defendant took an oath in rebuttal. The court then decided which party had to prove his case in the following session of the court. Sometimes the parties could do this by producing witnesses (compurgators) willing to swear, not to the justice of their principal's case, but simply that they believed he was truthful. (Truth-telling was a highly esteemed virtue among the Anglo-Saxons.) The number of compurgators required varied from six to twenty-four depending on the seriousness of the charge, and on rank.

Those accused of serious crimes were permitted to take the ordeals—a kind of appeal to the God of nature. Chief of these were the ordeal by water and by fire.

A. *Laws of King Ethelbert* (560?–616)

If a freeman steal from the king, let him pay nine-fold. . . .

If a freeman steal from a freeman, let him make three-fold 'bot'; and let the king have the 'wite' and all the chattels. . . .

If a man slay another, let him pay with his own money, and with any sound property whatever. . . .

If a shoulder be lamed, let 'bot' be made with xxx. shillings. . . .

If an ear be struck off, let 'bot' be made with xii. shillings. . . .

If an eye be struck out, let 'bot' be made with L. [fifty] shillings. . . .

Let him who breaks the chin-bone pay for it with xx. shillings. . . .

For each of the four front teeth, vi. shillings; for the tooth which stands next to them iv. shillings; for that which stands next to that, iii. shillings; and then afterwards, for each a shilling. . . .

If a thumb be struck off, xx. shillings. . . . If the shooting finger be struck off, let 'bot' be made with vii. shillings. If the middle finger be struck off, let 'bot' be made with iv. shillings. . . .

For every nail a shilling. . . .

If anyone strike another with his fist on the nose, iii. shillings. . . .

If a foot be cut off, let L. shillings be paid. If a great toe be cut off, let x. shillings be paid. For each of the other toes, let one half be paid like as is stated for fingers.

B. *Laws of the West Saxon King Ine* (688–726) *on Wood-Burning*

When anyone burns a tree in a wood, and it be found out against him who did it, let him pay the full 'wite'; let him give ix. shillings, because fire is a thief. If anyone fell in a wood a good many trees, and it be afterwards discovered; let him pay for iii. trees, each with xxx. shillings. He need not pay for more of them, were there as many of them as might be; because the axe is an informer, not a thief.

C. *Oath-taking of a Plaintiff*

By the Lord, I accuse not N. either of hatred or for envy, or for unlawful lust of gain; nor know I any thing soother; but as my informant to me said, and I myself in sooth believe, that he was the thief of my property.

D. *Oath of the Defendant*

By the Lord, I am guiltless, both in deed and counsel, of the charge of which N. accuses me.

E. *Compurgator's Oath*

By the Lord, the oath is clean and unperjured which N. has sworn.

F. *Trial by Ordeal*

And concerning the ordeal we enjoin by command of God, and of the archbishop, and of all bishops: that no man come within the Church after the fire is borne in with which the ordeal shall be heated, except the mass-priest, and with him who shall go thereto: and let there be measured nine feet from the stake to the mark, by the man's feet who goes thereto. But if it be water, let it be heated till it low to boiling. And be the kettle of iron or of brass, of lead or of clay. And if it be a single accusation, let the hand dive after the stone up to the wrist; and if it be three-fold, up to the elbow. And when the ordeal is ready, then let two men go in of either side; and be they agreed that it is so hot as we before have said. And let go in an equal number of men of either side, and stand on both sides of the ordeal, along the church; and let these all be fasting, and abstinent from their wives on that night; and let the mass-priest sprinkle holy water over them all, and let each of them taste of the holy water, and give them all the book and image of Christ's rood to kiss: and let no man mend the fire any longer when the hallowing is begun; but let the iron lie upon the 'stapela'; and let there be no other speaking within, except that they earnestly pray to Almighty God that he make

manifest what is soothest. And let him go thereto; and let his hand be enveloped, and be it postponed till after the third day, whether it be foul or
clean within the envelope. And he who shall break this law, be the ordeal
with respect to him void, and let him pay to the king cxx. [120] shillings as
'wite'.

7. ANGLES' AND SAXONS' SYSTEM OF LAND USAGE

> While the Anglo-Saxons were basically hunters and fishers and fierce war-
> riors inured to fatigue and hardship, it is their system of land usage which
> is most interesting. Julius Caesar (102–44 B.C.) describes it in his *Com-
> mentaries* in these words:

They do not pay much attention to agriculture, and a large portion of
their food consists in milk, cheese, and flesh; nor has anyone a fixed quantity
of land or his own individual limits; but the . . . leading men each year ap-
portion to the tribes and families, who have united together, as much land
as, and in the place in which, they think proper, and the year after compel
them to move elsewhere. For this enactment they advance many reasons—
lest seduced by long-continued custom, they may exchange their ardour in
the waging of war for agriculture; lest they may be anxious to acquire extensive estates, and the more powerful drive the weaker from their possessions;
lest they construct their houses with too great a desire to avoid heat and
cold; lest the desire of wealth spring up, from which cause divisions and discords arise; and that they may keep the common people in a contented state
of mind, when each sees his own means placed on an equality with those of
the most powerful.

8. THE COMING OF THE DANES

> At the end of the eighth century the Danes began their invasions of Eng-
> land, which lasted for almost three centuries. The greatest English leader
> during these centuries was King Alfred; the greatest of the Danes was
> King Cnut (also Knut or Canute). Alfred spent most of his reign (871–
> 899) in fighting against the Danes. After one of his successful battles, he
> negotiated the Treaty of Chippenham (often called Wedmore):

This is the peace that King Alfred, and King Guthrum, and the witan
of all the English nation, and all the people that are in East Anglia ordained,
and have sworn to, as well as for themselves as for their offspring.

1. First, concerning our land-boundries: along the Thames, and then
up on the Lea, and along the Lea unto its source, then right to Bedford, then
up on the Ouse unto Watling-Street.

2. And they ordained: if a man be slain, we estimate all equally dear, English and Danish, at viii. half-marks of pure gold; except the 'Ceorl' who resides upon 'gafol-land,' and their 'liesings:' they are also equally dear, either at cc. [200] shillings. . . .

9. LAWS OF KING CNUT (1017–1035)

In 1017 King Cnut became master of all England and later ruled Denmark and Norway as well. The following extracts from his laws reveal much about him, the Church, churchmen, and about eleventh-century English customs.

This is the ordinance that King Cnut . . . decreed, with the counsel of his witan to the praise of God, and to the honour and behoof of himself: and that was at the holy tide of Mid-winter at Winchester.

That then is first, that, above all other things, they should ever love and worship one God, and unanimously observe one Christianity, and love King Cnut with strict fidelity. . . .

And we will, that men of every order readily submit, each to that law which is becoming to him; and above all, let the servants of God, bishops and abbots, monks and mynchens, canons and nuns, submit to law, and live according to rule, and by day and by night . . . call to Christ, and fervently intercede for all Christian people. . . .

And Sunday marketing we also strictly forbid, and every folkmoot, unless it be for great necessity: and let huntings and all other worldly works be strictly abstained from on that holy day. . . .

And we instruct, that every one ever guard himself against foul lasciviousness, and against fornication, and against every kind of adultery.

And we also earnestly instruct every man, that he constantly have the dread of God in his mind, and, by day and by night, that he fear for sins, dread doomes-day, and shudder for hell, and ever suppose the end of his day near to him. . . .

And we command, that ye undertake diligently to cleanse the country on every side, and every where to desist from evil deeds: and if witches or diviners, 'morth-workers' or adulteresses, be any where found in the land, let them be diligently driven out of this country; or let them totally perish in the country, except they desist and the more thoroughly amend. . . .

Let manslayers and perjurers, violators of holy orders and adulterers, submit and make 'bot'; or with their sins retire from the country.

Let cheats and liars, robbers and reavers, have God's anger unless they desist, and the more thoroughly amend. . . .

And we will, that every man above twelve years make oath that he will neither be a thief nor cognizant of theft. . . .

And let no man buy anything above the value of four pence, either living or lying, unless he have the true witness of four men, be it within a 'burh,' be it up in the country. . . .

If during her husband's life, a woman lie with another man, and it become public, let her afterwards be for a worldly shame as regards herself, and let her lawful husband have all that she possessed; and let her then forfeit both nose and ears. . . .

If any one fight in the king's household, let him forfeit his life, unless the king will be merciful to him. . . .

And I will that every man be entitled to his hunting, in wood and in field on his own possession. And let every one forego my hunting: take notice where I will have it untrespassed on, under penalty of full 'wite'. . . .

May God Almighty have mercy on us all, as his will may be, and preserve us ever to all eternity. So be it. Amen.

SOURCE REFERENCES   *Chapter One*

1. A. Aristotle, *De Mundo*, 3, 393b 10-19, in *The Works of Aristotle,* ed. by W. D. Ross; trans. by E. S. Forster. Oxford: Clarendon Press, 1931.
   B. *Source Book of English History,* ed. by Guy C. Lee, p. 66. New York: Henry Holt, 1900.
2. *The Geography of Strabo,* trans. by H. C. Hamilton and W. Falconer, I, 297–298. London: G. Bell and Sons, 1912.
3. Caesar, Julius, *The Gallic War,* trans. by John Warrington, p. 103. Verona: Printed for the Limited Editions Club of Officina Bodoni, 1954.
4. *The Works of Gildas,* in *Six Old English Chronicles,* ed. by J. A. Giles, pp. 306–307. London: Henry G. Bohn, 1848.
5. *Bede's Ecclesiastical History of England,* ed. by J. A. Giles, Book I, c. 25. London: G. Bell and Sons, 1900.
6. *Ancient Laws and Institutes of England,* ed. by Benjamin Thorpe, I, 2–25, *passim;* 129; 181; 227–229. London: n.p., 1840.
7. *Commentaries of Caesar,* in Lee, *Source Book of English History,* p. 79.
8. *Ancient Laws and Institutes of England,* I, 153–154.
9. *Ancient Laws and Institutes of England,* I, 359–425, *passim.*

CHAPTER TWO

The Early Middle Ages
(1066-1307)

In 1066 William, Duke of Normandy, defeated Harold of Wessex and the witan at once proclaimed him king of England. The conquest accelerated the introduction into England of European constitutional, religious, economic, and cultural ideas. Perhaps the chief political effect was that it gave England a succession of able kings who successfully centralized the administration of the country.

10. DESCRIPTION OF WILLIAM THE CONQUEROR (1066–1087)

He was of just stature, extraordinary corpulence, fierce countenance; his forehead bare of hair: of such great strength of arm, that it was often matter of surprise, that no one was able to draw his bow, which himself could bend when his horse was on full gallop: he was majestic, whether sitting or standing, although the protuberance of his belly deformed his royal person: of excellent health, so that he was never confined with any dangerous disorder, except at the last: so given to the pleasures of the chase, that, as I have before said, ejecting the inhabitants, he let a space of many miles grow desolate, that, when at liberty from other avocations, he might there pursue his pleasures. He gave sumptuous and splendid entertainments, at the principal festivals. . . . At these times a royal edict summoned thither all the principal persons of every order, that the ambassadors from foreign nations might admire the splendour of the assemblage, and the costliness of the banquets. Nor was he at any time more affable or indulgent; in order that the visitants might proclaim universally, that his generosity kept pace with his riches. This mode of banqueting was constantly observed by his first successor; the second omitted it.

His anxiety for money is the only thing for which he can deservedly be blamed. This he sought all opportunities of scraping together, he cared not how; he would say and do some things, and, indeed, almost any thing, unbecoming such great majesty, where the hope of money allured him. . . .

11. SUMMONS TO MILITARY SERVICE

To effect a strong and efficient government, the Norman kings established the feudal political system used on the Continent. It was a system of personal relationships between a lord and his vassals. The former was obligated to protect his vassals who, in turn, had to render many services to their lord. Among these services was that of providing military service when summoned to do so. The following summons was issued by William I in 1072.

William, King of the English, to Aethelwig, abbot of Evesham, greeting. I command you to summon all those who are under your charge and administration that they shall have ready before me at Clarendon on the octave of Pentecost all the knights that they owe me. Come to me likewise yourself on that day, and bring ready with you those five knights that you owe me from your abbey.

Witness, Eudo the Steward. At Winchester.

12. FEUDAL RELIEFS

In addition to compulsory military service, vassals owed their lords certain "reliefs." When a vassal, as heir, succeeded to the fief, he paid a relief. Having done so, he gained the use of the land (the fief), the duty to perform homage, and to swear fealty to his lord. The following is an example of reliefs to be paid a feudal lord.

The relief of an earl, which comes to the king, is eight horses, of which four shall have saddles and bridles, and along with them four breastplates, four helmets, four lances, four shields, and four swords; and the other four horses are to be riding horses or hunting horses, with bridles and coverings.

The relief of a baron is four horses, of which two are to have saddles and bridles, and with them two breastplates, two shields, two helmets, two lances, and two swords; and of the other two horses one shall be a riding horse, the other a hunter, with bridles and coverings.

The relief of a vassal, which comes to his liege lord, is the horse of his father, such as he had it on the day of his death, and a breastplate, helmet, shield, lance, and sword. If perchance he did not have these, he shall be able to acquit himself of it by paying a hundred shillings.

The relief of a villein is his best beast; whether it is an ox or a horse, it shall be his lords.

He who holds the land for a yearly payment, his relief shall be as much as the payment of one year.

13. DOMESDAY BOOK

In order to know precisely what resources were at his disposal, William I sent royal commissioners into every English county to make a survey of all the manors. They were to record the names of owners of manors in the time of King Edward the Confessor and at the time of the inquest. The record was to show the number of hides and ploughs each manor contained, the number of all classes of people, the number of mills and ponds, the amount of meadow and forest, its value in 1066 and in 1086. The result was the famous Domesday Book. The nature of the survey is revealed in this extract:

Peter de Valence holds in domain Hecham, which Haldane a freeman held in the time of King Edward, as a manor, and as 5 hides. There have always been 2 ploughs in the demesne, 4 ploughs of the men. At that time there were 8 villeins, now 10; then there were 2 bordars, now 3; at both times 4 servi, woods for 300 swine, 18 acres of meadow. Then there were 2 fish ponds and a half, now there are none. At that time there was 1 ox, now there are 15 cattle and 1 small horse and 18 swine and 2 hives of bees. At that time it was worth 60s., now £4 10s. When he received this manor he found only 1 ox and 1 planted acre. Of those 5 hides spoken of above, one was held in the time of King Edward by 2 freemen, and was added to this manor in the time of King William. It was worth in the time of King Edward 10s., now 22s., and William holds this from Peter de Valence.

14. CHARACTER AND APPEARANCE OF WILLIAM II (1087-1100)

William I left three sons, Robert, William, and Henry, and a daughter, Adela, the wife of Count Stephen of Blois. The two older sons divided the Conqueror's domain, England for William and Normandy for Robert. Henry later inherited the English throne. William Rufus, whose nickname was prompted by his shock of red hair, was vengeful, devoid of compassion, vulgar, and greedy.

Greatness of soul was pre-eminent in the king, which, in process of time, he obscured by excessive severity; vices, indeed, in place of virtues, so insensibly crept into his bosom, that he could not distinguish them. . . . I may be allowed, with permission of the royal majesty, not to conceal the truth;

for he feared God but little, man not at all. . . . From apprehension of poverty, and of the treachery of others, . . . he was too much given to lucre, and to cruelty. . . . He was a man who knew not how to take off from the price of any thing, or to judge of the value of goods; but the trader might sell him his commodity at whatever rate, or the soldier demand any pay he pleased. He was anxious that the cost of his clothes should be extravagant, and angry if they were purchased at a low price. One morning, indeed, while putting on his new boots, he asked his chamberlain what they cost; and when he replied, "Three shillings," indignantly and in a rage he cried out, "You son of a whore, how long has the king worn boots of so paltry a price? . . . bring me a pair worth a mark of silver." He went, and bringing him a much cheaper pair, told him, falsely, that they cost as much as he had ordered: "Aye," said the king, "these are suitable to your royal majesty. . . ."

15. KING HENRY I (1100–1135)

> Henry I was one of the greatest of the Normans. The sternness, yet fairness, with which he settled disputes and subdued the turbulent barons, earned for him the title "Lion of Justice." A chronicler has left the following evaluation of the king, and the manner of his death and burial.

He was a person tall and strong, broad breasted, his limbes well knit, and fully furnished with flesh; his face well fashioned, his colour cleare, his eyes large and faire, his eye-browes large and thick, his haire black, and somewhat thinne towards his forehead; his countenance pleasant, specially when he was disposed to mirth. A private man, vilified, and thought to have but little in him: but come to the Crowne, never any man shewed more excellent abilities: so true is the saying, *Magistratus indicat virum.* His natural affection in a direct line was strong; in an oblique, but weake; for no man ever loved children more, nor a brother lesse. Though a King in act, yet he alwayes acted not a King; but in battels sometimes the part of a common Souldier, though with more than common valour. . . . A discontent of minde upon some differences between him and his sonne-in-law, the Earle of Anjou, brought upon him a distemper, which encreased by eating, against his Physicians advice, of a Lamprey; a meate always pleasing to him, but never agreeing with him; cast him into a Feaver, which in few dayes put a period to his life . . . though some write he tooke his death by the fall off his horse. . . . His bowels, braines, and eyes, were buried at Roan in Normandy where he died: the rest of his body was stuffed with Salt, wrapped in Oxe hides, and brought over into England, and with honourable Exequies, buried in the Monastery of Reading, which himselfe had Founded. His

Physician that tooke out his braines, with the intolerable stinch shortly after died. . . .

16. AGREEMENT ON INVESTITURE (1107)

The feudalization of the Church involved it in a protracted and acrimonious dispute with the crown over the question of who had authority to invest a bishop with his lay and spiritual symbols of office. Henry I and Anselm, Archbishop of Canterbury, reached the following compromise:

On the first of August an assemblage of bishops, abbots, and nobles of the realm was held at London in the king's palace. And for three successive days, in Anselm's absence, the matter was thoroughly discussed between king and bishops concerning church investitures, . . . Afterward, in the presence of Anselm and a large concourse, the king agreed and ordained that henceforward no one should be invested with bishopric or abbacy in England by the giving of a pastoral staff or the ring, by the king or any lay hand; Anselm also agreeing that no one elected to a prelacy should be deprived of consecration to the office undertaken on the ground of homage, which he should make to the king. After this decision, by the advice of Anselm and the nobles of the realm, bishops were appointed by the king, without any investiture of pastoral staff or ring, to nearly all the churches of England which had been so long widowed of their shepherds.

17. CHARACTER OF HENRY II (1154-1189)

The firm establishment of a regularized system of law and justice, and of court procedures, was the greatest achievement of Henry II. A chronicler extols the king in these words:

He was somewhat red of face, and broad breasted; short of body, and therewithal fat, which made him use much Exercise, and little meate. He was commonly called Henry Shortmantell, because he was the first that brought the use of short Cloakes out of Anjou into England. Concerning endowments of mind, he was of a Spirit in the highest degree Generous; which made him often say, that all the World sufficed not to a Courageous heart. He had the reputation of a wise Prince all the Christian World over. . . . His Custom was to be always in Action; for which cause, if he had no Reall Warres, he would have Faigned: and would transport Forces either into Normandy or Britaine, and goe with them himselfe, whereby he was alwayes prepared of an Army: and made it a Schooling to his Souldiers, and to himselfe an Exercise. To his Children he was both indulgent and hard: for out of indulgence he caused his Son Henry to be Crowned King in his owne time; and out of hardnesse he caused his younger Sonnes to Rebell against him. He was rather Superstitious, then not Religious; which he showed more by his carriage toward Becket being dead then while he lived. His incontinency was not so much that he used other Women besides his Wife, but that he used the affianced Wife of his owne Son: And it was commonly thought, he had a meaning to be divorced from his Wife Queene Eleanor, and to take the said Adela to be his Wife. Yet generally to speake of him, he was an excellent Prince. . . .

18. THE MARTYRDOM OF THOMAS BECKET

On Christmas day [1170], the archbishop of Canterbury mounted the pulpit to deliver a sermon to the people, which when he had finished, he excommunicated Nigel de Sackville, who had violently seized on the church of Herges, and the vicar of the same church Robert de Broc, who, in derision of the archbishop had maimed one of his horses loaded with provisions. After this, on the fifth day from Christmas-day, about the hour of vespers, as the archbishop was sitting with his clerks in his chamber, William de Tracy, Reginald Fitz-Urse, Hugh de Morville, and Richard Briton, coming from Normandy, burst into the room, as if impelled by madness, and commanded him, in the king's name, to restore the suspended bishops and absolve those whom he had excommunicated. To this the bishop answered that an inferior judge could not absolve from the sentence of his superior, and that no man could annul a decision of the apostolic see: if, however, the bishops of London and Salisbury and the other excommunicated persons would swear to comply with his mandate, he would, for the peace of the church and out of regard to the king, consent to absolve them. The men glowing with anger, and in haste to carry into effect what they had conceived, departed with violence; whilst the archbishop, by the advice of his clerks, and because the hour of vespers was at hand, entered the church for service. The four ministers of evil meanwhile had put on their armour, and following close upon the archbishop, found that the doors had been by his orders left open behind him. "For," said he, "the church of God should be open as a place of refuge to all men; let us not therefore convert it into a castle." The multitude now began to run together on all sides, and the four men irreverently entering the church, cried out, "Where is this traitor to his king?—where is the archbishop?" He, hearing himself called, turned back to meet them; for he had already mounted three or four steps of the presbytery, and said to them, "If you seek the archbishop, here he stands." Upon which they used harsh language towards him, mixed with threats. "I am ready to die," said he, "for I prefer the maintenance of justice and the liberties of the church to my own life; but these my adherents have done nothing for which they should be punished." The murderers now rushed on him with drawn swords, and he fell muttering these words, "To God and St. Mary, the patrons of this church, and to St. Dennis, I commend my soul and the cause of the church!" Thus was slain this glorious martyr before the altar of St. Benedict, by a wound received in that part of the body where he had formerly received the holy oil which consecrated him to the Lord; nor were they content to pollute the church with the blood of a priest and to profane that holy day, but they also cut off the crown of his skull, and with blood-stained swords scattered his brains over the pavement of the church.

19. THE KING'S HOUSEHOLD

Administration of government in medieval England rested primarily in the hands of the king and the members of his household, comprising a feudal court called the *curia regis*. The king relied upon its members to perform the day-to-day business of government. Its composition and the perquisites of some officials were as follows:

The Chancellor.

Five shillings daily and one royal simnel, and two [of dripping,] and one sextary of clear wine, and one sextary of household wine, and one wax-candle and forty candle-ends.

The Master of the Scriptorium.

Formerly tenpence daily, and one simnel [of dripping], and half a sextary of household wine, and one thick candle and twelve candle-ends. But King Henry increased Robert de Sigillo by so much, that on the day of the king's death he had two shillings, and one sextary of household wine, and one simnel [of dripping], and one taper and twenty-four candle-ends.

The Chaplain, Keeper of the Chapel and Relics.

The entertainment of two men and four serjeants of the Chapel, each a double ration; and two sumpter horses of the Chapel, each one penny daily and one penny to shoe them monthly. For the service of the Chapel, two wax-candles on Wednesday and two on Saturday; and every night one wax-candle at the Relics, and thirty candle-ends; and one gallon of clear wine at mass and one sextary of household wine on the Day of Absolution, to wash the altar. On Easter Day, at Communion, one sextary of clear wine and one of household wine.

The Clerk of the household bread and wine.

Two shillings daily, and simnel [of dripping], and one sextary of household wine, and one taper and twenty-four candle-ends.

Of the Stewards of the bread.

The regular Master Steward of the bread, if he shall eat without the king's house, two shillings and tenpence daily, and one simnel [of dripping], and one sextary of household wine, and candles fully.

Of the Sewers.

The Sewers the same as the Chancellor, if they shall eat without the house; if within, three shillings and sixpence, and two simnels [of dripping], and one sextary of household wine and candles fully.

Of the Stewards serving in turn.

If without the house, nineteen pence daily, and one simnel [of dripping], and one sextary of household wine, and one thick candle and twenty candle-ends. If within, tenpence and half a sextary of household wine and candles fully.

Of the Naperers.

The Naperer, the customary ration. To his man, three half-pence daily, and one penny for a sumpter-horse, and one penny monthly to shoe him.

The Usher of the Dispensary.

The same, the sumpter-horse excepted.

The Counter of the Bread.

The customary ration.

Of the four Bakers serving together in their turn.

Two who serve in the house shall eat in the house; and two who go abroad shall have forty pence to procure a measure of Rouen for which they should render forty royal simnels and a hundred and fifty [of dripping] and two hundred and seventy baker's loaves. A royal simnel to four, one [of dripping] to two, and a loaf to each.

Of the Waferers.

The Waferer, the customary ration; and three half-pence to his man daily.

The Keeper of the Tables.

So much as the above; and besides this a sumpter-horse with his allowance.

The bearer of the Alms-dish shall eat in the house.

Of the Stewards of the Larder.

The Master Steward of the Larder, the same as the Master Steward of the bread and wine, and in the same manner.

Likewise the Stewards of the Larder serving in turn, like also as the stewards of the bread and wine serve in turn. The Larderers who serve in turn, the customary ration, and their man three half-pence daily. The Usher of the Larder the same. The Slaughtermen the customary ration only. . . .

20. THE ASSIZE OF CLARENDON (1166)

To assure the repression of crime, security of life and property, and by improving the administration of justice to increase royal revenues, Henry II and his advisers promulgated many assizes. The term "assize" meant the sitting of a court or assembly, and from that definition the term was applied to the actions taken by such a court or assembly. One of the most important was the Assize of Clarendon.

Here begins the Assize of Clarendon, made by King Henry II, with the assent of the archbishops, bishops, abbots, earls, and barons of all England.

1. In the first place, the aforesaid King Henry, with the consent of all his barons, for the preservation of the peace and the keeping of justice, has enacted that inquiry should be made through the several counties and through the several hundreds, by twelve of the more legal men of the hundred and by four of the more legal men of each manor, upon their oath that they will tell the truth, whether there is in their hundred or in their manor any man who has been accused or publicly suspected of himself being a robber, or murderer, or thief, or of being a receiver of robbers, or murderers, or thieves, since the lord king has been king. And let the justices make this inquiry before themselves, and the sheriffs before themselves.

2. And let any one who has been found by the oath of the aforesaid to have been accused or publicly suspected of having been a robber, or murderer, or thief, or a receiver of them, since the lord king has been king, be arrested and go to the ordeal of water, and let him swear that he has not been a robber, or murderer, or thief, or receiver of them since the lord king has been king, to the value of five shillings, so far as he knows. . . .

12. And if any one is captured who has in his possession the fruits of robbery or theft, if he is of bad reputation and has an evil testimony from the public, and has not a warrant, let him not have law. And if he shall not have been accused on account of the possession which he has, let him go to the water. . . .

14. The lord king wills, moreover, that those who make their law and shall be absolved by the law, if they are of very bad testimony, and publicly and disgracefully spoken ill of by the testimony of many and legal men, shall abjure the lands of the king, so that within eight days they shall go over the sea, unless the wind shall have detained them; and with the first wind which they shall have afterward they shall go over the sea, and they shall not afterward return into England, except on the permission of the lord king; and then let them be outlaws if they return, and if they return they shall be seized as outlaws.

15. And the lord king forbids any vagabond—that is, a wandering or an unknown man—to be sheltered anywhere except in a borough, and even there he shall be sheltered only one night, unless he shall be sick there, or his horse, so that he is able to show an evident excuse.

16. And if he shall have been there more than one night, let him be arrested and held until his lord shall come to give securities for him, or until he himself shall have secured pledges; and let him likewise be arrested who has sheltered him.

21. THE ASSIZE OF ARMS (1181)

This assize reveals how confident Henry II was of his own position and the degree to which he trusted his subjects to keep the peace.

1. Whoever holds one knight's fee shall have a coat of mail, a helmet, a shield, and a lance; and every knight shall have as many coats of mail and helmets and shields and lances as he has knight's fees in his demesne.

2. Every free layman who has goods or rent to the value of sixteen marks shall have a coat of mail, a helmet, a shield, and a lance; every free layman who has in goods or rents ten marks shall have a shirt of mail and a headpiece of iron and a lance.

3. Likewise all burgesses and the whole body of freeman shall have padded coats and headpieces of iron and lances.

4. Every one of these shall swear that before the feast of St. Hilary he will have these arms, and will bear faith to his lord King Henry, son of Empress Matilda, and will keep these arms for his service according to his command and in fidelity to his lord the king and his realm. And no one of those who have these arms shall sell them or pawn them or give them away, or in any other way alienate them from himself; nor shall any lord alienate them in any way from his man; either by forfeiture, or by gift, or by pledge, or in any other way whatsoever. . . .

22. KING JOHN AND THE BARONS AT RUNNYMEDE (1215)

This Charter [known as *Magna Carta*] was first granted in Form by King John [1199–1216], in the sixteenth Year of his Reign, after a long Series of Civil War between him and his Barons, of which our Chronicles give a milancholy and terrible Description. The King being at last hard put to it by the Barons, deserted almost by every one, and having . . . only seven Lords about his Person, thought it high Time to sooth his other angry Nobles, and therefore sent William Mareschal, Earl of Pembroke, with some others, to the Lords, then at London, to tell them that he would grant the Laws and Liberties they desired. The Ambassador and his Message were received with great Joy by the Barons, who appointed a Time and Place, according to the King's Desire, for the meeting.

This great Assembly of the King and Barons was in a place betwixt Windsor and Stains, called Runingmede. . . .

23. "MAGNA CARTA" (1215)

Magna Carta was primarily designed to clarify and regularize the feudal contract, but the other groups which had taken action against the king at Runnymede were also included in its provisions. Here are the most significant clauses:

John, by the grace of God, King of England, Lord of Ireland, Duke of Normandy and Aquitaine, Count of Anjou, to the archbishops, bishops, abbots, earls, barons, justiciars, foresters, sheriffs, reeves, servants, and all bailiffs and his faithful people greeting. Know that by the suggestion of God and for the good of our soul and those of all our predecessors and of our heirs, to the honor of God and the exaltation of holy church, and the improvement of our kingdom, by the advice of our venerable fathers . . . and of the noblemen . . . and others of our faithful.

1. In the first place we have granted to God, and by this our present charter confirmed, for us and for our heirs forever, that the English church shall be free, and shall hold its rights entire and its liberties uninjured; and we will that it be thus observed; which is shown by this, that the freedom of elections, which is considered to be most important and especially necessary to the English church, we, of our pure and spontaneous will, granted, and by our charter confirmed, before the contest between us and our barons had arisen; and obtained a confirmation of it by the lord Pope Innocent III.; which we will observe and which we will shall be observed in good faith by

our heirs forever. We have granted moreover to all free men of our kingdom for us and our heirs forever all the liberties written below, to be had and holden for themselves and their heirs from us and our heirs. . . .

9. Neither we nor our bailiffs will seize any land or rent for any debt, so long as the chattels of the debtor are sufficient for the payment of the debt; nor shall the pledge of a debtor be distrained so long as the principal debtor himself has enough for the payment of the debt; and if the principal debtor fails in the payment of the debt, not having the wherewithal to pay it, the pledges shall be responsible for the debt; and if they wish, they shall have the lands and the rents of the debtor until they shall have been satisfied for the debt which they have before paid for him, unless the principal debtor shall have shown himself to be quit in that respect towards those pledges. . . .

13. And the city of London shall have all its ancient liberties and free customs, as well by land as by water. Moreover, we will and grant that all other cities and boroughs and villages and ports should have all their liberties and free customs. . . .

28. No constable or other bailiff of ours shall take anyone's grain or other chattels, without immediately paying for them in money, unless he is able to obtain a postponement at the good-will of the seller. . . .

35. There shall be one measure of wine throughout our whole kingdom, and one measure of ale, and one measure of grain, that is the London quarter, and one width of dyed cloth and of russets and of halbergets, that is two ells within the selvages; of weights, moreover it shall be as of measures.

36. Nothing shall henceforth be given or taken for a writ of inquisition concerning life or limbs, but it shall be given freely and not denied. . . .

38. No bailiff for the future shall place any one to his law on his simple affirmation without credible witnesses brought for this purpose. . . .

39. No free man shall be taken or imprisoned or dispossessed, or outlawed, or banished, or in any way destroyed, nor will we go upon him nor send upon him, except by the legal judgment of his peers or by the law of the land.

40. To no one will we sell, to no one will we deny, or delay right or justice. . . .

60. Moreover, all those customs and franchises mentioned above which we have conceded in our kingdom, and which are to be fulfilled, as far as pertains to us, in respect to our men; all men of our kingdom, as well clergy

as laymen, shall observe as far as pertains to them, in respect to their men. . . .

63. . . . Witness the above named and many others. Given by our hand in the meadow which is called Runnymede, between Windsor and Staines, on the fifteenth day of June, in the seventeenth year of our reign.

24. SUMMONSES TO PARLIAMENT (1295)

> While classes other than the lay and spiritual lords had previously been summoned by the king to meetings of the Great Council, in 1295 a more regular system was adopted, which became the standard and model for future Parliaments. The king summoned the archbishops, bishops, greater abbots, earls, and barons by private letter, or writ, addressed to each. He then sent a writ to the sheriff of each county directing him to see to the election of two knights to represent the county and two townsmen to represent each specified city or borough. All were ordered to come to the place of meeting. The following are examples of summonses to these groups to meet with the king to consider the threatening conduct of the king of France.

SUMMONS OF A BISHOP

The king to the venerable father in Christ, Robert, by the same grace archbishop of Canterbury, primate of all England, greeting. As a most just law, established by the careful providence of sacred princes, exhorts and decrees that what affects all, by all should be approved, so also, very evidently should common danger be met by means provided in common. . . . Because, therefore, darts seen beforehand do less injury, and your interest especially, as that of the rest of the citizens of the same realm, is concerned in this affair, we command you, strictly enjoining you in the fidelity and love in which you are bound to us, that on the Lord's day next after the feast of St. Martin, in the approaching winter, you be present in person at Westminster, citing beforehand the dean and chapter of your church, the archdeacons and all the clergy of your diocese, causing the same dean and archdeacons in their own persons, and the said chapter by one suitable proctor, and the said clergy by two, to be present along with you, having full and sufficient power from the same chapter and clergy, to consider, ordain and provide, along with us and the rest of the prelates and principal men and other inhabitants of our kingdom, how the dangers and threatened evils of this kind are to be met. Witness the king at Wangham the thirtieth day of September.

> Like summons were sent to the two archbishops, eighteen bishops and seventy abbots.

SUMMONS OF A BARON

The king to his beloved and faithful relative, Edmund, Earl of Cornwall, greeting. Because we wish to have a consultation and meeting with you and with the rest of the principal men of our kingdom, as to provision for remedies against the dangers which in these days are threatening our whole kingdom; we command you, strictly enjoining you in the fidelity and love in which you are bound to us, that on the Lord's day next after the feast of St. Martin, in the approaching winter, you be present in person at Westminster, for considering, ordaining and doing along with us and with the prelates, and the rest of the principal men and other inhabitants of our kingdom, as may be necessary for meeting dangers of this kind.

Witness the king at Canterbury, the first of October.

Like summons were sent to seven earls and 41 barons.

SUMMONS OF REPRESENTATIVES OF SHIRES AND TOWNS

The king to the sheriff of Northamptonshire. Since we intend to have a consultation and meeting with the earls, barons and other principal men of our kingdom with regard to providing remedies against the dangers which are in these days threatening the same kingdom; . . . we strictly require you to cause two knights from the aforesaid county, two citizens from each city in the same county, and two burgesses from each borough, of those who are especially discreet and capable of labouring, to be elected without delay, and to cause them to come to us at the aforesaid time and place.

Moreover, the said knights are to have full and sufficient power for themselves and for the community of the aforesaid county, and the said citizens and burgesses for themselves and the communities of the aforesaid cities and boroughs separately, then and there for doing what shall then be ordained according to the common counsel in the premises; so that the aforesaid business shall not remain unfinished in any way for defect of this power. And you shall have there the names of the knights, citizens and burgesses and this writ.

Witness the king at Canterbury on the third day of October.

The sheriffs of each county received the same summons.

25. DEVELOPMENT OF STATUTE LAW

Statutes, according to Edward P. Cheyney, "are written laws, not simply arising from custom, as the common law, nor issued as instructions to royal officials, as were the assizes of Henry II, but regularly drawn up and agreed to by both the king and his parliament." Many such statutes were passed during the reign of Edward I (1272–1307), two of which are the Statute of Mortmain (1279) which forbade the alienation of land to the Church, and the Statute of *Quia Emptores* (or Westminster III, 1290) which forbade the subinfeudation of land.

STATUTE OF MORTMAIN

Whereas of late it was provided, That Religious Men should not enter into the Fees of any without Licence and Will of the chief Lord, of whom such Fees be holden immediately; and notwithstanding such Religious Men have entered as well into their own Fees, as into the Fees of other Men, approprying and buying them, and sometime receiving them of the Gift of others, whereby the Services that are due of such Fees, and which at the Beginning were provided for Defence of the Realm, and wrongfully withdrawn, and the chief Lords do leese their Eschetes of the same: (2) We therefore to the Profit of our Realm, intending to provide convenient Remedy, by the Advice of our Prelates, Earls, Barons, and other our Subjects, being of our Council, have provided, made, and ordained, That no Person, Religious or other, whatsoever he be that will, buy or sell any Lands or Tenements, or under the colour of Gift or Lease, or that will receive by reason of any other Title, whatsoever it be, Lands or Tenements, or by any other Craft or Engine will presume to appropre to himself, under Pain of Forfeiture of the same, whereby such Lands or Tenements may any wise come into Mortmain. (3) We have provided also, That if any Person, Religious or other, do presume either by Craft or Engine to offend against this Statute, it shall be lawful to us and other chief Lords of the Fee immediate, to enter into the Land so aliened, within a Year from the Time of the Alienation, and to hold it in Fee as an Inheritance. . . .

STATUTE OF WESTMINSTER III ("QUIA EMPTORES")

Forasmuch as Purchasers of Lands and Tenements of the Fees of great Men and other lords, have many Times, heretofore entered into their Fees, to the Prejudice of the Lords, to whom the Freeholders of such great Men have sold their Lands and Tenements to be holden in Fee of their Feoffors, and not of the chief Lords of the Fees, whereby the same chief Lords have many Times lost their Escheats, Marriages, and Wardships of Lands and Tenements belonging to their Fees; which Thing seemed very hard and extream unto those Lords and other great Men, and moreover in this Case manifest

Disheritance: (2) Our Lord the King, in his Parliament at Westminster, after Easter . . . at the instance of the great Men of the Realm, granted, provided, and ordained, That from henceforth it shall be lawful to every Freeman to sell at his own pleasure his Lands and Tenements, or Part of them, so that the Feoffee shall hold the same Lands or Tenements of the chief Lord of the same Fee, by such Service and Customs as his Feoffor held before.

26. TOWN CHARTERS

One of the most important phenomena of the early Middle Ages was the growth and development of towns occasioned by a revival of commerce. These towns never lost their rural essence and by modern standards were never very large. In almost all cases the owners of lands on which the towns grew (crown, Church, or feudal lords) taxed them heavily and subjected them to feudal restrictions. The towns, therefore, sought to free themselves from these forms of control by means of charters permitting them to substitute a single tax for feudal dues. This tax they collected themselves, and hence excluded the overlord's tax collector. Sometimes they simply purchased a charter. By the thirteenth century many towns had also been given control of their own municipal institutions. For most towns the acquisition of such freedoms was the fruit of a long, hard struggle. The following charter was granted to the city of Ipswich by King John in 1200.

John, by the grace of God, king, etc. Know that we have granted and by our present charter have confirmed to our burgesses of Ipswich our borough of Ipswich, with all its appurtenances and with all its liberties and free customs, to be held of us and our heirs by them and their heirs in hereditary right, paying to our exchequer every year at Michaelmas term, by the hand of the reeve of Ipswich, the just and accustomed farm and, at the same time, the increment of 100s. sterling by tale that they used to pay. We have also granted that all burgesses of Ipswich are to be quit of toll, stallage, lastage, pontage, and all other customs throughout all our land and throughout the ports of the sea. We have granted to them that, with exception of our officials, none of them shall be impleaded in any plea outside the borough of Ipswich, save only in pleas concerning foreign tenures; and that they shall have their gild merchant and their hanse, that no one shall be lodged or shall take anything by force within the borough of Ipswich; that they shall justly have their lands and their pledges and all their debts, by whomsoever owed; that, with regard to their lands and tenures inside the borough, justice shall be assured them according to the custom of the borough of Ipswich and of our free boroughs; that, with regard to their debts established at Ipswich and their pledges made in the same place, the pleas shall be held at Ipswich; and that none of them shall be adjudged in mercy with respect to his chattels except according to the law of our free boroughs. We also forbid any one in all our land, on pain of £10 forfeiture to us, to exact toll, stallage, or any other custom from the men of Ipswich. Wherefore we will and straitly command that the aforesaid burgesses shall have and hold the aforesaid liberties and free customs well and in peace, as they have been and are best and most freely enjoyed by the other burgesses of our free boroughs in England, saving in all things to our citizens of London their liberties and free customs.

Furthermore, we will and grant that our said burgesses, by the common counsel of their town, shall elect two of the more lawful and discreet men of their town and present them to our chief justice at our exchequer; which men shall well and faithfully keep the reeveship (*preposituram*) of our aforesaid borough of Ipswich. And so long as they well conduct themselves in that office, they shall not be removed except by the common counsel of the aforesaid burgesses. We also will that in the same borough, by the common counsel of the aforesaid burgesses, four of the more lawful and discreet men of the borough shall be elected to keep the pleas of the crown and other matters that pertain to us and to our crown in the same borough, and to see that the reeves of that borough justly treat both rich and poor.

These are the witnesses. . . . May 25, in the second year of our reign.

27. MEDIEVAL GUILDS

Between the eleventh and fourteenth centuries economic activity in the towns came under the management of associations known as merchant or craft guilds. The merchant guilds developed first and there was but one such guild for each town. The craft guilds developed later. They were often, in fact, splinter groups from the merchant guilds and there were usually a number of them in the larger towns. In general, the merchant guilds were primarily engaged in trade, the craft guilds in the making of commodities. Rules or ordinances were drawn up by their leading members, and, when approved by the town authorities (often guild members), became the constitution of the guild.

Be it remembered that on Tuesday, the morrow of St. Peter's Chains, in the nineteenth year of the reign of King Edward III, the articles underwritten were read before John Hammond, mayor, Roger de Depham, recorder, and the other aldermen; and seeing that the same were deemed befitting, they were accepted and enrolled in these words.

In the first place, that no one of the trade of spurriers shall work longer than from the beginning of the day until curfew rung out at the church of St. Sepulcher . . . ; by reason that no man can work so neatly by night as by day. And many persons of the said trade, who compass how to practice deception in their work, desire to work by night rather than by day; and then they introduce false iron, and iron that has been cracked; for tin, and also they put gilt on false copper, and cracked. And further, many of the said trade are wandering about all day, without working at all at their trade; and then, when they have become drunk and frantic, they take to their work, to the annoyance of the sick, and all their neighborhood, by reason of the broils that arise between them and the strange folks who are dwelling among them.

And then they proceed to blow up their fires so vigorously that their forges begin all at once to blaze, to the great peril of themselves and of all the neighborhood around. And then, too, all the neighbors are much in dread of the sparks, which so vigorously issue forth in all directions from the mouths of the chimneys in their forges. By reason thereof it seems best that working by night should be put an end to, in order to avoid such false work and such perils; and therefore the mayor and the aldermen do will, by the assent of the good folks of the said trade, and for the common profit, that from henceforth such time for working, and such false work made in the trade, shall be forbidden. And if any person shall be found in the said trade to do the contrary hereof, let him be amerced, the first time in 40d., one-half thereof to go to the use of the Chamber of the Guildhall of London, and the other half to the use of the said trade; the second time, in half a mark, and the third time in 10s., to the use of the same Chamber and trade; and the fourth time, let him forswear the trade forever.

Also, that no one of the said trade shall hang his spurs out on Sundays, or any other days that are double feasts; but only a sign indicating his business; and such spurs as they shall so sell they are to show and sell within their shops, without exposing them without, or opening the doors or windows of their shops, on the pain aforesaid.

Also, that no one of the said trade shall keep a house or shop to carry on his business unless he is free of the city; and that no one shall cause to be sold, or exposed for sale, any manner of old spurs for new ones, or shall garnish them or change them for new ones.

Also, that no one of the said trade shall take an apprentice for a less term than seven years, and such apprentice shall be enrolled according to the usages of the said city.

Also, that if any one of the said trade, who is not a freeman, shall take an apprentice for a term of years, he shall be amerced as aforesaid.

Also, that no one of the said trade shall receive the apprentice, serving man, or journeyman of another in the same trade, during the term agreed upon between his master and him, on the pain aforesaid.

Also, that no alien of another country, or foreigner of this country, shall follow or use the said trade, unless he is enfranchised before the mayor, alderman, and chamberlain; and that, by witness and surety of the good folks of the said trade, who will undertake for him, as to his loyalty and his good behavior.

Also, that no one of the said trade shall work on Saturdays, after noon has been rung out in the city; and not from that hour until Monday morning following.

28. MEDIEVAL FAIRS

Commerce in the Middle Ages was either local or international. The hub of local trade was the town market, usually held one day a week, if the town's overlord had granted permission. The chief centers of international trade were the fairs, which were usually held once a year and lasted from three days to several weeks. As with the market, the right to hold a fair and to enjoy the profits from it (dues and fees) were dependent on a grant from the overlord of the place where it was held. An example of the regulation of fairs is the following statute of 1328.

Item it is established, That it shall be commanded to all the Sheriffs of England and elsewhere, where Need shall require, to cry and publish within Liberties and without, that all the Lords which have Fairs, be it for yielding certain Ferm [profits from courts and other royal revenues from the borough] for the same to the King, or otherwise, shall hold the same for the Time that they ought to hold it, and no longer; that is to say, such as have them by the King's Charter granted them, for the Time limited by said Charters; (2) and also they that have them without Charter, for the Time that they ought to hold them of Right. (3) And that every Lord at the Beginning of his Fair shall there do cry and publish how long the Fair shall endure, to the Intent that Merchants shall not be at the same Fairs over the Time so published, upon Pain to be grievously punished towards the King. (4) Nor the said Lords shall not hold them over the due Time upon pain to seize the Fairs into the King's Hands, there to remain till they have made a Fine to the King for the Offence, after it be duly found, that the Lords held the same Fairs longer than they ought, or that the Merchants have sitten above the Time so cried and published.

29. TREATMENT OF JEWS

The presence of an increasing number of Jews in England's major towns was a frequent source of town rioting. A chronicler records the events in one such riot that occurred in the city of York in 1190.

In the same year, during Lent, that is, that on the 15th of March, the Jews of the city of York, to the number of five hundred, besides women and children, through fear of an attack on the part of the Christians, by permission of the sheriff and the governor of the castle, shut themselves up in that fortress, and when the garrison required them to give up possession of it, they refused to do so. On this refusal, repeated attacks were made both by day and night, and at length the Jews after reflecting, offered a large sum of money for their lives, but this was refused by the people. Then one of them skilled in the law, rose and addressed his companions thus, "Oh, men of Israel, hear my counsel. It is better, as our law instructs us, to die for our law than to fall into the hands of our enemies." This being agreed to by all, each head of a family came with a sharp razor, and cut the throats first of his wife, sons, and daughters, and afterwards of all his family, and threw the dead bodies, which they considered as sacrificed to devils, on the Christians outside the castle; they then shut themselves up in the king's house, and setting fire to it, both living dead were burned together with the buildings. After this the citizens and soldiers burned the Jew's houses, with the papers of their debtors, but retained the money for their own use.

30. BANISHMENT OF JEWS FROM ENGLAND (1290)

Because the Jews were accused of usury (forbidden to Christians), extortion, and ridiculing Christian rites and beliefs, and because Edward I was greatly in debt to them, he decreed their expulsion from England in return for a parliamentary grant. It was centuries before they were allowed to return to England.

An Affair of Consequence came before this Parliament [in 1290], which was the entire Banishment of the Jews out of the Kingdom. The Nation had long desired it, but the Jews still found means to divert the Blow, by large Presents to the King and his Ministers. They wanted to play the same Game again now, but could not do it, the King being unable to protect them any longer, and unwilling to risque the disobliging his Parliament on their Accounts. Accordingly, the Act of Banishment was passed, whereby their immoveable Goods were confiscated; but they had Leave to carry away the rest with them.

There seems to be two different Transactions, in this Parliament, relating to the Jews; one to restrain their Usury, etc., and the other to ordain their Banishment. . . . The Number of these Banished Jews . . . were 16,160; and the Parliament were so well pleased to get rid of these Extortioners, that they readily and willingly granted the King an Aid of a Fifteenth, and the Clergy a Tenth, out of all their moveables; and joined with the Laity in granting a Fifteenth of all their Temporalities, up to their full Value, to make the King some small Amends for the great Loss he sustained by the Jews' Exile. . . .

31. GREGORY VII AND PAPAL POWER

Struggles between monarchs and the Church were constant sources of strife in the Middle Ages, for as the monarchs labored assiduously to establish their power and authority, so too did the Church. As early as 1075 Pope Gregory VII made clear what he regarded as papal prerogatives:

The Roman church was founded by God alone.

The Roman bishop alone is properly called universal.

He alone may depose bishops and reinstate them.

His legate, though of inferior grade, takes precedence, in a council, of all bishops and may render a decision of deposition against them.

He alone may use the insignia of empire.

The pope is the only person whose feet are kissed by all princes.

His title is unique in the world.

He may depose emperors.

No council may be regarded as a general one without his consent.

No book or chapter may be regarded as canonical without his authority.

A decree of his may be annulled by no one; he alone may annul the decrees of all.

He may be judged by no one.

No one shall dare to condemn one who appeals to the papal see.

The Roman church has never erred, nor ever, by the witness of Scripture, shall err to all eternity.

He may not be considered Catholic who does not agree with the Roman church.

The pope may absolve the subjects of the unjust from their allegiance.

32. THE PAPAL BULL, "CLERICIS LAICOS" (1296)

The papacy had reached the apogee of its power by the end of the thirteenth century, when Pope Boniface VIII declared in the papal bull, *Unam Sanctam,* that "subjugation to the Roman pontiff is absolutely necessary to salvation for every human creature." A few years earlier he had taken such umbrage at Edward I's taxation of the clergy that he issued the bull, *Clericis Laicos.*

We therefore desirous of preventing such wicked actions, do, with apostolic authority decree, with the advice of our brethren, that whatsoever prelates and ecclesiastical persons, religious or secular, of whatsoever orders, condition or standing, shall pay or promise or agree to pay to lay persons collections or taxes for the tithe, twentieth, or hundredth of their own rents, or goods, or those of the churches, or any other portion, proportion, or quantity of the same rents, or goods, at their own estimate or value, under the name of aid, loan, relief, subsidy, or gift, or by any other title, manner, or pretext demanded, without the authority of the same see.

And also whatsoever emperors, kings, or princes, dukes, earls, or barons, powers, captains, or officials, or rectors, by whatsoever names they are reputed, of cities, castles, or any places whatsoever, wheresoever situate, and all others of whatsoever rank, pre-eminence or state, who shall impose, exact, or receive the things aforesaid, or arrest, seize, or presume to occupy things anywhere deposited in holy buildings, or to command them to be arrested, seized, or occupied, or receive them when occupied, seized, or arrested, and also all who knowingly give aid, counsel, or favour, openly or secretly, in the things aforesaid, by this same should incur sentence of excommunication. Universities, too, which have been to blame in these matters, we subject to ecclesiastical interdict.

The prelates and ecclesiastical persons above mentioned we strictly command, in virtue of their obedience, and under pain of deposition, that they in no wise acquiesce in such things without express licence of the said see, and that they pay nothing under pretext of any obligation, promise, and acknowledgement whatsoever, made so far, or in progress heretofore, and before such constitution, prohibition, or order come to their notice, and that the seculars aforesaid do not in any wise receive it, and if they do pay, or the aforesaid receive, let them fall under sentence of excommunication by the very deed. . . .

33. EDWARD I's EDICT OUTLAWING THE CLERGY (1297)

The reply of Edward to the *Clericis Laicos* and papal interference with his demands for money came quickly. The bull had proclaimed the excommunication of those clerics who paid the money the king demanded; the king outlawed those who did not pay it. The following is a description of the proceedings:

But we find that the King was not so much afraid of the Pope's Bull as the Archbishop pretended; for he had no sooner heard the Clergy's Answer to his Demand, but he thundered out an Excommunication, indeed, against them all. He immediately put the Archbishop, and the whole Body of the English Clergy, out of his Protection and Defence; and ordered that all their Lands and Possessions, throughout the whole Realm, should be seized to his use. This Edict had the Consent of the Earls, Barons, and others who constituted this Parliament, which continued to sit whilst all the Bishops were excluded. The Chief Justice of the King's Bench, John de Metingham, sitting in his Tribunal, says Knyghton, pronounced Sentence against the Clergy in these words:

'You that are the Proctors, or Attornies, for the Archbishops, Bishops, Abbots, and Priors, with the rest of the Clergy, take Notice to acquaint all your Masters, that, for the future, no Manner of Justice shall be done them in any of the King's Courts, on any Cause whatsoever; but Justice shall be had against them to every one that will complain and require it of us!

O mirabile & inauditum, Auribus horribile! cries the Canon of Leicester; and others of the Monkish Writers of those Times exclaim as loud against this Proceeding. The Miseries that the Clergy suffered, along with their Archbishop, on Account of the aforesaid Sentence against them, were very great; insomuch that a poor Vicar or Parson, when they had Occasion to go abroad, were glad to cloath themselves like Laymen, to pass through the Country with Safety; for if they were robbed or spoiled on the King's Highway, they could have no Restitution or Redress. Indeed, the whole Body of them were struck into a dreadful Panic by this Blow; but most of them compounded the matter with the King for a Fine, and received the King's Letters of Protection; which must have raised a vast Sum of Money in those Days.

34. THE ORDER OF CISTERCIANS

The numerous religious houses founded in the eleventh to the thirteenth centuries all followed the Benedictine Rule. As there was a natural tendency for monasteries to become rich and for monks to become lazy, reforms had periodically to be instituted. Inspired by the Cluniac reforms, a group of monks established the Order of Cistercians at Citeaux, France, in 1098. They had no thought originally of founding a new order, but rather to found a monastery where they could strictly enforce the Benedictine Rule. The result was that they had to devote a part of each day to manual labor. To enable themselves to live if they were not to accept gifts, tithes, feudal dues, or rents, they had to work on their own lands. The Order of Cistercians came to England in 1128, established many houses, and assiduously cultivated their lands, drained the swamps and marshes, and engaged in agricultural experimentation. The mortification of the flesh, characteristic of monasticism, was designed to defend human weaknesses from the wiles of the devil.

Certainly many of their regulations seem severe, and more particularly these: they wear nothing made with furs or linen, nor even that finely spun linen garment which we call *staminium*: neither breeches, unless when sent on a journey, which at their return they wash and restore. They have two tunics with cowls, but no additional garments in winter, though, if they think fit, in summer they may lighten their garb. They sleep clad and girded, and never after matins return to their beds; but they so order the time of matins that it shall be light ere the lauds begin. So intent are they on their rule that they think no jot or tittle of it should be disregarded. Directly after these hymns they sing the prime, after which they go out to work for stated hours. They complete whatever labor or service they have to perform by day without any other light. No one is ever absent from daily services or from complines except the sick. The cellarer and hospitaller, after complines, wait upon the guests, yet observing the strictest silence. The abbot allows himself no indulgence beyond the others. He is everywhere present, everywhere attending to his flock; except that he does not eat with the rest, because his table is with the strangers and the poor. Nevertheless, be he where he may, he is equally sparing of food and of speech; for never more than two dishes are served either to him or to his company; butter and meat never but to the sick.

From the Ides of September till Easter they do not take more than one meal a day, no matter what festival it may be, except on Sunday. They never leave the cloister but for the purpose of labor, nor do they ever speak, either there or elsewhere, save only to the abbot or prior. They pay unwearied attention to the canonical services, making no addition to them except the vigil for the dead. They use in their divine service the Ambrosian chants and hymns, as far as they have been able to learn them at Milan. While they bestow care on the stranger and the sick, they inflict intolerable mortifications on their own bodies, for the health of their souls. . . .

35. THE STATUTE OF CARLISLE (1307)

This statute is important because it reveals the nature of monastic services, the evils which developed with increasing concentration on money-making activities, and the need for regulation.

Of late it came to the Knowledge of our Lord the King, by the grievous Complaint of the honourable Persons, Lords, and other Noblemen of his Realm, that whereas Monasteries, Priories, and other Religious Houses were founded to the Honour and Glory of God, and the Advancement of the Holy Church, by the King and his Progenitors, and by the said Noblemen and their Ancestors; (2) and a very great portion of Lands and Tenements have been given by them to the said Monasteries, Priories, and Houses, and the Religious Men serving God in them, to the Intent that Clerks and Laymen might be admitted . . . according to their sufficient Ability, and that sick and feeble Men might be maintained, Hospitality, Almsgiving, and other charitable Deeds might be done, and that in them Prayers might be said for the Souls of the said Founders and their Heirs; (3) the Abbots, Priors, and Governors of the said Houses, and certain Aliens their Superiors, as the Abbots and Priors of Cestercienses, and Premonstratenses, and of the Order of St. Augustine, and St. Benedict, and many more of other Religion and Order, have at their own Pleasures set divers unwonted, heavy and intollerable Tallages, Payments, and Impositions upon every of the said Monasteries and Houses in Subjection unto them in England, Ireland, Scotland, and Wales, without the Privity of our Lord the King and his Nobility, contrary to the Laws and Customs of the said Realm; (4) and thereby the number of Religious Persons, and other Servants in the said Houses and Religious Places being oppressed by such Tallages, Payments, and Impositions, the Service of God is diminished, Alms being not given to the Poor, the Sick, and Feeble, the Healths of the Living and the Souls of the Dead be miserably defrauded, Hospitality, Almsgiving, and other godly Deeds do cease; (5) and so that which in Times past was charitably given to godly Uses, and to the Increase of the Service of God, is now converted to an evil End; by Permission whereof there groweth great Scandal to the People. . . .

Wherefore our aforesaid Lord the King . . . hath ordained and enacted, That no Abbot, Prior, Master, Warden, or other Religious Person, of whatsoever Condition, State, or Religion he be, being under the King's

Power or Jurisdiction, shall by himself, or by Merchants or others, secretly or openly, by any Device or Means, carry or send, or by any means cause to be sent, any Tax imposed by the Abbots, Priors, Masters, or Wardens of Religious Houses their Superiors, or assessed amongst themselves, out of his Kingdom and his Dominion . . . ; (2) neither shall depart into any other Country for Visitation, or upon any other Colour, by that Means to carry the Goods of their Monasteries and Houses out of the Kingdom and Dominions aforesaid. . . .

36. THE MEDIEVAL UNIVERSITY PROFESSOR

Several medieval towns were distinguished by the fact of the presence of a great scholar, such as Abelard and others, whose fame drew students from far and near to the towns where the scholars lectured. It was not long before teachers and students became so numerous that they organized themselves into guilds, or corporations, which became the universities. The University of Bologna became famous for the study of law, Paris for theology, Salerno for medicine. Oxford and Cambridge concentrated on the arts curriculum. The professors in all universities usually lectured on *a* book and rarely suffered from undue modesty, as the following discourse of Odofredus at the conclusion of his lectures on the *Old Digest* at Bologna illustrates.

Now Gentlemen, we have begun and finished and gone through this book as you know who have been in the class, for which we thank God and His Virgin Mother and all His Saints. It is an ancient custom in this city that when a book is finished mass should be sung to the Holy Ghost, and it is a good custom and hence should be observed. But since it is the practice that doctors on finishing a book should say something of their plans, I will tell you something but not much. Next year I expect to give ordinary lectures well and lawfully as I always have, but no extraordinary lectures, for students are not good payers, wishing to learn but not to pay, as the saying is: All desire to know but none to pay the price. I have nothing more to say to you beyond dismissing you with God's blessing and begging you to attend the mass.

37. MEDIEVAL UNIVERSITY STUDENTS

In the early Middle Ages, the greatest need of students was money for books, lodging, clothes, and food. Hence it followed that many took to begging, borrowing, and importuning parents and relatives for aid. This letter from an Oxford student to his father illustrates the point.

This is to inform you that I am studying at Oxford with the greatest diligence, but the matter of money stands greatly in the way of my promotion, as it is now two months since I spent the last of what you sent me. The city is expensive and makes demands; I have to rent lodgings, buy necessaries, and provide for many other things which I cannot now specify. Wherefore I respectfully beg of your paternity that by the promptings of divine pity you may assist me, so that I may be able to complete what I have well begun. . . .

> In his *Rise of Universities,* from which this letter is taken, Charles H. Haskins does not include the reply of the father, but he does give a reply of a father to his son who was studying at Orleans, and who had requested money.

I have recently discovered that you live dissolutely and slothfully, preferring license to restraint and play to work and strumming a guitar while the others are at their studies, whence it happens that you have read but one volume of law while your more industrious companions have read several. Wherefore I have decided to exhort you herewith to repent utterly of your dissolute and careless ways, that you may no longer be called a waster and your shame may be turned to good repute.

38. TOWN AND GOWN RIOTS

> Medieval students, far from their homes, without serious responsibilities, short of money, careless, and pleasure-seeking, often engaged in disreputable brawls and riots. At Oxford, writes Charles E. Mallet in his *History of the University of Oxford* (I, 156), "There were fights with King's foresters, fights with the officers of justice, fights with the monks of Abingdon, fights between clerks and laymen, fights among the clerks themselves. And the offenders were not only rowdy boys, but Masters, Friars, beneficed clergymen, Heads of Halls, principalities and powers." The chief cause of the riots between the town and the students was the latter's complaint that they were over-charged for food, drink, and lodging, though almost any incident could serve as an excuse for a fight. The first serious clash at Oxford occurred in 1209 and during the next century and a half they occurred with increasing frequency and violence. The following is an account of an attack on a papal legate in 1238.

[A.] Ottobone the Popes Legat here in England, lying at the Abbey of Oseney, there happened a difference between his servants and the Schollers of Oxford; in which contention, a brother of his was slain, and the Legat himselfe faine to fly into the Steeple for safegard of his life: whereupon after

being gotten from thence by the King's safe conduct, he thundered out
curses against the Schollers, and interdicted the University, so as the Colleges
grew desolate, and the Students were dispersed abroad into other places,
for the space of halfe a yeare: till the Monkes of Oseney, and the Regent
Masters of Oxford were faine to goe bare-foote and bare-head through
London, as farre as Durham house, where the Legat lay; and there upon
their humble submission, and great mens intercession, they were absolved,
and the University restored to its former estate. . . .

> Another serious riot, which erupted in 1298, started with nothing but a
> mere servants' quarrel, but lasted four days.

[B.] They [the townsmen] seized and imprisoned all scholars on
whom they could lay hands, invaded their inns, made havoc of their goods
and trampled their books under foot. In the face of such provocation the
Proctors sent their bedels about the town, forbidding the students to leave
their inns. But all commands and exhortations were in vain. By nine o'clock
next morning, bands of scholars were parading the streets in martial array.
If the Proctors failed to restrain them, the mayor was equally powerless to
restrain his townsmen. The great bell of S. Martin's rang out an alarm; ox-
horns were sounded in the streets; messengers were sent into the country
to collect rustic allies. The clerks, who numbered three thousand in all,
began their attack simultaneously in various quarters. They broke open
warehouses in the Spicery, the Cutlery and elsewhere. Armed with bows
and arrows, swords and bucklers, slings and stones, they fell upon their
opponents. Three they slew, and wounded fifty or more. One band, led
by Fulk de Neyrmit, Rector of Piglesthorne, and his brother, took up a
position in High Street between the Churches of S. Mary and All Saints',
and attacked the house of a certain Edward Hales. This Hales was a long-
standing enemy of the clerks. There were no half measures with him. He
seized his crossbow, and from an upper chamber sent an unerring shaft into
the eye of the pugnacious rector. The death of their valiant leader caused
the clerks to lose heart. They fled, closely pursued by the townsmen and
country-folk. Some were struck down in the streets, and others who had
taken refuge in the churches were dragged out and driven mercilessly to
prison, lashed with thongs and goaded with iron spikes.

Complaints of murder, violence and robbery were lodged straight-way
with the King by both parties. The townsmen claimed three thousand
pounds' damage. The commissioners, however, appointed to decide the

matter, condemned them to pay two hundred marks, removed the bailiffs, and banished twelve of the most turbulent citizens from Oxford. Then the terms of peace were formally ratified.

SOURCE REFERENCES   Chapter Two

10. *William of Malmesbury's Chronicle of the Kings of England from the Earliest Times to the Reign of King Stephen,* trans. by J. A. Giles, pp. 308-309. London: Henry G. Bohn, 1847.

11. Stephenson, Carl, and Marcham, Frederick G., eds., *Sources of English Constitutional History. A Selection of Documents from A. D. 600 to the Present,* pp. 58-59. New York: Harpers, 1937.

12. *Laws of William the Conqueror* and the *Laws of Henry I,* quoted in Edward P. Cheyney, ed., *Readings in English History,* pp. 131-132. Boston: Ginn and Co., 1908.

13. Domesday Book, II, 78b, in Lee, *Source Book of English History,* p. 121.

14. *William of Malmesbury's Chronicle,* pp. 334-336.

15. *Chronicle of the Kings of England from the Time of the Romans Government unto the Raigne of our Soveraigne Lord King Charles,* collected by Richard Baker, p. 60. London: Daniel Frere, 1641.

16. Lee, *Source Book of English History,* p. 129.

17. Baker, *Chronicle of the Kings of England,* p. 81.

18. *Roger of Wendover's Flowers of History,* trans. by J. A. Giles, II, 16-18, London: Henry G. Bohn, 1849.

19. Hall, Hubert, *Court Life Under the Plantagenets,* Appendix, pp. 244-249. New York: Macmillan and Co., 1890.

20. Cheyney, *Readings in English History,* pp. 141-142.

21. Cheyney, *Readings in English History,* p. 143.

22. *The Parliamentary or Constitutional History of England, from the Earliest Times to the Restoration of King Charles II,* 2nd ed., several collectors and translators, I, 21. London: various publishers, 1762.

23. *Translations and Reprints from the Original Sources of European History,* 1st series, I (number 6), 6ff. Philadelphia: University of Pennsylvania Press, 1894.

24. *Lord's Report on the Dignity of a Peer,* trans. by E. P. Cheyney, in Lee, *Source Book of English History,* pp. 181-183.

25. *Statutes at Large, from Magna Carta to the End of the Eleventh Parliament of Great Britain,* 7 Edward I, CAP. 2; 18 Edward I, CAP. 1. London: Danby, Pickering, 1762. Hereafter cited *Statutes at Large.*

26. Gross, C., *The Gild Merchant,* II, 115ff., in Stephenson and Marcham, *Sources of English Constitutional History,* pp. 96-97.

27. Cheyney, *Readings in English History,* pp. 209-211.

28. *Statutes at Large,* 2 Edward III, CAP. 15.

29. *Roger of Wendover's Flowers of History,* II, 89-90.

30. *Parliamentary History,* I, 95.

31. Gregory's *Dictatus,* translated in James Harvey Robinson, *Readings in European History,* I, 274–275. New York: Ginn and Co., 1904.

32. Gee, Henry, and Hardy, William J., eds., *Documents Illustrative of English Church History,* pp. 87–88. London: Macmillan and Co., 1896.

33. *Parliamentary History,* I, 116–117.

34. Cheyney, *Readings in English History,* pp. 206–207.

35. *Statutes at Large,* 35 Edward I, CAPS. 1, 2, 4.

36. As quoted in Haskins, Charles H., *The Rise of Universities,* pp. 60–61. New York: Henry Holt and Co., 1923.

37. Haskins, *The Rise of Universities,* pp. 104–105; 107–108.

38. A. Baker, *Chronicle of the Kings of England,* p. 122.
    B. Headlam, Cecil, *The Story of Oxford,* pp. 234–235. London: J. M. Dent and Co., 1907.

CHAPTER THREE

The Later Middle Ages
(1307-1485)

Among the most important developments of the later Middle Ages was the steady expansion in the power of Parliament, the regularization of procedures for parliamentary elections, and the establishment of qualifications for voting and holding office.

39. ABDICATION OF EDWARD II (1327)

The reasons for Parliament's compelling Edward II (1307–1327) to abdicate, and the abdication itself, are revealed in the following account:

I. That the Person of the King was not sufficient to govern; for in all his Time he was led and governed by others, who gave him evil Counsel, to the Dishonour of himself, and the Destruction of Holy Church and all his People, not considering or knowing whether it was good or evil; nor would remedy these Things, when he was requested by the Great and Wise Men of his Realm, or suffer them to be amended.

II. That in all his Time he would not give himself to good Counsel, nor take it, nor to the good Government of his Kingdom; but always gave himself to Works and Employments not convenient, neglecting the Business of his Realm.

III. That, for want of good Government, he lost the Kingdom of Scotland, and other Lands and Dominions in Gascoigny [Gascony] and Ireland, which his Father left him in Peace and Amity with the King of France, and many other Great Persons.

IV. That, by his Pride and Cruelty, he destroyed Holy Church, and the Persons of Holy Church, putting some in Prison, and others in Distress; and also put to Shameful Death, and imprisoned, banished, and disinherited, many Great and Noble Men of the Land.

V. That whereas he was bound, by his Oath, to do Right to all, he would not do it, thro' his own Lucre and the Covetousness of him and his evil Counsellors which were with him; neither regarded the other Points of the Oath which he made at his Coronation, as he was obliged.

VI. That he abandoned his Realm, and did as much as he could to destroy it and his People; and, what is worse, by his Cruelty and the Default of his Person, he was found incorrigible, without Hopes of Amendment. . . .

After this Deputation from the Grand Committee had softened and brought the King to their own Temper, the whole Body of them was introduced. The King came out of his Bed-Chamber, in a Morning-Gown, to meet them; but no sooner had he heard their Message, and the Articles against him, than he swooned away, and had fallen to the Ground, had he not been supported by the Earl of Lancaster and the Bishop of Winchester. However, coming to himself, he answered, with tears in his Eyes, That he was very sorry he had so misbehaved himself towards his People, and asked Pardon for it of all that were present; but, seeing now it could not be otherwise, he returned them Thanks for chusing his first-born Son in his Room. He then made his Resignation, by delivering up his Royal Ensigns of Sovereignty, the Crown and Scepter, which the Commissioners had taken Care to bring for that Purpose; after which, one Sir William Trussel, supplying the Place of Chief Justice of England, and chosen as Procurator, was ordered, by the whole Committee to pronounce their Resignation of Homage to the King. . . .

40. GRANT OF SUPPLIES AND REDRESS OF GRIEVANCES (1348)

Edward III (1327–1377) had demanded large grants from Parliament without having redressed the grievances of the House of Commons. Therefore, when he demanded additional subsidies early in his reign, the Commons declared:

That when this Aid should be levied, that then, for the future, no Subsidy upon Wooll may be granted by the Merchants; and that no Imposition, Loan, or other Tallage, or Charge whatsoever, shall be put upon them (the Commons) by the Privy Council, without their grant and Consent in Parliament; and that two Prelates, two Lords, and two Justices might be assigned to hear and dispatch their Petitions, which were not answered in the last Parliament; and that their Petitions in this Parliament might also be answered according to Reason, and the Answers to remain in Force, without being changed or altered. . . .

Upon these conditions, and not otherwise, as also that they may be entered in the Parliament-Roll, as Matter of Record, by which they might have Remedy, if any Thing should be done to the contrary in Time to come, the said poor Commonalty, to their very great Mischief, grant to the King three-Fifteenths, to be levied in three Years, to begin at Michaelmas next coming, so as every Year one-Fifteenth may be levied, and no more, at two Terms in the Year, viz. St. Michael and Easter, by even Portions; and that this Aid may be assigned and reserved only for the War, and not to pay Debts; and if the War should cease, or a Truce be made, then the Fifteenth of the last Year not to be levied. . . .

41. SPEAKER OF THE HOUSE OF COMMONS (1378)

Another Affair, which we must not omit, is, That this is the first Parliament in which we find a Speaker of the House of Commons expressly named as such; and here Sir Thomas de Hungerford, Knt. was appointed Speaker by the Evidence of the Record itself [1378]. There is no Doubt to be made but that, in former Parliaments, and perhaps in all ever since the Commons were called to sit there, a public Orator, or one that was chosen by the rest to deliver their Petitions to the King, was elected; but no one is particularized in the Records, for having that Office, before the last-named Gentleman; tho', for the future, the Records go very regularly on in giving us their Names. . . .

42. THE ABDICATION OF KING RICHARD II (1399)

In the name of God Amen: I Richard by the Grace of God, king of England and of France, &c: lord of Ireland, acquit and assoile all archbishops, bishops, and other prelats, secular or religious, of what dignitie, degree, state, or condition so ever they be; and also all dukes, marquesses, earles, barons, lords, and all my liege men, both spirituall and secular, of what manner or degree they be, from their oth of fealtie and homage, and all other deeds and privileges made unto me, and from all manner bonds of allegiance, regalitie and lordship, in which they were or be bounden to me, or anie otherwise constreined; and them, their heires, and successors for evermore, from the same bonds and oths I release, deliver, and acquit, and set them for free, dissolved and acquit, and to be harmelesse, for as much as longeth to my person by anie manner waie or title of right, that to me might follow of the foresaid things, or anie of them. And also I resigne all my kinglie dignitie, majestie and crowne, with all the lordships, power, and privileges to the foresaid kinglie dignitie and crowne belonging, and all other lordships and possessions to me in anie maner of wise perteining, of what name, title, qualitie, or condition soever they be, except the lands and possessions for me and mine obits purchased and bought. And I renounce all right, and all maner of title of possession, which I ever had or have in the same lordships and possessions, or anie of them, with anie manner of rights belonging or apperteining unto anie part of them. And also the rule and governance of the same kingdome and lordships, with all ministrations of the same, and all things and everie each of them, that to the whole empire and jurisdictions of the same belongeth of right, or in anie wise may belong.

And also I renounce the name, worship, and regaltie and kinglie highnesse, clearelie, freelie, singularlie and wholie, in the most best maner and forme that I may, and with deed and word I leave off and resigne them, and go from them for evermore; saving alwaies to my successors kings of England, all the rights, privileges and appurtenances to the said kingdome and lordships abovesaid belonging and apperteining. For well I wote and knowledge, and deeme my selfe to be, and have beene insufficient and unable, and also unprofitable, and for my open deserts not unworthie to be put downe. And I sweare upon the holie evangelists here presentlie with my hands touched, that I shall never repugne to this resignation, demission or yeelding up, nor never impugne them in anie maner by word or deed, by my selfe nor none other: nor I shall not suffer it to be impugned, in as much as in me is, privilie or apertlie. But I shall have, hold, and keepe this renouncing, demission, and giving up for firme and stable for evermore in all and everie part thereof, so God me helpe and all saints, and by this holie evangelist, by me bodilie touched and kissed. And for more record of the same, here openlie I subscribe and signe this present resignation with mine owne hand.

43. ELECTIONS OF KNIGHTS OF SHIRES TO PARLIAMENT (1429)

ITEM, Whereas the elections of knights of shires to come to the parliaments of our lord the king, in many counties of the realm of England, have now of late been made by very great, outragious, and excessive number of people dwelling within the same counties of the realm of England, of the which most part was of people of small substance, and of no value, whereof every of them pretended a voice equivalent, as to such elections to be made, with the most worthy knights and esquires dwelling within the same counties, whereby manslaughters, riots, batteries, and divisions among the gentlemen, and other people of the same counties, shall very likely rise and be, unless convenient and due remedy be provided in this behalf; (2) our lord the King, considering the premisses, hath provided, ordained, and established, by authority of this present Parliament, That the knights of the shires to be chosen within the same realm of England to come to the Parliaments of our lord the King hereafter to be holden, shall be chosen in every county of the realm of England, by people dwelling and resident in the same counties, whereof every one of them shall have free land or tenement to the value of forty shillings by the year at the least above all charges; (3) and that they which shall be so chose shall be dwelling and resident within the same counties; (4) and such as have the greatest number of them that may expend forty shillings by year and above, as afore is said, shall be returned by the sheriffs of every county, knights for the parliament, by indentures sealed betwixt the said sheriffs and the said choosers so to be made. (5) And every sheriff of the realm of England shall have power, by the said authority, to examine upon the evangelists every such chooser, how much he may expend by the year; (6) and if any sheriff return knights to come to the parliament contrary to the said ordinance, the justices in their sessions of assizes shall have power, by the authority aforesaid, thereof to inquire. . . .

Provided always, That he which cannot expend forty shillings by year, as afore is said, shall in no wise be chooser of the knights for the parliament; (2) and that in every writ that shall hereafter go forth to the sheriffs to choose knights for the parliament, mention be made of the said ordinances.

44. DUTIES OF JUSTICES OF THE PEACE (1360)

> This statute, as with so many other statutes, was in succeeding years reissued and frequently amended so that the duties of justices of the peace were greatly increased from time to time.

First, that in every county of England shall be assigned for the keeping of the peace, one lord, and with him three or four of the most worthy of the county, with some learned in the law; (2) and they shall have power to restrain the offenders, rioters, and all other barators, and to pursue, arrest, take, and chastise them according to their trespass or offence; (3) and to cause them to be imprisoned and duly punished according to the law and customs of the realm, and according to that which to them shall seem best to do by their discretions and good advisements; (4) and also to inform them, and to inquire of all those that have been pillors and robbers in all the parts beyond the sea, and be now come again, and go wandering, and will not labour as they were wont in times past; (5) and to take and arrest all those that they may find by indictment, or by suspicion, and to put them in prison; (6) and to take of all them that be not of good fame, where they shall be found, sufficient surety and mainprise of their good behaviour towards the King and his people, and the other duly to punish, to the intent that the people be not by such rioters or rebels troubled nor endamaged, nor the peace blemished, nor merchants nor other passing by the highways of the realm disturbed, nor put in the peril which may happen of such offenders. (7) And also to hear and determine at the King's suit all manner of felonies and trespasses done in the same county, according to the laws and customs aforesaid: (8) and that writs of Oyer and Determiner be granted according to the statutes thereof made, and that the justices which shall be thereto assigned be named by the court, and not by the party. (9) And the King's will, that all general inquiries before this time granted within any seignories, for the mischiefs and oppressions which have been done to the people by such inquiries, shall cease utterly and be repealed; (10) and that fines, which are to be made before justices for a trespass done by any person, be reasonable and just, having regard to the quantity of the trespass, and the causes for which they be made.

45. QUALIFICATIONS FOR JUSTICES OF THE PEACE (1439)

Item, Whereas by statutes made in the time of the King's noble progenitors, it was ordained, That in every county of England justices should be assigned of the most worthy of the same counties, to keep the peace, and to do other things, as in the same statutes fully is contained; which statutes notwithstanding now of late in many counties of England, the greatest number have been deputed and assigned, which before this time were not wont to be, whereof some be of small having, by whom the people will not be governed nor ruled, and some for their necessity do great extortion and oppression upon the people, whereof great inconveniencies be likely to rise daily if the King thereof do not provide remedy: (2) the King willingly against such inconveniencies to provide remedy, hath ordained and established, by authority aforesaid, That no justice of the peace within the realm of England, in any county, shall be assigned or deputed if he have not lands or tenements to the value of £20 by year. . . .

46. QUALIFICATIONS OF KNIGHTS OF THE SHIRE (1445)

Knights of the shire for the parliament thereafter to be chosen, shall be notable knights of the same counties for the which they shall be chosen, or otherwise such notable esquires, gentlemen of birth of the same counties, as shall be able to be knights; and no man to be such knight which standeth in the degree of a yeoman and under. . . .

47. THE STATUTE OF LABOURERS (1351)

One evidence of the increasing attention paid by Parliament to matters of national concern was the number of statutes which it passed to regulate various aspects of the nation's life. The Black Death of 1347–1348 had decimated the population, thereby putting labor in short supply. Workers naturally sought to take advantage of their favorable position by demanding higher wages. The following statute was intended to control this situation, and to freeze the *status quo* both as to wages and prices.

CAP. I

That every man and woman of our realm of England, of what condition he be, free or bond, able in body, and within the age of threescore years, not living in merchandize, nor exercising any craft, nor having of his own whereof he may live, nor proper land, about whose tillage he may himself occupy, and not serving any other, . . . he shall be bounden to serve him which so shall him require. And take only the wages, livery, meed, or salary which were accustomed to be given in the places where he oweth to serve, the xx. year of our reign of England or five or six other common years next before. . . . And if any such man or woman, being so required to serve, will not the same do, that proved by two true men before the sheriff or the bailiffs of our sovereign lord the King, or the constables of the town where the same shall happen to be done, he shall anon be taken by them or any of them, and committed to the next gaol, there to remain under strait keeping, till he find surety to serve in the form aforesaid.

CAP. II

Item, If any reaper, mower, or other workman or servant, of what estate or condition that he be, retained in any man's service, do depart from the said service without reasonable cause or licence, before the term agreed, he shall have pain of imprisonment. And that none under the same pain presume to receive or to retain any such in his service.

CAP. III

Item, That no man pay, or promise to pay, any servant any more wages, liveries, meed, or salary than was wont, as afore is said. . . .

CAP. IV

Item, If the lords of the towns or manors presume in any point to come against this present ordinance either by them, or by their servants, then pursuit shall be made against them in the counties, wapentakes, tithings, or such other courts, for the treble pain paid or promised by them or their servants in the form aforesaid. . . .

CAP. V

Item, That sadlers, skinners, white-tawers, cordwainers, taylors, smiths, carpenters, masons, tilers, shipwrights, carters, and all other artificers and workmen, shall not take for their labour and workmanship above the same that was wont to be paid to such persons the said twentieth year, and other common years next before, as afore is said, in the place where they shall happen to work. And if any man take more, he shall be committed to the next gaol, in the manner as afore is said.

CAP. VI

Item, That butchers, fishmongers, regrators, hostelers, brewers, bakers, pulters, and all other sellers of all manner of victual, shall be bound to sell the same victual for a reasonable price, having respect to the price that such victual be sold at in the places adjoining, so that the same sellers have moderate gains, and not excessive, reasonably to be required according to the distance of the place from whence the said victuals be carried. . . .

> During the century and more in which England and France fought the Hundred Years' War (1337–1453), important religious developments occurred. The English laity became particularly hostile to the Church and this animosity was reflected in the enactments of Parliament. In 1343 it forbade anyone to bring orders from Avignon (then the headquarters of the Church) prejudicial to the king. As long as popes ruled from Avignon they were very much under French influence. On the outbreak of the war with France, the English suspected that money paid to the pope found its way into the war chests of the French king. After the first English victories they boasted, in the words of Professor M. M. Knappen, that "if the Pope was French, Jesus was English." Since the Avignonese popes needed money as much as secular states, they sought to make England a source of income and thus established the practice of provisors.

48. THE STATUTE OF PROVISORS OF BENEFICES (1351)

> A provisor was the grant of the next succession to a Church living (benefice). The evil was that an official in the papal curia appointed to a living in England performed the duties of the benefice indirectly through a vicar but drew a large part of its income as salary for services which he performed in Rome. English resentment at this practice grew so great that Parliament passed this statute:

Our lord the king . . . hath ordained and established, that the free elections of archbishops, bishops, and all other dignities and benefices elective in England, shall hold from henceforth in the manner as they were granted by the king's progenitors, and founded by the ancestors of other lords. And that all prelates and other people of holy Church, which have advowsons of any benefices of the king's gift, or of any of his progenitors, or of other lords and donors, to do divine services, and other charges thereof ordained, shall have their collations and presentments freely to the same, in the manner as they were enfeoffed by their donors. And in case that reservation, collation, or provision be made by the court of Rome, of any archbishopric, bishopric, dignity, or other benefice, in disturbance of the elections, collations, or presentations aforenamed that at the same time of the voidance, when such reservations, collations, and provisions shall take effect, our lord the king and his heirs shall have and enjoy for the same time the collations to the archbishoprics, bishoprics, and other dignities elective, which be of his advowry, such as his progenitors had, before that free election was granted. . . . And if any such reservation, provision, or collation be made of any house of religion of the king's advowry, in disturbance of free election, our sovereign lord the king and his heirs, shall have for that time the collation to give this dignity to a convenient person. . . .

49. THE STATUTE OF PRAEMUNIRE (1353)

First, Because it is showed to our lord the King, by the grievous and clamorous complaints of the great men and commons aforesaid [Parliament], how that diverse of the people be, and have been drawn out of the realm to answer of things, whereof the cognizance pertaineth to the King's court; (2) and also that the judgements given in the same court be impeached in another court, in prejudice and disherison of our lord the King, and of his crown, and of all the people of his said realm, and to the undoing and destruction of the common law of the same realm at all times used. (3) Whereupon, good deliberation had with the great men and other of his said council, it is assented and accorded by our lord the King, and the great men and commons aforesaid, That all the people of the King's ligeance, of what condition that they be, which shall draw any out of the realm in plea, whereof the cognizance pertaineth to the King's court, or of things whereof judgements be given in the King's court, or which do sue in any other court, to defeat or impeach the judgements given in the King's court, shall have a day, containing the space of two months, by warning to be made to them in the place where the possessions be, which be in debate, or otherwise where

they have lands or other possessions by the sheriffs or other the King's ministers, to appear before the King and his council, or in his chancery, or before
the King's justices in his places of the one bench or the other, or before other
the King's justices which to the same shall be deputed, to answer in their
proper persons to the King, of the contempt done in his behalf. (4) And if
they come not at the said day in their proper person to be at the law, they,
their procurators, attornies, executors, notaries, and maintainors, shall from
that day forth be put out of the King's protection, and their lands, goods,
and chattels forfeit to the King, and their bodies, wheresoever they may be
found, shall be taken and imprisoned, and ransomed at the King's will: (5)
And upon the same a writ shall be made to take them by their bodies, and to
seise their lands, goods, and possessions, into the King's hands; (6) and if
it be returned, that they be not found, they shall be put in exigent, and outlawed.

    II. Provided always, That at what time they come before they be out-
lawed, and will yield them to the King's prison to be justified by the law,
and to receive that which the court shall award in this behalf, that they shall
be thereto received; the forfeiture of the lands, goods, and chattels abiding in
their force, if they do not yield them within the said two months, as afore is
said.

50. JOHN WYCLIFFE (1320–1384)

> Wycliffe was one of the greatest schoolmen of his day and he organized a
> group of followers (the Lollards) to teach how the Scriptures could be
> preached honestly. Students at Oxford, where he was the Master of Balliol
> College, supported his views because they liked the man, because they de-
> sired Church reform, and because they resented the practice of begging. A
> chronicler has this to say of Wycliffe's activities:

. . . towards the end of his [Edward III's] Raigne, there fell a disturbance in
matter of Doctrine, for a certain Divine, named John Wickliffe, inveighed in
his Sermons, and other Acts in the Schooles, against the abuses of Churchmen, Monks, and other religious Orders; and had by his Doctrine wonne
many Disciples unto him, (who after were called Lollards) professing
poverty, going bare-foot, and poorely clad in Russet; amongst other his Doctrines, he taught that neither King nor other secular Lord, could give any
thing in perpetuity unto Church-men; and that Temporall Lords, if they
needed, might lawfully take the Goods of Religious Persons to relieve them
in their necessities, by the example of William Rufus and others. . . .

51. CONDEMNATION OF WYCLIFFE'S PROPOSITIONS AT THE OXFORD CONVOCATION (1408)

Wycliffe had advanced many ideas repugnant to the Church, among which were the following: (1) that a bishop in mortal sin cannot ordain, consecrate, or baptize; (2) that Christ had not ordained the Mass; (3) that it was unscriptural for the clergy to have temporal possessions; (4) that tithes are pure alms which parishioners can withhold because of the sins of their curates; (5) that friars must get their living by the honest labor of their hands, not by begging. These ideas of Wycliffe were all condemned at the Convocation of Canterbury held at Blackfriars in 1382. In 1408 a convocation at Oxford condemned all his works.

This yeare certeine learned men in Oxford and other places, publikelie in their sermons mainteined and set foorth the opinions and conclusions of Wickliffe. This troubled the bishops and other of the clergie sore, insomuch that in their convocation house, the six and twentith of June, by a speciall mandat of the lord chancellor in presence of the procurators, regents, and others, as Richard Courtneie, Richard Talbot, Nicholas Zouch, Walter Midford, and such like in great multitude: sentence was pronounced by John Wels, doctor of the canon law against the books of John Wickliffe doctor of divinitie. . . . These books and the conclusions in the same conteined, the chancellor of the universitie of Oxford by common consent and assent of the regents and non regents of the same universitie, reproved, disanulled and condemned, inhibiting on paine of the great cursse and deprivation of all degrees scholasticall, that none from thenceforth should affirme, teach, or preach by anie manner of meanes or waies. . . .

52. SERMON BY JOHN BALL (D. 1381)

Another reformer, the poor priest John Ball, though not as famous as Wycliffe, preached sermons in and around London which bred popular discontent and led partly to the Peasants' Rebellion of 1381.

A crazy priest in the county of Kent, called John Ball, who, for his absurd preaching, had been thrice confined in the prison of the archbishop of Canterbury, was greatly instrumental in inflaming them with those ideas. He was accustomed, every Sunday after mass, as the people were coming out of the church, to preach to them in the market place and assemble a crowd around him; to whom he would say: "My good friends, things cannot go on well in England, nor ever will until everything shall be in common; when there shall neither be vassal nor lord, and all distinctions levelled: when the lords shall be no more masters than ourselves. How ill they have used us! and for what reason do they thus hold us in bondage? Are we not all descended from the same parents, Adam and Eve? and what can they show, or what reasons give, why they should be more the masters than ourselves? except, perhaps, in making us labor and work for them to spend. They are clothed in velvets and rich stuffs, ornamented with ermine and other furs, while we are forced to wear poor cloth. They have wines, spices, and fine bread, when we have only rye and the refuse of the straw; and, if we drink, it must be water. They have handsome seats and manors, when we must brave the wind and rain in our labors in the field; but it is from our labor they have wherewith to support their pomp. . . . Let us go to the king, who is young, and remonstrate with him on our servitude, telling him we must have it otherwise, or that we shall find a remedy for it ourselves. If we wait on him in a body, all those who come under the appellation of slaves, or are held in bondage, will follow us. . . . When the king shall see us, we shall obtain a favorable answer, or we must then seek ourselves to amend our condition."

With such words as these did John Ball harangue the people, at his village . . . for which he was much beloved by them. . . .

53. STATUTE AGAINST ALIENS HOLDING ENGLISH BENEFICES
(1383)

> An indication of the popular criticism of the Church, as it relates to the rising national sentiment of the times, is the following statute against alien clergymen enacted under Richard II (1377–1399):

ITEM, whereas late in the parliament holden at Westminster, the third year of the reign . . . , at the request of the commons, . . . it was ordained and assented, and upon a grievous pain prohibited, That no subject of the King nor other person, of what estate or condition he were, should take, neither receive from thenceforth, within the realm of England, procuracy, letter of attorney . . . nor any other administration by indenture, or in any other manner, of any person concerning any benefice of holy church within the realm, but only of the King's subjects of the same realm, without the especial grace and express licence of . . . the King, upon a certain pain contained in the said statute; (2) it is assented and agreed . . . That the same statute shall keep his force and effect in all points. (3) And moreover it is assented, That if any alien have purchased, or from henceforth shall purchase any benefice of holy church, dignity, or other thing, and in his proper person take possession of the same, or occupy it himself within the realm, whether it be to his own proper use, or to the use of another, without special licence of the King, he shall be comprised within the same statute: (4) and moreover shall incur all pains and forfeitures in all points as is before ordained by another statute made the five and twentieth year of the noble King Edward the Third. . . .

54. STATUTE ON THE BURNING OF HERETICS (1401)

With the suppression of the peasants' rebellion in 1381 and the flight of Wycliffe, the Lollard heresy was sternly repressed by means of statutes providing severe punishments for its proponents, including this statute prescribing the burning of heretics:

And if any person within the said realm and dominions, upon the said wicked preachings, doctrines, opinions, schools, and heretical and erroneous informations or any of them be before the diocesan of the same place or his commissaries sententially convict, and the same wicked sect, preachings, doctrines, and opinions, schools and informations, do refuse duly to abjure, or by the diocesan of the same place or his commissaries after the abjuration made by the same person pronounced fall into relapse, so that according to the holy canons he ought to be left to the secular court, whereupon credence shall be given to the diocesan of the same place, or to his commissaries in this behalf, then the sheriff of the county of the same place, and mayor and sheriff or sheriffs, or mayor and bailiffs of the city, town and borough, of the same county next to the same diocesan or the said commissaries shall be required: and they the same persons and every of them, after such sentence promulgate, shall receive, and them before the people in an high place do to be burnt, that such punishment may strike fear to the minds of other . . . [persons].

55. THE EXECUTION OF SIR JOHN OLDCASTLE FOR HERESY (1417)

On the accession of Henry V (1413–1422), those who thought to take advantage of the new king revived Lollardy as part of their program. The movement had gained many adherents among those sections of the middle class which were critical of the Church. Their leader, Sir John Oldcastle, brought about a Lollard uprising in London in 1414, for which he was later burned at the stake.

In the beginning of his Reigne [Henry V], the Wicliffs increased greatly, of whom Sir John Oldcastle was a Chiefe; who by mariage of a kinswoman of the Lord Cobhams of Cooling in Kent, obtained that Title: This knight, being very valorous, and in great favour with the King, was in a Synod at London accused for maintaining of Wicliffs doctrine: whereof

the King being informed, sent for him, and instantly dealt with him to submit himselfe to the censure of the Church: But Sir John Oldcastle told the
King, that he owed his subjection onely to his Majestie; and as for others, he
would stand for the truth against them, to the uttermost of his life. Upon
this, he was served by Processe, to appeare in the Archbishops Court; and
not appearing, was condemned of Contumacy, and afterwards in a Synod at
Rochester, was by the Archbishop pronounced to be an Heretick; who then
enacted that Decree, That the Holy Scriptures ought not to be translated
into the English tongue: But marke the judgement that fell upon his owne
tongue, whose rootes and blade shortly after (as is recorded) grew so bigge
in his mouth and throat that he could neither speake, nor swallow downe
meat, but in horrour lay languishing, till at last starved by famine, he so
dyed. In the meane time, Sir John Oldcastle wrote his Beliefe, and presented
it himselfe to the King; which the King would in no wise receive, but
suffered him, in his presence, and Privy chamber, to be summoned; who appearing before the Archbishop, after divers examinations, he was condemned
of Heresie, and committed to the Tower of London, from whence shortly
after he escaped, and got into Wales. The king, by his Proclamation, promised a thousand Marks to any that should bring him in: but so much was his
doctrine generally favoured, that the kings offer was not much regarded, but
he continued foure yeares after undiscovered: At last he was taken in the
borders of Wales, within a Lordship belonging to the Lord Powes, who
brought him to London, before the Duke of Bedford Regent of the Realme;
where in the end he was condemned, and finally was drawn from the Tower
to St. Giles field, and there hanged in a chaine by the middle, and after consumed with fire, the gallowes and all. . . .

56. THE BATTLE OF CRÉCY (1346)

The Hundred Years' War between England and France began in 1337
when Edward III (1327–1377) revived the English claim to the French
throne. The war lasted until 1453, but the fighting was not continuous and
there were long intervals of peace. Although the war began in 1337, the
first battle was fought three years later at Sluys. This English victory was a
land fight on ships, won by the archers. Nine years were to elapse before
the decisive land battle at Crécy, the chief consequence of which was the
English capture of Calais. The following is a detailed, if not altogether
accurate, account of the events at Crécy:

King Edward had now encamped in a Village called Cressy, his Army
consisted of thirty thousand men, which he divided into three battalions.

. . . In the third the King was himselfe, having about him seven hundred men at Armes, and three thousand Archers. The battels thus ordered, mounted on a white Hobby, he rode from ranke to ranke . . . encouraging every man that day to have regard to his right and honour. The French Kings Army was farre greater, consisting of above sixty thousand combatants well armed. . . . The Vauntguard he commits to his brother the Count de Alanson, the Reere to the Earle of Savoy, the maine battell he leads himselfe; his heate out of confidence of victory was so great, that it scarce permitted time for a little counsell what was fit to be done. The old King of Bohemia advised that the Army should take some repast, and that the Infantry consisting of Genouese (which were above fifteene thousand Crossebowes, and sure men) should make the first Front, and the Cavallery to follow; which was agreed on. But the Count of Alanson, contrary to this order, tooke it ill that the Genouese were in the first ranke, and in fury caused them to change place; which bred that discontentment, that it irritated them more against the Leader, then the enemy; besides there fell at the instant, such a showre of raine, as dissolved their strings, and made their Bowes of little use; and at the breaking up of the showre, the Sun shone full in the face of the French (dazling their fight) and on the backe of the English, as if all made for them. K. Edward who had gotten to a Windmill, beholding as from a Sentinell, the countenance of the Enemy, and discovering the disturbance made by the change of place; instantly sends to charge that part, without giving them time to re-accommodate themselves; whereupon the discontented Genouese recoyle; which the Count de Alanson perceiving, he comes on with the horse, and in great rage cries out, On, on, Let us make way upon the bellies of these Genoueses, who doe but hinder us: and instantly pricks on with a full careere through the midst of them . . . and never staies till he came up to the English battell, where the Prince was; the fight grew hot and doubtfull, in so much as the Commanders about the Prince send to King Edward to come up with his power to aide him. The King askes the messengers whether his son were slaine or hurt: who answering, no; but that he was like to be over-laid: Well then (said the King) returne, and tell them who sent you, that so long as my sonne is alive, they send no more to me what ever happen; for I will that the honour of this day be his. And so being left to try for themselves, they wrought it out with the Sword; the rather by reason the French King having his horse slaine under him, and in danger to be trodden to death, had he not been recovered by the Lord Beaumont; was to the great discouragement of his people, withdrawne out of the field: whereof notice being once taken by the English, the day was soone after theirs, and the greatest victory they ever had yet against the

French, and so bloudy, as there is no mention made of any one prisoner taken in the battell, but all slaine out-right; onely some few troopes that held together, saved themselves by retiring to places neare adjoyning. . . . The number of the slaine are certified to be thirty thousand. . . . This memorable Victory happened upon the Saturday after Bartholomew day [August 24], in the yeare 1346. The next day, earely in the morning, being Sunday, he sent out 300. Lances, and 2000. Archers, to discover what was become of the Enemy, who found great Troopes comming from Abbevile, Saint Requier, Roan, and Beauvoyes (ignorant of what had happened) led by the Arch-Bishop of Roan, and the Priour of France: whom they likewise defeated, and slew seven thousand.

57. THE BATTLE OF AGINCOURT (1415)

At this battle the English repeated the tactics used so successfully at Crécy in 1346 and at Poitiers in 1356. It was a smashing victory for the English whose king, Henry V (1413–1422), had carefully planned the strategy and taken up a strong defensive position. The following is how the chronicler Holinshed described it:

Thus the king having ordered his battels, feared not the puissance of his enimies, but yet to provide that they should not with the multitude of horssemen breake the order of his archers, in whome the force of his armie consisted (For in those daies the yeomen had their lims at libertie, sith their hosen were then fastened with one point, and their jackes long and easie to shoot in; so that they might draw bowes of great strength, and shoot arrowes of a yard long, beside the head) he caused stakes bound with iron sharpe at both ends, of the length of five or six foot to be pitched before the archers, and of ech side the footmen like an hidge, to the intent that if the barded horsses ran rashlie upon them, they might shortlie be gored and destroied. Certeine persons also were appointed to remoove the stakes, as by the mooveing of the archers occasion and time should require, so that the footmen were hedged about with stakes, and the horssemen stood like a bulwarke betweene them and their enimies, without the stakes. This devise of fortifieng an armie, was at this time first invented: but since that time they have devised caltraps, harrowes, and other new engins against the force of horssemen; so that if the enimies run hastilie upon the same, either are their horsses wounded with the stakes, or their feet hurt with the other engins, so as thereby the beasts are gored, or else made unable to mainteine their course.

King Henrie, by reasons of his small number of people to fill up his battels, placed his vauntgard so on the right hand of the maine battell, which himselfe led, that the distance betwixt them might scarse be perceived, and so in like case was the rereward joined on the left hand, that the one might the more readilie succour an other in time of need. When he had thus ordered his battels, he left a small companie to keepe his campe and cariage, which remained still in the village, and then calling his capteins and soldiers about him, he made to them a right grave oration, mooving them to plaie the men, whereby to obteine a glorious victorie, as there was hope certeine they should, the rather if they would but remember the just cause for which they fought, and whome they should incounter, such faintharted people as their ancestors had so often overcome. To conclude, manie words of courage he uttered, to stirre them to doo manfullie, assuring them that England should never be charged with his ransome, nor anie Frenchman triumph over him as a captive; for either by famous death or glorious victorie would he (by Gods grace) win honour and fame. . . .

There were taken prisoners, Charles duke of Orleance nephue to the French king, John duke of Burbon, the lord Bouciqualt one of the marshals of France . . . with a number of other lords, knights, and esquires, at the least fifteene hundred, besides the common people. There were slain in all the French part to the number of ten thousand men. . . .

Of Englishmen, there died at the battell, Edward duke of Yorke, the earle of Suffolke, Sir Richard Kikelie, and Davie Gamme esquier, and of all other not above five and twentie persons, as some doo report; but other writers of greater credit affirme, that there were slaine about five or six hundred persons. . . .

58. THE TRIAL OF JOAN OF ARC (1431)

The Hundred Years' War died out in a series of sieges in which the French showed greater skill in the use of a new weapon—the cannon. The best known of these sieges was that at Orleans made famous by the exploits of the peasant girl Joan of Arc. She was betrayed by her own countrymen, tried by a court presided over by a French bishop, and put to death by the English.

Asked concerning the place of her origin, she replied that she was born in the village of Domremy.

Asked concerning the name of her parents, she replied that her father was called Jacques d'Arc, her mother Isabella. . . .

Asked how old she is, she replied that so far as she knows she is about nineteen. . . .

She confessed that when she was thirteen years of age she had a voice from God, to aid her in how to act. And the first time she had great fear. The voice came about noontime, in summer, in her father's garden; and the said Joan had been fasting the previous day. She heard the voice on the right hand in the direction of the church, and she seldom heard it without there being a light. The light came from the same direction the voice was heard from, and usually it was a very great light. And when the same Joan came into France she often heard that voice. . . .

She said that when she was in the woods she heard a voice coming toward her. She said, moreover, that it seemed to her to be a good voice, and she believed that the voice was sent from God; and after she heard the voice three times she knew that it was the voice of an angel. She said, besides, that that voice always kept her safe, and that she understood the voice very well.

Asked what proof she had that that voice was for the good of her soul, she said that it taught her to act rightly, to attend church, and said to the same Joan that it was necessary for her to go into France. She confessed that that voice said to her twice or three times in a week that the same Joan must go into France, and she said that her father knew nothing of her departure. Moreover, the voice told her that she should raise a siege laid against the city of Orleans. She said that the voice said to her farther that the same Joan should go to Robert de Baudricourt, at the city of Vaucouleurs, captain of that place, and he would give her men to go with her; and the said Joan then replied that she was a poor girl, who did not know how to ride, nor to carry on war. . . .

Asked whether it was the voice of an angel which spoke to her, or of a man or a woman saint, or of God directly, she replied that that voice was of St. Catherine and of St. Margaret, and that their forms were crowned with beautiful crowns, very rich and precious.

Asked what was the first voice that came to her when she was thirteen years old, she said that it was St. Michael.

Asked whether she saw St. Michael and the angels bodily, she replied, "I saw them with my bodily eyes, as well as I see you, and when they left me I cried and would have liked them to take me away with them."

Asked whether when she went to Orleans she had a banner, and of what color it was, she replied that she had a banner of which the field was sowed with lilies, and there was on it the figure of the world and two angels at the side. It was of white color made of linen, and the words "Jesus, Mary" were written on it, and it was embroidered with silk.

Asked which she liked best, her banner or her sword, she replied that she liked much better, yes, forty times better, her banner than her sword. She said, moreover, that she herself carried the banner when she attacked the enemy, so that she would not have to kill any one, and she said she had never killed a man, so far as she knew.

59. THE PIEPOWDER COURTS

Merchants attending medieval fairs, sometimes having come a considerable distance, could not afford to waste time awaiting action in regular courts arising from dishonesty and other crimes committed at the fairs. The following reading shows the nature of these crimes and the decisions reached in the piepowder court (from the French *pied poudre,* meaning dusty feet).

Pleas of the fair held at Carnarvon on Saturday the morrow of Michaelmas in the nineteenth year [1325].

Cadogan, Adam's son, plaintiff appeared against Meredith, Llowarch's son, in a plea of trespass. And the said Meredith came and acknowledged; therefore he is in mercy (12d.).

Meredith, Llowarch's son, was arraigned for that he carried arms at the fair of the lord king at Carnarvon on the feast of St. James in the aforesaid year contrary to the prohibition of the justices. And the said Meredith came and acknowledged; therefore he and his pledges are in mercy (a half-mark).

Jevan, Traherne's son, was arraigned for the same. And he came and acknowledged; therefore, he is in mercy (40d.).

Sum total, 11s.

During the years in which England was waging war with France (1337–1453), great changes were occurring in the nation's economy. Business was active; merchants aggressively sought wider markets and higher profits. As a result, Parliament devoted an increasing amount of time to the enactment of regulative statutes. The following are just a few examples of the degree to which Parliament attempted to regulate the economic life of the country, to protect it from foreign competition, and to standardize weights and measures.

60. STATUTE RELATING TO WOOL (1337)

CAP. I

It is accorded by our Sovereign Lord the King, his Prelates, Earls, and Barons, with the Assent of the Commons in the Parliament summoned at

Westminster, the Monday next after the Feast of Saint Mathew the Apostle
in the xi Year of the Reign of our Sovereign Lord the King, That no
Merchant foreign or denizen, nor none other of what Estate or Condition
that he be, upon Pain of Forfeiture of Life and of Member, and of as much
as he may forfeit towards our . . . King, shall bring or cause to be brought,
by himself nor by other, privily nor apertly from henceforth any Wools out
of the Realm, till by the King and his Council it be thereof otherwise provided.

CAP. 2

ITEM, it was accorded, That no Man nor Woman great nor small of England,
Ireland, nor Wales, nor of our Sovereign Lord the King's Power in Scotland,
of what Estate or Condition he be, the King, Queen, and their Children only
except, shall wear no cloth, which shall be bought after the Feast of Saint
Michael next coming, other than is made in England, Ireland, Wales, or Scotland. . . .

CAP. 3

ITEM, it is accorded and established, That no Merchant, foreign nor Denizen,
nor none other shall bring . . . into the said Lands of England, Ireland,
Wales, and Scotland, within the King's Power, any Clothes made in any
other Places than in the same. . . .

CAP. 4

ITEM, it is accorded, That no Man nor Woman of the said Lands . . . of
what Estate or Condition that he be, the King, Queen, and their Children,
the Prelates, Earls, Barons, Knights, and Ladies, and People of Holy Church,
which may expend by year an C. li. [£100] of their Benefices at the least, to
the very Value, only except, shall wear no Fur in his Clothes, that shall be
bought after the said Feast of Saint Michael, upon the Forfeiture of the said
Fur. And further to be punished at the King's Will.

61. STATUTE ON STANDARDIZATION OF WEIGHTS AND MEASURES (1340)

ITEM, Where it is contained in the Great Charter, that one Measure and one
Weight be throughout England; (2) and also it is contained in a Statute
made in the Time of King Edward, Grandfather to the King that now is,

that none shall sell by the Bushel, if it be not marked with the King's Seal, and that it be according to the King's Standard; (3) and also it is contained, that he which shall be attainted for having double Measure, that is to say, one greater to buy, and another less to sell, shall be imprisoned as false, and grievously punished; which Things have not been holden nor used after the said Establishment, to the great Grief of the People; (4) it is assented and accorded, That from henceforth one Measure and one Weight shall be throughout the Realm of England. . . .

62. STATUTE ON FORESTALLING (1353)

ITEM, we have ordained and established, that all merchants, aliens and denizens, and other that do bring wines and other wares or merchandises whatsoever they be to the staples, cities, boroughs, and good towns, or to ports of the sea within our said realm and lands, may falsely and without challenge and impeachment of any sell them in gross or at retail, or by parcels at their will, to all manner of people that will buy the same. (2) And that no merchant, privy nor stranger, nor other of what condition that he be, go by land nor by water toward such wines, wares, or merchandises, coming into our said realm and lands in the sea, nor elsewhere, to forestal or buy them, or in other manner, to give earnest upon them before that they come to the staple, or to the port where they shall be discharged, nor enter into the ships for such cause, till the merchandises be set to land to be sold, upon the pains and forefeitures contained in the [law]. . . .

63. STATUTE OF THE STAPLE (1353)

> Most of these statutes were subsequently altered in many respects and reissued. This is also illustrated in the next three selections on staples, wages, and malt.

First, That the staple of wools, leather, woolfels, and lead, growing or coming forth within our said realm and lands, shall be perpetually holden at the places underwritten; that is to say, for England at Newcastle upon Tine, York, Lincoln, Norwich, Westminster, Canterbury, Chichester, Winchester, Exeter, and Bristol: (2) for Wales, at Kaermerdyn: (3) and for Ireland at Devylen, Waterford, Cork and Drogheda, and not elsewhere. (4) And that all the said wools, as well old as new, woolfels, leather and lead, which shall be carried out of the said realm and lands, shall be first brought to the said staples, and there the said wool and lead betwixt merchant and merchant, or merchant and others, shall be lawfully weighed by the standard. (5) And

that every sack and sarpler of the same wools so weighed, be sealed under
the seal of the mayor of the staple. (6) And that all the wools so weighed
and sealed at the staple of York, Lincoln, Norwich, Westminster, Canterbury and Winchester; and also leather, woolfels, and lead which shall come
there, (the customs of the staple thereof paid,) shall be witnessed by bill,
sealed with the seal of the mayor of the staple, and brought to the ports under written, that is to say, from York to Hull, from Lincoln to saint Botolf,
from Norwich to great Yarmouth, from Westminster to London, from
Canterbury to Sandwich, and from Winchester to Southampton. . . . (8)
And an indenture shall be made betwixt the mayor of the staple being in the
port of the sea, and our customers there, of all the wools and lead so
weighed, and also of all the leather and woolfels which shall come to the
said staples to pass there. . . .

64. STATUTE OF WAGES (1388)

ITEM, because that servants and labourers will not . . . serve and labour
without outragious and excessive hire, and much more than hath been given
to such servants and labourers in any time past, so that for scarcity of the
said servants and labourers, the husbands and landtenants may not pay their
rents, nor hardly live upon their lands, to the great damage and loss as well
of the lords as all the commons: . . . It is accorded and assented that the
bailiff for husbandry shall take by year xiii.s. iii.d [thirteen shillings and
three pence] and his clothing once by year at the most. The master hine x.s.
the carter x.s. the shepherd x.s. the oxherd vi.s. viii.d. the cowherd vi.s. viii.d.
the swineherd vi.s. a woman labourer vi.s. a day a driver of the plough vii.s.
at the most. And every other labourer and servant according to his degree,
and less in the country where less was wont to be given without clothing,
courtesie, or other reward by covenant. And that no servant or artificer nor
victualler within city, borough, nor other town, shall take more than the
servants and labourers above named after their estate without vesture,
courtesie, or other reward by covenant as is aforesaid . . . .

65. STATUTE OF MALT (1393)

ITEM, That the malt which shall be made in the counties of Huntingdon,
Cambridge, Northampton, and Bedford, that shall be sold and brought to
the city of London, to victual the King's household, and other lord's house-
holds, and gentlemen's there dwelling and repairing, and also for sustenance
of all the people of the said city, shall be well and sufficiently sifted, cleansed,
and purified, before the sale of the same, from dust and all other filth, so that

the buyers may have eight bushels of clean malt for the quarter. And that the mayors, bailiffs, and wardens of towns and places where such malt shall be sold, shall have power at every man's suit that will complain, to see and search the said malt, and if default be found thereof, to make due redress.

> The fourteenth and fifteenth centuries were a time of wars, of great economic changes, and of constitutional developments. They were also a time of very great social upheaval occasioned by the wars, the Black Death, and peasants' rebellions. The succeeding readings are descriptive of these important events and other developments.

66. THE ORDER OF THE GARTER (1344)

He [Edward III] instituted the Order of the Garter, upon what cause is not certaine; the common opinion is, that a Garter of his owne queene, or (as some say) of the Lady Joane Countesse of Salisbury, slipping off in a Dance, King Edward stooped and tooke it up; whereat some of his Lords that were present, smiling, as at an amorous action; he seriously said, it should not be long ere Sovereigne honour should be done to that Garter; whereupon he afterward added the French Motto, *Honi soit qui maly pense;* therein checking his Lords' sinister suspicion. Some conjecture that he instituted the Order of the Garter, for that in a battell wherein he was victorious, he had given the word Garter, for the word or signe: and some againe are of opinion, that the institution of this Order is more ancient, and begunne by King Richard the first, but that this King Edward adorned it, and brought it into splendour. The number of knights of this Order is twenty sixe, whereof the King himself is alwayes one, and president; and their Feast yearely celebrated at Windsor on Saint Georges day, the Tutelar Saint of that Order. The lawes of the Order are many, whereof there is a booke of purpose . . . .

67. THE BLACK DEATH (1348)

Then the grievous plague penetrated the seacoasts from Southampton, and came to Bristol, and there almost the whole strength of the town died, struck, as it were, by sudden death; for there were few who kept their beds more than three days, or two days, or half a day; and after this the fell death broke forth on every side with the course of the sun. There died at Leicester in the small parish of St. Leonard more than 380; in the parish of Holy Cross, more than 400; in the parish of St. Margaret of Leicester, more than 700; and so in each parish a great number. Then the bishop of Lincoln sent through the whole bishopric, and gave general power to all and every priest,

both regular and secular, to hear confessions, and absolve with full and entire episcopal authority except in matters of debt, in which case the dying
man, if he could should pay the debt while he lived, or others should certainly fulfill that duty from his property after his death. Likewise, the pope
granted full remission of all sins to whoever was absolved in peril of death,
and granted that this power should last till next Easter, and every one could
choose a confessor at his will. In the same year there was a great plague of
sheep everywhere in the realm, so that in one place there died in one
pasturage more than 5000 sheep, and so rotted that neither beast nor bird
would touch them. And there were small prices for everything on account of
the fear of death. For there were very few who cared about riches or anything else; for a man could have a horse, which before was worth 40s., for 6s.
8d., a fat ox for 4s., a cow for 12d., a heifer for 6d., a fat wether for 4d., a
sheep for 3d., a lamb for 2d., a big pig for 5d., a stone of wool for 9d. Sheep
and cattle went wandering over fields and through crops, and there was no
one to go and drive or gather them, so that the number cannot be reckoned
which perished in the ditches and hedges in every district, for lack of herds-
men; for there was such a lack of servants that no one knew what he ought
to do. In the following autumn no one could get a reaper for less than 8d.
with his food, a mower for less than 12d. with his food. Wherefore many
crops perished in the fields for want of some one to gather them; but in the
pestilence year, as is above said of other things, there was such abundance of
grain that no one troubled about it . . . .

Meanwhile the king sent proclamation into all the counties that reapers
and other laborers should not take more than they had been accustomed to
take under a penalty appointed by statute. But the laborers were so lifted up
and obstinate that they would not listen to the king's command: if any one
wished to have them he had to give them what they wanted, and either lose
his fruit and crops, or satisfy the lofty and covetous wishes of the workmen.
And when it was known to the king that men had not observed his command, and had given greater wages to the laborers, he levied heavy fines
upon abbots, priors, knights, greater and lesser, and other great folk and
small folk of the realm, of some 100s., of some 40s., of some 20s., from each
according to what he could give. He took from each plowland of the realm
20s., and, notwithstanding this, a fifteenth. And afterwards the king had
many laborers arrested and sent them to prison; many withdrew themselves
and went into the forests and woods; and those who were taken were
heavily fined. Their ringleaders were made to swear that they would not
take daily wages beyond the ancient custom, and then were freed from

prison. And in like manner it was done with the other craftsmen in the boroughs and villages. . . . After the aforesaid pestilence many buildings, great and small, fell into ruins in every city, borough, and village for lack of inhabitants, likewise many villages and hamlets became desolate, not a house being left in them, all having died who dwelt there; and it was probable that many such villages would never be inhabited. In the winter following there was such a want of servants in work of all kinds, that one would scarcely believe that in times past there had ever been such a lack . . . . And so all necessaries became so much dearer that what in times past had been worth a penny was then worth 4d. or 5d.

Magnates and lesser lords of the realm who had tenants made abatements of the rent in order that the tenants should not go away on account of the want of servants and the general dearness, some half the rent, some more, some less, some for two years, some for three, some for one year, according as they could agree with them. Likewise, those who received of their tenants day work throughout the year, as is the practice with villains [villeins], had to give them more leisure and remit such works, and either entirely to free them or give them an easier tenure at a small rent, so that homes should not be everywhere irrecoverably ruined, and the land everywhere remain entirely uncultivated.

68. STATUTE AGAINST BEGGING (1349)

ITEM, because that many valiant beggars, as long as they may live of begging, do refuse to labour, giving themselves to idleness and vice, and sometimes to theft and other abominations; none upon the said pain of imprisonment shall, under the colour of pity or alms, give anything to such, which may labour, or presume to favour them towards their desires, so that thereby they may be compelled to labour for their necessary living: Wherefore our said sovereign lord the King, the xiiii. [fourteenth] day of June, the xxiii. yeare of his reign, hath commanded to all sheriffs of England by divers writs, that they shall do openly to be proclaimed and holden, all and singular the premises in the counties, boroughs, merchant-towns, sea-ports, and other places in their bailiwicks, where to them shall seem expedient: and that they do thereof due execution, as afore is said.

69. THE POLL TAX (1378)

Imposed by King Richard II, this tax, levied on everyone in accordance with his ability to pay, was one of the principal causes of the Peasants' Rebellion.

The Lords and Commons, taking into Consideration the dangerous State of the Nation, at this Crisis, from the Malice of its Enemies, both of France and elsewhere, and the great Necessities of the Kingdom, to raise Monies to be able to withstand them; first, agreed that the Mark laid upon every Sack of Wooll, and the Six-Pence in the Pound for all Merchandize, which was given in the last Parliament, should be remitted; and, in Lieu thereof, they granted the old Subsidy on Wooll, as it was before that Parliament, for one Year from Michaelmas next. They likewise granted a certain Poll-Tax, to be paid by Persons of different Sexes, Ranks, Estates, and Degrees in the Kingdom; which being a Tax quite new, and the Act itself expressing, very particularly, what Sum each Man or Woman should pay, as well as the several Qualities and Conditions of the whole English Nation, in those Days, we shall give at Length, as translated from the original French; and we are persuaded it cannot be unacceptable to a curious Reader.

After the Recital, in the Act of what is mentioned before, the Particulars of this Capitation-Tax begin with

The Dukes of Lancaster and Bretaigne, each ten Marks.

Also every Earl of England £4.

The Countesses, who were Widows, the same as the Earls, £4.

Every Baron, Banneret, or Knight, who had as good an Estate as the Barons, 40s.

Every Baroness, who is a Widow, as a Baron; and a Banneress as a Banneret, 40s.

Every Batchelor and every Esquire, who by Estate ought to be made a Knight, 20s.

Every Widow that was the Wife of a Batchelor, or Esquire, 20s.

Every Esquire of less Estate, 6s. 8d. . . .

Every Esquire without Possessions, Lands, Rents, or Goods, that is in Service, or bears Arms, 3s. 4d. . . .

Every Justice, as well of the one Bench as of the other, and the Chief Baron of the Exchequer, each 100s.

Every Serjeant and great Apprentice of the Law, 40s.

Other Apprentices which follow the Law, 20s.

All other Apprentices of less Estate, and Attorneys, each 6s. 8d.

The Mayor of London shall pay as an Earl, £4.

The Aldermen of London, each as a Baron, 40s.

All other Mayors of great Towns in England, each as a Baron, 40s.

Other Mayors of smaller Towns, according to the Value of their Estate, 20s., 10s. or 6s. 8d.

And all Jurats of good Towns, and great Merchants of the Realm, shall pay as Batchelors, each 20s. . . .

All lesser Merchants, and Artificers, Husbandmen, or who live upon Tillage according to the Value of their Estate, 4s. 8d., 3s. 4d., 1s. or 6d.

Every Serjeant and Freeman of the Country, according to their Estate, 6s. 8d., or 40d.

The Farmers of Manors, Parsonages, and Granges, Merchants of Beasts, and other Buyers and Sellers, according to their Estate, 6s. 8d., 40d., 2s. or 12d.

All Advocates, Notaries, and Proctors, who are married, shall pay as Serjeants of the Law, and Apprentices of the Law, and Attorneys, each according to their Estate, 40s., 20s. or 6s. 8d. . . .

Every married Man, for himself and his Wife, that have not the Estates above named, and above the Age of sixteen, except very Beggars, 4d.

And every Man and Woman unmarried, of such an Estate, and above the Age aforesaid, 4d.

Also every strange Merchant, of what Condition soever, shall pay according to his Ability, as other Denizens.

Walsingham and Knyghton also tell us, That the Clergy were not exempt from this Tax, but, according to their own Custom, taxed themselves very high, viz. every Archbishop, Bishop, and Mitred Abbot, as much as a Baron; every Abbot was to pay forty Pence for each Monk in his Monastery; and the Beneficed Clergy six Shillings and Eight-pence. All which together must needs amount to a vast Sum, tho' how it was disposed of is hard to tell; for we do not find that the warlike Preparations, at that Time, either by Sea or Land, were any ways adequate to so great a Tax.

70. THE PEASANTS' REBELLION (1381)

When tax-collectors put pressure on the evaders of the Poll Tax of 1378 (which had been levied to pay for the war with France and bore with great severity on the poor, who therefore evaded paying it), rioting broke out. In each case where rioting occurred, it began with resistance to tax-collectors or to those whose duty it was to punish tax-evaders. Wage-earners, though better off than formerly, were annoyed by attempts to enforce the Statute of Labourers, which they thought unjust, and their improved condition only served to arouse their discontent. The villeins, also better off than in former times, were dissatisfied with their bondage, sought social equality, and insisted that it was morally wrong for them to be bound to the soil. Peasants, whose services were in great demand after the Black Death, began to unite in combinations for securing higher wages and reduced rents. In addition, there was general disgust at the incompetence of King Richard II. Froissart, the chronicler, describes the rebellion in these words:

This day, all the rabble were again assembled, under the conduct of Wat Tyler, Jack Straw, and John Ball, to parley at a place called Smithfield, where, every Friday, the horse-market is kept. They amounted to upward of twenty thousand, all of the same sort. Many more were in the city, breakfasting and drinking Rhenish, Malmsey and Madeira wines, in taverns and at the houses of the Lombards, without paying for anything; and happy was he who could give them good cheer. Those who were collected in Smithfield had king's banners, which had been given to them the preceding evening; and these reprobates wanted to pillage the city the same day, their leaders saying, "that hitherto they had done nothing. The pardons which the king has granted will not be of much use to us: but, if we be of the same mind, we shall pillage this large, rich and powerful town of London, before those from Essex, Suffolk, Cambridge, Bedford, Warwick, Reading, Lancashire, Arundel, Guilford, Coventry, Lynne, Lincoln, York and Durham shall arrive; for they are on the road, and we know for certain that Vaquier and Lister will conduct them hither. If we now plunder the city of the wealth that is in it, we shall have been beforehand, and shall not repent of so doing; but, if we wait for their arrival, they will wrest it from us." To this opinion all had agreed, when the king appeared in sight, attended by sixty horse. He was not thinking of them, but intended to have continued his ride without coming into London: however, when he came before the abbey of St. Bartholomew, which is in Smithfield, and saw the crowd of people, he stopped, and said he would not proceed until he knew what they wanted; and, if they were troubled, he would appease them.

The lords who accompanied him stopped also, as was but right, since the king had stopped; when Wat Tyler, seeing the king, said to his men, "Here is the king: I will go and speak with him: do not you stir from hence until I give you a signal." He made a motion with his hand, and added, "When you shall see me make this sign, then step forward, and kill every one except the king; but hurt him not, for he is young, and we can do what we please with him; for, by carrying him with us through England, we shall be lords of it without any opposition." There was a doublet-maker of London, called John Ticle, who had brought sixty doublets, with which some of the clowns had dressed themselves; and on his asking who was to pay, for he must have for them thirty good marks, Tyler replied, "Make thyself easy man; thou shalt be well paid this day: look to me for it: thou hast sufficient security for them." On saying this, he spurred the horse on which he rode, and, leaving his men, galloped up to the king, and came so near that his horse's head touched the crupper of that of the king. The first words he said, when he addressed the king, were, "King, dost thou see all those men there?" "Yes," replied the king: "why dost thou ask?" "Because they are all under my command, and have sworn by their faith and loyalty to do whatever I shall order." "Very well," said the king: "I have no objections to it." Tyler, who was only desirous of a riot, answered, "And thinkest thou, king, that those people and as many more who are in the city, also under command, ought to depart without having had thy letters? Oh no, we will carry them with us." "Why," replied the king, "so it has been ordered, and they will be delivered out one after the other: but, friend, return to thy companions, and tell them to depart from London: be peaceable and careful of yourselves, for it is our determination that you shall all of you have your letters by villages and towns, as it had been agreed on."

As the king finished speaking, Wat Tyler, casting his eyes around him, spied a squire attached to the king's person bearing his sword. Tyler mortally hated this squire; formerly they had had words together, when the squire ill-treated him. "What are thou here?" cried Tyler; "give me thy dagger." "I will not," said the squire: "why should I give it thee?" The king, turning to him, said "Give it him, give it him;" which he did, though much against his will. When Tyler took it, he began to play with it and turn it about in his hand, and, again addressing the squire, said, "Give me that sword." "I will not," replied the squire; "for it is the king's sword, and thou are not worthy to bear it, who art but a mechanic; and, if only thou and I were together thou wouldst not have dared to say what thou hast for as large a heap of gold as this church." "By my troth," answered Tyler, "I will not eat this day before I have thy head." At these words, the mayor of London, with about twelve more, rode forward, armed under their robes, and, pushing through the crowd, saw Tyler's manner of behaving: upon which, he said, "Scoundrel, how dare you thus behave in the presence of the king, and utter such words? It is too impudent for such as thou." The king then began to be enraged, and said to the mayor, "Lay hands on him."

While the king was giving the order, Tyler had addressed the mayor, saying, "Hey, in God's name, what I have said, does it concern thee? what dost thou mean?" "Truly," replied the mayor, who found himself supported by the king, "does it become such a stinking rascal as thou art to use such speech in the presence of the king, thy natural lord? I will not live a day, if thou pay not for it." Upon this, he drew a kind of cimeter he wore, and struck Tyler such a blow on the head as felled him to his horse's feet. When he was down, he was surrounded on all sides, so that his men could not see him; and one of the king's squires, called John Standwich, immediately leaped from his horse, and, drawing a handsome sword which he bore, thrust it into his belly, and thus killed him.

His men advancing, saw their leader dead, when they cried out, "They have killed our captain: let us march to them, and slay the whole." On these words, they drew up in a sort of battle-array, each man having his bent bow before him. The king certainly hazarded much by this action, but it turned out fortunate: for, when Tyler was on the ground, he left his attendants, ordering not one to follow him. He rode up to these rebellious fellows, who were advancing to revenge their leader's death, and said to them, "Gentlemen, what are you about? you shall have no other captain but me: I am your king: remain peaceable." When the greater part of them heard these words, they were quite ashamed, and those inclined to peace began to slip away. The riotous ones kept their ground, and showed symptoms of mischief, and as if they were resolved to do something.

71. STATUTE REGULATING HUNTING (1389)

ITEM, forasmuch as divers artificers, labourers, and servants, and grooms, keep greyhounds and other dogs, and on the holy days, when good christian people be at church, hearing divine service, they go hunting in parks, warrens, and connigries of lords and others, to the very great destruction of the same, and sometime under such colour they make their assemblies, conferences, and conspiracies for to rise and disobey their allegiance; (2) it is ordained and assented, That no manner of artificer, labourer, nor any other layman, which hath not lands or tenements to the value of xl s. [forty shillings] by year, nor any priest, nor other clerk, if he be not advanced to the value of x l. [ten pounds] by year, shall have or keep from henceforth any greyhound, hound, nor other dog to hunt; (3) nor shall they use ferrets, heys, nets, harepipes, nor cords, nor other engines for to take or destroy deer, hares, nor conies, nor other gentlemen's game, upon pain of one year's imprisonment; (4) and that the justices of peace have power to enquire, and shall enquire of the offenders in this behalf, and punish them by the pain aforesaid.

72. STATUTE OF MAINTENANCE AND LIVERIES (1390)

We have already seen that in the latter half of the fourteenth century peasants and townsmen were often rebellious. So, too, were the powerful barons who had a great many retainers whom they held in line by pay in-

stead of by the old system of land tenure. The fighting men among them
received livery and maintenance from the lord, who thus had at his beck
and call a private little army which wore his livery and coat of arms. These
groups formed the bulk of the English armies in the Hundred Years' War.
During the intervals of peace they were busily engaged in brawling, fighting
the forces of some rival lord, or simply in terrorizing the countryside. It was
to check this evil that the following statute was passed.

Whereas . . . grievous complaint and great clamor hath been made
unto us, as well by the lords spiritual and temporal as by the commons of
our said realm, of great and outrageous oppressions and maintenances made
to the damage of us and of our people, in divers parts of the same realm, by
divers maintainors, instigators, barrators, procurors, and embraceors of quarrels and inquests in the country, whereof many are the more encouraged and
bold in their maintenance and evil deeds aforesaid, because that they be of
the retinue of lords and others of our said realm, with fees, robes, and other
liveries, called liveries of company; We have ordained and straitly forbidden,
by the advice of our great council, that no prelate, nor other man of holy
Church, nor bachelor, nor esquire, nor other of less estate, give any manner
of such livery called livery of company; and that no duke, earl, baron, or
banneret give such livery of company to knight or esquire, if he be not retained with him for the term of his life for peace and for war, by indenture,
without fraud or evil device, or unless he be a domestic and familiar abiding
in his household; nor to any valet called yeoman archer, nor to other of less
estate than esquire, if he be not, in like manner, a familiar abiding in his
household. And that all lords spiritual and temporal, and all others of what
condition or estate they be, shall utterly oust all such maintainors, instigators,
barrators, procurors, and embraceors of quarrels and inquests from their
fees, robes, and all manner of liveries, and from their service, company, and
retainer, without receiving any such on their retainer, in any manner, in time
to come; and that no lord spiritual nor temporal, nor any other, that hath or
shall have people of his retinue, shall suffer any that belong to him, to be a
maintainor, instigator, barrator, procuror, or embraceor of quarrels and inquests in the country, in any manner, but shall put them away from his service and retinue, as afore is said, as soon as it can be discovered; and that if
any lord do oust any such maintainor, instigator, barrator, procuror, or embraceor from his company for this cause, that then no other lord do retain or
receive him of his retinue nor of his company in any manner; and that none
of our lieges, great nor small, of what condition or estate he be, whether he
be of the retinue of any lord, or other person whatever who belongeth not to

any retinue, shall not undertake any quarrel other than his own, nor shall maintain it, by himself nor by other, privily nor openly; and that all those who use and wear such livery called livery of company, contrary to this our ordinance, shall leave them off altogether within ten days after the proclamation of this same ordinance, without using or wearing them any more afterwards . . . .

73. LAWLESSNESS OF THE FIFTEENTH-CENTURY NOBILITY

The statute of maintenance and liveries did not succeed in putting an end to the lawlessness, and great lords with their armed retainers ambushed people on the king's highways, seized disputed lands by force, browbeat local officials, and prevented the administration of justice. An example of this type of disorderly conduct is given in the personal and private correspondence of the Pastons, a substantial middle-class family of Norfolk. Margaret Paston writes to her husband John in 1465:

On Tuesday in the morwyn whas John Botiller, otherwyse callid John Palmer, and Davy Arnald your cook, and William Malthows of Aylsham, takyn at Heylesdon be the balyf of Ey callid Bottisforth, and led for to Cossey, and ther thei kepe hem yet with ought any warant or autoryte of Justice of Peas. And thei saye thei will carie hem forth to Ey preson, and as many as thei may gete more of your men and tenaunts, that thei may know that owe yow good wyll or hath be to you ward, thei be thret to be slayn or presoned. The Duke came to Norwich on Tuesday at x. of clok with the nombre of v. hundred men. And he sent after the Meyr and Alderman with the Sherefs desiryng hem in the Kyngs name that thei shuld take an enqueraunce of the constablys of every ward with in the cyte what men shuld a go on your party to have holpyn or socowryd your men at any tyme of thes gaderyngs, and if any thei cowde fynde, that thei shuld take and arest hym and correct hym, and also certifie hym the names on Wyndenesse day [*Wednesday*] be viij. of clok. Which the Meyr dede, and wull do anythyng that he may for hym and his. And her up on the Meyr hath arestid on that was with me callid Roberd Lovegold, braser, and threte hym that he shall be hanged be the nek; wherfor I wuld that ther myght come down a writ too remeve hym if ye thynk it be to do. He was not with me not save that Harleston and other mad the assaught up on me and Lammesse; he is right good and feythfull on to you, and therefore I wuld he had help. I have non man . . . to avayte upon me that dare be avowyb but Litill John. . . .

The logge and the remenaunte of your place was betyn down on Tuesday and Wednesday, and the Duke rode on Wednysday to Drayton and so for to Cossey whille the logge at Heylesdon was in the betyng down. And this nyght at mydnyght Thomas Sleyforth, Grene Porter, and Joh. Botesforth the Baly of Eye, and other had a cart and fetched awey fetherbeddes, and all the stuffe that was left at the parsones, and Thom Wateres hows to be kept of owrs. I shall send you billes er after, as ner as I may, what stuffe we have forborn. I pray you send me word how ye will that I be demened, wheder ye wull that [I] abide at Cayster or come to you to London. I have no leyser to write more. God have yow in His kepyng. Wretyn at Norwich on Sent Lukes Evyn.   M. P.

> Ten days later (October 27, 1465), Margaret once more wrote to her husband, this time about a sacrilegious act by a nobleman's guards:

Ryght wyrshypfull hosbond, I recomand me to you. Please it you to wyte that I was at Haylesden uppon Thersday laste passyd, and sey the place ther, and in gode feyth ther wyll no cryatur thynke how fowle and orubelly it ys arayed but yf they sey it. . . . The Duck ys men rensackyd the church, and bare a way all the gode that was lefte ther, both of ours and of the tenaunts, and lefte not so moch but that they stode uppon the hey awter, and ransackyd the images, and toke a way such as they myght fynd, and put a way the parson owte of the church till they had don, and ransackyd every mans hous in the towne v. or vj. tymys. . . .

74. A FIFTEENTH-CENTURY WEDDING AGREEMENT

> In the fifteenth century there was a constant fusion of classes. Impoverished country gentry hoped to arrange marriages with prosperous town merchants and the latter sought social status by marriages with the landed families. Squires built houses for themselves in neighboring boroughs, became traders, and often held public office. John Paston, to whom previous reference has been made, married the daughter of a London draper and one of his brothers desired to wed the widow of a worsted-cloth merchant who had been left one hundred marks in money, one hundred marks in plate and furniture, and ten pounds in land. The following is an example of such a wedding contract:

This indenture, made betwix Anneys that was the wyfe of William Paston, John Paston hir sone, and John Dam on the one partie, and William Clopton, Squyer, on the other partie, witnesseth that accord is take attwyn the seid parties that John Clopton, sone and heir of the seid William Clopton, by the grace of God, shall wedde Elizabeth, the doughter of the seid Anneys. For which mareage the said Anneys, &c. shall paye to the seid John

Clopton CCCCth marc in hand of lawfull mony of England; and over that, yf the seid mareage be holdyn with the seid Anneys, the seid Anneys shall bere the costages therof the day of the weddyng, with swech chaumbeyr as shall be to the plesir of the seid Anneys; and the seid William Clopton shall do his feffees make a lawfull estate to the seid William of londs, tenementz, rentz, and servysez to the yerly value of xl*li*. over all chargez born, to have and to hold to hym terme of his lyfe, withoutyn empechement of wast, the remaindr therof to the seid John and Elizabeth, and to his heirs male of hir body lawfully begotyn, withoute impechement of wast, withynne xij. dayes after the seid weddyng.

And over that, withynne the seid xij. dayes the seid John shall do lawfull estate to be made to the seid William of londs, tenementz, rentz, and servysez to the yerly value of xl. marc over all charges born; to have and hold to the seid William terme of his lyfe, withoute empechement of wast; the remayndre therof to the seid Elizabeth, to have and hold to hir terme of hir lyfe withoute empechement of wast.

Also it is accorded that the seid William shall make estate of all the residue of his londs which he is sesid of, or any other man to his use, to swech personys as the seid John shall name, to the use of the seid John.

Also the seid John Clopton shall do lawfull estate to be made to the seid Elizabeth of londs, tenementz, rentz, and servysez to the yerly value of xxx*li*. over all chargez born, to have and to hold to hir duryng the lyfe of the seid William.

And moreover the seid John permytteth and ensureth be the feith of his body that he shall leve, over the xl*li*. worth lond aboveseid to his heirs and issue male of the body of the seid Elizabeth begotyn, londes in fee symple or in taill to the yerly value of xl. marc, in cas the same issue male be governyd to the seid John as the sone oweth to be to the fadir. And, &c.

75. MANAGEMENT OF FAMILY AFFAIRS

The correspondence between Margaret Paston and her husband, John, reveal the problems of family management when John was off on government business and Margaret was left to run the family's affairs. Money was then, as now, a constant source of concern. Margaret writes to John (probably in the 1460's):

Ryth reverent and worcepfful husbonde, I recomande me to yow, desyryng hertely to here of yowre welle fare, thankyn yow for yowr letter and for the thyngys that ye sent me ther with. And towchyn John Estegate,

he com nowdyr non sent hedyr nowt zyt; wer for I sopose I must borrowyn
money in schorte time but zyf [*unless*] ye come sone home; for I sopose I
xal non have of hym, so Godd helpe me. I have but iiijs. and I howhe nerr as
meche mony as com to the for seyd some. I have do yowr herrendys to my
modyr and my hunckyl and as for the feffeys of Stokysby, my hunckyll syth
that ther be no mo than he wrot to yow of that he knowit. And also I hauwe
delyvyrit the todyr thyng that ye sent me inselyd in the boxe as ye comaundit
me, and the man seyt, that I delyverid it to, that he wylle nowt of the
bargeyne that ye sent hym, but sweche thynggys be do or he come ther that
ye sent hym worde of, he seyth that he wold nowt be noysyd with no sweche
thyngis of that is, that it wer do in hesse tyme for xx. marke. I sopose he xal
send yow word in shorte time ho he wylle do. I pray yow that ye wylle
weche save to beyn for me swech lacys os I send yow exsaumpyll of in this
letter and j. pesse of blac lacys; as for cappys that ye sent me for the chyl-
deryn they be to lytyl for hem. I pray yow bey hem feyner cappys and larger
than tho wer. . . .

It is obvious from the next letter that John expected a good deal of his wife.

I pray yow, see to the god governaunce of my housold and guydynge of
other thynges touchyng my profite, and that ye, with Daubeney and Richard
Calle, and with other such of my frendis and servauntis as can avise yow aftir
the mater requireth, wekely take a sad comunecacion of such thynges as be for
to do, or oftener and nede be, takyng avise of the master, and of the viker
and Sir Jamis, that is for to say, as well for provision of stuffe for myn
howsold as for the gaderyng of the revenew of my livelode or greynes, or for
setting awerk of my servauntis, and for the more poletik meane of sellyng
and carryng of my malt, and for all other thynges necessari for to be do; and
that whanne I come home I have not an excuse, seying that ye spoke to my
servauntis and that Daubeney and Calle exkuse them that thei were so besy
thei myght not attende; for I woll have my mater so guided that if on many
may not attend a nother shall be comaunded to do it; and if my servauntis
faile I had lever wages some other man, for a jorny or a season, thanne my
mater should be on sped.

76. CHARACTER OF RICHARD III (1483-1485)

Sir Thomas More and historians who wrote under the Tudors, and a long
list of later historians, have represented Richard III as a monster of iniquity.
Though he was undoubtedly unscrupulous, cruel, and violent, he was probably no worse than contemporary princes on the Continent or many of his
predecessors in England, and probably no worse than his brother Edward

IV (1461–1483), or his successor, Henry Tudor. A seventeenth-century chronicler described Richard in these words:

There never was in any man greater uniformity of Body and Minde than was in him; both of them equally deformed. Of Body he was but low, crooke-backt, hook-shouldered, splay-footed, and goggle-eyed, his face little and round, his complexion swarthie, his left arm from his birth dry and withered: born a monster in nature, with all his teeth, with haire on his head, and nailes on his fingers and toes. And just such were the qualities of his minde: One quality he had in ordinary, which was, to look fawningly when he plotted, sternly when he executed. Those vices which in other men are Passions, in him were Habits: and his cruelty was not upon occasion, but naturall. If at any time he shewed any virtue, it was but pretence; the truth of his Minde was onely lying and falsehood. He was full of courage and yet not valiant; valour consisting not only in doing, but as well in suffering, which he could not abide. He was politick and yet not wise, Policie looking but to the middle, wisdome to the end: which he did, and did not. And it was not so much ambition that made him desire the Crown, as cruelty, that it might be in his power to kill at his pleasure: and to say the truth, he was scarce of the number of men who consist of flesh and blood, being nothing but blood. . . .

77. THE MURDER OF THE TWO PRINCES (1483)

Shortly after Richard III came to the throne, Edward V and his brother, aged nine and thirteen, disappeared, and though their fate is not certain, it was commonly believed that Richard had them put to death in the Tower of London. Of course, Richard was entirely capable of such a deed, but so was Henry Tudor, who would also gain by their removal from the scene. Charlotte M. Yonge describes the deed in this fashion:

No one knew them to be alive; but beyond dark rumour, and a quiet sad certainty on the part of those to whom they were nearest and dearest, nothing more was ascertained, though throughout the country people were singing the ballad of the Babes in the Wood, with an under-current of thought as to the cruel uncle and the two ruffians who slew the innocent children.

And the manner of their death has remained a "historic doubt." Whether they were really murdered is sometimes questioned; but this seems certain, since their uncle would otherwise have produced them to silence the outcry against him. To have sent them abroad, as was sometimes alleged, would have been very unlike so able a man as Richard, who would thus only have raised enemies against himself and his son; for boys of thirteen and nine were not like to forget their rank and right, and many a foreign sovereign would have delighted to avail himself of their quarrel, as Philippe Auguste had done of that of Arthur of Brittany [d. 1203]. Perhaps popular belief inclined to the mysterious and dreary wanderings hand in hand in the forest, with lips stained with blackberries, and the final sleep beneath the pious redbreasts' leafy pile; but about nine years later, a confession was published, said to have been made by two of the four persons concerned in the murder.

According to this confession, King Richard sent one John Green to Sir Robert Brackenbury, the Constable of the Tower, commanding him to make away with the children. Brackenbury refused; and Richard being overheard lamenting the difficulty, his page suggested one Sir James Tyrrell as fitted for the purpose.

Tyrrell was summoned, and agreed to do the King's bidding; whereupon Brackenbury was commanded to give up the keys of the Tower to him for one night. During the night, he brought in two servants, John Dighton and Miles Forrest, big powerful men, who smothered the two boys by pressing pillows on their faces as they lay asleep. Edward, it was said, had apprehended his fate for some days past, had paid no attention to his dress, and spent his time in weeping and lamentation; but both seem to have been peacefully sleeping when their lives were actually taken.

Sir James Tyrrell was called in to see the corpses, and they were buried at once at the foot of the staircase, but were afterwards removed from thence by Brackenbury's priest to another portion of the Tower by the King's desire.

Such was the story told by Tyrrell and Dighton, and published by command of Henry VII. . . .

As for the bodies, they could not be found when search was made for them where Dighton had buried them, at the base of the Bloody Tower, but he believed them to have been removed; and another search was made without effect under Queen Elizabeth. However, in 1674, under the White Tower, about ten feet under ground, a great chest was discovered containing the bones of two children, corresponding in age to Edward and Richard of York; and these were by command of Charles II. placed in a marble urn among the tombs of the kings in Westminster Abbey.

78. FOUNDING OF ALL SOULS COLLEGE, OXFORD (1437)

During the troubled times of the fifteenth century, continuing interest in education is revealed in the founding of grammar schools and colleges. The next document relates the origin of All Souls College, what it was like, and describes a fascinating All Souls tradition.

All Souls was built by Henry Chichly, Archbishop of Canterbury año dni 1437. Mr Henry Stedman, my worthy friend, one of that society, told me that this Archbishop, advising the king in those days to a war wth ffrance in wch many English were slaine, to Attone for that & æternise what in him lay their memory; he caused this Colledge to be built and gave it the name of All Souls, erecting there a fair Chappell, in which they were to pray for the soules of those deceased gallants. But, as a man may say, 'twas well for him he had money to do it. . . .

All Souls stands in the heart of the City. Between Brasenose & this Colledge Archbishop Laud had a design to open the great square, that was, to take away the houses between them as far as the schools, as you may find in that Bishops diary, printed by Mr Prin, who was commanded to sease his paper when a prisoner in the Tower. Here is in the Colledge one fair Quadrangle & the onely one that is paued with stone in Town. At the upper end of this Court against the wall is a sumptuous dial lately set up.

It has a very good Chappel pau'd with black and white Marble, & on the wall at ye East end since the King's Restauration is painted ye Resurrection, among the rest old Chichly rising out of his Tombe. But the colors haue now lost much of their beauty, and I believe People in these days haue not the skill to paint on walls as in former times, for I haue seen on the walls of a Church at Bilbo painting retaine its Pristine beauty, & doubtless there painted a great many years before, and in the Cloyster of Ashridge, the Lord Bridgewaters house in Hertfordshier, wch was a Religious house, you may there see Monkish stories painted on the wall, wch Colours do yet look pretty well fresh. But to proceed, here is a fair Hall, an excellent Common fire roome, & a very good Buttery, where the fellows of the house do often treat their friends, and there among other plate you may see Sr William Portman's great guilt Bowl of silver. . . .

Here, before I leave this Colledge and the good people in it, I must remember their mallard night. . . .

As touching the first institution of this Ceremony (which is uery ancient; saith Mr Stedman) I cannot give any account of it, but when they have a mind to keep it, the time is always within a night or two of All Souls.

Then there are six Electors wch nominate ye Lord of the Mallard, wch Lord is to beare the expences of the Ceremony. When he is chosen, he appoints six officers, who march before him with white staues in their hands, and meddalls hanging upon their breasts tied with a large blew ribbond. Upon ye meddalls is cut on the one side the Lrd of the Mallard wth his officers, on the other ye mallard as he is carried upon a long Poll. When ye L^d is seated in his chair with his officers of state (as aboue s^d) before him, they carry him thrice about the Quadrangle and sing this song:

> Griffin Turkey Bustard Capon
> Let other hungry mortalls gape on
> And on their bones wth stomacks fall hard
> But let All Souls men haue the mallard
> Hough the bloud of King Edward, by ye bloud of
> King Edward
> It was a swapping swapping Mallard.

> Stories strange were told I trow
> By Baker, Holinshead, and Stow
> Of Cocks & Bulls & other quere things
> That were done in the Reignes of their kings
> Hough the blood &c.

> Swapping he was from bill to eye
> Swapping he was from wing to thigh
> His swapping toole of generation
> Out swap'd all the winged Nation
> Ho the bloud &c.

> The Romans once admir'd a Gander
> More than they did their Chiefe Comānder
> Because it sau'd if some don't foole us
> The p[lace] called from ye head of Tolus
> Ho the bloud &c.

> Then let us sing & dance a Galliard
> To the remembrance of the mallard
> And as the mallard does in Poole
> Let's dabble diue and duck in Bowle
> Ho the bloud &c.

SOURCE REFERENCES   Chapter Three

39. *Parliamentary History*, I, 200–203.
40. *Parliamentary History*, I, 289–290.
41. *Parliamentary History*, I, 351.
42. *Holinshed's Chronicles Richard II. 1398–1400, Henry IV. and Henry V.*, pp. 37–39. Oxford: Clarendon Press, 1923.
43. *Statutes at Large,* 7 Henry VI, CAP. 7.
44. *Statutes at Large,* 33 Edward III, CAP. 1.
45. *Statutes at Large,* 17 Henry VI, CAP. 11.
46. 2 *Statutes of the Realm*, p. 342, in George B. Adams and H. Morse Stephens, eds., *Select Documents of English Constitutional History*, p. 195. New York: Macmillan and Co., 1929.
47. *Statutes at Large,* 23 Edward III, CAPS. 1 to 6.
48. *1 Statutes of the Realm*, p. 329, in Adams and Stephens, *Select Documents of English Constitutional History*, pp. 117–121.
49. *Statutes at Large,* 27 Edward III, CAP. 1.
50. Baker, *Chronicle of the Kings of England*, p. 175.
51. *Holinshed's Chronicles*, pp. 84–85.
52. Froissart, Sir John, *Chronicles of England, France, Spain, and the Adjoining Countries from the Latter Part of the Reign of Edward II. to the Coronation of Henry IV.*, trans. by Thomas Johnes, p. 283. New York: George A. Leavitt, 1852.
53. *Statutes at Large,* 7 Richard II, CAP. 12.
54. *Statutes at Large,* 2 Henry IV, CAP. 15.
55. Baker, *Chronicle of the Kings of England*, pp. 57–58.
56. Baker, *Chronicle of the Kings of England*, pp. 163–164.
57. *Holinshed's Chronicles*, pp. 34ff.
58. Cheyney, *Readings in English History*, pp. 293–295.
59. Selden Society, *Select Cases Concerning the Law Merchant, A.D. 1270–1638*, ed. by Charles Gross, I, 108; 115. London: Bernard Quaritch, 1908.
60. *Statutes at Large,* 11 Edward III, CAPS. 1, 2, 3, and 4.
61. *Statutes at Large,* 14 Edward III, CAP. 12.
62. *Statutes at Large,* 27 Edward III, CAP. 11.
63. *Statutes at Large,* Edward III, CAP. 1.
64. *Statutes at Large,* 12 Richard II, CAP. 4.
65. *Statutes at Large,* 17 Richard II, CAP. 4.
66. Baker, *Chronicle of the Kings of England*, p. 173.
67. From the account written by Henry Knighton, a Leicester clergyman, as given in Cheyney, *Readings in English History*, pp. 255–257.
68. *Statutes at Large,* 23 Edward III, CAP. 7.
69. *Parliamentary History*, I, 367–370.
70. Froissart, *Chronicles*, pp. 287–288.
71. *Statutes at Large,* 13 Richard II, CAP. 13.
72. 2 *Statutes of the Realm*, p. 74, as given in Adams and Stephens, *Select Documents*, pp. 153–154.

73. *The Paston Letters, A. D. 1422–1509,* ed. by James Gairdner, New Complete Library Edition, IV, 204–206. London: Chatto and Windus, 1904.

74. *Paston Letters,* II, 315–316.

75. *Paston Letters,* III, 255–256; IV, 121–122.

76. Baker, *Chronicle of the Kings of England,* p. 137.

77. Yonge, Charlotte M., *Cameos From English History,* pp. 175–176. London: Macmillan and Co., 1877.

78. *Collectanea,* 4th series, ed. by the Committee of the Oxford Historical Society, pp. 199–202. Oxford: Clarendon Press, 1905.

CHAPTER FOUR

The Tudor Period (1485-1603)

The Tudor period may be characterized as one of increasing sophistication and growing national wealth, great religious changes and overseas expansion. It was also an age of brilliant intellectual achievement such as England had never known, and of monarchical supremacy. The latter is traceable partly to the fact that the crown no longer had to share control of society with nobles and churchmen, and therefore it became almost the sole legal authority. And yet Tudor power was not absolute, for the monarchs relied on popular support and were careful to enlist the approval of their subjects and to curry favor with the increasingly important middle classes. Fundamental change in many areas of endeavor was so much the order of the day that scholars regard this period as the beginning of the "modern era" of English history.

79. THE COURT OF STAR CHAMBER (1487)

This court had exercised jurisdiction for some time as a prerogative court to handle those cases which the ordinary courts had not been strong enough to settle. It continued to function as a part of the privy council after it was formally constituted in 1487. Here is the most important part of the statute that formalized its existence:

First, The King our said sovereign lord remembereth, how by unlawful maintenances, giving of liveries, signs and tokens, and retainders by indentures, promises, oaths, writings, or otherwise embraceries of his subjects, untrue demeanings of sheriffs in making of panels, and other untrue returns, by taking of money, by juries, by great riots, and unlawful assemblies, the policy and good rule of this realm is almost subdued, (2) and for the not punishing of these inconveniencies, and by occasion of the premises, little or nothing may be found by inquiry, whereby the laws of this land in execution may take little effect, to the increase of murderers, robberies, perjuries, and unsureties of all men living, and losses of the lands and goods, to the great displeasure of almighty God: (3) Therefore it is ordained, for reformation of the premisses, by authority of the said parliament, That the chancellor and treasurer of England for the time being, and keeper of the King's privy seal, or two of them, calling to them a bishop, and a temporal lord of the King's most honorable council, and the two chief justices of the King's bench, and common place, for the time being, or other two justices in their absence, upon bill or information put to the said chancellor for the King, or any other, against any person for any misbehaviour afore rehearsed, have authority to call before them by writ, or by privy seal, the said mis-doers, and them, and other by their discretion, by whom the truth may be known to examine, and such as they find therein defective, to punish them after their demerits, after the form and effect of statutes thereof made, in like manner and form as they should and ought to be punished, as if they were thereof convict after the due order of the law. . . .

80. YEOMEN OF THE GUARD (1487)

In order to secure the safety of his own person and to provide for internal peace and order, Henry VII (1485–1509) created this special guard, which a chronicler has described:

Kyng Henry beyng made wise and expert with troubles and mischiefes before past, remembered that it was wisedome to feare and prouide for the crafty wyles and lurkyng traps of hys secret enemies, remembryng all men for the most part embrued and exercised in planting of diuision and sowyng dissencion, can not lightly leaue their pestiferous appetite, and sedicious occupation: Wherefore, for the sauegarde and preseruacion of his owne body, he constituted and ordayned a certayne number aswell of good archers as of diuers other persons beyng hardye, strong and of agilitie to geue dayly attendaunce on his body, whome he named Yomen of the crowne, which president men thought that he learned of y french kyng when he was in Fraunce: For men remembre not anye king of Englande before that tyme which vsed such a furniture of daylye souldiours. Yet forasmuch as to auoyde and eschew all doubtfull daungers and perilles vnloked for, lytle auayleth outwarde warre, except there be a sure stay, and a stedfast backstande at home, aswel for the sauegarde and securitie, as for the good gouernaunce of such as be left behynde . . . .

81. EMPSON AND DUDLEY, ROYAL AGENTS

Henry VII, greatly in need of revenue, for the treasury was entirely depleted, put councillors Morton, Empson, and Dudley in charge of his finances and insisted that they make the crown lands, feudal dues, and customs duty as productive as possible. He also ordered that they impose heavy fines upon men who had unwittingly violated obscure statutes. They did their work so well that they were accused of extortion and were thoroughly hated by the well-to-do. To gain favor with the latter, Henry VIII (1509–1547) had Empson and Dudley executed early in his reign.

King Henry having gotten as much honour as the Estimation of neighbouring Princes could give him, began now to be intentive to getting of wealth; wherein he quickly found instruments fit for his purpose, but specially two, Empson & Dudley both Lawyers; Dudley of a good family, but Empson the son of a Sieve-maker. These two persons being put in Authority, turned Law and Justice into Rapine. For first, their manner was, to cause divers Subjects to be indicted of Crimes, and then presently to commit them; and not produce them to their answer, but suffer them to languish long in Prison; and by sundry artificiall devices and terrors, extort from them great Fines, which they termed Compositions and Mitigations. Neither did they (towards the end) observe so much as the halfe face of Justice, in proceeding by Indictment; but sent forth their Precepts to attach men, and convent them before themselves and some others at their private houses, and there used to shuffle up a Summary proceeding by examination, without tryall of Jury; affirming to themselves, to deale both in Pleas of the Crowne, and controversies Civill. Then did they also use to enthrall and charge the Subjects lands with Tenures in capite, by finding false Offices; refusing upon divers pretexts and delays, to admit men to traverse those false Offices, as by Law they might. Nay the Kings Wards, after they had accomplished their full age, could not be suffered to have livery of their lands, without paying excessive Fines, farre exceeding all reasonable rates. When men were outlawed in personall actions, they would not permit them to purchase their Charters of Pardon, except they paid great and intolerable summes; standing upon the strict point of Law, which upon Outlawries gives forfeiture of goods. Nay, contrary to all Law and colour, they maintained, the King ought to have the halfe of mens lands and rents during the space of full two yeeres, for a Paine in case of Outlawry. They would also ruffle with Jurors, and enforce them to finde as they would direct; and if they did not, then convent, imprison, and fine them. These and many other courses they had of preying upon the people: but their principall working was upon Penall Statutes; wherein they considered not whether the Law were obsolete, or in use; and had ever a rabble of Promoters and leading Jurors at their command, so as they could have any thing found, either for Fact or Valuation.

82. DESCRIPTION OF HENRY VIII IN 1515

The Venetian ambassadors to England during the sixteenth and seventeenth centuries were among the most astute commentators on contemporary affairs, as this description by Giustinian amply illustrates.

King Henry was 29 years old, and much handsomer than any other Sovereign in Christendom,—a great deal handsomer than the King of France. He was very fair, and his whole frame admirably proportioned. Hearing that King Francis wore a beard, he allowed his own to grow, and as it was reddish, he had then got a beard which looked like gold. He was very accomplished and a good musician; composed well; was a capital horseman, and a fine jouster; spoke good French, Latin, and Spanish; was very religious; heard three masses daily when he hunted, and sometimes five on other days, besides hearing the office daily in the Queen's chamber, that is to say, vespers and compline. He was extremely fond of hunting, and never took that diversion without tiring eight or ten horses, which he caused to be stationed beforehand along the line of country he meant to take. He was also fond of tennis, at which game it was the prettiest thing in the world to see him play . . . .

He was affable and gracious; harmed no one; did not covet his neighbour's goods, and was satisfied with his own dominions . . . . He seemed extremely desirous of peace.

He was very rich. His father left him ten millions of ready money in gold, of which he was supposed to have spent one half in the war against France, when he had three armies on foot; one crossed the Channel with him; another was in the field against Scotland; and the third remained with the Queen in reserve.

His revenues amounted to about 350,000 ducats annually, and were derived from estates, forests, and meres, the customs, hereditary and confiscated property, the duchies of Lancaster, York, Cornwall, and Suffolk, the county palatine of Chester and others, the principality of Wales, the export duties, the wool staple, the Great Seal, the annates yielded by church benefices, the Court of Wards, and from new year's gifts; for on the first day of the year it is customary for his Majesty to make presents to everybody, but the value of those he receives in return greatly exceeds his own outlay.

A subject of all-absorbing interest during the sixteenth century in England and on the Continent was religion. Like other institutions, the Church could not hope to escape from hostile criticism. Church abuses such as

simony, nepotism, clerical immorality, pluralism and absenteeism existed, as
well as ignorance and laxity among the lower clergy, and wealth and corruption among the hierarchy. These abuses and a revival of heresies had led
to the Protestant Reformation. The prestige of the papacy had declined as
the Renaissance spirit shook men's faith in the supremacy of the popes and
brought into question many Church doctrines and practices. Its need for
money had caused the Church to resort to questionable methods of obtaining revenue exactly as it had caused monarchs to do. The Wycliffe heresy,
the work of the Oxford reformers, and centuries of troubled relations between England and the Church at Rome set the stage for change. Henry
VIII shrewdly won Parliament's support in his quarrel with the Church,
and thus gave to the English Reformation during the remainder of the century a national character. Unlike the circumstances on the Continent, the
quarrel in England was not at its inception a matter of doctrine, but primarily a question of papal supremacy.

83. HENRY VIII HONORED AS DEFENDER OF THE FAITH (1521)

About this time the king wrote in Latine a vehement booke against Martyn
Luther and confuted his judgement, touching Indulgences, and defendeth
the Bishop of Romes aucthority, and in the ende reproueth all his dis-
putacions concerning the Sacraments of the Church. The which booke the
Pope liked so well that the seconde daye of February, the king being at
Grenewich, came thether the Cardinall with a Legation from Leo Bishop of
Rome, and also his Ambassador, on whome waighted many a noble man,
the king met wyth them at his chamber doore welcoming them as though
they had both come from Rome. Then sayd the Cardinall, high and vic-
toryous king it hath pleased our Lorde God to indue your grace with a great
multitude of manifolde graces as king elect in fauour of the High Heauen,
and so appereth presently by your noble person, so formed & Figured in
shape and stature with force and pulcritude, which signifieth the present
pleasure of our Lorde God wrought in your noble grace. And further he
praysed his wisedome, prudence, and learning, with many other goodly
wordes in the praise of his most noble grace. And finally the Cardinall declared how the sayd Bishoppe of Rome had sent his highnesse an Acte in
Bull vnder leade, declaring therein his grace to be the defendor of the Christian fayth and his successors for euermore.

84. THOMAS WOLSEY BECOMES A CARDINAL (1515)

Wolsey, chief adviser to Henry VIII until 1529, was born in 1471, the son of
a butcher. After being educated at Magdalen College, his rise to prominence

was rapid and brilliant. From almoner to the king, he became a royal councillor, Registrar of the Order of the Garter, Dean of York, Bishop of Lincoln, and Archbishop of York. In 1515 he was given his Cardinal's hat. The chronicler Holinshed re-creates the scene in these words:

No lesse adoo was there at the bringing of the cardinals hat, who on a sundaie (in S. Peters church at Westminster) received the same, with the habit, the piller, and other such tokens of a Cardinall. And now that he was thus a perfect cardinall, he looked above all estates, which purchased him great hatred and disdaine on all sides. For his ambition was no lesse discernable to the eies of the people, than the sunne in the firmament in a cleere and cloudlesse summer daie; which procured against him the more hatred among the noble and popular sort; for that his base linage was both noted and knowne, in so much that his insatiable aspring to supereminent degrees of dignitie kindled manifest contempt and detestation among such as pretended a countenance of good will and honorable dutie to him, though in verie deede the same parties (if freelie and without checke they might have spoken their fansie) would have intituled him a proud popeling; as led with the like spirit of swelling ambition, wherwith the rable of popes have beene bladder like puffed and blowne up; a divelish and luciferian vice, in the judgements of men and abhominable, and in the sight of God most damnable . . . .

85. DESCRIPTION OF CARDINAL WOLSEY IN 1519

Wolsey was soon the recipient of other honors and offices, and as his power increased, so did his wealth and his pride. In 1519, the Venetian ambassador wrote of him:

The Cardinal of York had been styled Orion in a work composed by the ambassador. He was of low origin, and had two brothers, one of whom held an untitled benefice, and the other was pushing his fortune. He ruled both the King and the entire kingdom. On Giustinian's first arrival in England he used to say to him, "His Majesty will do so and so." Subsequently, by degrees, he went forgetting himself, and commenced saying, "We shall do so and so." He had then reached such a pitch that he used to say, "I shall do so and so."

He was about 46 years old, very handsome, learned, extremely eloquent, of vast ability, and indefatigable. He transacted alone the same business as that which occupied all the magistrates, offices, and councils of Venice, both civil and criminal; and all state affairs were managed by him.

He was pensive, and had the reputation of being extremely just. He favoured the people exceedingly, and especially the poor, hearing their suits, and seeking to despatch them instantly. He also made the lawyers plead gratis for all poor men.

He was in very great repute; seven times more so than if he were Pope. He had a very fine palace, where one traversed eight rooms before reaching his audience chamber. They were all hung with tapestry, which was changed once a week. Wherever he was, he always had a sideboard of plate worth 25,000 ducats. His silver was estimated at 150,000 ducats. In his own chamber there was always a cupboard with vessels to the amount of 30,000 ducats, as was customary with the English nobility. He was supposed to be very rich indeed in money, plate, and household stuff.

The archbishopric of York yielded him about 14,000 ducats, and the bishopric of Bath 8,000. One-third of the fees derived from the Great Seal were his; the other two were divided between the King and the Chancellor. The Cardinal's share amounted to about 5,000 ducats. By new year's gifts he made about 15,000 ducats.

86. THE "DIVORCE" CASE OF HENRY VIII AND CATHERINE (1527–1533)

Many considerations entered into this celebrated case. Henry had no male heir; all his children by Catherine had died in infancy save a daughter, Mary. Uncertainty about the succession might plunge England into a bloody conflict. Catherine was not only older than Henry, she was also sickly. Why had Catherine not given him a son? As Henry pondered this question, he concluded that God was displeased with his marriage to his brother Arthur's widow and that the pope ought not to have granted the dispensation permitting that marriage. His conscience bothered him, he said, and his desire to have the marriage annulled was quickened by his attachment to Anne Boleyn. Baker, the chronicler, gives the following account of the conduct of Henry and Catherine before the examining commissioners, and of Wolsey's discomfiture.

And now King Henry began to be troubled in mind about his marriage with Queen Katherin; but whether his trouble of minde grew for scruple of conscience, or from desire of change, was by many men doubted; some thought he had set his affection upon the Lady Anne Bullen whom afterward he maried, and to make way for that mariage, moved his scruple, that he might be divorced; but this is not likely, for he maried not the said Lady, til above three yeers after this doubt had bin moved; and three yeers was a long time to have affection be delaid, which comonly is impatient of any delay: if King Henries own protestation may be taken, it was very scruple of conscience that troubled his mind; but then by what meanes this scruple came first into his head, is another doubt . . . . He allowed the Queene to make choyce of what councell she thought best; who thereupon chose William Warham Archbishop of Canterbury, and Nicholas West Bishop of Elye . . . ; and in the mean time, sent to all the Universities in Italie & France to have their opinions, but specially to the Court of Rome, desiring the Pope to send his Legat to hear the cause; who thereupon sent Cardinall Campeius [Campeggio], and joyned Cardinall Woolsey in Commission with him. . . . The Court being set, the Judges commanded silence, whilst their Commission was read; which done, the Scribes commanded the Cryer to call the King, by the name of King Henry of England . . . ; then called he the Queene, by the name of Katherine . . . : the Queen though present, yet answered not, but rising from her seat, went to the place where the King sat, and kneeling down, said in effect; Sir, I humbly desire you to take pity upon me, for I am a poor woman & a stranger, & have here no indifferent Councel, where all are your Subjects, and lesse assurance of friendship when they all depend upon your favour; I have bin your wife these twenty yeers, and have borne you divers children, if you can charge me with dishonesty or undutifulnesse, I am content to depart from you to my shame; but if you cannot, I then desire you to do me justice, and to spare me untill I may know what councel my friends in Spain will give me; but if you will not, then your pleasure be fulfilled . . . . The King being advertised that she was going out of the House, commanded the Cryar to call her again . . . ; wel (she said) it makes no matter, I will not tarry . . . : and thus she departed, and never after would appear in any Court, but appealed from the Cardinals to the Pope himselfe. The Queen being gone, the King said, I confesse she hath bin to me, the most dutifull and loving wife, that ever Prince had; and if it were not for this scruple of my conscience, I would not leave her for any woman living: and having now referred the judgement of the cause to these Commissioners, I should be most glad they could finde the marriage between us to be in such sort lawfull, that with obedience to the Law of God, we might continue together; for I take God to witnesse, there is nothing I more desire. This said, the King rose, and the Court was adjourned to another day; for notwithstanding the Queens Appeal (from which she would by no meanes be drawn) the Cardinals continued their Session weekly, & heard all of both sides: the Point that was chiefly stood on, was, whether Prince Arthur had ever had carnall knowledge of her, or no; the Kings Councell alleadged, he had, and proved it; first, by Prince Arthurs speech, the next morning after his mariage, that he had bin that night in the midst of Spain; and then by the words of the last dispensation . . . : the Queens Advocates alleadged the contrary . . . . But whilest Arguments were thus urged on both sides, . . . the king sent the two Cardinals to the Queene . . . to perswade her, she should submit her selfe to the Kings pleasure, and not stand so peremptorily to her Appeale. . . . [She said] that in all other things she would willingly submit her selfe to the Kings will, but in this which concerned her honesty, and the legitimatenesse of her children, she durst not, but would relye upon the wisdom . . . [of the pope]. Upon their returne to the King, when he perceived she could not be removed from her opinion; he commanded the Court to goe on; so that at last it came to judgement, which every man expected should be the next day. At which day . . . Cardinall Campeius . . . said; I finde the case very doubtfull, and the party Defendant standing to her Appeale, I will therefore give no Judgement . . . and therefore I adjourne the Court for this time, according to the order of the Court of Rome, which heares no Causes judicially from the last of July till the fourth of October; at which protraction of time, King Henry was not a little angry . . . . Soon after this, the Cardinall tooke his leave of the King, and returned to Rome . . . . Whilst these things were in acting, Cardinall Woolsey had an inkling of the Kings affection to Anne Bullen, daughter of the Viscount Rochford; and that the Divorce once passed, he ment to marry her; which Match, because for many reasons, he misliked; one perhaps, because she was a Lutheran, he sent privily to the Pope, that by no means he should give sentence for the Divorce, till he had framed the Kings minde another way . . . . This packing of Woolsey was not so closely carried, but that it soone came to the Kings knowledge; and the King finding him a rubbe in his way, whom he expected to have expedited his proceeding, began to thinke it necessary to remove him, and to take him off from that greatnesse which had made him so presuming; and indeed he made short worke with him; for soone after he sent the Dukes of Norfolke and Suffolke to him for the Seale, which yet he would not deliver to them, till they brought him a Warrant under the Kings owne hand. When the Seale was brought to the King, he delivered it to Sir Thomas Moore, Speaker then of the Parliament (the first Lay-man that bore that Office in any memory;) and in his roome was chosen Speaker Thomas Audley, Attourney of the Dutchie. Woolsey now removed from his Chauncellourship; was in the Parliament then holden, charged with points of treason; but that charge was so cleerely taken off by his servant Thomas Cromwell, who was then of the House, that the Cardinall was acquitted, to the great commendation of Cromwell . . . .

87. LETTER OF HENRY VIII TO ANNE BOLEYN

The cause of my writeing at this time (good sweetheart) is wonly to understand off your good health and prosperity, whereof to know I would be as glad in manner myne awne, praying God, that and it be his pleasure, to send us shortly togydder, for I promise you I long for it, howbeit, trust it shall not be long to; and seeing my darling is absent, I can no less do, than to send her some fleshe representing my name, which is harts fleshe for Henry, prognosticating, that hereafter God willing you must enjoy some of mine, which if he pleased I wolde were now. As touching your sisters matter, I have caused Walter Welche to write to my lord mine mind therein, whereby I trust that Eve shall not have power to deceave Adam. . . . No more to you at this tyme, mine own darling, but that with a wishe I would we were togydder one evening with the hand of your, H.R.

88. CHARGES AGAINST CARDINAL WOLSEY (1529)

Indecision during the "divorce" proceedings gained for Wolsey the displeasure of Henry and the hatred of Anne. His many powerful enemies took advantage of his predicament to revive popular indignation against him because of his oppressive taxation and his arbitrary administration. Although he was successfully defended by Cromwell against an impeachment in the House of Lords, the charge that he had violated the Statute of Praemunire stood, and his property was declared forfeit to the crown. He then retired to his archdiocesan seat at York, but in 1530 he was arrested on a charge of high treason. On route to London to stand trial, he died at Leicester Abbey on November 29, 1530. The articles of impeachment against him the previous year were as follows:

First, that without the Kings assent, he hath procured himselfe to be made a Legat by reason whereof he tooke away the right of all Bishops and spirituall persons.

Secondly, that in all his writings which he wrote to Rome, or to any foraign Prince he wrote *Ego et Rex meus*, I and my King; so preferring himselfe before the King.

Thirdly, that without the Kings assent, hee carried the great Seale of England with him into Flanders.

Fourthly, that having the French-pox, he presumed to come and breath upon the King.

Fifthly, that he caused the Cardinals-hat to be put upon the Kings Coyne.

Sixthly, that he would not suffer the Kings Clerke of the Market to sit at Saint Albanes.

Seventhly, that he had sent infinite store of treasure to Rome, for purchasing of his dignity.

89. ANNULMENT OF MARRIAGE BETWEEN HENRY AND CATHERINE (1533)

Thomas Cranmer, Archbishop of Canterbury, gave an account of the annulment in a letter he wrote to Mr. Hawkyns, ambassador at the Imperial Court.

Ande fyrste as towchyng the small determynacion and concludyng of the matter of devorse betwene my Lady Kateren and the Kyngs Grace, whiche said matter after the Convocacion in that behalf hadde determyned and aggreed accordyng to the former consent of the Vniversities, yt was thowght convenient by the Kyng and his lernyd Councell that I shuld repayre unto Dunstable, which ys within iiij. myles vnto Amptell, where the said Lady Kateren kepeth her howse, and there to call her before me, to here the fynall Sentance in this said mateir. Nothwithstandyng she would not att all obey therunto, for whan she was by doctour Lee cited to appear by a daye, she utterly refused the same, sayinge that inasmoche as her cause was before the Pope she would have none other judge; and therfore woulde not take me for her judge. Nevertheless the viijth daye of Maye, accordyng to the said appoyntment, I came vnto Dunstable, . . . and soo there at our commyng kepte a Courte for the apperance of the said Lady Kateren, where were examyned certeyn witnes whiche testified that she was lawfully cited and called to appere, whome for fawte of apperance was declared contumax; procedyng in the said cause agaynste her *in poenam contumaciam* as the processe of the Lawe thereunto belongeth; whiche contynewed xv. dayes after our cummyng thither. And the morrow after Assension daye I gave finall Sentance therin, howe that it was indispensable for the Pope to lycense any suche marieges.

Henry VIII summoned Parliament in 1529 to consider national grievances against the Church, and, in the succeeding five years, it passed a series of statutes to reform those "evils" against which popular complaints had often been voiced. The statutes were designed to gain popularity for the king and as a sort of blackmail to force the pope to give him a "divorce" from Catherine. In 1529 a Mortuary Act restricted fees that could be collected at burials, a Probate Act fixed fees for probating wills, and a Pluralities Act substantially restricted plural livings—all to the detriment of the clergy. The king informed them in 1532 that they must agree to enact no laws, canons, or ordinances without royal license. In the same year Parliament conditionally abolished annates—the payment due to the pope by incumbents of ecclesiastical benefices. It was left to Henry to decide whether to apply the rule or not. In 1533 the Restraint of Appeals Act declared that henceforth all cases should be finally determinable in England without the right of appeal to any foreign prince or power. Shortly thereafter the payment of Peter's pence to Rome was abolished and an Act of Succession was passed vesting the succession to the throne in the heirs of Henry and Anne. Parliament concluded its work by enacting the following statute.

90. ACT OF SUPREMACY (1534)

Albeit the King's majesty justly and rightfully is and ought to be the supreme head of the church of England, and so is recognized by the clergy of this realm in their convocations, yet nevertheless for corroboration and confirmation thereof, and for increase of virtue in Christ's religion within this realm of England, and to repress and extirp all errors, heresies, and other enormities and abuses heretofore used in the same: be it enacted by authority of this present parliament, That the King our sovereign lord, his heirs and successors, Kings of this realm, shall be taken accepted and reputed the only supreme head in earth of the church of England, called *Anglicana Ecclesia;* (2) and shall have and enjoy, annexed and united to the imperial crown of this realm, as well the title and stile thereof, as all honours, dignities, preheminences, jurisdictions, privileges, authorities, immunities, profits and commodities to the said dignity of supreme head of the same church belonging and appertaining; (3) and that our said sovereign lord, his heirs and successors, Kings of this realm, shall have full power and authority from time to time to visit, repress, redress, reform, order, correct, restrain and amend all such errors, heresies, abuses, offences, contempts and enormities, whatsoever they be, which by any manner spiritual authority or jurisdiction ought or may lawfully be reformed . . . most of the pleasure of Almighty God, the increase of virtue in Christ's religion, and for the conservation of the peace, unity and tranquility of this realm; any usage, custom, foreign laws, foreign authority, prescription, or any other thing or things to the contrary hereof notwithstanding.

91. EXECUTIONS FOR HERESY AND FOR DENYING THE ROYAL HEADSHIP (1535)

After the Act of Supremacy had been passed, the Church in England had a new head, King Henry VIII, who insisted that those who did not take the oath to observe the Act be declared guilty of treason. But the creed of the

Church had not been changed; the ritual remained, and Henry permitted
the execution of those found guilty of heresy.

The five and twentieth daie of Maie [1535], was in saint Paules church
at London examined nineteene men and six women borne in Holland,
whose opinions were, first, that in Christ is not two natures, God and man:
secondlie, that Christ tooke neither flesh nor bloud of the virgin Marie:
thirdlie, that children borne of infidels shall be saved: fourthlie, that baptisme of children is to none effect: fiftlie, that the sacrament of Christs bodie
is but bread onelie: sixtlie, that he, who after his baptisme sinneth wittinglie,
sinneth deadlie, and cannot be saued. Fourteene of them were condemned, a
man and a woman of them were burned in Smithfield, the other twelue
were sent to other townes there to be burnt.

On the nineteenth of June were three monkes of the Charterhouse
hanged, drawne, and quartered at Tiburne, and their heads and quarters set
up about London, for denieng the king to be supreme head of the church.
. . . Also the one and twentith of the same moneth, and for the same cause,
doctor John Fisher bishop of Rochester was beheaded for denieng of the
supremacie, and his head set upon London bridge . . . . On the sixt of Julie
was Sir Thomas Moore beheaded for the like crime . . . . And then the
bodie of doctor Fisher was . . . buried with Sir Thomas Moore in the
Tower . . . .

92. DISSOLUTION OF THE MONASTERIES (1536–1539)

The customary payments to the pope had been diverted to the crown, but,
as Henry needed more money, Cromwell's responsibility was to find it.
Hence, Cromwell directed a visitation of all religious houses, which he and
others assumed to be richer than they actually were. It was also generally
believed that they were centers of superstition and vice. The commissioners,
some of whose reports follow, found enough monastic corruption to justify
in Henry's mind the confiscation of their property. In 1536, therefore, Parliament decreed the dissolution of 376 small monasteries (with an income of
less than £200 each per year). All their property was turned over to the
king. After the Pilgrimage of Grace (1536), an uprising in the North partly
caused by the dissolution, the larger monasteries were also dissolved. Estimates of the total value of these confiscations vary, but Professor Conyers
Read says that the king received about one-sixth of all the land of England,
yielding an annual value of about £100,000. Those who were granted lands
by the king paid about £800,000 for them. Henry disposed of about two-
thirds of these lands in this way; the remainder was let out on lease. The
residents of these monastic houses, male and female, were on the whole well

treated; they were given pensions, gratuities, or Church positions. The following examples of commissioners' reports to Cromwell reveal their work and the conditions in the various religious houses.

A. *Commissioner Layton to Cromwell:*

Pleasit your mastershipe to understonde, that yesternyght, late we came from Glassynburie to Bristowe to Saint Austins, wheras we begyn this mornyng, intendyng this day to dispache bothe this howse here, beyng but xiiij chanons, and also the Gawntes [hospital] wheras be iiij or v. By this bringar, my servant, I sende yowe relyqwis, fyrste, two flowres wrapped in white and blake sarcenet that one Christynmas evyn *hora ipsa qua Christus natus fuerat* will spring and burgen and bere blossoms, *quod expertum esse,* saith the prior off Maden Bradeley; ye shall also receve a bage of reliquis, wherin ye shall se straingeis thynges, as shall appere by the scripture, as Godes cote, Oure lades smoke, Parte of Godes supper *in cena domini, Pars petre super qua natus erate Jesus in Bethlehem,* belyke ther is in Bethlehem plentie of stones and sum quarrie, and makith ther maingierres off stone. . . .

I sende yowe also oure lades gyrdell of Bruton [a priory] rede silke, wiche is a solemne reliquie sent to women travelyng, wiche shall not miscarie *in partu.* I sende yowe also Mare Magdalens girdell, and that is wrappyde and coveride with white, sent also with gret reverence to women traveling, wiche girdell Matilda the empresse, fownder of Ferley [a small house dependent on the priory of Lewes] gave unto them, as saith the holy father of Ferley. I have crosses of silver and golde, sum wiche I send yow not now bycause I have mo that shalbe delivered me this nyght by the prior of Maden Bradeley hym self . . . .

B. *Commissioner Rice to Cromwell:*

Please it your mastership, fforasmoche as I suppose ye shall have sute made unto yow touching Burie er we retourne, I thought convenient to advertise yow of our procedinges there, and also of the compertes of the same. As for thabbot, we found nothing suspect as touching his lyving, but it was detected that he laye moche forth in his granges, that he delited moche in playng at dice and cardes, and therin spent moche money, and in buylding for his pleasure. He did not preche openly. Also that he converted divers fermes into copie holdes, wherof poore men doth complayne. Also he seemeth to be addict to the mayntenying of suche supersticious ceremonies as hathe ben used hertofor.

As touching the convent, we coulde geate litle or no reportes amonge theym, although we did use moche diligence in our examinacion, and therby, with some other argumentes gethered of their examinacions, I fermely beleve and suppose that they had confedered and compacted bifore our commyng that they shulde disclose nothing. And yet it is confessed and proved, that there was here suche frequence of women commyng and re-assorting to this monastery as to no place more. Amongest the reliques we founde moche vanitie and superstituion, as the coles that Saint Laurence was tosted withall, the paring of S. Edmundes naylles, S. Thomas of Canterbury penneknyff and his bootes, and divers skulles for the hedache; peces of the holie crosse able to make a hole crosse of; other reliques for rayne and cer-tain other superstitiouse usages, for avoyding of wedes growing in corne, with suche other . . . .

C. *Commissioners in Northamptonshire to Sir R. Rich:*

Ryght honorable, after all humble recommendacions, theis shalbe to ad-vertyse you that we have byn yn execusion off the kynges commission di-rected unto us, begyngnyng at Chacumbe, wher we accomplysshed alle thynges accordyng unto our commyssion, and frome thens we repayred to Assheby, where after on days tarreyng we werr ffayne to departe thens unto Catesby nunrey. . . . Which howse of Catesby we ffounde in verry perfett order, the prioress a sure, wyse, discrete, and very religyous woman, with ix nunnys under her obedyencye as relygious and devoute and with as good obedyencye as we have in tyme past seen or belyke shall see . . . . Where-fore yf yt shulde please the kynges highnesse to have eny remorse that eny suche relygous house shall stande, we thynke his grace cannot appoynt eny house more mete to shewe his most gracious charitie and pitey on than one the said howse of Catesby . . . .

93. THE SIX ARTICLES (1539)

By 1539 it was deemed essential to define doctrines of the Church in Eng-land. This was done by the following Six Articles, which were basically a reiteration of existing Roman Catholic belief on these points.

First, That in the most blessed sacrament of the altar, by the strength and efficacy of Christ's mighty word (it being spoken by the priest) is present really, under the form of bread and wine, the natural body and blood of our Saviour Jesus Christ, conceived of the Virgin Mary; and that after the con-secration there remaineth no substance of bread or wine, nor any other sub-stance: but the substance of Christ, God and man.

Secondly, That communion in both kinds is not necessary *ad salutem,* by the law of God, to all persons; and that it is to be believed, and not doubted of, but that in the flesh, under the form of bread, is the very blood; and with the blood, under the form of wine, is the very flesh; as well apart, as though they were both together.

Thirdly, That priests after the order of priesthood received, as afore, may not marry by the law of God.

Fourthly, That vows of chastity or widowhood, by man or woman made to God advisedly, ought to be observed by the Law of God; and that it exempteth them from other liberties of christian people, which without that they might enjoy.

Fifthly, That it is meet and necessary, that private masses be continued and admitted in this the King's English church and congregation, as whereby good christian people, ordering themselves accordingly, do receive both godly and goodly consolations and benefits; and it is agreeable also to God's law.

Sixthly, That auricular confession is expedient and necessary to be retained and continued, used and frequented in that church of God.

94. THE ACT OF UNIFORMITY (1549)

Edward VI (1547–1553), the sickly ten-year-old son of Henry VIII, succeeded to the throne at the same time that leadership in the privy council passed to the Duke of Somerset. He secured legislation which liberalized the Treasons Act of 1534, rescinded the Six Articles, and permitted the clergy to marry. The capstone of his religious policy was the Act of Uniformity, requiring the use in all churches of Thomas Cranmer's *Book of Common Prayer* and removing many remaining Roman Catholic practices.

Where the King's most excellent majesty hath of late set forth and established by authority of parliament, an uniform, quiet and godly order for common and open prayer, in a book, intituled, the Book of Common Prayer and Administration of the Sacraments, and other Rites and Ceremonies of the Church, after the Church of England, to be used and observed in the said church of England, agreeable to the order of the primitive church, much more comfortable unto his loving subjects than other diversity of service, as heretofore of long time hath been used, being in the said book ordained, nothing to be read but the very pure word of God, or which is evidently grounded upon the same; (2) and in the other, things corrupt, untrue, vain and superstitious, and as it were a preparation to superstition; which for that they be not called in, but permitted to remain undefaced, do not only give occasion to such perverse persons as do impugn the order and godly meaning of the King's said book of common prayer, to continue in their old accustomed superstitious service, but also minister great occasion to diversity of opinions, rites, ceremonies and services: (3) be it therefore enacted . . . That all books called Antiphoners, Missals, Grailes, Processionals, Manuals, Legends, Pies, Portuasses, Primers in Latin or English, Couchers, Journals, Ordinals or other books or writings whatsoever heretofore used for service of the church, written or printed in the English or Latin tongue, other than such as are or shall be set forth by the King's majesty, shall be by authority of this present act clearly and utterly abolished, extinguished and forbidden for ever to be used or kept in this realm, or elsewhere within any the King's dominions.

II. And be it further enacted . . . That if any person or persons, of what estate, degree or condition soever he, she or they be, body politick or corporate, that now have or hereafter shall have in his, her or their custody, any the books or writings of the sorts aforesaid, or any images of stone, timber, alabaster or earth, graven, carved or painted, which heretofore have been taken out of any church or chapel, or yet stand in any church or chapel, and do not before the last day of June next ensuing deface and destroy, . . . the same images and every of them, and deliver or cause to be delivered all and every the same books to the mayor, bailiff, constable or church-wardens of the town where such books then shall be, to be by them delivered over openly within three months next following . . . to the archbishop, bishop, chancellor or commissary of the same diocese, to the intent the said . . . cause them immediately either to be openly burnt or otherwise defaced and destroyed; shall for every such book or books willingly retained in his, her or their hands or custody within this realm, or elsewhere within any the King's dominions, and not delivered . . . after the said last day of June, and be thereof lawfully convict, forfeit and lose to the King our sovereign lord, for the first offence xx.s. and for the second offence shall forfeit and lose . . . iv. li [£4] and for the third offence shall suffer imprisonment at the King's will. . . .

95. PRINCESS MARY AND THE MASS (1550)

The majority of Englishmen accepted the liturgical and doctrinal changes effected under Edward VI. Some reformers, however, wished further changes from Romanism, while Roman Catholics, although accepting royal supremacy, much preferred the old Latin mass. Mary was one of them, as can be seen from these two entries in Edward's diary.

June 22. The Lady Mary sent Letters to the Council marvelling at the Imprisonment of Dr. Mallet her Chaplain for saying of Mass before her household seeing it was promised the Emperors Ambassadour she should not be molested in Religion but that she and her Household should have the Mass said before them continually.

Aug. 29. Certain Pinaces were prepared to see that there should be no conveyance over sea of the Lady Mary secretly done. Also appointed that the Lord Chancellor, Lord Chamberlain, the Vice Chamberlain and the Secretary Petre should see by all means they could whether she used the Mass; and if she did that the Laws should be executed on her chaplains. Also that when I came from this Progress to Hampton Court or Westminster both my sisters should be with Me till further Orders were taken for this purpose.

96. QUEEN MARY RESTORES ROMAN CATHOLICISM (1553–1558)

Mary had been brought up in the Roman Catholic faith by her mother Catherine. In the years of Mary's suffering and mistreatment because she steadfastly adhered to her religion, she became convinced that all the ills she had been heir to were attributable to England's departure from the old faith. When she came to the throne, therefore, she began to restore that faith. Bishops imprisoned in Edward's reign were released; the Roman Catholic Bishop Stephen Gardiner was made Lord Chancellor and chief adviser to the queen; and her first Parliament, while it did not restore papal supremacy nor the confiscated Church lands, did repeal the anti-Catholic legislation of Edward's Parliaments, and declared her legitimate and the "divorce" of Henry and Catherine illegal. A later Marian Parliament restored papal jurisdiction in England and renewed the laws against heresy. Clauses 24 and 53 of the statute of 1554 read in part:

That all clauses, sentences and articles of every other statute or act of parliament, made sithence the said twentieth year of the reign of King Henry the Eighth, against the supream authority of the pope's holiness, or see apostolick of Rome, or containing any other matter of the same effect only, that is repealed in any of the statutes aforesaid, shall be also by authority hereof from henceforth utterly void, frustrate and of none effect. . . . (3) and the pope's holiness and see apostolick to be restored, and to have and enjoy such authority, preheminence and jurisdiction, as his holiness used and exercised, or might lawfully have used and exercised, by authority of his supremacy, the said twentieth year of the reign of the King your father, within this your realm of England, and other your dominions, without diminution or inlargement of the same, and none other; and . . . the ecclesiastical jurisdictions of the archbishops, bishops and ordinaries, to be in the same state for process of suits, punishment of crimes, and the execution of censures of the church, with knowledge of causes belonging to the same, and as large in these points as the said jurisdictions was the said twentieth year . . . .

97. CHARGES AGAINST RIDLEY AND LATIMER (1554)

> Bishops Nicholas Ridley and Hugh Latimer refused to conform to the reestablished Catholicism, and continued to be vigorous exponents of Protestantism. They were arrested and charged in these words:

In the name of God, Amen. We, John of Lincoln, James of Gloucester, and John of Bristol, bishops, &c.

1. We do object to thee, Nicholas Ridley, and to thee, Hugh Latimer, jointly and severally, first, that thou, Nicholas Ridley, in this high University of Oxford, in the year 1554, hast affirmed, and openly defended, and maintained, and in many other times and places besides, that the true and natural body of Christ, after the consecration of the priest, is not really present in the sacrament of the altar.

2. Item. That in the year aforesaid thou hast publicly affirmed and defended that in the sacrament of the altar remaineth still the substance of bread and wine.

3. Item. That in the said year thou hast openly affirmed, and obstinately maintained, that in the mass is no propitiatory sacrifice for the quick and the dead.

4. Item. That in the year, place, and months aforesaid, these the aforesaid assertions solemnly had been condemned, by the scholastical censure of this school, as heretical and contrary to the catholic faith, by Dr. Weston, prolocutor then of the Convocation House, as also by other learned men of both the universities.

5. Item. That the premises be true and openly known by public fame, as well to them near hand as also to them in distant places.

98. STATEMENT OF ARCHBISHOP CRANMER (1556)

> Ridley and Latimer had been burned at the stake at Oxford in 1555, and Cranmer followed them to the same death in 1556. Mary, of course, had reason to oppose him, for he had supported the cause of Lady Jane Grey, he had been the author of the *Book of Common Prayer,* and he had given the sanction of the Church to Henry's "divorce." Before being put to the fire he made a stirring statement to the assembled crowd which restored the dignity he had lost by earlier recantations.

And now, forasmuch as I am come to the last end of my life, where-upon hangeth all my life past, and all my life to come, either to live with my Master Christ for ever in joy, or else to be in pain for ever with wicked devils in hell, and I see before mine eyes presently either heaven ready to receive me, or else hell ready to swallow me up: I shall therefore declare unto you my very faith how I believe, without any colour or dissimulation; for now is no time to dissemble, whatsoever I have said or written in time past.

First, I believe in God the Father Almighty, maker of heaven and earth, etc. And I believe every article of the catholic faith, every word and sentence taught by our Saviour Jesus Christ, his apostles and prophets, in the New and Old Testament.

And now I come to the great thing, which so much troubleth my con-science, more than anything that ever I did or said in my whole life, and that is the setting abroad of a writing contrary to the truth; which now here I renounce and refuse, as things written with my hand, contrary to the truth which I thought in my heart, and written for fear of death, and to save my life if it might be; and that is, all such bills and papers which I have written or signed with my hand since my degradation; wherein I have written many things untrue. And foreasmuch as my hand offended, writing contrary to my heart, my hand shall first be punished there-for; for may I come to the fire, it shall be first burned.

And as for the pope, I refuse him, as Christ's enemy, and antichrist, with all his false doctrine.

And as for the sacrament, I believe as I have taught in my book against the bishop of Winchester, the which my book teacheth so true a doctrine of the sacrament, that it shall stand at the last day before the judgment of God, where the papistical doctrine contrary thereto shall be ashamed to show her face.

99. MARTYRDOM OF PROTESTANTS UNDER MARY (1555–1558)

John Foxe, whose necrology of Protestant martyrs deeply influenced the at-titudes of Englishmen of his age, gives these reasons for persecution of Protestants:

Of these five prisoners, the first two were uncondemned; the other three last were condemned, and should have been burned, but suffered no less torments than if they had abided the fire, being macerated and pined to death by famine. What their articles and answers were, I need not here to recite, seeing all they, in the time of queen Mary, commonly suffered for one manner and sort of cause, that is, for holding against the seven sacraments; against the reality of Christ's being in his supper; for speaking against the church of Rome, and determinations of the same; against images set up and worshipped in the church; for not coming to church, and other like, etc.

100. ELIZABETHAN OATH OF SUPREMACY (1559)

> Elizabeth I (1558-1603), having lived through the troubled years of Edward and Mary, had seen to what misery a nation could be forced by religious bigotry and intolerance. She decided, therefore, to pursue a middle-of-the-road policy, but being a strong nationalist, she naturally accepted the break with Rome as basic to her religious settlement. To achieve this, Parliament passed an Act of Supremacy and an Act of Uniformity (1559). By these statutes Anglicanism was restored, the pope's authority in England ended, and Elizabeth became the "governor" of the Church of England. The mass was abolished and the *Book of Common Prayer* was reintroduced. The ornaments, forms, and services used in churches were ordered to be the same as during Edward's reign. Despite protests, all clergymen and officers of the crown were compelled to take the following oath of supremacy:

I A.B. do utterly testify and declare in my conscience, That the Queen's highness is the only supreme governor of this realm, and of all other her Highness dominions and countries, as well in all spiritual or ecclesiastical things or causes, as temporal; and that no foreign prince, person, prelate, state or potentate, hath or ought to have any jurisdiction, power, superiority, preheminence, or authority ecclesiastical or spiritual, within this realm; and therefore I do utterly renounce and forsake all foreign jurisdictions, powers, superiorities and authorities, and do promise, that from henceforth I shall bear faith and true allegiance to the Queen's Highness, her heirs and lawful successors, and to my power shall assist and defend all jurisdictions, preheminences, privileges and authorities granted or belonging to the Queen's highness, her heirs and successors, or united and annexed to the imperial crown of this realm. So help me God, and by the contents of this book.

101. PROCLAMATION AGAINST ANABAPTISTS (1560)

> The Anabaptists, believing in the imminence of the second coming of Christ, denying the efficacy of infant baptism, and opposing the union of Church and State, were hated by virtually all religious groups. The persecution to which they were subjected on all sides in the Low Countries caused many of them to flee to England. Elizabeth also detested their doctrines and hence had the following proclamation issued.

The Queen's Majesty understanding that of late time sundry persons, being infected with certayn dangerous and pernicious opinions, in matters of religion, contrary to the fayth of the Church of Chryst, as Anabaptists, and such lyke, are come from sundry parts beyond the seas into this her realme, and speciallye into the citie of London, and other maritime townes, under the colour and pretence of flying from persecution against the professors of the Gospel of Chryst: whereby if remedy be not speedily provided, the Church of God in this realme shall susteyne great daunger of corruption, and sects to encrease contrary to the unitie of Chryst's Church here established.

For redresse whereof, her Majestie, by advice of her Counsayle, having commanded the Archbishop of Canterbury, Byshop of London, and other Byshops to see the parishes in London, and other places herewith suspected, to be severely visited, and all persons suspected to be openly tried and examined, touching such phanatical and heretical opinions; willeth and chargeth all manner of persons born eyther in forreigne parts, or in her Majesties dominions, that have conceaved any manner of such heretical opinion as the Anabaptists do hold, and meaneth not by charitable teaching to be reconciled, to depart out of this realme within twenty days after this proclamation, upon payne of forfeiture of all their goods and cattelles, and to be imprisoned, and further punyshed, as by the laws eyther ecclesiastical or temporal in such case is provided.

And her Majesty also chargeth and commaundeth upon payne of imprisonment, that no Minister, nor other person, make any conventicules or secret congregations, eyther to read, or to preache, or to minister the Sacraments, or to use any maner of divine service, but that they shall resort to open chappels or churches, and there to preach, teach, minister, or pray, according to the order of the Church of England. . . .

102. STATUTE FORBIDDING THE PUBLISHING IN ENGLAND OF ANY PAPAL BULLS (1570)

The Elizabethan Religious Settlement of 1559 was followed by approximately ten years of quiet. However, the flight of Mary Stuart to England in 1567 and talk of a Roman Catholic plot to overthrow Elizabeth in favor of Mary worried Elizabeth. Moreover, after considerable hesitation, the pope decided to excommunicate her and a bull to that effect was published in London in May 1570. In reprisal against the bull, Parliament passed the following statute:

II. For remedy and redress whereof, and to prevent the great mischiefs and inconveniences that thereby may ensue, be it enacted by the Queen's most excellent majesty, with the assent of the lords spiritual and temporal, and the commons, in this present parliament assembled, and by the authority of the same, That if any person or persons, after the first day of July next coming, shall use or put in use in any place within this realm, or in any the Queen's dominions, any such bull, writing or instrument written or printed, of absolution or reconciliation, at any time heretofore obtained and gotten, or at any time hereafter to be obtained or gotten from the said bishop of Rome or any his successors, or from any other person or persons authorized or claiming authority by or from the said bishop of Rome, his predecessors or successors, or see of Rome; (2) or if any person or persons after the said first day of July, shall take upon him or them, by colour of any such bull, writing instrument or authority, to absolve or reconcile any person or persons, or to grant or promise to any person or persons within this realm, or any other the Queen's majesty's dominions any such absolution or reconciliation, by any speech, preaching, teaching, writing or any other open deed; (3) or if any person or persons within this realm . . . after the said first day of July shall willingly receive and take any such absolution or reconciliation:

III. Or else if any person or persons have obtained or gotten since the last day of the parliament holden in the first year of the Queen's . . . reign, or after the said first day of July shall obtain or get, from the said bishop of Rome, . . . any manner of bull writing or instrument . . . containing any thing, matter or cause whatsoever; (2) or shall publish, or by any ways or means put in use any such bull, writing or instrument; (3) that then all and every such act . . . shall be deemed and adjudged by the authority of this act to be high treason; (4) and the offender and offenders therein, their procurers, abetters and counsellers to the fact and committing of the said offence or offences, shall be deemed and adjudged high traitors to the Queen and the realm; (5) and being thereof lawfully indicted and attainted according to the course of the laws of this realm, shall suffer pains of death, and also lose and forfeit all their lands, tenements, hereditaments, goods and chattels, as in cases of high treason by the laws of this realm ought to be lost and forfeited. . . .

103. STATUTE AGAINST PERSONS BECOMING ROMAN CATHOLICS (1581)

Despite the statute of 1570, says the preamble of this statute of 1581, "diverse evil-affected persons have practiced . . . by other means than bulls or instruments . . . to withdraw divers of the Queen's Majesty's subjects from their natural obedience to her Majesty, to obey the said usurped authority of Rome, and . . . to perswade great numbers to withdraw their due obedience from her Majesty's laws, established for the due service of Almighty God."

II. For reformation whereof, and to declare the true meaning of the said law, be it declared and enacted . . . That all persons whatsoever, which have or shall have, or shall pretend to have power, or shall by any ways or means put in practice to absolve, perswade or withdraw any of the Queen's Majesty's subjects, or any within her Highness realms and dominions, from their natural obedience to her Majesty: (2) or to withdraw them for that intent from the religion now by her Highness authority established within her Highness dominions, to the Romish religion, (3) or to move them or any of them to promise any obedience to any pretended authority of the see of Rome, or of any other prince, state or potentate, to be had or used within her dominions, (4) or shall do any overt act to that intent or purpose; and every of them shall be to all intents adjudged to be traitors, and being thereof lawfully convicted shall have judgment, suffer and forfeit, as in case of high treason. (5) And if any person shall after the end of this session of parliament, by any means be willingly absolved or withdrawn as aforesaid, or willingly be reconciled, or shall promise any obedience to any such pretended authority, prince, state or potentate, as is aforesaid, that then every such person, their procurers and counsellors, . . . shall be taken, tried and judged, and shall suffer and forfeit, as in cases of high treason. . . .

104. ACT AGAINST JESUITS AND SEMINARY PRIESTS (1585)

During the 1570's a strong anti-Catholic, anti-Spanish attitude developed in England. This was attributable to the pope's unwise excommunication of Elizabeth, to Roman Catholic support of Mary, Queen of Scots, who craved the English throne, and to the numerous plots which her coreligionists planned against Elizabeth. Catholic seminaries on the Continent trained Englishmen for the priesthood, and many of them returned to England to bolster the faith of Roman Catholics and to win Anglicans and Protestants back to the fold. In 1580 the pope sent Jesuits to aid in this work. Elizabeth and her advisers believed, rightly or wrongly, that the Jesuits had been commissioned to rouse the Roman Catholics against her, which the Babington Plot later appeared to prove. Parliament, agreeing with the queen, quickly passed a statute against Jesuits and other priests, the main parts of which are the following:

That all and every jesuits, seminary priests, and other priests whatsoever made or ordained out of the realm of England or other her Highness dominions, or within any of her Majesty's realms or dominions, by any au-

thority . . . from the see of Rome, since the feast of the nativity of St. John
Baptist in the first year of her Highness reign, shall within forty days next
after the end of this present session of parliament depart out of this realm of
England, . . . if the wind, weather and passage shall so serve.

III. . . . That it shall not be lawful to or for any jesuit, seminary priest,
or other such priest, deacon, or religious or ecclesiastical person whatsoever,
being born within this realm . . . to come into, be or remain in any part of
this realm, . . . after the end of the same forty days, other than in such special cases, and upon such special occasions only, and for such time only, as is
expressed in this act; and if he do, that then every such offence shall be taken
and adjudged to be high treason; and every person so offending shall for
his offence be adjudged a traitor, and shall suffer, lose and forfeit, as in case
of high treason.

IV. And every person which after the end of the same forty days, and
after such time of departure as is before limited and appointed, shall wit-
tingly and willingly receive, relieve, comfort, aid or maintain any such jesuit,
seminary priest or other priest, deacon or religious or ecclesiastical person,
. . . being at liberty, or out of hold, knowing him to be a jesuit, seminary
priest or other such priest, deacon, or religious or ecclesiastical person, as is
aforesaid, shall also for such offence be adjudged a felon, without benefit of
clergy, and suffer death, lose and forfeit, as in case of one attainted of
felony. . . .

105. ELIZABETH'S COMPLAINTS AGAINST PURITANS (1576)

While Roman Catholics attacked the Established Church from one direction, the Puritans in the Church of England attacked it from another. They
thought the Church still too Catholic in its ceremonies, ritual, and government. They preferred a form of Church government in which the laity
could take a greater part. These Puritans were strong in the House of
Commons, and influential in intellectual and mercantile circles. Elizabeth
did not like them even though they were passionately loyal to her. When
they were excluded from pulpits, they held public services outside the
church, a practice which Elizabeth ordered the Archbishop of Canterbury
to stop.

All this pains did the Archbishop take to rectify and take away the
abuses of these religious exercises, rather than wholly to abolish them. However the Queen liked not of them, nor would have them continued; as seeing
probably how very apt they were to be abused. Nor did she like that the laity
should neglect their secular affairs by repairing to these meetings; which she

thought also might fill their heads with notions, and so occasion dissensions and unquiet disputes, and it may be seditions in the state. And the Archbishop being at Court, she particularly declared herself offended at the numbers of preachers, as well as at the exercises, and warned him to redress both: urging, that it was good for the Church to have few preachers, and that, three or four might suffice for a county; and that the reading of the homilies to the people was enough. In short, she required him to do these two things, viz. to abridge the number of preachers, and to put down the religious exercises. The speeches she used to him were somewhat sharp; and she was very resolute to have no more exercises of this sort, and cared not for any great increase of preachers; but that the licences for preaching should be more sparingly granted out; and she expected the Archbishop should give especial orders for both.

106. ELIZABETHAN PERSECUTION OF PURITANS

The following item, taken from G. B. Harrison's *An Elizabethan Journal* and dated March 11, 1591, shows how firmly the government dealt with the Puritans.

There is much discontent at this time amongst those that favour the Puritan principles; for the labouring and striving to bring in a uniformity cause, and seems likely to cause, nothing but desolation. The best and faithfullest preachers, say they, are cast into prison, sometimes being closely shut up from the speech and company of their dearest friends, degraded and deprived of their livings, some even having six or seven children, who are sent begging, for all the pillars of the church would do for them. Mr. Cartwright has lain in the Fleet since September; Mr. Fenne of Coventry with many more is in the Clink; Udall, a profitable preacher of Kingston-on-Thames, lies sentenced to be hanged for a book called *Demonstrations of Discipline*; and having been condemned before as its author, they now try to make him acknowledge it as his doing. His life is spared hitherto by the intercession of Sir Walter Ralegh. All these things seem but a way to bring in popery, for atheism is here already, and soon will overflow the land. It is rumoured that a general demand is proposed not only of the ministry but of all who bear public office throughout the land to subscribe that the authority of the bishops is lawful by God's Word. When the Lord Treasurer was asked to subscribe to it, he answered, "It is lawfully the positive law; but to say it is lawful by the Word of God, that is another matter." There the matter stayed for the time.

107. MARY STUART FOUND GUILTY OF TREASON (1587)

When Mary was caught red-handed in the Babington Plot, her fate, long a matter of great concern to Elizabeth, was sealed. Mary had been the focal point, sometimes unwittingly, of all the plots by Catholics against Elizabeth. Had these plots succeeded, they would have given Mary the English throne and seen the death of Elizabeth. Parliament recommended that Mary should be executed, but before the date was set, Bellièvre, a special ambassador, was sent from France to try to save her life. He failed. Elizabeth wrote to Bellièvre:

The wickedness of the Queen of Scotland is unwonted, and unwonted should be the example offered to the world as a warning to live well; on this point I have been admirably advised by my Councillors that the King has no reason to complain, for sound justice is being done and as that is pleasing to God it ought to be pleasing to the King, for this justice is being done on a bad woman, protected by bad men, enemies of his Majesty and of the peace of France. It is absolutely necessary for Mary to die if Elizabeth is to live, or for Elizabeth to die if Mary is to live. On every occasion I have shown how great is the love I bear to the King, and now on this occasion as well I will give another proof by suspending execution for fifteen days, and thus will demonstrate to the King how just my claim and my resolve is.

108. DEATH OF MARY STUART (1587)

After this, the two Earls, and the Sheriff of the County leading the way, she came to the Scaffold, which was set up at the upper end of the Hall, where was a Chayre, a Cushion, and a Block, all covered with Mourning. Then the Dean of Peterborough going to Prayers, she falling upon her knees, and holding up the Crucifix in both her hands, prayed with her Servants in Latine, out of the Office of the blessed Virgin. Prayers being ended, she kissed the Crucifix, and signing her self with the Sign of the Crosse, said, As thy arms, of Christ, were spread forth upon the Crosse, so embrace me with the open arms of thy mercy, and forgive me my sins. Then the Executioner asking her pardon, she forgave him. And now her women helping off her outer Garments, and breaking forth into shrikes and cryes, she kissed them, signed them with the Crosse, and willed them to leave lamenting, for now an end of her sorrows was at hand; and then shadowing her face with a Linnen Cloth, and lying down on the Block, she repeated the Psalm, In te Domine speravi, ne confundar in aeternum; at which words she stretching forth her Body, her head at two blows was taken off. Her Body was afterward Royally buried in the Cathedrall Church at Peterborough; but since that, her Noble Son James, King of Great Britain, erected a Royall Monument for her, in King Henry the seventh's Chappell at Westminster. This end had Mary Queen of Scots . . . .

> In matters of national government, the Tudors in general got along well with Parliament. To be sure, Henry VII, Henry VIII, and Elizabeth had an antipathy to that body. They regarded it as a necessary evil, called it as infrequently as possible, and often browbeat it. But it wanted exactly what they did: an England free from foreign involvements, safe from invasion, possessing internal peace and order. They demanded of their advisers absolute loyalty, and sound and successful advice on solutions to national problems. Those who failed suffered the consequences—dismissal, punishment, or, in some cases, death.

109. ELIZABETH APPOINTS LORD BURGHLEY HER CHIEF MINISTER (1558)

I give you this charge that you shall be of my privy council, and content yourself to take pains for me and my realm. This judgment I have of you, that you will not be corrupted by any manner of gift, and that you will be faithful to the state; and that, without respect to my private will, you will give me that counsel which you think best, and if you shall know anything necessary to be declared to me of secrecy, you shall shew it to myself only, and assure yourself I will not fail to keep taciturnity therein, and therefore herewith I charge you.

110. ELIZABETH'S FIRST MESSAGE TO PARLIAMENT (1558)

> This document reveals, as well as anything could, the method used by the queen to court the favor and support of Parliament.

But for the more plain declaration of her highness's disposition in this matter, her Highness hath commanded me to say unto you, even from her own Mouth, that were it not for the preservation of your selves, and the surety of the State, her Highness would sooner have adventured her Life, (which our Lord long preserve) than she would have adventured to trouble her Loving Subjects with any offensive matter, or that should be burthenous or displeasant unto them; And for the further Notifying of her Highness's mind herein, she hath commanded me to say unto you, That albeit you your selves see, that this is not matter of will, no matter of displeasure, no private Cause of her own, which in times past have been sufficient for Prince's Pretences, . . . but a matter for the universal Weal of this realm, the defence of our Country, the preservation of every man, his house and Family particularly; yet her Majestie's Will and Pleasure is, that nothing shall be demanded or required of her Loving Subjects, but that, which they, of their own free wills and Liberalities, be well contented, readily and gladly, frankly and freely to offer; so great is the trust that she reposeth in them, and the love and affection that her Highness beareth toward them, nothing at all doubting, but that they will so lovingly, carefully and prudently consider and weigh this great and weighty Matter, that such provision out of hand be taken therein, as her Highness shall be preserved in all Honour and Royal Dignity, and you, and the rest of her Loving Subjects, in common quiet and surety.

III. PRIVILEGES OF PARLIAMENT (1562)

The following communication to the queen clearly states what privileges the members of Parliament wished her to guarantee to them. These privileges were important to Parliament not only because they had been won strenuously over several centuries from successive monarchs, but also because these privileges conflicted sometimes with what the crown considered to be its prerogatives.

Further I am to be a Suitor to your Majesty, that when matters of importance shall arise, whereupon it shall be necessary to have your Highness Opinion, that then I may have free access unto you for the same; and the like to the Lords of the Upper House.

Secondly, That in repairing from the nether House to your Majesty, of the Lords of the Upper House, to declare their meanings, and I mistaking on uttering the same contrary to their meaning, that then my fault or imbecillity in declaring thereof be not prejudicial to the House, but that I may again repair to them, the better to understand their meanings, and so they to reform the same.

Thirdly, That the Assembly of the Lower House, may have frank and free Liberties to speak their Minds, without any Controulment, Blame, Grudge, Menaces or Displeasure, according to the old antient Order.

Finally, That the old Priviledge of the House be observed, which is, that they and theirs might be at Liberty, frank and free, without Arrest, molestation, trouble or other damage to their Bodies, Lands, Goods or Servants, with all other their Liberties, during the time of the said Parliament; whereby they may the better attend, and do their Duty; all which Priviledges I desire may be Inrolled, as at other times it hath been accustomed.

And thus having been tedious unto you with my Speech, void of Eloquence, I crave your Pardon, and desire your Majesty to accept of my Heart, and good Will, as well at this time as after, and I will pray as I am bounden, for your Honour long to Reign over us.

112. DESCRIPTION OF PARLIAMENT IN ACTION (1583)

In like manner in the lower house the speaker sitting in a seate or chaire for that purpose somewhat higher, that he may see and be seene of them all, hath before him in a lower seate his Clarke, who readeth such bils as be first propounded in the lower house, or be sent down from the Lords. For in that point ech house hath equal authoritie, to propounde what they think meete, either for thabrogating of some law made before, or for making of a newe. All bils be thrise in three diverse dayes read and disputed upon, before they come to the question. In the disputing is a marvelous good order used in the lower house. He that standeth uppe bareheadded is understanded that he will speake to the bill. . . . He that once hath spoken in a bill though he be confuted straight, that day may not replie, no though he would chaunge his opinion. So that to one bill in one day one may not in that house speake twise, for else one or two with altercation woulde spende all the time. The next day he may, but then also but once.

No reviling or nipping wordes must be used. . . . At the afternoone they keepe no parliament. The speaker hath no voice in the house, nor they will not suffer him to speake in any bill to moove or diswade it. If the commons doe assent to such billes as be sent to them first agreed upon from the Lords thus subscribed, *Les commons ont assentus,* so if the Lords doe agree to such billes as be first agreed uppon by the Commons, they sende them downe to the speaker thus subscribed, *Les Seigneurs ont assentus.* If they cannot agree, the two houses (for everie bill from whence soever it doth come is thrise reade in each of the houses) if it be understoode that there is any sticking, sometimes the Lordes to the Commons, sometime the Commons to the Lords doe require that a certaine of each house may meete together, and so each part to be enformed of others meaning, and this is alwaies graunted. After which meeting for the most part not alwaies either parte agrees to other billes . . . .

While the Tudor age was one of profound preoccupation with religious matters, economic affairs were not in any way ignored. As trade and industry expanded, medieval industrial and commercial patterns broke down. In the towns prices rose sharply and caused a great deal of distress. The rise in prices was due largely to the heavy influx of precious metals from the new world. Also, the inflation of the currency under Henry VII and Henry VIII was accelerated by increasing the amount of alloy in English coins, so that, as Professor Conyers Read points out, "in the end not more than a quarter of the English shilling was precious metal." The now "bad money" drove the good out of circulation—into safe depositories or overseas.

As to enclosures, the picture is not so clear. In general, lords of manors began to enclose the common lands and to convert the arable lands of their holdings into pastures for sheep. Hence they evicted their customary tenants to make room for flocks. The concentration on sheep-raising resulted in a decreasing production of foodstuffs and the consequent increase in prices.

113. RESULTS OF ENCLOSURES

The following extracts from John Hales' *A Discourse of the Common Weal of this Realm of England,* written in manuscript in 1549 and printed in 1581, explain the nature of the problem. In a dialogue a husbandman says to a merchant:

Yea, those shepe is the cause of all theise mischeives, for they haue driven husbandrie oute of the countrie, by the which was encreased before all kynde of victuall, and now altogether shepe, shepe. It was far better whan theare was not only shepe enoughe, but also oxen, kyen, swyne, pigges, geese and capons, egges, butter and chese, yea, and bred corne and mault corne enoughe besides, and altogether rered vpon the same land.

And a doctor and capper engage in this conversation:

DOCTOR. I will tell youe my mynde therin hereafter. But first let vs beate out the cause of this Dearth. Therefore let me learne what other thinge should be the cause therof.

CAPPER. Marie, these Inclosurs and great pasturs are a great cause of the same, wherby men doe turne theire arable land, beinge a livinge for divers poore men before tyme, nowe to one mans hande. And wheare bothe corne of al sortes, and also cattaile of all kinde, weare reared afore tyme, nowe is there nothinge but only shepe. And in stead of some C. or CC. parsons, that had their livinges theron, now be theare but thre or foure sheppards, and the maister only, that hathe a livinge therof.

DOCTOR. Youe touch a matter that is much to be considered, albeit I take not that only [to be] the cause of this dearth at this time; but this I thincke in my mind, that yf that kinde of inclosures doe asmuch increase in xx^{tie} yeres to come as it hath done xx^{tie} yeres past, it maie come to the great dissolucion and weakninge of the kinges straingthe of this Realme, which is more to be feared then dearth. . . .

114. STATUTE LIMITING NUMBER OF SHEEP (1533)

Parliament enacted a statute in order to quiet the popular agitation against enclosures and to check the sheep-raising mania. The preamble to this Act is especially revealing.

Forasmuch as divers and sundry persons of the King's subjects of this realm, to whom God of his goodness hath disposed great plenty and abundance of moveable substance, now of late within few years have daily studied, practised, and invented ways and means how they might accumulate and gather together into few hands, as well great multitude of farms as great plenty of cattle, and in especial sheep, putting such lands as they can get to pasture, and not to tillage; (2) whereby they have not only pulled down churches and towns, and enhanced the old rates of the rents of the possessions of this realm, or else brought it to such excessive fines that no poor man is able to meddle with it, but also have raised and enhanced the prices of all manner of corn, cattle, wool, pigs, geese, hens, chickens, eggs, and such order, almost double above the prices which have been accustomed; (3) by reason whereof a marvellous multitude and number of the people of this realm be not able to provide meat, drink and clothes necessary for themselves, their wives and children, but be so discouraged with misery and poverty, that they fall daily to theft, robbery and other inconveniences, or pitifully die for hunger and cold; (4) and as it is thought by the King's most humble and loving subjects, that one of the greatest occasions that moveth and provoketh those greedy and covetous people so to accumulate and keep in their hands such great portions and parts of the grounds and lands of this realm from the occupying of the poor husbandman, and so to use it in pasture, and not in tillage, is only the great profit that cometh of sheep, which now be come to a few persons hands of this realm, in respect of the whole number of the King's subjects; . . . (8) it may therefore please the King's highness, of his most gracious and godly disposition, and the lords spiritual and temporal . . . with the assent of the commons . . . to ordain and enact . . . That no person . . . from the feast of Saint Michael the archangel, which shall be in the year of our Lord God 1535 shall keep, occupy or have in his possession, in his own proper lands, nor in the possession, lands nor grounds of any other which he shall have or occupy in farm, nor otherwise have of his own proper cattle, in use, possession, or property, by any manner of means, fraud, craft or covin, above the number of two thousand sheep at one time, within any part of this realm, of all sorts and kinds, (9) upon pain to lose and forfeit for every sheep that any person or persons shall have or keep above the number limited by this act, iii. s. iv. d. [three shillings four pence] the one half to the King . . . , and the other half to such person as will sue for the same, by original writ of debt, bill, plaint or information in any court of record . . . .

115. DECAY OF ENGLAND ATTRIBUTED TO THE VAST NUMBER OF SHEEP

> Henry VIII found it impossible to enforce the sheep-limiting statute, and it proved equally impossible for the Duke of Somerset to do so during Edward VI's reign. The following is a supplication to the privy council and Parliament relative to the evils of sheep-farming.

The fyrst Article and poynt, as we do thynke, it is great pyttye (so the will of God it were) that there is not corne ynough within this Realme . . . necessary to certyfy and suffyce the Kynges subiectes for the space of one yere, two, or thre, yf there were no corne sowen in this Realme by the sayde space.

We do saye that the Kinges Maiestie, mercifully hearing the peticion of these his graces poore subiectes, maye at al tymes remedy it, when it shall please hys Maiestie, being for a common wealth for his graces subiectes, and to the greate encrease of this noble realme of England.

We saye, as reason doeth leade vs, that shepe and shepemasters doeth cause skantyte of corne, whiche we do thynke it maye be well approued, by reason of six prouerbes; for and yf all our lyuynges, and all our commodities, were diuyded in partes, by reason of the same syx prouerbes, we that be the Kynges Maiestyes poore subiectes do lose syx of our commodityes; then haue we thre losses, whiche make nyne; by reason of the same thre losses, we, the Kynges Magestyes subiectes, do lose the third part of our lyuinge; then haue we the tenth part, which we cal a remedy, beseching your noble grace to remedye when your Maiestye shall please.

As touchyng the fyrste prouerbe of the syx, we do thynke

> The more shepe, the dearer is the woll.
> The more shepe, the dearer is the motton.
> The more shepe, the dearer is the beffe.
> The more shepe, the dearer is the corne.
> The more shepe, the skanter is the whit meate.
> The more shepe, the fewer egges for a peny.

116. THE MINES ROYAL (1568)

While the cloth trade was of first importance in sixteenth-century England, the extractive industries were not neglected. Patents such as the one below were issued to certain operators of mining industries necessary to the nation's economy.

ELIZABETH by the Grace of God, etc. To all unto whom these presents shall come, Greeting:

WHERE We by our Letters Patents bearing date at Westminster the tenth day of October in the sixth year of our reign have, for the considerations therein mentioned, given and granted full power licence and authority to THOMAS THURLAND, Clerk, one of our Chaplains and Master of our Hospital of the Savoy, and to DANIEL HOUGHSETTER, a German born, their heirs and assigns and every of them forever, by themselves their servants labourers and workmen or any of them to search dig open roast melt stamp wash drain or convey waters or otherwise work for all manner of mines or ores of gold, silver, copper and quicksilver within our counties of York, Lancaster, Cumberland, Westmorland, Cornwall, Devon, Gloucestershire and Worcestershire and within our Principality of Wales or in any of them,

And the same to try out convert and use to their most profit and commodity and the commodity of every of them forever, as well within our own lands, grounds and possessions as also within the lands grounds and possessions of any of our subjects set lying or being within our said counties and principalities or in any of them, without any let or perturbation of Us, our heirs or successors or of any other person or persons whatsoever, together with divers other powers authorities licences privileges benefits and immunities specified in the said Letters Patents for and concerning the effectual obtaining and enjoying of the premises, as by the same Letters Patents amongst divers other clauses and articles therein contained more plainly and at large it may and doth appear; . . .

117. ALIEN WORKERS IN ENGLAND

In 1564, the Mayor of Norwich requested that the cloth-makers from Flanders, who had come to England to escape persecution from the Catholic Duke of Alva, might be sent to Norwich to keep the industry in that city.

Master Thomas Sotherton, Maior of the Citye of Norwiche. In the year . . . 1564 . . . by reason that the commodities of woorsted makyinge is greatelye decayed, by the whiche manye cittyzens bothe marchauntes and

artizans that befor that tyme hadd (of the geyne therof) their whoale
lyvinges, and greate nombre of poore of the cyttye were sette on worke by
spninge, weavinge, dyenge, callendringe and shearinge theseyde clothes
which nowe were owte of estimation and vente, that the makers and woork-
ers therof in all the exercises aforeseyde were fayne to geve themselves to
other exercises and trades to maynteyne their families whiche was nothinge
so proffytable, wherebye people became poore, manye lefte ther howses and
dwelte in the countrye, that howses decayed for lacke of fearmes, and that
they were letten at small prises, and the citye lyke to decaye yf prudente
polici did not assyste the same. And after manye consultacons and devices
what trades might be practized to redresse this poor state, was geven intelligence that dyverse strangers of the Lowe Countryes were nowe come to
London and Sandwiche and had gotte lyscens of the Quenis Maiestye to exercize the makynge of Flaunders comodityes made of woolle, which
straungers came over for refuge ageynste the persecution then raysed
agaynste them by the power of the Duke Alva, principall for the Kynge of
Spayne. And bycause the poore here might be excercized in theyr spynninge
and woolle worke a motion was made to Thomas, then Duke of Norffolke,
then lodged at his housse in this citye, that at his retorne to London he
obtayned of the Quenis Maiestye, who of her gracious goodnes and mercifull
clemencye havinge compassyon of the poore state of this her highnes citye,
dyd tollerate and admytte to be and inhabite within this her highnes Citye of
Norwiche thirtye master workemen, to have eyther of them tenne servauntes
to exercize the makynge of those comodityes with warraunte to the Maiour
and citezns to permitte them so to do. Whiche being done under her highnes
lettres pattents (at seyde Duke his charges) was sente downe to the
foreseyde Maiour to be putte in execution.

> Throughout the sixteenth century English maritime enterprise grew stead-
> ily. It took the form of seeking lands as yet unclaimed and of finding new
> and shorter routes to the Far East, being careful not to encroach upon
> Spanish and Portuguese preserves. True to character, the Tudors took little
> interest in ventures that did not profit them immediately, and unlike Euro-
> pean monarchs, expected to gain by voyages of discovery, not to subsidize
> them.

118. MARTIN FROBISHER'S THIRD VOYAGE FOR THE DISCOVERY OF CATHAY (1578)

> This carefully planned voyage consisted of forty mariners, thirty miners
> (for digging the gold they expected to find), and thirty soldiers to guard

the group which was to stay for a year. There were fifteen sailing ships and twelve of these were to return to England "with their loading of gold ore in the end of the summer." On May 27, 1578, the expedition gathered at Harwich, the captain of each ship receiving the following orders and instructions:

1. IMPRIMIS, to banish swearing, dice, and card-playing, and filthy communication, and to serve God twice a-day, with the ordinary service usual in Churches of *England,* and to clear the glass according to the old order of *England.*

2. The Admiral shall carry the light, and after his light be once put out no man to go ahead of him, but every man to fit his sails to follow as near as they may without endangering one another.

3. That no man shall by day or by night depart further from the Admiral than the distance of one English mile, and as near as they may without danger one of another.

4. If it chance to grow thick, and the wind contrary, either by day or by night, that the Admiral be forced to cast about, before her casting about she shall give warning by shooting off a piece: and to her shall answer the Vice-Admiral and the Rear-Admiral, each of them with a piece, if it be by night or in a fog; and that the Vice-Admiral shall answer first and the Rear-Admiral last.

5. That no man in the fleet, descrying any sail or sails, give upon any occasion any chase before he have spoken with the Admiral.

6. That every evening all the fleet come up and speak with the Admiral, at seven of the clock, or between that and eight; and if the weather will not serve them all to speak with the Admiral, then some shall come to the Vice-Admiral, and receive the order of their course of Master *Hall,* Chief Pilot of the Fleet, as he shall direct them.

7. If to any man in the fleet there happen any mischance, they shall presently shoot off two pieces by day, and if it be by night, two pieces, and shew two lights.

8. If any man in the fleet come up in the night, and hail his fellow, knowing him not, he shall give him this watchword, BEFORE THE WORLD WAS GOD. The other shall answer him, if he be one of our fleet, AFTER GOD CAME CHRIST HIS SON. So that if any be found amongst us, not of our own company, he that first descrieth any such sail or sails, shall give warning to the Admiral by himself or any other that he can speak to, that sails better than he, being nearest unto him.

9. That every ship in the fleet in the time of fogs, which continually

happen with little winds, and most part calms, shall keep a reasonable noise with trumpet, drum, or otherwise, to keep themselves clear one of another.

10. If it fall out so thick or misty that we lay it to hull, the Admiral shall give warning with a piece, and putting out three lights one over another, to the end that every man may take in his sails; and at his setting of sails again do the like, if it be not clear.

11. If any man discover land by night, that he give the like warning that he doth for mischances, two lights and two pieces; if it be by day, one piece, and put out his flag, and strike all his sails he hath aboard. . . .

119. SIR FRANCIS DRAKE'S VOYAGE TO THE WEST INDIES (1585)

The greatest of all English seamen of the sixteenth century was Sir Francis Drake. He circumnavigated the globe from 1577 to 1580 and made numerous other voyages. In 1585 he left for the West Indies. His armada took the cities of Santiago, Santo Domingo, Cartagena, and St. Augustine, and stopped in Virginia to visit the Englishmen sent to that place by Sir Walter Raleigh in the previous year. He offered to leave them supplies or to take them back to England. They chose the latter, but the ship given to them was wrecked in a storm. Captain Biggs' narrative of this journey ends in these words:

Notwithstanding, after all this, the General offered them, with consent of his captains, another ship with some provisions, although not such a one for their turns as might have been spared them before, this being unable to be brought into their harbour: or else, if they would, to give them passage into England, although he knew he should perform it with greater difficulty than he might have done before. But Master Lane, with those of the chiefest of his company which he had then with him, considering what should be best for them to do, made request unto the General under their hands, that they might have passage for England: the which being granted, and the rest sent for out of the country and shipped, we departed from that coast the 18. of June. And so, God be thanked, both they and we in good safety arrived at Portsmouth the 28. of July, 1586, to the great glory of God, and to no small honour to our Prince, our country, and ourselves. The total value of that which was got in this voyage is esteemed at three score thousand pounds, whereof the companies which have travailed in the voyage were to have twenty thousand pounds, the adventurers the other forty. Of which twenty thousand pounds (as I can judge) will redound some six pounds to the single share. We lost some 750 men in the voyage; above three parts of them only by sickness. . . .

120. QUEEN ELIZABETH (1558-1603)

The queen so dominated the last half of the sixteenth century that it is commonly called the "Elizabethan Age." This description of her, written in the early seventeenth century, is too laudatory and not altogether convincing, but it is illustrative of the esteem in which she was held.

She was in stature indifferent tall, slender and straight, fair of Complexion, her hair inclining to pale yellow, her fore-head large and fair, her eyes lively and sweet, but short sighted; her nose somewhat rising in the midst; the whole compasse of her countenance somewhat long, yet of admirable beauty, but the beauty of her minde was far more admirable: She had been a subject, which taught her to rule; she had been in misery, which taught her to be mercifull; and indeed, never Prince ruled with more Justice, and with her Justice mingled more mercy. She had more Valour in her then was fit for a woman, but that she was a Ruler over men; and more Humility in her then was fit for a Prince, but that she meant to be a President to women. She delighted in nothing so much, as in the love of her People, which she procured by ordaining good Magistrates, and forbearing Impositions. Her way not to need them was frugality; and her way to have them when she needed them, was liberality. She made Honour in her time the more honourable, by not making it common; and indeed, knowing it to be an influence from her self, she kept it, as her self, a Virgin, and would not prostitute it to unworthy persons. She declined being a mother of children, to the end she might be a mother of her Countrey; and indeed, no mother ever loved her children more, then she did her people; and therefore never children loved a mother more, then her people did her. She coveted not so much to be an owner of riches, as of rich Subjects; for she thought money did as well in their Coffers, as in her own: and indeed, she never wanted it, when they had it; and they always had it, when she needed it. Never Prince had a wiser Counsell than she, yet never Prince needed it lesse; for she was her self a Counsellor to her Counsell. In sum, whatsoever may in flattery be said of a wise, just, mercifull, religious, and learned Prince, may truely be said of her; in all which, if ever she had an equall, yet she never certainly had a superiour. In playing her game of Fortune, she loved not an after-game; for she liked Preventions, better then Remedies. . . .

121. ELIZABETH'S CHARACTER AND RULE

A. *The Marriage Question*

Parliament was anxious that Elizabeth should marry in order to provide an heir for the Tudor family line and the throne, but Elizabeth preferred to

remain unmarried so that she could use her position as a tool in diplomacy
to control relations with France, Spain, and other powers. On one occasion
she wrote to the French ambassador:

It is not yet decided that I shall ever marry; and whoever the man may
be, if he had not great means, he would acquire great power by his marriage,
to execute any ill designs he might possess. Therefore I have decided never
to give up to my husband anything, neither property, nor power, nor opportunities for acquiring it, for I want to make use of him only to leave a successor to my subjects.

And to the Spanish ambassador Elizabeth wrote this brief note:

I promise you, if I could to-day appoint such a successor to the Crown as
would please me and the country, I would not marry, as that is a thing for
which I have never had any inclination.

B. *Elizabeth's Temperament*

Sir Christopher Hatton, a royal favorite, desired Hatton Place in Holborn.
The Bishop of Ely, Dr. Cox, refused to give it up and an angry queen
wrote to him:

Proud Prelate,
    You know what you were before I made you what you are now. If you
do not immediately comply with my request, I will unfrock you, by God.

C. *Elizabeth's Letter to Sir Nicholas Bacon*

In her view, Bacon had mishandled the inquiry into the guilt of Mary
Stuart in the Darnley murder and bungled the trial of the Duke of Norfolk
in 1572, although Bacon had taken no part in the latter. She angrily wrote
to him:

I have followed your advice, these two years past, in all the affairs of my
kingdom, and I have seen nothing but trouble, expense, and danger. From
this hour, for the same length of time, I am going to follow my own opinion, and see if I find I do any better.

122. ELIZABETH'S SPEECH TO HER TROOPS (1588)

Elizabeth delivered this rousing speech to her troops gathered at Tilbury,
on the Thames below London, to defend England against the Spanish
Armada. Her remarks help to explain her tremendous popularity.

My Loving People:
    We have been perswaded by some that are careful of our safety, to take
heed how we commit ourselves to armed multitudes, for fear of treachery;

but I assure you, I do not desire to live to distrust my faithful and loving people.

Let tyrants fear; I have always so behaved myself that, under God, I have placed my chiefest strength and safeguard in the loyal hearts and good will of my subjects, and therefore I am come amongst you, as you see, at this time, not for my recreation and disport, but being resolved in the midst and heat of the battle to live or die amongst you all, to lay down for my God and for my kingdoms and for my people, my honour and my blood, even in the dust.

I know I have the body but of a weak and feeble woman; but I have the heart and stomach of a king, and of a king of England, too; and think foul scorn that Parma [Duke of Parma] or Spain or any prince of Europe should dare to invade the borders of my realm; to which rather than any dishonour should grow by me, I myself will take up arms, I myself will be your general, judge, and rewarder of every one of your virtues in the field. . . .

123. PRAISE OF ELIZABETH AT HER DEATH (1603)

Sweet virgin, she was born on the eve of that blessed Virgin's nativity, holy Mary, Christ's mother; she died on the eve of the annunciation of the same most holy Virgin; a blessed note of her endless blessedness, and her society in heaven with those wise virgins, that kept oil ever in their lamps, to await the bridegoom. She came unto the crown after her royal sister's death, like a fresh spring even in the beginning of winter, and brought us comfort, as the clear sun doth to storm-pressed mariners; she left the crown likewise in the winter of her age, and the beginning of our spring; as if the ruler of heaven had ordained her coronation in our sharpest winter, to bring us happiness, and uncrowned her in our happiest spring, to leave us in more felicity by her successor. O happy beginning, and more happy end; which, notwithstanding, as natural sons and subjects, let her not go unwept for to her grave . . . ; she came amongst them mounted at Tilbury, being gathered into a royal army against the Spanish invasion; promising to share with them in all fortunes, if the enemy durst but shew his face on land. Let citizens likewise shed tears for her loss, especially those of London, to whom she was ever a kind sovereign, and bountiful neighbour.

An age of profound political, economic, and religious change is certain to be one of great social change as well. Perhaps the chief social problem of the Tudor period was poverty and the care of the poor. Sheep-raising and enclosures, price inflation, and the dissolution of the monasteries had led to vagabondage and begging. The Tudors and their government officers at all levels were deeply concerned with these problems.

124. ACT AGAINST VAGABONDS AND BEGGARS (1495)

I. For asmoche as the Kyngis grace moost entierly desireth amonges all erthly thingis the prosperite and restfulnes of this his land and his subgettis . . . to leve quietly and surefully . . . willing and alweiss of his pitie intending to reduce theym therunto by softer meanes then by such extreme rigour therfor proveied in a Statute made in the tyme of King Richard the second, considering also the great charges that shuld growe to his subgettis for bringing of vagabondes to the Gaoles according to the same Statute and the long abiding of theym therin, wherby for likelehede many of theym shuld lose their lives, In modring [moderating] of the seid estatute his highnes wull by thauctorite of this present parliament it be ordeyned and enacted, that where suche mysdoers shuld be by examinacion commytted to the comen gaole ther to remayne as is aforseid, that the Shiref Maires Baillifs High Constables and Pety Constables and all other Governors and Officers of Citees Burghes Townes Townshipps Villages and other placis, within iij daies after this acte proclamed, make due serch, and take or cause to be taken all suche vagaboundes idell and suspecte persones lyvyng suspeciously, and theym so taken to sette in stokkes, ther to remayne by the space of iij daies and iij nyghtes and ther to have noon other sustenaunce but brede and water; and after the seid iij daies and iij nyghtes to be had oute and set at large and then to be commaunded to avoide the Towen; And if eftsones he be taken in suche defaute in the same Town or Township then he to be sette in the like wise in Stokkis by the space of vj daies with like diete as is before reherced; and if eny persone or persones geve any other mete or drinke to the seid mysdoers being in stokkes in fourme aforseid, or the same prisoners favour in their mysdoyng, that then they forfeite for every tyme so doing xij *d.*

II. And also it is ordeyned by the seid auctorite that all maner of beggers not able to worke, within vj wekis next after proclamacion made of this acte, goe rest and abide in his hundred where he last dwelled, or ther where he is best knowen or born, ther to remayne or abide without begging out of the said Hundred, upon payne to be punyshed as is beforeseid, And that no man be excused by that he is a Clerke of on Unyversite or of other, without he shewe the letters of the Chaunceller of the Unyversite from whens he seeth he commyth, nor none other calling himself a Souldeour Shipman or travelyngman without he bringe a letter from his Captayn or from the Town where he landed, and that he then to be commaunded to go the steight high wey into his Country. . . .

125. DUKE OF NORFOLK TO CROMWELL ON VAGABONDS AND MONASTERIES (1537)

My veray good Lorde . . . forasmoche as I do now wryght to the Kinges maiestie I shall not molest you with nothing conteyned in my lettre sent to his highnes. And where I do understand his maiestie hath now sent lettres to thiese parties concernyng vacabonds, your good lordship shall perceyve by copies of lettres which I have a good tyme past sent to all the justice of pease and religouse houses in thies parties, that I haue not neglected that matier; surely I never sawe so many as be in thiese cuntrees. . . .

126. STATUTE FOR PUNISHING VAGABONDS AND FOR RELIEF OF THE POOR (1547)

While this statute provided severe punishments for vagabonds, section eleven did give a modicum of relief for the aged and infirm.

If any person shall bring to two justices of peace, any runagate servant, or any other which liveth idly and loiteringly, by the space of three days, the said justices shall cause the said idle and loitering servant or vagabond, to be marked with an hot iron on the breast, with the mark of *V*. (3) and adjudge him to be slave to the same person that brought or presented him, to have to him, his executors or assigne, for two years after, who shall take the said slave, and give him bread, water or small drink, and refuse meat, and cause him to work, by beating, chaining or otherwise, in such work and labour as he shall put him unto, be it never so vile: (4) and if such slave absent himself from his said master, within the said term of two years, by the space of fourteen days, then he shall be adjudged by two justices of peace to be marked on the forehead, or the ball of the cheek, with an hot iron, with the sign of an *S*. and further shall be adjudged to be slave to his said master for ever: (5) and if the said slave shall run away the second time, he shall be adjudged a felon. . . . (9) A justice of peace and constable may bind a beggar's man-child apprentice to the age of fourteen years, and a woman-child to the age of twenty years, to any that will require them. (10) And if the said child run away, then his master may retain and use him for the term aforesaid, as his slave. (11) All impotent, maimed and aged persons, who cannot be taken for vagabonds, shall have convenient houses provided for them, and otherwise be relieved in the cities, boroughs or towns where they were born, or were most conversant by the space of three years, by the willing and charitable dispositions of the parishioners: and none other shall be suffered to beg there.

127. THE ELIZABETHAN POOR LAW (1601)

> Monasteries had been the main dispensers of charity. With their dissolution, the government assumed part of this responsibility. But, aside from enacting laws against begging and vagabondage, it actually did little for the poor. In 1563 Parliament empowered local authorities to collect weekly payments from all who would not voluntarily give alms to the poor. Other enactments followed until, in 1601, a comprehensive poor law (incorporating the provisions of several earlier laws) was passed. It remained the basis for relief of the poor by the state until 1834. The following are the main provisions of the statute.

Be it enacted . . . That the church-wardens of every parish . . . shall be called overseers of the poor of the same parish: and they, or the greater part of them, shall take order from time to time, . . . for setting to work the children of all such whose parents shall not by the said church-wardens and overseers . . . be thought able to keep and maintain their children; and also for setting to work all such persons, married or unmarried, having no means to maintain them, and use no ordinary and daily trade of life to get their living by: and also to raise weekly or otherwise (by taxation of every inhabitant, parson, vicar and other, and of every occupier of lands, houses, tithes impropriate, propriations of tithes, coal-mines, or saleable underwoods in the said parish, in such competent sum and sums of money as they think fit) a convenient stock of flax, hemp, wool, thread, iron and other necessary ware and stuff, to set the poor on work: and also competent sums of money for and towards the necessary relief of the lame, impotent, old, blind, and such other among them, being poor and not able to work, and also for the putting out of such children to be apprentices, to be gathered out of the same parish, according to the ability of the same parish, and to do and execute all other things, as well for the disposing of the said stock as otherwise concerning the premisses, as to them shall seem convenient:

II. Which said church-wardens and overseers so to be nominated, . . . shall within four days after the end of their year . . . make and yield up to such two justices of peace . . . a true and perfect account of all sums of money by them received . . . , and of all other things concerning their said office; (3) and such sum . . . of money as shall be in their hands, shall pay and deliver over to the said church-wardens and overseers newly nominated and appointed as aforesaid; (4) upon pain that every one of them . . . being negligent in their office, or in the execution of the orders aforesaid . . . forfeit for every such default . . . twenty shillings.

III. . . . That if the said justices of peace do perceive, that the inhabitants of any parish are not able to levy among themselves sufficient sums of money for the purposes aforesaid; That then the said two justices shall and may tax, rate and assess as aforesaid, any other of other parishes, or out of any parish, within the hundred where the said parish is, to pay such sum and sums of money to the church-wardens and overseers of the said poor parish for the said purposes, as the said justices shall think fit. . . .

V. And be it further enacted, That it shall be lawful for the said church-wardens and overseers, or the greater part of them, by the assent of any two justices of the peace aforesaid, to bind any such children, as aforesaid, to be apprentices, where they shall see convenient, till such man-child shall come to the age of four and twenty years, and such woman-child to the age of one and twenty years, or the time of her marriage; . . . (2) And to the intent that necessary places of habitation may more conveniently be provided for such poor impotent people; (3) be it enacted . . . That it shall and may be lawful for the said church-wardens and overseers . . . by the leave of the lord or lords of the manor, whereof any waste or common within their parish is or shall be parcel . . . to erect, build, and set up in fit and convenient places of habitation in such waste or common, at the general charges of the parish, or otherwise of the hundred or county, . . . to be taxed, rated, and gathered in manner before expressed, convenient houses of dwelling for the said impotent poor; (4) and also to place inmates, or more families than one in one cottage or house; . . . (5) which cottages and places for inmates shall not at any time after be used or employed to or for any other habitation, but only for impotent and poor of the same parish. . . .

XII. And be it further enacted . . . That the justices of peace of every county or place corporate, or the more part of them, in their general sessions to be holden next after the feast of Easter next, and so yearly as often as they shall think meet, shall rate every parish to such a weekly sum of money as they shall think convenient; (2) so as no parish be rated above the sum of six-pence, nor under the sum of a half-peny, weekly to be paid, and so as the total sum of such taxation of the parishes in every county amount not above the rate of two-pence for every parish within the said county: (3) which sums so taxed shall be yearly assessed by the agreement of the parishioners within themselves, or in default thereof, by the church-wardens and petty constables of the same parish. . . .

As can readily be seen through the last document, the Tudor period saw a more efficient administration of law and order. The prerogative courts, such as the Star Chamber and High Commission, on the whole administered justice fairly, even if arbitrarily. Treason trials were notably unjust, however, and the punishment brutal. For other crimes, the courts ordered punishment prescribed in the laws themselves. Apart from the fact that the treatment of those guilty of treason was perhaps more cruel in the Tudor period than in earlier periods, there was not much significant change in the administration of law and justice in other respects.

128. CRIMES AND PUNISHMENTS

Sir Thomas Smith, writing in the mid-sixteenth century, describes the penalties for various crimes in this manner:

For any felonie, manslaughter, robberie, murther, rape, and such capitall crimes as touch not treason and *laesam maiestatem,* we have by the Lawe of England no other punishment, but to hang till they be dead: when they be dead, everie man may burie them that will, as commonly they be. Heading, tormenting, demembring, either arme or legge, breaking upon the wheele, empailing, and such cruel torments, as be used in other nations by the order of their law, we have not: and yet as few murthers committed as any where: nor it is not in the Judges or the Justices power, to aggravate or mitigate the punishment of the Lawe, but in the Prince onely and his privie Counsell, which is marvelous seldom done. Yet notable murtherers many times by the Princes commaundement, after they be hanged with corde till they bee dead, bee hanged with chaines while they rotte in the ayre. If the wife kill her husbande, shee shall bee burned alive. If the servaunt kill his master, hee shalbee drawen on a hurdle to the place of execution: it is called *petit treason.* Impoisoners, if the person die thereof, by a new lawe made in King Henrie the eights time shalbe boyled to death: but this mischiefe is rare and almost unknowen in England. . . . And againe, when a man is murthered, all be principals and shall die, even he that doth but hold the candel to give light to the murderers. For mitigation and moderation of paines, is but corruption of Judges, as we thinke. Likewise, torment . . . to put a malefactor to excessive paine, to make him confesse of him selfe, or of his fellowes or complices, is not used in England, it is taken for servile. . . . The nature of Englishmen is to neglect death, to abide no torment: And therefore he will confesse rather to have done any thing, yea, to have killed his own father, than to suffer torment, for death our nation doth not so much esteem as a mean torment. . . . The nature of our nation is free, stout, haulte prodigall of life and bloud: but contumelie, beatings, servitude and servile torment and punishment it will not abide. . . . The xij [twelve jurors] as soone as they have given their verdict are dismissed to goe whither they will, and have no manner commoditie and profit of their labour and verdict, but onely do service to the Prince and common wealth. . . .

The same order touching trial by enquest of xij men is taken in Treason, but the paine is more cruell. First to be hanged, taken downe alive, his bowels taken out and burned before his face, then to be beheaded, and quartered, and those set up in diverse places. . . .

129. A SCHOOL FOR CRIME (1585)

Recorder Fleetwood wrote this letter to Lord Treasurer Burghley.

Uppon Frydaie last we sate at the Justice hall att Newgate from vij [seven] in the morninge untill vij att night, where were condempned certen horstealers, cutpurses, and such lyke, to the number of x., whereof ix. were executed, and the tenthe stayed by a meanes from the Courte. These were executed uppon Saterdaye in the morninge. The same day . . . [we spent] searchinge out of sundrye that were receptors of ffelons, where we found a greate manye aswell in London, Westminster, Sowthwarke, as in all other places abowte the same. Amongst our travells this one matter tumbled owt by the waye, that one Wotton a gentilman borne, and sometyme a merchauntt man of good credyte, who fallinge by tyme into decaye, kepte an Alehouse att Smarts keye neere Byllingsgate, and after, for some mysdemeanor beinge put downe, he reared upp a newe trade of lyffe, and in the same Howse he procured all the Cuttpurses abowt this Cittie to repaire to his said howse. There, was a schole howse sett upp to learne younge boyes to cutt purses. There were hunge up two devises, the one was a pockett, the other was a purse. The pockett had in yt certen cownters and was hunge abowt with hawkes bells, and over the toppe did hannge a litle sacring bell; and he that could take owt a cownter without any noyse, was allowed to be a *publique ffoyster:* and he that could take a peece of sylver owt of the purse without the noyse of any of the bells, he was adjudged a *judiciall Nypper.* Nota that a ffoister is a Pick-pockett, and a Nypper is termed a Pickpurse, or a Cutpurse. . . .

130. ORDER TO SEND FELONS TO THE GALLEYS (1586)

To my very loving frend Mr. Egerton, her Ma[tles] Sollicitor Generall.

Sir. Her Maty fynding that the lawes of the realm do not cary severity enough to represse the insolency of all sortes of fellows, the number wherof by such meanes doth daily increase, yt hath pleased her of late to devise that

such offendors, being repryved from execution, shalbe bestowed in her
gallyes, wherof one is already built, and more are meant to be built; the use
of which kind of punishment will both terrify ill disposed persons from
offending, and make thos that shall hazard them selves to offend in some
sorte proffitable to the common wealthe. For which purpose her Ma^{tys}
meaning is to direct a Commission unto any sixe of her Counsell, wherof the
L. Chancellor, the L. Thrir, and the L. Admirall to be alwayes one, authoriz-
ing them to repryve from tyme to tyme such fellows as they shall fynd to be
of hable bodyes to serve in gallyes, and then to commit to the said gallyes for
the space of three yeares, or longer tyme, as to them shalbe thought
meete. . . .

Your assured frend,
Fra Walsyngham.

131. AN ACCUSATION OF WITCHCRAFT IN ENGLAND (1570)

> Sir Thomas Smith, a secretary of state to Edward VI and Elizabeth, retired
> to County Essex in 1567 and served there as a justice of the peace. While in
> that office he conducted an examination of a woman accused of witchcraft.

The examination of [a malter's wife] . . . he took in April 1570: against
whom one evidence deposed, that about two years past she bore her husband
in hand that he was bewitched: and as a remedy thereof, she caused a trivet
to be set, and certain pieces of elder and white hazle wood to be laid upon
the trivet across, with a fire under it; and then him, who was at that time
not well in his wits, to kneel down and say certain prayers, as she taught
him: and thereby, she said, he should be delivered of his bewitching, or his
witch should consume as the fire did; which, when this evidence rebuked
her for doing, as using witchcraft, she conceived an ill-will towards him.
And he having a sheep-shearing about that time, and not inviting her thereto, being his neighbour, she, as he supposed, bewitched two of his sheep; for
immediately after they were taken with sickness, their hinder legs so indis-
posed that they only could crawl, and died. The same man had a sow, being
well when the sun went down, which the next morning was found dead,
with her nose lying upon the groundsel of this woman's house, where she
never was fed, nor wont to come before. . . .

132. PERSECUTION OF WITCHES IN SCOTLAND (1591)

Within the towne of Trenent, in the kingdome of Scotland, there
dwelleth one David Seaton, who, being deputie bailiffe in the said towne,
had a maid called Geillis Duncane, who used secretlie to absent and lie forth

of hir maister's house every other night: This Geillis Duncane tooke in hand to helpe all such as were troubled or grieved with anie kinde of sicknes or infirmitie, and in short space did perfourme many matters most miraculous; which things, for asmuche as she began to do them upon a sodaine, having never done the like before, made her maister and others to be in great admiration, and wondered thereat: by means whereof, the saide David Seaton had his maide in great suspition that shee did not those things by naturall and lawful waies, but rather supposed it to bee done by some extraordinarie and unlawfull meanes. Whereupon, her maister began to grow verie inquisitive, and examined hir which way and by what means shee was able to performe matters of so great importance; whereat shee gave him no aunswere: nevertheless, her maister, to the intent that hee might the better trie and finde out the truth of the same, did with the help of others torment her with the torture of the pilliwinkes [an instrument of torture similar to the thumb-screws later in use] upon her fingers, which is a grievous torture; and binding or wrinching her head with a cord or roape, which is a most cruell torment also; yet would she not confess anie thing; whereuppon, they suspecting that she had beene marked by the Devill (as commonly witches are), made diligent search about her, and found the enemies mark to be in her fore crag, or fore part of her throate; which being found, she confessed that all her doings was done by the wicked allurements and entisements of the Devil, and that she did them by witchcraft. After this her confession, she was committed to prison, where shee continued a season, where immediately shee accused these persons following to be notorious witches, and caused them forthwith to be apprehended . . . in those parts, . . . of whom some are alreadie executed, the rest remaine in prison to receive the doome of judgment at the Kinges Majesties will and pleasure.

133. THE SWEATING SICKNESS

This was an acute, infectious, and often fatal disease that occurred in fifteenth- and sixteenth-century England. Particularly severe outbreaks occurred in 1506, 1517, 1528, and 1551.

"This sweat (writes Du Bellay, the French Ambassador to Montmorency), which has made its appearance within these four days, is a most perilous disease. One has a little pain in the head and heart; suddenly a sweat breaks out, and a doctor is useless; for whether you wrap yourself up much or little, in four hours, and sometimes in two or three, you are despatched without languishing, as in those troublesome fevers. However, only about two thousand have caught it in London. Yesterday we saw them

as thick as flies rushing from the streets and shops into their houses, to take
the sweat, whenever they felt ill. I found the Ambassador of Milan leaving
his lodgings in great haste because two or three had been suddenly attacked.
In London, I assure you, the priests have a better time of it than the doctors,
except that the latter do not help to bury. If the thing goes on corn will soon
be cheap. . . . The King keeps moving about for fear of the plague. . . . Of
40,000 attacked in London, only 2,000 are dead, but if a man only put his
hand out of bed during twenty-four hours it becomes as stiff as a pane of
glass."

Various remedies were employed, and it may amuse modern pharmacy
to study a few of the prescriptions then made out to check the ravages of the
pestilence. "Take endive," says one, "sowthistle, marygold, m'oney, and
nightshade, three handfuls of all, and seethe them in conduit water from a
quart to a pint, then strain it in a fair vessel, then delay it with a little sugar
to put away the tartness, and then drink it when the sweat taketh you, and
keep you warm; and by the grace of God ye shall be whole."

134. THE PRACTICE OF MEDICINE AND ITS REGULATION (1543)

In 1512, a statute had been passed stating that no one could claim to be a
physician or surgeon unless he had been licensed by the Bishop of London.
But, as usual, people who were sick made use of the services and skills of
anyone they believed might aid them, whether licensed practitioners or not.
The following regulatory statute was therefore passed in 1543. The preamble has a peculiarly modern ring to it.

Where in the parliament holden at Westminster in the third year of the
King's . . . reign, amongst other things, for the avoiding of sorceries, witchcraft, and other inconveniencies, it was enacted, That no person within the
city of London, nor within seven miles of the same, should take upon him to
exercise and occupy as physician or surgeon, except he be first examined, approved, and admitted by the bishop of London and other, under and upon
certain pains and penalties in the same act mentioned: (2) sithence the
making of which said act, the company and fellowship of surgeons of London, minding only their own lucres, and nothing the profit or ease of the
diseased or patient, have sued, troubled, and vexed divers honest persons, as
well men as women, whom God hath endued with the knowledge of the
nature, kind, and operation of certain herbs, roots and waters, and the using
and ministering of them to such as been pained with customable diseases, as
womens breasts being sore, a pin and the web in the eye, uncomes of hands,
burnings, scaldings, sore mouths, the stone, strangury, saucelim and

morphew, and such other like diseases; and yet the said persons have not taken anything for their pains or cunning, but have ministred the same to poor people only for neighbourhood and God's sake, and of pity and charity. (3) And it is now well known, that the surgeons admitted will do no cure to any person, but where they shall know to be rewarded with a greater sum or reward than the cure extendeth unto: for in case they would minister their cunning unto sore people unrewarded, there should not so many rot and perish to death for lack or help of surgery, as daily do; but the greatest part of surgeons admitted been much more to be blamed, than these persons that they trouble.

II. For although the most part of the persons of the said craft of surgeons have small cunning, yet they will take great sums of money, and do little therefore, and by reason thereof they do oftentimes impair and hurt their patients, rather than do them good: (2) in consideration whereof, and for the ease, comfort, succour, help, relief, and health of the King's poor subjects, inhabitants of this realm, now pained or diseased, or that hereafter shall be pained or diseased;

III. Be it ordained . . . That at all time from henceforth it shall be lawful to every person being the King's subject, having knowledge and experience of the nature of herbs, roots and waters, . . . to practise, use, and minister in and to any outward sore, uncome, wound, apostemations, outward swelling or disease, any herb or herbs, ointments, baths, pultess and emplaisters, according to their cunning, experience and knowledge in any of the diseases, sores and maladies beforesaid, and all other like to the same, or drinks for the stone, strangury or agues, without suit, vexation, trouble, penalty, or loss of their goods, the foresaid statute in the foresaid third year of the King's most gracious reign, or any other act, ordinance, or statute to the contrary heretofore made in any wise notwithstanding.

135. A CURE FOR GOUT

In January 1593 the Earl of Shrewsbury wrote to Lord Burghley:

My especiall good Lord, at this present I have no particuler matter wherwith to trouble your Lordship, and yet I cannot satisfye myself with silence, but hereby to recommend myself to your Lordship in all trew affection of harte, being allway more ready and desirous to express the same by any other means if it lay in my power. I heard your Lordship was, of late, somewhat visited with the Goute; I hope before this you are well ryd thereof, as I most heartily wish. I would your Lordship wolde once make trial of MY OYLE OF STAGS BLUD, for I am strongly persuaded of the rare and great vertu thereof. In the beginninge of this Wynter I was touched with the Goute in the joynte of my great toe, and it began sumwhat sharpely, and yet was I spedely eased, and for that tyme cured by that oyle only. I know it to be a moste safe thynge. Some offence there is in the smell thereof; and yet it is wrytten of it that the very smell therof is comfortable and yeldeth streyngeth to the brayne. I am afrayd to troble your Lordship overlonge therefore with the remembrance of my Wyves truble and moste harty commendacions to your Lordship. . . .

> As the Renaissance aroused increased interest in education, during the six-
> teenth century many grammar schools were founded. Here sons of trades-
> men and farmers mingled with sons of gentlemen in pursuit of an educa-
> tion that was largely classical, administered by schoolmasters who were
> often better disciplinarians than teachers. At the two universities of Oxford
> and Cambridge additional colleges were founded, but the level of instruc-
> tion was low and scholars were too largely oriented toward ecclesiastical
> studies. And, in Elizabeth's reign, the heavy hand of censorship served to
> impede learning.

136. GRAMMAR SCHOOLS (*ca.* 1509)

> Judging by Erasmus' account, he did not think highly of these schools or of
> their teachers.

The citizen's sons were educated in such schools . . . but the grammar teachers of the middle age did not treat the boys kindly. Erasmus, in his "Praise of Folly," singles them out as "a race of men the most miserable, who grow old in penury and filth in their schools—*schools,* did I say? *prisons! dungeons!* I should have said, among their boys, deafened with din, poisoned by a fetid atmosphere; but, thanks to their folly, perfectly self-satisfied, so long as they can bawl and shout to their terrified boys, and box, and beat, and flog them, and so indulge in all kinds of ways their cruel disposition." And elsewhere Erasmus says: "What can such masters do in their schools but get through the day by flogging and scolding? I once knew a divine, and intimately too, a man of reputation . . . who seemed to think that no cruelty to scholars could be enough, since he would not have any but flogging masters. He thought this was the only way to crush the boy's un-ruly spirits, and to subdue the wantonness of their age. Never did he take a meal with his flock without making the comedy end in a tragedy. So at the end of the meal one or another boy was dragged out to be flogged. . . ."

137. THE FOUNDING OF CORPUS CHRISTI COLLEGE, OXFORD (1518)

This yeare, and about this time, Richard Fox bishop of Winchester builded and founded Corpus Christie college in Oxford. . . . Bishop Fox was of the mind and determination to have made the college for religious men. But bishop Oldom (whether it was bicause he favoured not those sects of cloistered moonks, or whether hee foresaw anie fall towards of those sects) disuaded bishop Fox what he could from that his purpose and opinion, and said unto him; "What my lord, shall we build houses, and provide livelodes for a companie of bussing moonks, whose end and fall we our selves maie live to see? No, no it is more meet a great deale, that we should haue care to provide for the increase of learning, and for such as who by their learning shall doo good in the church and commonwealth." To this bishop Fox at length yeelded, and so they proceeded in their buildings. Wherein Oldom reserving to Fox the name of the founder, was contented with the name of benefactor, and verie liberallie did contribute great masses of monie to the same: and since (according to his wish and desire) the same college hath bene and is the nurse of manie notable good scholers.

138. COMPLAINT AGAINST THE PROVOST OF KING'S COLLEGE, CAMBRIDGE (1569)

At this very time a matter happened, that gave the godly Bishop occasion to shew his concern for the good estate of the University. One Mr. Colpots, Fellow of King's college in Cambridge, was now come up to Town in the name of the college, to make complaint to Sir William Cecil, Chancellor of that University, against their Provost Dr. Baker, one who was very negligent of religion, and of the good government of the college: of which, complaint had been made four years before: which occasioned the Bishop of Lincoln, their visitor, to enter upon a visitation of that college, *viz.* in the year 1565, and to give them certain injunctions to be observed. By them the Provost was enjoined to destroy a great deal of Popish stuff, as mass-books, legends, couchers, and grails, copes, vestments, candlesticks, crosses, pixes, paxes, and the brazen rood: which the Provost did not perform, but preserved them in a secret corner.

(1566)

139. ORDINANCE ESTABLISHING CENSORSHIP OF THE PRESS

I. That no person should print . . . or bring . . . into the realm printed any book against the force and meaning of any ordinance . . . contained in any the statutes or laws of this realm or in any injunctions, letters patente or ordinances set forth by the Queen's authority.

II. That whosoever should offend against the said ordinances should forfeit all such books, and from thenceforth should never exercise . . . the feat of printing; and to sustain three months' imprisonment.

III. That no person should sell, bind or sew any such books, upon pain to forfeit all such books and for every book 20*s*.

IV. That all books so forfeited should be brought into Stationers' Hall . . . and all the books so to be forfeited to be destroyed or made waste paper.

V. That it should be lawful for the wardens of the [Stationers'] Company . . . to make search in all workhouses, shops . . . and other places of printers, booksellers and such as bring books into the realm . . . ; and all books to be found against the said ordinances to seize and carry to the Hall to the uses abovesaid and to bring the persons offending before the Queen's Commissioners in causes ecclesiastical.

VI. Every stationer, printer, bookseller . . . should . . . enter into several recognizances of reasonable sums of money to her Majesty . . . that he should truly observe all the said ordinances. . . .

140. FOUNDING OF THE BODLEIAN LIBRARY IN OXFORD (1598)

The end of the reign of Elizabeth was marked by the foundation of the Bodleian Library. Sir Thomas Bodley, being tired of Court life, came back to his old haunts, and resolved to restore Duke Humphry's library. He wrote to the Vice-Chancellor in 1598, offering that whereas "there hath bin heretofore a public library in Oxford, which is apparent by the room itself remaining, and by your statute records, I will take the charge and cost upon me, to reduce it again to its former use, and to make it fit and handsome with seates and shelfes and deskes, and all that may be needful, to stir up other men's benevolence to help to furnish it with books." His own college, Merton, offered timber, and during the next two years the beautiful roof was put up. It was ready for use in 1600, and opened in 1602, and Bodley afterwards endowed it with lands. The bell which he gave still rings for the library to be closed, and his iron chest with three locks is now exhibited in the Picture Gallery.

141. BACON'S ESSAY ON THE VIRTUE OF STUDY (1597)

Sir Francis Bacon (1560–1626), son of Elizabeth's chancellor, Sir Nicholas Bacon, was a typical Renaissance courtier-scholar who excelled in classics, philosophy, science, and government service. While he is better known as one of the queen's favorites, the antagonist of Sir Edward Coke, and as James I's lord chancellor, he made his scholarly reputation through the publication of his celebrated *Essays*. Part of one of these *Essays* is reprinted here.

OF STUDIES

Studies serve for delight, for ornament, and for ability. Their chief use for delight, is in privateness and retiring; for ornament, is in discourse; and for ability, is in the judgment and disposition of business; for expert men can execute, and perhaps judge of particulars, one by one; but the general counsels, and the plots and marshalling of affairs, come best from those that are learned. To spend too much time in studies is sloth; to use them too much for ornament, is affectation; to make judgment wholly by their rules, is the humour of a scholar. They perfect nature, and are perfected by experience; for natural abilities are like natural plants, that need proyning [pruning] by study; and studies themselves do give forth directions too much at large, except they be bounded in by experience. Crafty men condemn studies; simple men admire them; and wise men use them. For they teach not their own use; but that is a wisdom without them, and above them, won by observation.

Read not to contradict and confute, nor to believe and take for granted, nor to find talk and discourse, but to weigh and consider. Some books are to be tasted, others to be swallowed, and some few to be chewed and digested. That is, some books are to be read only in parts; others to be read, but not curiously; and some few to be read wholly, and with diligence and attention. . . .

Reading maketh a full man; conference a ready man; and writing an exact man; and, therefore, if a man write little, he had need have a great memory; if he confer little, he had need have a present wit; and if he read little, he had need have much cunning, to seem to know that he doth not. . . .

SOURCE REFERENCES   *Chapter Four*

79. *Statutes at Large,* 3 Henry VII, CAP. 1.
80. *Grafton's Chronicle; or, History of England. To which is added His Table of the Bailiffs, Sheriffs, and Mayors of the City of London. From the Year 1189 to 1558 Inclusive,* II, 160. London: J. Johnson, *et al.,* 1809.
81. Baker, *Chronicle of the Kings of England,* p. 155.
82. *Calendar of State Papers and Manuscripts Relating to English Affairs Existing in the Archives and Collections of Venice, and in Other Libraries of Northern Italy,* ed. by Rowdon Brown, II, 559. London: Longmans, Green and Co., 1867.
83. *Grafton's Chronicle,* II, 316.
84. *Holinshed's Chronicles,* III, 613.
85. *Calendar of State Papers, Venetian,* II, 560.
86. Baker, *Chronicle of the Kings of England,* pp. 33–35.
87. *A Selection from the Harleian Miscellany of Tracts, which Principally Regard English History,* p. 145. London: C. and G. Kearsley, 1793.
88. Baker, *Chronicle of the Kings of England,* p. 37.
89. Ellis, Henry, ed., *Original Letters, Illustrative of English History Including Numerous Royal Letters: From Autographs in the British Museum and One or Two Other Collections,* II, 35–36. London: Harding, Triphook, and Lepard, 1824.
90. *Statutes at Large,* 26 Henry VIII, CAP. 1.
91. *Holinshed's Chronicles,* III, 793.
92. *Three Chapters of Letters Relating to the Suppression of the Monasteries from the Originals in the British Museum,* ed. by Thomas Wright, pp. 58–59, 85, 129. London: J. B. Nichols and Son, 1843.
93. *Statutes at Large,* 31 Henry VIII, CAP. 14.
94. *Statutes at Large,* 3 Edward VI, CAP. 10.
95. Ponsonby, Arthur, ed., *English Diaries. A Review of English Diaries from the Sixteenth Century to the Twentieth Century,* 2nd ed., p. 57. London: Methuen and Co., 1923.
96. *Statutes at Large,* 2 Mary, CAP. 8.
97. Foxe, John, *The Book of Martyrs. Revised with Notes and an Appendix by Rev. William Bramley-Moore,* p. 462. London: Cassell, Petter and Galpin, n. d.
98. *The Acts and Monuments of John Foxe,* 4th ed., rev. and corrected by Rev. Josiah Pratt, VIII, 88. London: Religious Tract Society, n. d.
99. *The Acts and Monuments of John Foxe,* VIII, 254.
100. *Statutes at Large,* 1 Elizabeth, CAP. 1.
101. Strype, John, *The History of the Life and Acts of Edmund Grindal, the First Bishop of London, and the Second Archbishop of York and Canterbury,* pp. 181–182. Oxford: Clarendon Press, 1821.
102. *Statutes at Large,* 12 Elizabeth, CAP. 2.
103. *Statutes at Large,* 23 Elizabeth, CAP. 1.
104. *Statutes at Large,* 27 Elizabeth, CAP. 2.
105. Strype, *History of the Life and Acts of Edmund Grindal,* pp. 328–329.
106. Harrison, G. B., ed., *An Elizabethan Journal; Being a Record of Those Things*

Most Talked About During the Years 1591-1594, pp. 14-15. New York: Cosmopolitan Book Corporation, 1929.

107. Chamberlin, Frederick, *The Sayings of Queen Elizabeth,* pp. 246-247. New York: Dodd, Mead and Co., 1923.
108. Baker, *Chronicle of the Kings of England,* p. 75.
109. Chamberlin, *Sayings of Queen Elizabeth,* p. 164.
110. D'Ewes, Sir Simonds, *A Compleat Journal of the Votes, Speeches, and Debates both of the House of Lords and House of Commons Throughout the Whole Reign of Queen Elizabeth, of Glorious Memory,* 2nd ed., p. 14. London: Paul Bowes, 1693.
111. D'Ewes, *A Compleat Journal,* pp. 65-66.
112. Smith, Sir Thomas, *De Republica Anglorum,* ed. by Leonard Alston, pp. 54-55. Cambridge: University Press, 1906.
113. *A Discourse of the Commonweal of this Realm of England,* ed. by Elizabeth Lamond, pp. 20; 48-49. Cambridge: University Press, 1929.
114. *Statutes at Large,* 25 Henry VIII, CAP. 13.
115. Tawney, R. H., and Power, Eileen, eds., *Tudor Economic Documents Being Select Documents Illustrating the Economic and Social History of Tudor England,* III, 51-52. London: Longmans, Green and Co., 1924.
116. Tawney and Power, *Tudor Economic Documents,* I, 250-251.
117. Tawney and Power, *Tudor Economic Documents,* I, 298-299.
118. *Voyages of the Elizabethan Seamen, Select Narratives from the 'Principle Navigations' of Hakluyt,* ed. by Edward John Payne, pp. 136-139. Oxford: Clarendon Press, 1907.
119. Payne, *Voyages of the Elizabethan Seamen,* pp. 270-271.
120. Baker, *Chronicle of the Kings of England,* pp. 118-119.
121. A. Chamberlin, *Sayings of Elizabeth,* pp. 68-69.
     B. Harrison, *Elizabethan Journal,* p. 121.
     C. Chamberlin, *Sayings of Elizabeth,* p. 171.
122. As quoted in Cheyney, *Readings in English History,* pp. 410-411.
123. Cited in *A Selection from the Harleian Miscellany,* p. 209.
124. Tawney and Power, *Tudor Economic Documents,* II, 298-299.
125. Tawney and Power, *Tudor Economic Documents,* II, 301.
126. *Statutes at Large,* 1 Edward VI, CAP. 3.
127. *Statutes at Large,* 43 Elizabeth I, CAP. 2.
128. Smith, *De Republica Anglorum,* pp. 104-107.
129. Ellis, *Original Letters,* II, 296-298.
130. Egerton, Lord Francis, *The Egerton Papers. A Collection of Public and Private Documents, Illustrative of the Times of Elizabeth and James I,* pp. 116-117. London: John B. Nichols and Son, 1840.
131. Strype, John, *The Life of the Learned Sir Thomas Smith Kt. D.C.L. Principal Secretary of State to King Edward the Sixth, and Queen Elizabeth,* pp. 97-98. Oxford: Clarendon Press, 1820.
132. *Translations and Reprints from the Original Sources of European History,* III, 19-20. Philadelphia: University of Pennsylvania, 1902.

133. Ewald, Alexander Charles, *Stories from the State Papers,* pp. 95–96. Boston: Houghton, Mifflin and Co., 1882.

134. *Statutes at Large,* 34 Henry VIII, CAP. 8.

135. Ellis, *Original Letters,* 1824 ed., III, 38–39.

136. Boase, Charles W., *Historic Towns, Oxford,* pp. 76–77. London: Longmans, Green and Co., 1903.

137. *Holinshed's Chronicles,* III, 617.

138. Strype, *History of the Life and Acts of Edmund Grindal,* p. 210.

139. *Select Statutes and other Constitutional Documents Illustrative of the Reigns of Elizabeth and James I,* ed. by G. W. Prothero, p. 168. Oxford: Clarendon Press, 1894.

140. Boase, *Historic Towns, Oxford,* pp. 133–134.

141. *The Essays of Lord Bacon,* pp. 90–91. New York: Frederick Warne and Co., 1889.

CHAPTER FIVE

The Seventeenth Century (1603-1714)

The seventeenth century was a period of intense religious conflict, civil war, experimentation in government, rebellion, and revolution. Its turbulence and discontent were reflected in the execution of one king and the expulsion of another; in wars in Ireland, Scotland and abroad; and in increased activity in trade and colonial expansion. It was also an age of solid intellectual achievements. Between 1603 and 1714 England experienced a tremendous "shaking up and settling down"—a process logically resulting from the shift from the medieval world to the modern world.

142. DESCRIPTION OF JAMES I (1603–1625)

One of the reasons for the many troubles that plagued James' reign was that he neither looked nor acted as Englishmen expected a king to look and act. Many persons thought he was peculiar. On seeing the king (the first king in fifty years) many people were keenly disappointed.

He was of middle stature, more corpulent through his clothes than in his body, yet fat enough; his clothes ever being made large and easy, the doublets quilted for stiletto proof; his breeches in plaits and full stuffed: he was naturally of a timorous disposition, which was the reason of his quilted doublets: his eyes large, ever rolling after any stranger came in his presence; insomuch as many for shame have left the room, as being out of countenance: his beard was very thin; his tongue too large for his mouth, and made him drink very uncomely, as if eating his drink, which came out into the cup of each side his mouth; his skin was as soft as taffeta sarsenet; which felt so because he never washed his hands, only rubbed his fingers' ends slightly with the wet end of a napkin. His legs were very weak; having, as some thought, some foul play in his youth; or, rather, before he was born, that he was not able to stand at seven years of age; that weakness made him ever leaning on other men's shoulders; his walk was ever circular.

143. THE GUNPOWDER PLOT (1605)

At once James encountered difficulties with the Puritans because he foolishly denied almost all their petitions for reforms in the Church. He also offended Catholics by retaining the penal laws. As a result, a small group, led by Robert Catesby and including Guy Fawkes, plotted to kill the king, ministers, and members of Parliament by blowing up Parliament when it met on November 5. A warning given in time foiled the plot, and led to the arrest and execution of the plotters as well as several innocent Roman Catholics such as the Jesuit Henry Garnet.

A. *Warning to Lord Monteagle*
My Lord,
Out of the love I bear to some of your friends, I have a care of your preservation: therefore I would advise you, as you tender your life, to devise some excuse to shift off your attendance at this parliament; for God and man have concurred to punish the wickedness of this time. And think not slightly of this advertisement, but retire yourself into your own country, where you may expect the event in safety: for, though there be no appearance of any stir, yet, I say, they shall receive a terrible blow this parliament, and yet they shall not see who hurt them. This counsel is not to be contemned, because it may do you good, and can do you no harm; for the danger is past, as soon as you shall have burned this letter; and I hope God will give you the grace to make good use of it; to whose holy protection, I commend you.

B. *Involvement and Trial of Father Henry Garnet*
The Jesuit, certainly a man of ability, and apparently more of a Machiavelian politician than a bigot or enthusiast, conducted his defence with courage, moderation and presence of mind; and he availed himself of all the nice distinctions, crafty turns and dexterous evasions, of which his education, state and calling had taught him the habitual and skilful use. That he was in part at least acquainted with the meditated treason, he did not now venture, in the face of all the testimonies which had been adduced, to deny; but he sought to rest his justification on the plea of his having come to this knowledge solely through the medium of confession, which a catholic priest is forbidden under pain of perdition to reveal. It is obvious that such a

defence could not be legally admissible in any protestant court of justice; but the crown lawyers contented themselves with showing that it was false in fact. Garnet had clearly been consulted out of confession; he had given letters of recommendation, and lent assistance in various cautious but efficacious methods to the conspirators; had sent a gentleman to apprize the pope of the plot, as of a thing which he could not but approve; and had absolved, encouraged, and relieved from scruples those engaged in it. . . .

C. Guy Fawkes Day (November 5)

The following is an excerpt from an Act of Parliament ordering public thanksgiving services every year on November 5.

Be it therefore enacted . . . That all and singular ministers in every cathedral and parish church, or other usual place for common prayer, within this realm of England and the dominions of the same, shall always upon the fifth day of November say morning prayer, and give unto Almighty God thanks for this most happy deliverance: (2) and that all and every person and persons inhabiting within this realm of England and the dominions of the same, shall always upon that day diligently and faithfully resort to the parish church or chapel accustomed, or to some usual church or chapel where the said morning prayer, preaching, or other service of God shall be used, and then and there to abide orderly and soberly during the time of the said prayers, preaching, or other service of God there to be used and ministred.

144. JAMES RESORTS TO SELLING TITLES AND DIGNITIES (1610-1625)

Because James was inordinately extravagant and Parliament parsimonious, he resorted to new devices to raise revenue. In addition to benevolences (gifts), forced loans, and the sale of monopolies, he sold titles and dignities.

Amongst the ways and means resorted to by the king, are to be mentioned the revival of an obsolete law compelling all persons possessed of 40 £. a year in land to compound for not receiving the order of knighthood; and the introduction of the dignity of baronet, which was offered for the sum of 1000 £. to any person who thought fit to become a purchaser. Salisbury is said by some to have been the author of this latter device, though it more probably originated with sir Robert Cotton: he was however accounted a promoter of it; for, when the king hesitated, from the fear of offending the

gentry by creating a new rank above them, the minister is said to have replied; "Tush, sir! the money will do you good, and the honor will do them
very little." It was indeed barely and simply a patent of precedency above
knights and esquires, and, being made attainable by money and money only,
scarcely deserved at its first institution even the name of an honor or a dignity. Yet the vanity of mankind swallowed the bait; the royal promise of
restricting the whole number of baronets to 200, kept up the price and augmented the eagerness of purchasers; but no sooner was the number completed than the limitation was forgotten, and no one who could produce the
requisite fee of admission had ever cause to lament that his application came
too late.

Even the peerage was set to sale with almost equal publicity; twenty
thousand pounds would purchase the title of an earl, ten thousand that of
viscount, and five thousand that of baron. Monopolies increased to a fright-
ful degree, and the star-chamber fines became more than ever exorbitant. All
these expedients, however, fell far short of producing supplies equal to the
royal expenditure, and James sought further to relieve himself by cutting off
the access of his needy and importunate countrymen, whose petitions he
could neither deny without doing violence to his nature, nor grant without
exciting the jealous murmurs of his English subjects; . . .

145. TRIAL AND PUNISHMENT OF SIR FRANCIS BACON (1621)

Bacon, the brilliant lawyer, philosopher, and natural scientist, had by hard
work and by flattering the king and his favorites, been created Viscount St.
Albans and given the lord chancellorship. In 1621 the House of Commons
charged him with bribery for allegedly having accepted gifts from litigants
while their suits were still pending. The House of Lords found him guilty
and asked the king to punish him.

The following day, on demand of the speaker of the lower house, the
peers proceeded to pronounce their sentence in the absence of the delinquent,
who pleaded sickness. It consisted of four articles: "That the lord viscount St.
Albans, lord chancellor of England, shall undergo fine and ransom of 40,-
000 £.: That he shall be imprisoned in the Tower during the king's pleasure:
That he shall be for ever uncapable of any office, place, or employment, in
the state or commonwealth: That he shall never sit in parliament, nor come
within the verge of the court. . . .

James had shed tears on the first intelligence of his chancellor's being
accused: he speedily liberated him from the Tower; remitted his fine, and, in
the end, absolved him from all the other parts of his sentence and granted

him a very considerable pension; though his own distresses often interfered with the payments.

146. THE DUKE OF BUCKINGHAM (1592–1628)

To James the government was his personal affair and he therefore chose as his advisers his close personal friends. The first to be chosen was Robert Carr, Earl of Somerset. When the latter was found guilty of poisoning a man, he disappeared from court. The next favorite, the witty, gay, and attractive George Villiers, was knighted in 1616 and finally raised to the peerage as Duke of Buckingham. Although he served the crown well, his haughty manner, consummate control of national affairs, grasping for privileges for himself and his family, and bungling of military affairs aroused the enmity of most of the country.

In less than three years from the date of his knighthood, he had obtained for himself the order of the garter, the titles of baron, viscount, earl, and finally that of marquis of Buckingham. Shortly after, his mother had been created countess of Buckingham in her own right; of his brothers, one was made a baronet and the other was knighted and appointed president of Munster; a third, after marrying the daughter of sir Edward Coke, as has been mentioned, was created baron Villiers and viscount Purbeck; and a fourth received the titles of earl of Anglesey and baron of Daventry. One of his sisters was married to lord Butler, another to the earl of Denbigh. To enumerate all the offices of trust and profit held by the favorite and his friends, with the grants, donations and privileges of various kinds which they received, would be endless; suffice it to state, that Buckingham himself was first gentleman of the bed-chamber, and afterwards privy-councillor and master of the horse; that on his expressing a desire for the post of lord-high admiral, the old earl of Nottingham,—the vanquisher of the Spanish armada—was dismissed with a pension to make room for him; and that he afterwards added to these high offices, those of chief-justice in eyre of all the parks and forests south of Trent, master of the king's-bench office, high-steward of Westminster, and constable of Windsor-Castle.

147. THE SPANISH AND FRENCH MARRIAGE QUESTIONS (1623–1625)

As James' daughter, Elizabeth, had married the Protestant Prince Frederick, Elector Palatine, James decided to increase his power and prestige abroad by arranging a marriage of his son Charles to Maria, daughter of

Philip III of Spain. James expected that Maria would bring with her a dowry large enough to pay off many of his debts. Failing to accomplish this marriage by protracted negotiations beginning in 1611, it was at last decided to send Charles, accompanied by Buckingham, to Spain in 1623 to woo the princess in person. The venture failed and Charles and Buckingham returned to England without a bride or a dowry. But, in 1625, James arranged a marriage between Charles and Henrietta Maria, a sister of Louis XIII of France. The following documents reveal the attitude of the English toward these marriage questions and a good deal about the relationship between the king and his "dear boys"—Charles and Buckingham.

A. *Letter to Buckingham*

Thus, my Lord, I have made bold to lay my poor single mite at your feet. The many talents you have cannot be better employed than thus to make you here and ever hereafter a good faithful servant to both your Masters. For if you would lay in wait for an opportunity . . . for advancing God's glory and your honour, you cannot find or invent an occasion more pleasing to God, and more plausible to the best and most men, than in dissuading privately by humble entreaties, and opposing publickly by your solid reasons, this *Spanish* match. Since whatsoever the occasions and necessities of the Crown are, it will find more support by casting itself into the arms of the subjects (which are the two Houses of Parliament) than by seeking to any foreign fawning foe, or envious enemy; whereunto whenever we lean or trust, we shall find them *Egyptian* reeds, and their intentions bent rather to supplant us than supply us.

> By him, that is not ambitious (because not worthy) nor yet afraid (because not ashamed) to be known to your Lordship in this business.
>
>   Tho. Alured.

B. *Letter of James to the Speaker of the House (1621)*

Mr. Speaker; We have heard, by divers reports, to our great grief, that the far distance of our person, at this time, from our high court of parl. caused by our want of health, hath emboldened some fiery and popular spirits in our house of commons, to debate and argue publickly on matters far beyond their reach or capacity; and so tending to our high dishonour, and to the trenching upon our prerogative royal. You shall therefore acquaint that house with our pleasure, that none therein shall presume to meddle with any thing concerning our government or mysteries of state, namely not to speak of our dearest son's match with the daughter of Spain, nor to touch the honour of that king, or any other our friends or confederates: and also not to meddle with any men's particulars, which have their due motion in any of our ordinary courts of justice. . . .

C. Letter from Buckingham ("Steenie") to James (1623)

Dear Dad and Gossip,

This bearer hath staid for the Infanta's and other letters, a day longer than was resolved of, which hath given me this occasion, by stealth from your Baby [Charles], to assure your Majesty, by this last night's rest, of my perfect recovery. Nothing dejected me so much in my sickness, as my absence from you; nor nothing was so great a cordial to me in my recovery, as this thought, that in a few days we shall step towards you; yet I beseech your Majesty to believe this truth, that I so far prefer this business, and your service, before any particular of my own, that this resolution hath not been taken with precipitation, but when we saw there was no more to be gained here, we thought it then high time with all diligence to gain your presence. Sir, my heart and very soul dances for joy; for the change will be no less than to leap from trouble to ease, from sadness to mirth, nay, from hell to heaven. I cannot now think of giving thanks for friend, wife, or child; my thoughts are only bent of having my dear Dad and Master's legs soon in my arms; which sweet Jesus grant me, and your Majesty all health and happiness; so I crave your blessing.

Your Majesty's most humble slave and dog,

Steenie

D. James to Charles and Buckingham (1623)

My sweet Boys,

Your letter by Cottington, hath strucken me dead; I fear it shall very much shorten my days, and I am the more perplexed that I know not how to satisfy the people's expectation here, neither know I what to say to our Council, for the fleet that staid upon a wind this fortnight. Rutland, and all aboard must now be staid, and I know not what reason I shall pretend for the doing of it [1] . . . but as for my advice and directions that ye crave, in case they [the Spanish] will not alter their decree, it is in a word, to come speedily away, and if ye can get leave, and give over all treaty. And this I speak without respect of any security they can offer you, except ye never look to see

---

[1] Here were five lines blotted so as not to be read. [Original footnote.]

your old Dad again, whom I fear ye shall never see, if you see him not before Winter: Alas, I now repent me sore, that ever I suffered you to go away.
I care for Match, nor nothing, so I may once have you in my arms again;
God grant it, God grant it, God grant it, amen, amen, amen. I protest ye
shall be as heartily welcome, as if ye had done all things ye went for, so that
I may once have you in my arms again, and God bless you both, my only
sweet son, and my only best sweet servant, and let me hear from you quickly
with all speed, as ye love my life; and so God send you a happy and joyful
meeting in the arms of your dear Dad.

James, R.

148. MARRIAGE OF KING CHARLES I TO HENRIETTA MARIA OF FRANCE (1625)

Dr. Meddus to Rev. Joseph Mead

It were but lost labour to tell you the queen arrived on Sunday at
Dover; that on Monday, at ten o'clock, the king came from Canterbury
thither to visit her; and though she were unready, so soon as she heard he
was come, she hastened down a pair of stairs to meet him, and offering to
kneel down and to kiss his hand, he wrapt her up in his arms, and kissed her
with many kisses. . . . At dinner, being carved pheasant and venison, by his
majesty, (who had dined before) she eat heartily of both, notwithstanding
her confessor (who all the while stood by her) had forewarned her that it
was the even of St. John Baptist, and was to be fasted, and that she should
take heed how she gave ill examples or scandal at her first arrival. . . .

Yesterday, I saw them coming up from Gravesend, and never beheld the
king to look so merrily. In stature, her head reached just to his shoulder; but
she is young enough to grow taller. Those of our nation that know best her
disposition are very hopeful his majesty will have power to bring her to his
own religion. Being asked, not long since, if she could abide an Huguenot,
"Why not?" said she; "Was not my father one?"

149. THE LAST DAYS OF BUCKINGHAM (1625–1628)

When Charles I came to the throne in 1625, Buckingham became increasingly influential. Though he was not without considerable ability, he was
rich and arrogant; he badly mismanaged a war with Spain (1625–1631)
and one with France (1626–1629). As often happens, he was blamed for all
the misfortunes of the day, was impeached by the Commons, and in 1628
murdered. In 1625, when he went to Paris to get Henrietta Maria, he took

with him a veritable army of well over 300 persons—knights, cooks, grooms, yeomen, laborers, pages, coachmen, and musicians.

A. *The Duke's Appearance*

His Grace hath for his body, twenty-seven rich suits embroidered and laced with silk and silver plushes; besides one rich white satin uncut velvet suit, set all over, both suit and cloak, with diamonds, the value whereof is thought to be worth fourscore thousand pounds, besides a feather made with great diamonds; with sword, girdle, hatband and spurs with diamonds, which suit his Grace intends to enter into Paris with. Another rich suit is of purple satin, embroidered all over with rich orient pearls; the cloak made after the Spanish fashion, with all things suitable, the value whereof will be 20,000 £. and this is thought shall be for the wedding-day in Paris. . . .

B. *Buckingham Charged with Treason* (*1626*)

The dismal failure of Buckingham's foreign policies and projects led to a treason charge against him. Martin Stuteville described the circumstances in this letter to Rev. Joseph Mead:

On Monday last, being May-day, my Lord of Bristol appearing at the upper house bar as a delinquent, Mr. Attorney-General intimated to the lords, that he was there to accuse him [Buckingham] of high treason. Then said the Earl of Bristol, "My lords, I am a freeman, and a peer of the realm unattainted. Somewhat I have to say of high consequence for his majesty's service; and therefore I beseech your lordships give me leave to speak." Which being granted—"Then, my lords, I accuse that man . . . , the Duke of Buckingham, of high treason; and I will prove it!" and so presented the articles to the duke most boldly, so he spoke most contemptuously: and whilst he delivered his accusation in the upper house, his son did the like in the House of Commons.

The judges and the king's learned counsel having since met to frame an indictment against the Earl of Bristol, cannot fasten any reason upon him. . . . Whereupon yesternight was a night of great joy and triumph at the Earl of Bristol's.

C. *Calumny Against Buckingham* (*1626*)

The king saved the Duke by dissolving Parliament, but the attacks on him increased in violence. On June 19, 1626, Joseph Mead wrote to Martin Stuteville:

On Thursday June 19th was a Libel taken down from a Post in Colman Street by a Constable, and carried to my Lord Mayor; by his Lordship considered on in a Court of Aldermen; and by the two Sherifs sent to the King, with charge they should deliver it to none but his Majesty. Some part whereof (we hear saith mine author) ran thus presumptuously. "Who rules the Kingdome? The King. Who rules the King? The Duke. Who rules the Duke? The Devil." And that the Libellers there professe, Let the Duke look to it; for they intend shortly to use him worse than they did his Doctor [Lamb, who was murdered in the streets of London], and if things be not shortly reformed, they will work reformation themselves. . . .

D. *Assassination of Buckingham* (*1628*)

King Charles had been able to save Buckingham from Parliament's wrath, but he was unable to protect him from assassination. On August 23, 1628, he was fatally stabbed by John Felton. Sir Henry Wotton concludes a description of the event in these words:

One thing in this enormous accident is, I must confess, to me beyond all wonder . . . that, within the space of not many minutes after the fall of the body, and removal thereof into the first room, there was not a living creature in either of the chambers, no more than if it had lain in the sands of Ethiopia: whereas commonly, in such cases, you shall note everywhere a great and sudden conflux of people unto the place, to hearken and to see: but it should seem the very horror of the fact had stupified all curiosity, and so dispersed the multitude, that it is thought even the murderer himself might have escaped, for who gave the blow none could affirm, if he had not lingered about the house below. . . .

150. THE PETITION OF RIGHT (1628)

The Petition of Right was a statement of constitutional principles, in the form of a petition, designed permanently to settle the troublesome question of forced loans and benevolences, and the means employed in collecting them. After a long recitation of their grievances, Parliament petitioned:

That no man hereafter be compelled to make or yield, any gift, loan, benevolence, tax, or such like charge, without common consent by act of Parliament; and that none be called to make answer, or take such oath, or to give attendance, or be confined, or otherwise molested or disquieted concerning the same, or for refusal thereof: and that no freeman, in any such manner as is before-mentioned, be imprisoned or detained: and that your maj.

will be pleased to remove the said soldiers and mariners; and that your people may not be so burdened in time to come: and that the aforesaid commissions for proceeding by martial law, may be revoked and annulled; and that hereafter no commissions of like nature may issue forth to any person or persons whatsoever, to be executed as aforesaid, lest, by colour of them, any of your majesty's subjects be destroyed or put to death, contrary to the laws and franchise of the land. —All which they most humbly pray of your most excellent maj. as their Rights and Liberties, according to the laws and statutes of this realm: and that your maj. would also vouchsafe to declare, That the awards, doings and proceedings, to the prejudice of your people, in any of the premises, shall not be drawn hereafter into consequence or example: and that your maj. would be also graciously pleased for the further comfort and safety of your people, to declare your royal will and pleasure, that, in the things aforesaid, all your officers and ministers shall serve you, according to the laws and statutes of this realm, as they tender the honour of your maj. and the prosperity of this kingdom.

151. THE SHIP-MONEY CASE (1637)

After the House of Commons had passed the Three Resolutions (1629) declaring that anyone bringing in a change in religion, advising the collection of tunnage and poundage, or voluntarily paying it, a capital enemy of the realm, Charles was forced to seek new sources of revenue, for he had decided not to call another Parliament. Between 1629 and 1640, when no Parliament sat, the government was hard pressed for money, and resorted to imposing taxes and fines without the consent of Parliament. The most troublesome tax during this period of Charles' personal government was ship-money. An old law had compelled coastal cities and littoral counties to provide ships for the navy. Charles now revived the law and extended it to inland areas as well. As these could send no ships, provision was made for the collection of equivalent sums of money from each county. There was little opposition to the first writ for its collection (1634), but as successive collections were made people became convinced that the king was using the money at his pleasure instead of for the defense of the country. Charles insisted that it was his prerogative to judge when the nation was in peril, which was one of the pre-conditions for the collection of ship-money. John Hampden refused to pay the small sum he was assessed and the matter was taken to the Court of Exchequer where the judges handed down the following decision:

We are of opinion, that when the good and safety of the kingdom in general is concerned, and the whole kingdom in danger, your majesty may

by writ under the great seal of England, command all your subjects of this
your kingdom, at their charge, to provide and furnish such number of ships
with men, victuals, and ammunition, and for such time as your majesty shall
think fit, for the defence and safeguard of the kingdom from such peril and
danger. And that by law your majesty may compel the doing thereof in case
of refusal or refractoriness. And we are also of opinion, that in such case
your majesty is the sole judge, both of the dangers, and when and how the
same is to be prevented and avoided.

152. CAUSES OF THE DISPUTE BETWEEN CHARLES I AND PARLIAMENT THAT LED TO THE CIVIL WAR

In his *Origin and Progress of the Revolutions in England*, M. Wren writes
as follows:

King James being dead his Son at once succeeded to his Crowns and
cares. The first storm that fell upon him was from the house of Commons,
about the Duke of Buckingham; to bear off which the King was fain to use
the right hand of authority. And truly matters were presently come to that
pass, that the Parliament house was but a field of battle, where the King's
prerogative was combated by the People's pretended privilege. In which con-
tests the King was always loser: for, either he was forced to recede from
some of his rights, or was put to defend them by dissolving the Parliament,
or clapping up some of the seditious Members: Which courses were highly
improved by the Malecontents for rendering the King odious to the People.

This turbulent Spirit of the lower House having made the summoning
of Parliaments unsafe for the Crown, it was necessary to think of some other
way to procure monies. Ship money, Enquiry into Forest Lands, and
Monopolies were fixt upon, as the most ready and considerable. The first of
these, if it were not law, was so like it, that most of the Judges, and great
Lawyers of the Nation mistook it for law. The second was a revival of
odious and almost obsolete laws, which, being accompanied perhaps with
some insolence in the Ministers of it, did very much disoblige the Gentry in
divers counties. The last I take to be the least justifiable either in law or
prudence; for by these Monopolies the price of divers necessary commodities
being enhanced, the common people first, and most, underwent the oppression; who were taught the odious names of Excise, and Gabells [taxes on
salt and other necessities], and made to cry out upon a design of introducing
the Government of France. Besides, the profit came not into the Exchequer,
but was swallowed up by those greedy Courtiers, who had begged them of

the King. Divers refused the payment of these taxes and, being severely proceeded with, were cryed up as the people's Martyrs: Though the tameness of the nation afterwards in bearing excise and contribution makes it appear the King wanted only an army to justify his proceedings.

About the middle of King Charles's reign, the highest place both in the Church and the King's favour, came to be possessed by Archbishop Laud; who resolved to improve his interest for the restauration of Ecclesiastical discipline, and the settling of a decent uniformity in divine worship through the Kingdom. This gave a mighty alarm to the whole Puritan faction, who saw themselves reduced to a necessity of conformity, or undergoing those censures, that would be fulminated against them. The way of procedure was chiefly by Visitations in particular dioceses; where order was taken for the suppressing of lectures, and all clancular meetings under pretence of spiritual exercise; for restoring the full use of the Liturgy, where it had been omitted; for the wearing the Surplice, railing in the Communion Table, and some other ceremonies; for punishing those who absented themselves from Church, or behaved themselves irreverently in it; and for many other particulars of the like nature. The execution of all this was committed to the Ecclesiastical courts, where they proceeded to excommunication, suspension, etc. etc. sometimes, but very rarely to deprivation. . . .

153. DISPUTES BETWEEN THE CROWN AND PARLIAMENT (1640–1642)

As Charles did not summon Parliament for eleven years (1629–1640), he governed the country with the aid and advice of able and devoted councillors, notably Thomas Wentworth (Earl of Strafford), Archbishop William Laud, and Richard Weston (Earl of Portland). Try as they might to cope with national problems without resorting to Parliament, everything went wrong. Treasurer Weston had to resort to technically legal but archaic and unpopular means of raising revenue. Strafford advised Charles to follow a policy of thoroughness and efficiency. When Strafford did so Parliament accused him in 1640 of giving the king bad advice, and the Earl was executed by Act of Attainder. Laud, in trying to establish much-needed order and reform in the Anglican Church, aroused the Puritans and helped to provoke a war with the Presbyterian Scots in 1638–1640. When the war went against the king, he was forced to summon Parliament to ask for funds to pay for military expenses. Parliament, angry over many unanswered grievances, abolished the prerogative courts of Star Chamber, High Commission, and Wards and Liveries; declared ship-money illegal; made it incumbent upon the king to summon Parliament at least every three years; and passed a Grand Remonstrance against the king. In 1642, radicalism in the House of Commons provoked Charles unwisely to go to the Commons with some troops in order to arrest five leaders of the opposition to his policies. Edmund Ludlow, a pro-Parliament and anti-Catholic leader, describes the scene as follows:

The King, finding his instruments thus discouraged, and being resolved to remove all obstructions in his way, went in person to the House of Commons, attended not only with his ordinary guard of pensioners, but also with those desperadoes that for some time he had entertained at Whitehall, to the number of three or four hundred, armed with partizans, sword and pistol. At the door of the House he left his guard commanded by the Lord Roxberry, entring accompanied only by the Prince Palatine [Prince Rupert]; where taking possession of the Speaker's chair, and not seeing those that he looked for, he said, "The birds are flown." For upon notice given by a lady of the court of the King's intention, they were retired into the city. The King then demanded of the Speaker where such and such were, naming the five members: to which he answered in these words: "I have neither eyes to see, ears to hear, nor tongue to speak in this place, save what this House gives me." The King replied, "I think you are in the right": and then addressing himself to the House, said; that he was sorry he had been necessitated to come thither: that no King of England had been more careful to preserve the privileges of Parliament than he desired to be; but that those five members being dangerous persons, he had been obliged to pursue them, not by force, but by the ordinary forms of justice: that he hoped the Parliament would send them to him, to justify themselves, if they could; if not, he knew how to find them: which said, he retired. The Parliament sensible of this violation of their privileges, and fearing they might be further intrenched upon, ordered a committee of the House to sit in the city of London, whither their five members were gone before for protection. The king followed them thither with a slender, or rather no guard, (so far was he from fearing either Parliament or City) designing to engage the citizens to deliver up the five members to him, and to stand by him in this horrid enterprise; but they would not be perswaded to comply with his desires in that matter. This violent attempt proving unsuccessful, the Parliament, to assert their just rights, voted it to be a breach of their privileges; and that the like might be prevented for the future, after the committee had sat a few days in the city, they returned to Westminster, accompanied with guards from the city both by land and water. Which the King being informed of, and finding that the design which he had laid had highly provoked the Parliament and people, he retired to Hampton-Court, whither those that he had formerly entertained at Whitehall soon repaired; and at Kingston upon Thames appeared in a military posture, with the Lord Digby and Colonel Lunsford at the head of them. The two Houses having notice thereof, desired the King to disperse the said troops, and to return to the Parliament. The Lord Digby was also required to attend his duty in the House: but he being conscious of his own guilt, and knowing that the King's affairs were not yet in a posture to bid open defiance to the Parliament, chose rather to betake himself to flight; as the Queen did soon after, upon notice that the two Houses were about to accuse her of high treason. . . .

154. A LETTER BY OLIVER CROMWELL (1644)

In the midst of the cares, anxieties, and problems of war, Cromwell took time to send the following letter to the father of a soldier who had been killed in the battle of Marston Moor.

Sir, God hath taken away your eldest Son by a cannonshot. It brake his leg. We were necessitated to have it cut off, whereof he died.

Sir, you know my own trials this way: but the Lord supported me with this, That the Lord took him into the happiness we all pant for and live for. There is your precious child full of glory, never to know sin or sorrow any more. He was a gallant young man, exceedingly gracious. God give you His comfort. Before his death he was so full of comfort that to Frank Russel and myself he could not express it, "It was so great above his pain." This he said to us. Indeed it was admirable. A little after, he said, One thing lay upon his spirit. I asked him, What that was? He told me it was, That God had not suffered him to be any more the executioner of His enemies. At his fall, his horse being killed with the bullet, and as I am informed three horses more, I am told he bid them, Open to the right and left, that he might see the rogues run. Truly he was exceedingly beloved in the Army, of all that knew him. But few knew him; for he was a precious young man, fit for God. You have cause to bless the Lord. He is a glorious Saint in Heaven; wherein you ought exceedingly to rejoice. Let us drink up your sorrow; seeing these are not feigned words to comfort you, but the thing is so real and undoubted a truth. You may do all things by the strength of Christ. Seek that, and you shall easily bear your trial. Let this public mercy to the Church of God make you to forget your private sorrow. . . .

155. THE BATTLE OF NASEBY (JUNE 14, 1645)

After the victory at Marston Moor, Cromwell had written to his brother: "Give glory, all the glory, to God." Now, after the great victory at Naseby, he wrote to William Lenthall, Speaker of the House:

Beinge commanded by you to this service, I thinke my selfe bound to acquaint you with the good hand of God towards you and us. Wee marched yesterday after the Kinge whoe went before us from Daventree to Haverbrowe [Harborough], and quartered about six miles from him. This day wee marched towards him. Hee drew out to meete us. Both Armies engaged. Wee, after three howers fight, very doubtfull, att last routed his Armie, killed and tooke about five thousand, very many officers, but of what qualitye wee yet know not. Wee tooke alsoe about two hundred carrages, all hee had, and all his gunnes, . . . Wee persued the enimie from three miles short of Haverb [Harborough] to nine miles beyond, even to sight of Leic. [Leicester] whether the Kinge fled. Sir this is non other but the hand of God, and to him alone belongs the glorie, wher in none are to share with him. The Generall has served you with all faythfullness and honor, and the best commendations I can give him is that I dare say hee attributes all to God, and would rather perish than assume to himselfe; which is an honest and a thrivinge way, and yett as much for bravery may bee given to him in this action as to any man. Honest men served you faythfully in this action. Sir they are trusty. I beseech you in the name of God not to discourage them. I wish this action may begett thankfullnesse and himilitye in all that are concerned in itt. Hee that venters his life for the libertye of his countrie, I wish hee trust God for the libertye of his conscience and you for the libertye hee fights for. . . .

156. DEMANDS OF THE SOLDIERS (1645)

The king had suffered from the niggardliness of Parliament, and so also did Cromwell, for it had not made provision for the payment of his soldiers. The latter, under the immediate command of Samuel Luke, wrote to Cromwell demanding their pay.

Wee are fully resolved that you are not ignorant of our wants and grievances, in regard that our pay is soe long kept from us; and who is the occasion, it is unknowne to us. In the meane tyme wee find many commaunds from your Honor which except speedily redressed will prove very disadvantagious to the State. As for those that concerne our dutyes in martiall discipline, it is best knowne to your Honor how ready wee have beene to obay; but for those that concerne our quartering in the country, wee may have just cause to feare that the people may rise and cutt our throates, if an enemy approach from whom they may expect some releife from such op-pression; as by their continuall murmering appeares that their grievances are soe greate that their generall expressions are that wee eate the meate out of their childrens mouthes, they paying their contribution and wee neither re-ceiving any pay to give some small satisfaction for quarter, nor they expect-ing any abatement out of their taxe, having beene soe long deceived by fayre promises; which is probably as greate oppression to the country as Pharoh's demaunding the full tayle of bricke, without allowance of straw. Your Honor may bee pleased to consider the crye of the Country which is dayly in our eares, and our wants likewise, which wee are very sensible is likely to bee greater if wee march further without mony. Wee are not ignorant of the ex-traordinary sums of mony that are allowed by the Parliament for the pay-ment of the garrison, which wee conceive should amount to above four weeks pay in four months at 14s. per weeke; and the most of us paying a months quarters out of it, our desire is that yor Honor would speedily redresse it, considering that wee can neither have apparell for our selves nor necessarye for our horse, noe nor soe much as powder and bullett, from the garrison, although to secure it from the approach of the enemy, without mony or security; and finally wee desire that your Honor may understand, that, if upon this reasonable declaration, wee cannot have our pay upon rea-sonable tearmes, that wee shall more fully declare our selves, and appeale to the honorable the High Court of Parliament. In the meane tyme until wee have an answer from your Honor wee rest at our quarters at Cosgrave. . . .

Our demaunds is ten weekes pay at the least, and therefore put us not of with the cocking of a pistol, or stearne threatening, as upon the like occasion hath beene formerly.

157. CHARGES AGAINST KING CHARLES I (JANUARY 27, 1649)

Having lost the war and been taken prisoner, Charles was tried before a Commission on the following charges:

That Charles Stuart being admitted King of England, and therein trusted with a Limited Power to govern by, and according to the Laws of the Land, and not otherwise: And by his Trust, Oath, and Office, being obliged to use the Power committed to him for the good and benefit of the People, and for the preservation of their Rights and Liberties; yet neverthe-less out of a wicked Design to erect and uphold in himself an unlimited and tyrannical Power to rule according to his Will, and to overthrow the Rights and Liberties of the People; yea to take away and make void the Foundations thereof, and of all redress and remedy of Misgovernment, which by the fundamental Constitutions of this Kingdom were reserved on the People's behalf, in the Right and Power of frequent and successive Parliament's, or national Meetings in Council; he the said Charles Stuart for accomplishment of such his Designs, and for the protecting of himself and his Adherents in his and their wicked Practices to the same ends, hath traitorously and maliciously levyed War against the present Parliament, and the People therein represented . . . .

All which wicked Designs, Wars, and evil Practices of him the said Charles Stuart, have been and are carried on for the advancing and upholding of the personal Interest Will and Power, and pretended Prerogative to himself and his Family, against the Publick Interest, Common Right, Liberty, Justice, and Peace of the People of this Nation, by and for whom he was intrusted as aforesaid.

By all which it appeareth, that he the said Charles Stuart has been and is the Occasioner, Author and Contriver of the said unnatural, cruel, and bloody Wars, and therein guilty of all the Treasons, Murders, Rapines, Burnings, Spoils, Disolations, Damage and Mischief to this Nation acted or committed in the said Wars, or occasioned thereby.

158. TRIAL AND EXECUTION OF CHARLES I (1649)

The following is an excerpt from the trial of Charles, and a warrant for beheading him.

Then the Clerk of the Court read as followeth: CHARLES STUART, King of England, you have been accused on the behalf of the People of England, of High Treason, and other high Crimes; the Court have determined, that you ought to answer the same. King. "I will answer the same, as soon as I know by what Authority you do this."

President. If this be all that you will say, then, Gentlemen, you that brought the Prisoner hither, take charge of him back again.

King. "I do require that I may give in my Reasons why I do not Answer, and give me time for that."

President. Sir 'Tis not for Prisoners to require.

King. "Prisoner? Sir, I am not an ordinary Prisoner."

President. The Court hath considered of their Jurisdiction, and they have already affirmed their Jurisdiction; if you will not answer, we shall give order to Record your default.

King. "You never heard my Reasons yet."

President. Sir, your Reasons are not to be heard against the highest Jurisdiction.

King. "Shew me that Jurisdiction where Reason is not to be heard."

President. Sir, We shew it you here, the Commons of England; and the next time you are brought, you will know more of the pleasure of the Court, and, it may be, their final determination.

King. "Shew me wherever the House of Commons was a Court of Judicature of that kind."

President. Serjeant, take away the Prisoner.

King. "Well, Sir, remember that the King is not suffered to give his Reasons, for the Liberty and Freedom of all his Subjects."

President. Sir, you are not to have liberty to use this language: How great a Friend you have been to the Laws and Liberties of the People, let all England and the World judge.

King. "Sir, under favour, it was the Liberty, Freedom, and Laws of the Subject that ever I took—defended my self with Arms, I never took up Arms against the People, but for my People and the Laws."

President. The command of the Court must be obeyed; no answer will be given to the Charge.

The Warrant for Beheading the King

At the High-Court of Justice for the Trying and Judging
of Charles Stuart King of England, January 29, 1648 [o.s.].

Whereas Charles Stuart King of England, is, and standeth convicted, Attainted and Condemned of High Treason, and other high Crimes, and Sentence upon Saturday last was pronounced against him by this Court, to be put to Death by the severing of his Head from his Body; of which Sentence, Execution yet remains to be done; These are therefore to Will and Require you to see the Sentence Executed in the open Street before White-Hall, upon the Morrow, being the 30th Day of this Instant Month of January, between the Hours of Ten in the Morning, and Five in the Afternoon of the same Day with full Effect: And for so doing, this shall be your sufficient Warrant. And these are to require all Officers and Soldiers, and other the good People of this Nation of England, to be assisting unto you in this Service.

159. THE BATTLE OF DROGHEDA (1649)

After Charles was executed the Rump Parliament abolished the monarchy and the House of Lords, and on May 19, 1649, declared England a republic.

However, real power was in the hands of Cromwell and the Army. On the
execution of the king, Ireland declared for Charles II, whereupon an English army commanded by Cromwell and his son-in-law, Henry Ireton, invaded Ireland, defeated the Irish and thoroughly subdued the island. The
most famous battle of the campaign, and one which led to accusations of
brutality against Cromwell, was at Drogheda, which Ludlow describes:

The Lieutenant-General well knowing the importance of this action, resolved to put all upon it; and having commanded some guns to be loaded
with bullets of half a pound, and fired upon the enemy's horse, who were
drawn up somewhat in view; himself with a reserve of foot marched up to
the breach, which giving fresh courage to our men, they made a second attack with more vigour than before: whereupon the enemy's foot being abandoned by their horse, whom our shot had forced to retire, began to break
and shift for themselves; which ours perceiving, followed them so close, that
they overtook them at the bridg that lay cross the river, and separated that
part where the action was from the principal part of the town; and preventing them from drawing up the bridg entred pell-mell with them into the
place, where they put all they met with to the sword, having positive orders
from the Lieutenant-General to give no quarter to any souldier. Their works
and fort were also stormed and taken, and those that defended them put to
the sword also, and amongst them Sir Arthur Ashton, governour of the
place. A great dispute there was amongst the souldiers for his artificial leg,
which was reported to be of gold, but it proved to be but of wood, his girdle
being found to be the better booty; wherein two hundred pieces of gold
were found quilted. The slaughter was continued all that day and the next;
which extraordinary severity I presume was used, to discourage others from
making opposition.

160. CROMWELL'S "PURGE" OF THE HOUSE OF COMMONS (1653)

By 1653 the Long Parliament had been sitting for thirteen years without
reelection. It was by now thoroughly unpopular, and therefore, when Cromwell heard it was about to pass a law perpetuating itself, he dismissed it.

A. *Bulstrode Whitelocke on the Dismissal*

In this manner [accompanied by a troop of soldiers] entering the house,
he, in a furious manner, bid the Speaker leave his chair; told the house
"That they had sat long enough, unless they had done more good; that some
of them were whoremasters, (looking then towards Henry Martyn and Sir

Peter Wentworth) that others of them were drunkards, and some corrupt and unjust men, and scandalous to the profession of the Gospel; and that it was not fit they should sit as a parliament any longer, and desired them to go away." The Speaker not stirring from his seat, col. Harrison, who sat near the chair, rose up and took him by the arm, to remove him from his seat; which when the Speaker saw, he left his chair. Some of the members rose up to answer Cromwell, but he would suffer none to speak but himself; which he did with so much arrogance in himself, and reproach to his fellow-members, that some of his privadoes were ashamed of it, but he and his officers and party would have it so; and among all the parliament men, of whom many wore swords, and would sometimes brag high, not one man offered to draw his sword against Cromwell, or to make the least resistance against him; but all of them tamely departed the house. He bid one of his soldiers to take away that fool's bauble, the mace, and stayed himself to see all the members out of the house, himself the last of them, and then caused the doors of the house to be shut up.

B. *Ludlow on Cromwell's Behavior at the Dismissal*

"Come, come, I will put an end to your prating," [Cromwell said] then walking up and down the house like a mad-man, and kicking the ground with his feet, he cried out, "You are no parliament; I say you are no parliament: I will put an end to your sitting: call them [soldiers] in, call them in."

161. THE FUNERAL OF CROMWELL (1658)

The diarist, John Evelyn, a High Church Tory who abhorred the Cromwellian regime, records the ceremonies attending the Lord Protector's elaborate funeral. Although he had refused to be called a king, he nevertheless was buried like one.

22d October, 1658. Saw the superb funeral of the protector. He was carried from Somerset House in a velvet bed of state, drawn by six horses, housed with the same; the pall held by his new lords; Oliver lying in effigy, in royal robes, and crowned with a crown, sceptre, and globe, like a king. The pendants and guidons were carried by the officers of the army; the imperial banners, achievements, etc., by the heralds in their coats; a rich caparisoned horse, embroidered all over with gold; a knight of honor, armed *cap-a-pie,* and, after all, his guards, soldiers, and innumerable mourners. In this equipage, they proceeded to Westminster: but it was the most joyful

funeral I ever saw; for there were none that cried but dogs, which the soldiers hooted away with a barbarous noise, drinking and taking tobacco in
the streets as they went.

162. THE RESTORATION OF CHARLES II (1660)

After nine years of exile on the Continent, Charles II, who had undergone
hardship and privation, returned triumphantly to England, his friend and
adviser, Edward Hyde, later Earl of Clarendon, at his side. The next reading records Charles' joyous entry into London on his thirtieth birthday.

29th May, 1660. This day, his Majesty, Charles II. came to London, after
a sad and long exile and calamitous suffering both of the King and Church,
being seventeen years. This was also his birthday, and with a triumph of
above 20,000 horse and foot, brandishing their swords, and shouting with inexpressible joy; the ways strewn with flowers, the bells ringing; the streets
hung with tapestry, fountains running with wine; the Mayor, Aldermen,
and all the companies, in their liveries, chains of gold, and banners; Lords
and Nobles, clad in cloth of silver, gold, and velvet; the windows and bal-
conies, all set with ladies; trumpets, music, and myriads of people flocking,
even so far as from Rochester, so as they were seven hours in passing the
city, even from two in the afternoon till nine at night.

163. ACT OF PARDON, INDEMNITY AND OBLIVION (1660)

After agreeing to Charles II's demand for the punishment of the regicides
responsible for his father's death (thirteen by death and twenty-five by life
imprisonment), and to the disinterring and hanging of the corpses of
Cromwell, Bradshaw, and Ireton, the Convention Parliament passed this
statute:

The King's most excellent Majesty . . . out of a hearty and pious desire
to put an end to all suits and controversies that by occasion of the late dis-
tractions have arisen or may arise between all his subjects; (3) and to the
intent that no crime whatsoever committed against his Majesty or his royal
father, shall hereafter rise in judgment, or be brought in question, against
any of them to the least endamagement of them, either in their lives, liberties,
estates, or to the prejudice of the reputations, by any reproach or term of
distinction; (4) and to bury all seeds of future discords and remembrance
of the former . . . , be it enacted . . . That all and all manner of treasons,
misprisions of treasons, murders, felonies, offences, crimes, contempts and
misdemeanors, counselled, commanded, acted or done since the first day of

January in the year . . . [1637] by any person . . . before the twenty-fourth day of June in the year . . . [1660], other than the persons hereafter by name excepted, in such manner as they are hereafter excepted, by virtue or colour of any command, power, authority, commission, warrant or instructions from his late Majesty King Charles, or his Majesty that now is . . . or of or from any convention or assembly, called or reputed, or taking on them the name of a parliament, or by, from or under any authority stiled or known by the name of the keepers of liberty of England by authority of parliament, or by virtue or colour of any writ, commission, letters patents, instruction . . . from any person or persons, tituled, reputed or taken to be lord protector of the commonwealth . . . or reputed to be chief magistrate of the commonwealth, or commander in chief of the forces or armies of this nation . . . or by any pretence, warrant or command whatsoever, from them or any of them, or their or either of their respective council or councils, or any member of such council . . . , or from any person . . . whatsoever deriving or pretending to derive authority from them or any of them, be pardoned, released, indemnified, discharged and put in utter oblivion . . . .

III. And be it further enacted, That all appeals, and all personal actions, suits, molestations and prosecutions whatsoever, for or by reason of any act of hostility, trespass, assault, imprisonment or breach of the peace, advised, counselled, commanded, appointed, happened, acted or done, by reason of the late troubles, or the late wars, in his Majesty's dominions, or relating thereunto, and all judgments and executions thereupon had before the first day of May in the year of our Lord one thousand six hundred fifty and eight, stand and be from henceforth discharged . . . .

164. THE CORPORATION ACT (1661)

The strongly Royalist and ardently Anglican Parliament elected in 1661 made certain of their hold on local government by means of the Corporation Act, which excluded Dissenters who refused to take Communion once a year according to the Anglican rite and to obey the Act of Uniformity confirming Anglicanism as the state religion.

IV. And be it further enacted . . . That all persons who upon . . . [December 24, 1661] shall be mayors, aldermen, recorders, bailiffs, town-clerks, common council-men, and other persons then bearing any office or offices of magistracy, or places, or trusts, or other employment relating to or concerning the government of the said respective cities, corporations and boroughs, and cinque ports and their members and other port-towns, shall at any time before . . . [March 25, 1663], when they shall be thereunto required by the said respective commissioners or any three or more of them, take the oaths of allegiance and supremacy, and this oath following:

V. I A.B. do declare and believe, That it is not lawful, upon any pretence whatsoever, to take arms against the King; and that I do abhor that traitorous position of taking arms by his authority against his person, or against those that are commissioned by him: So help me God.

VI. And also at the same time shall publickly subscribe, before the said commissioners or any three of them, this following declaration:

I A.B. do declare, That I hold that there lies no obligation upon me or any other person, from the oath commonly called, The solemn league and covenant; and that the same was in it self an unlawful oath, and imposed upon the subjects of this realm against the known laws and liberties of the kingdom.

VII. And that all such of the said mayors and other the persons aforesaid, by whom the said oaths are to be taken, and declaration subscribed as aforesaid, who shall refuse to take and subscribe the same within the time and in manner aforesaid, shall, from and immediately after such refusal, be by authority of this act . . . removed . . . from the said offices . . . ; (2) and the said offices and places from and immediately after such refusal, shall be and are hereby declared and adjudged to be void to all intents and purposes, as if the said respective persons so refusing were naturally dead . . . .

165. THE TRIENNIAL ACT (1664)

Because serious problems had often developed when Parliament had not met for long periods (England had not forgotten Charles I's eleven-year period of personal government, 1629–1640), Parliament passed the Triennial Act, the chief part of which is as follows:

III. And because by the ancient laws and statutes of this realm, made in the reign of King Edward the Third, parliaments are to be held very often: your Majesty's humble and loyal subjects the lords . . . and . . . commons . . . beseech your most excellent Majesty, That it may be declared and enacted; (2) and be it declared and enacted . . . That hereafter the sitting and holding of parliaments shall not be intermitted or discontinued above three years . . . ; (3) but that within three years from and after the determination of this present parliament, and so from time to time within three years after the determination of any other parliament or parliaments or if there be occasion more often, your Majesty, your heirs and successors, do issue out your writs for calling, assembling and holding of another parliament, to the end there may be a frequent calling, assembling and holding of parliaments once in three years at the least.

166. CHARLES II AND THE MARRIAGE OF WILLIAM OF ORANGE TO MARY (1677)

Perhaps nowhere is there a better example of the diplomatic skill of Charles II and of the type of planning that was a part of royal marriages than in the following account. De Barillon, a French diplomat who had negotiated with Charles, reported to King Louis XIV what Charles had said:

I judge it [the marriage] very necessary for my interests, and I believe I shall draw considerable advantages from it now, and greater hereafter. This alliance will quiet the suspicions which my subjects have, that the alliance I preserve with France, hath no other foundation than a change of religion. It is my brother, the Duke of York's conduct, that has given rise to all these suspicions. All the jealousy and passion which people have in this country against the prosperities of France, comes from the Duke's declaring his [Catholic] religion. In the first war of 1667, they looked here upon all the conquests [by France] that were made in Flanders with indifference, and cared little about them; but since the Duke of York professed the Catholic religion, all England has been in motion, and apprehensive that I have other designs, and am taking measures for changing the government and religion of my country. This is the rock against which I must guard myself, and I assure you that I need every thing to enable me to resist the continual efforts of the whole English nation; for, in fine, I am the only one of my party, except it be my brother. I am assured that the Prince of Orange's marriage with my niece will dissipate a part of these suspicions, and infinitely serve to shew that I have no design which is not conformable to the established laws and religion of England. It will destroy the cabals that might be made, and put my nephew in my interest. I confound thereby the hopes of those who only seek a pretence to rise against me, and who would endeavour to get the Prince of Orange on their side, by making him entertain pretensions, which now he will rest on no other foundation than my friendship, and a true attachment to my interests.

167. THE DUKE OF MONMOUTH (1685)

Charles II died on February 6, 1685, and was succeeded by his brother, James, Duke of York. A small group of men, thinking James ought not to be king because he was a Roman Catholic, rallied to the cause of Monmouth, the so-called "Protestant Duke," who was an illegitimate son of Charles. Monmouth claimed the throne, and led a disastrous rebellion against James, for which he was executed along with many other rebels. On July 15, 1685, Evelyn described his appearance, condemnation, and execution.

Monmouth was this day brought to London and examined before the King, to whom he made great submission, acknowledged his seduction by Ferguson, the Scot, whom he named the bloody villain. He was sent to the Tower, had an interview with his late Duchess, whom he received coldly, having lived dishonestly with the Lady Henrietta Wentworth for two years. He obstinately asserted his conversation with that debauched woman to be no sin; whereupon, seeing he could not be persuaded to his last breath, the divines who were sent to assist him thought not fit to administer the Holy Communion to him. For the rest of his faults he professed great sorrow, and so died without any apparent fear. He would not make use of a cap or other circumstance, but lying down, bid the fellow to do his office better than to the late Lord Russell [executed for complicity in an earlier plot to assassinate Charles II], and gave him gold; but the wretch made five chops before he had his head off; which so incensed the people, that had he not been guarded and got away, they would have torn him to pieces.

The Duke made no speech on the scaffold (which was on Tower Hill), but gave a paper containing not above five or six lines, for the King, in which he disclaims all title to the Crown, acknowledges that the late King, his father, had indeed told him he was but his base son, and so desired his Majesty to be kind to his wife and children. This relation I had from Dr. Tenison (Rector of St. Martin's) who, with the Bishops of Ely and Bath and Wells, were sent to him by his Majesty, and were at the execution.

Thus ended this quondam Duke, darling of his father and the ladies, being extremely handsome and adroit, an excellent soldier and dancer, a favorite of the people, of an easy nature, debauched by lust; seduced by crafty knaves, who would have set him up only to make a property, and taken the opportunity of the King being of another religion, to gather a party of discontented men. He failed and perished. . . .

168. TROUBLES IN THE ARMY AND NAVY (1688)

When James attempted to secure the support of the army and navy for the abrogation of the Test Act of 1673, which made it obligatory on all holders of civil and military offices to receive Communion according to the Anglican rite and take an oath against transubstantiation, he met with stout resistance. Dalrymple cites two instances of opposition to the king:

Finding the civil and ecclesiastical courts insufficient for the accomplishment of his will, James gave orders to sound the different regiments at
Blackheath, if they would stand by him in the abrogation of the tests. The
major of Litchfield's regiment made a speech to the soldiers, and ordered all
those to lay down their arms who would not comply with their sovereign's
desire. The whole regiment, except a few, threw their arms upon the ground.
The King was on the field. He was struck motionless at the sight. But, after
some pause, he ordered them to take up their muskets, and said, with sullen
ambiguity, "That he would do them the honour to ask their advice another
time." Experience should have taught him how little his military force was
to be depended upon in matters of religion. For the year before, Admiral
Strickland, who was a papist, having directed the priests to say mass on
board his ship, the seamen, a class of men not famous in England for attention to religious controversy, rose in a mutiny, and insisted to throw the
priests over board. Strickland proceeded to severity: The severity added rage
to mutiny; and both flew from ship to ship. The King was obliged to repair
to Portsmouth, to pacify the seamen. He in vain called them his children and
old friends. Though more easily affected with concessions, and with kindness of expression than other men, it was impossible to satisfy them until the
priests were removed from the ships.

169. THE REVOLUTION OF 1688 AND THE COMING OF
WILLIAM OF ORANGE

King James had aroused great opposition in the country because of his pro-
Catholic religious policy and a succession of unconstitutional actions, such
as violation of the penal laws, the imprisonment of the seven bishops who
had petitioned him to absolve them from promulgating the second Declaration of Indulgence, and interference with elections to Parliament and local
government. For these reasons and others, a number of prominent Whig
and Tory courtiers and politicians negotiated with William of Orange,
stadtholder of Holland, to invade England in order to depose James. After
long and careful preparations, William landed his army in Dorsetshire,
gained many English supporters, and marched toward London without any
significant opposition. James, deserted by practically everyone, fled the country.

Hourly expectation of the Prince of Orange's invasion heightened to
that degree, that his Majesty [James II] thought fit to abrogate the Commission for the dispensing Power (but retaining his own right still to
dispense with all laws) and restore the ejected Fellows of Magdalen Col-

lege, Oxford. In the meantime, he called over 5,000 Irish, and 4,000 Scots, and continued to remove Protestants and put in Papists at Portsmouth and other places of trust, and retained the Jesuits about him, increasing the universal discontent. It brought people to so desperate a pass, that they seemed passionately to long for and desire the landing of that Prince, whom they looked on to be their deliverer from Popish tyranny, praying incessantly for an east wind, which was said to be the only hindrance of his expedition with a numerous army ready to make a descent. To such a strange temper, and unheard of in former times, was this poor nation reduced, and of which I was an eyewitness. The apprehension was (and with reason) that his Majesty's forces would neither at land nor sea oppose them with that vigor requisite to repel invaders.

170. THE NEW SOVEREIGNS: WILLIAM AND MARY (1689–1702)

With the expulsion of James II by William and his English allies, the English throne was offered jointly to William and Mary. They at once moved to Whitehall Palace to assume the administration of the country. The scene was witnessed by John Evelyn, who wrote:

I saw the new Queen and King proclaimed the very next day after her coming to Whitehall, Wednesday, 13th February [1689], with great acclamation and general good reception. Bonfires, bells, guns, etc. It was believed that both, especially the Princess, would have shown some (seeming) reluctance at least, of assuming her father's crown, and made some apology, testifying by her regret that he should by his mismanagement necessitate the nation to so extraordinary a proceeding, which would have shown very handsomely to the world, and according to the character given of her piety; consonant also to her husband's first declaration, that there was no intention of deposing the King, but of succoring the nation; but nothing of all this appeared; she came into Whitehall laughing and jolly, as to a wedding, so as to seem quite transported. She rose early the next morning, and in her undress, as it was reported, before her women were up, went about from room to room to see the convenience of Whitehall; lay in the same bed and apartment where the late Queen lay [Mary of Modena], and within a night or two sat down to play at basset, as the Queen, her predecessor used to do. She smiled upon and talked to everybody, so that no change seemed to have taken place at Court since her last going away, save that infinite crowds of people thronged to see her, and that she went to our prayers. This carriage was censured by many. She seems to be of a good nature, and that she takes nothing to heart: while the Prince, her husband, has a thoughtful countenance, is wonderfully serious and silent, and seems to treat all persons alike gravely, and to be very intent on affairs: Holland, Ireland, and France calling for his care.

171. THE SCOTTISH REBELS IN 1689

William and Mary were not accepted as legitimate rulers by the Irish or the Scottish rebels. William defeated the Irish commanded by James II at the Battle of the Boyne (July, 1690), and James returned to France for good. When a convention in Scotland offered the crown to William and Mary, a minority (chiefly Highland Catholics), who remained loyal to the Catholic Stuarts, took up arms. William's troops defeated them at Dunkeld. The next reading is a description of the Scottish rebels.

Their dress, which was the last remains of the Roman habit in Europe, was well suited to the nature of their country, and still better to the necessities of war. It consisted of a roll of light woollen, called a plaid, six yards in length, and two in breadth, wrapped loosely around the body, the upper lappet of which rested on the left shoulder, leaving the right arm at full liberty; a jacket of thick cloth, fitted tightly to the body; and a loose short garment of light woollen, which went around the waist and covered the thigh. In rain, they formed the plaid into folds, and, laying it on the shoulders were covered as with a roof. When they were obliged to lie abroad in the hills, in their hunting parties, or tending their cattle, or in war, the plaid served them both for bed and for covering; for, when three men slept together, they could spread three folds of cloth below, and six above them. The garters of their stockings were tied under the knee, with a view to give more freedom to the limb; and they wore no breeches, that they might climb mountains with the greater ease. The lightness and looseness of their dress, the custom they had of going always on foot, never on horseback, their love of long journeys, but above all, that patience of hunger, and every kind of hardship, which carried their bodies forward, even after their spirits were exhausted, made them exceed all other European nations in speed and perserverance of march. Montrose's marches were sometimes sixty miles in a day, without food or halting, over mountains, along rocks, through morasses. In encampments, they were expert at forming beds in a moment, by tying together bunches of heath, and fixing them upright in the ground: An art, which, as the beds were both soft and dry, preserved their health in the field, when other soldiers lost theirs.

Their arms were a broad sword, a dagger, called a durk, a target, a musket, and two pistols: So that they carried the long sword of the Celts, the pugio of the Romans, the shield of the ancients, and both kinds of modern fire arms altogether. In battle, they threw away the plaid and under garment, and fought in their jackets, making thus their movements quicker, and their strokes more forcible.

172. THE REVOLUTIONARY SETTLEMENT (1689–1701)

This settlement was accomplished by the enactment of a series of statutes, the first and most important of which was the Bill of Rights of 1689. It enumerated the faults of which the Stuart monarchs were guilty, and settled the crown on William and Mary with the understanding that these faults were not to be repeated. The only wholly new constitutional principle enunciated in the Bill of Rights was the statement that standing armies in time of peace were illegal. The great constitutional contest between the king and Parliament for sovereignty, a contest that had consumed most of the seventeenth century, had finally been resolved. No future sovereign who violated the fundamental laws of the land could hope to keep the throne. As Parliament had made a king, it could also unmake one. Hence the theory of divine-right monarchy was dead. After 1689 other statutes were passed which are regarded as part of the Revolutionary Settlement.

A. *Bill of Rights* (*1689*)

1. That the pretended power of suspending of laws, or the execution of laws, by regal authority, without consent of parliament, is illegal.

2. That the pretended power of dispensing with laws, or the execution of laws, by regal authority, as it hath been assumed and exercised of late, is illegal.

3. That the commission for erecting the late court of commissioners for ecclesiastical causes, and all other commissions and courts of like nature are illegal and pernicious.

4. That levying money for or to the use of the crown, by pretence of prerogative, without grant of parliament, for longer time, or in other manner than the same is or shall be granted, is illegal.

5. That it is the right of the subjects to petition the King, and all commitments and prosecutions for such petitioning are illegal.

6. That the raising or keeping a standing army within the kingdom in time of peace, unless it be with consent of parliament, is against law.

7. That the subjects which are protestants, may have arms for their defence suitable to their conditions, and as allowed by law.

8. That election of members of parliament ought to be free.

9. That the freedom of speech, and debates or proceedings in parliament, ought not to be impeached or questioned in any court or place out of parliament.

10. That excessive bail ought not to be required, nor excessive fines imposed; nor cruel and unusual punishments inflicted.

11. That jurors ought to be duly impanelled and returned, and jurors which pass upon men in trials for high treason ought to be freeholders.

12. That all grants and promises of fines and forfeitures of particular persons before conviction, are illegal and void.

13. And that for redress of all grievances, and for the amending, strengthening, and preserving of the laws, parliaments ought to be held frequently.

And they do claim, demand, and insist upon all and singular the premisses, as their undoubted rights and liberties; and that no declarations, judgments, doings or proceedings, to the prejudice of the people in any of the said premisses, ought in any wise to be drawn hereafter into consequence or example.

To which demand of their rights they are particularly encouraged by the declaration of his highness the prince of Orange, as being the only means for obtaining a full redress and remedy therein.

Having therefore an entire confidence, That his said highness the prince of Orange will perfect the deliverance so far advanced by him, and will still preserve them from the violation of their rights, which they have here asserted, and from all other attempts upon their religion, rights, and liberties. . . .

> Other parts of the Bill of Rights bestowed the English throne on William and Mary, abrogated the oaths of allegiance and supremacy, substituted for them a simple oath of fealty to the crown and another oath denying that "princes excommunicated or deprived by the pope . . . may be deposed or murdered by their subjects," settled the succession on Mary's sister Anne, and debarred Roman Catholics from the throne of England.

B. *Act for Frequent Parliaments* (*1694*)

Whereas by the ancient laws, and statutes of this kingdom, frequent parliaments ought to be held; and whereas frequent and new parliaments tend very much to the happy union and good agreement of the King and people . . . it is hereby declared . . . That from henceforth a parliament shall be holden once in three years at the least.

II. And be it further enacted . . . That within three years at the farthest, from and after the dissolution of this present parliament, and so from time to time for ever hereafter, within three years at the farthest, from and after the determination of every other parliament, legal writs under the great seal shall be issued by directions of your Majesties, your heirs and successors, for calling, assembling and holding another new parliament.

III. And be it further enacted . . . That from henceforth no parliament whatsoever, that shall at any time hereafter be called, assembled or held, shall have any continuance longer than for three years only at the farthest, to be accounted from the day on which by the writs of summons the said parliament shall be appointed to meet . . . .

C. *Act Regulating Treason Cases* (*1695*)

Whereas nothing is more just and reasonable, than that persons prosecuted for high treason and misprision of treason, whereby the liberties, lives, honour, estates, blood, and posterity of the subjects, may be lost and destroyed, should be justly and equally tried, and that persons accused as offenders therein should not be debarred of all just and equal means for defence of their innocencies in such cases; in order thereunto, and for the better regulation of trials of persons prosecuted for high treason and misprision of such treason; be it enacted . . . That from and after . . . [March 25, 1696], all and every person . . . that shall be accused and indicted for high treason, whereby any corruption of blood may or shall be made to any such offender . . . or for misprision of such treason, shall have a true copy of the whole indictment, but not the names of the witnesses, delivered unto them, . . . five days at the least before he or they shall be tried for the same, whereby to enable them, and any of them respectively, to advise with counsel thereupon, to plead and make their defence, his or their attorney . . . requiring the same, and paying the officer his reasonable fees for writing thereof, not exceeding five shillings for the copy of every such indictment; and that every such person so accused and indicted, arraigned or tried for any such treason, as aforesaid, or for misprision of such treason, from and after the said time, shall be received and admitted to make his and their full defence, by counsel learned in the law, and to make any proof that he or they can produce by lawful witness or witnesses, who shall then be upon oath, for his and their just defence in that behalf; and in case any person . . . so accused or indicted shall desire counsel, the court before whom such person . . . shall be tried, or some judge of that court, shall and is hereby authorized and required immediately, upon his or their request, to assign to such person . . .

such and so many counsel, not exceeding two, as the person or persons shall desire, to whom such counsel shall have free access at all seasonable hours; any law or usage to the contrary notwithstanding.

II. And be it further enacted, That from and after the said . . . [March 25, 1696], no person or persons whatsoever shall be indicted, tried, or attainted of high treason . . . but by and upon the oaths and testimony of two lawful witnesses, either both of them to the same overt act, or one of them to one, and the other of them to another overt act of the same treason; unless the party indicted . . . shall willingly . . . in open court, confess the same, or shall stand mute, or refuse to plead, or in cases of high treason shall peremptorily challenge above the number of thirty five of the jury . . . .

III. Provided always, That any person or persons, being indicted . . . for any of the treasons . . . may be outlawed, and thereby attainted of or for any of the said offences of treason, or misprision of treason; and in cases of the high treasons aforesaid, where by the law, after such outlawry, the party outlawed may come in, and be tried, he shall, upon such trial, have the benefit of this act . . . .

VII. And that all and every person and persons, who shall be accused, indicted, and tried for such treason as aforesaid, or for misprision of such treason, after the said . . . [March 25, 1696], shall have copies of the panel of the jurors who are to try them, duly returned by the sheriff, and delivered unto them and every of them so accused and indicted respectively, two days at the least before he or they shall be tried for the same; and that all persons so accused and indicted for any such treason . . . shall have the like process of the court where they shall be tried, to compel their witnesses to appear for them at any such trial or trials, as is usually granted to compel witnesses to appear against them . . . .

D. *Act of Settlement* (*1701*)

That the crown and regal government of the said kingdoms [England, France, and Ireland], and the dominions thereunto belonging, with the royal state and dignity of the said realms, and all honours, stiles, titles, regalities, prerogatives, powers, jurisdictions and authorities, to the same belonging and appertaining, after the decease of your Majesty, and of the said princess Anne of Denmark [older daughter of James II, married to George of Denmark], and in default of issue of the said princess Anne . . . , and of your Majesty respectively, should be, remain, and continue to the most excellent princess Sophia, electress and duchess dowager of Hanover, daughter of the most excellent princess Elizabeth [daughter of James I, wife of Frederick,

Elector of the Rhenish Palatinate] . . . late Queen of Bohemia, and the heirs of the body of the said princess Sophia, being protestants . . . .

173. QUEEN ANNE (1702–1714)

On the death of William in 1702 (Mary having died in 1694), Anne, wife of George of Denmark, came to the throne in accordance with the Act of Settlement. In his *Memoirs of the Court of England,* John H. Jesse describes Anne.

The great Duke of Marlborough, in his secret correspondence, both with the Electress Sophia of Hanover, and with the exiled court of St. Germains [where the Catholic Stuarts resided], speaks familiarly of his royal mistress as a "very good sort of woman." Were the character of Queen Anne to be described in a single sentence, it could not be done more effectively than in these words:—As a wife her conduct was exemplary; she was pious without affectation; she was a tender mother; an attached friend, and a generous and indulgent mistress. As a sovereign she had less merit. If, on the one hand, she was without ostentation and without ambition, she was also weak, indolent, and irresolute; devoid of all genius and political courage; open to the grossest flattery from every designing sycophant; and easily led by persons who were more artful, but whose capacities were scarcely superior to her own. Slavish, however, as was her submission to the reigning favorite, she is said to have been peculiarly jealous of her prerogative, and singularly vindictive to those who infringed on it. In every other respect she seems to have been eminently forbearing: indeed, her conduct, on many trying occasions, was distinguished by that constitutional good-humor—the only quality, excepting indolence, which descended conspicuously to her from the Stuarts.

Queen Anne, whether from the consolations which she derived from religion, or from a natural coldness of temperament, bore her numerous domestic sorrows with an extraordinary equanimity of mind. Few, indeed, have had afflictions heaped more thickly on their head. The misfortunes of her father could scarcely fail to have been felt by her; she was also deprived of her husband while yet in his prime; and of her numerous progeny not one was left to be the solace of her declining years. On the other hand, she was peculiarly favored by Providence, not only in the exceeding splendor of her sovereignty, but in being able to retain the quiet possession of a throne, to which she had no legitimate right [Jesse here assumes that the Catholic Stuart Pretender had the right to the throne]. During the few years that she wielded the British sceptre, her arms triumphed gloriously abroad, and literature blazed in its zenith at home. Her reign, indeed, was the Augustan age of England: unlike, however, the celebrated Roman era from which it takes its name, it flourished independent of sovereign favor. The galaxy of genius which has rendered so illustrious the reign of Anne, owed as little to her fostering munificence as a Queen, as to her individual taste.

By her husband, Prince George of Denmark, Anne was the mother of nineteen children. . . .

174. THE DUKE OF MARLBOROUGH (1650–1722)

John Churchill, later Duke of Marlborough, and one of England's greatest generals, had fought in Ireland under William III, and at the latter's death was the close friend and confidant of Queen Anne. Honors, including command of the army, were conferred on him by the queen. His chief weakness was his avarice. Stories about his love of money are both numerous and amusing. It is said that his first purchase in life was a box in which to keep his money, and late in life, when he was infirm, he would walk from the rooms in Bath to his lodgings on a cold and dark night to save sixpence cab fare. Evelyn has this to say of him:

After the excess of honor conferred by the Queen on the Earl of Marlborough, by making him a Knight of the Garter and a Duke, for the success of but one campaign, that he should desire £5,000 a year to be settled on him by Parliament out of the Post Office, was thought a bold and unadvised request, as he had, besides his own considerable estate, above £30,000 a year in places and employments, with £50,000 at interest. He had married one daughter to the son of my Lord Treasurer Godolphin, another to the Earl of Sunderland, and a third to the Earl of Bridgewater. He is a very handsome person, well-spoken and affable, and supports his want of acquired knowledge by keeping good company.

175. ACT OF UNION (1707)

Throughout the seventeenth century there had been continuous friction between England and Scotland. In 1703 the Scottish Parliament passed an Act making succession to the throne of Scotland different from that to the throne of England, whereupon the English Parliament retaliated with additional restrictions on Scottish trade. For the next four years a joint committee sought to end the difficulties by an Act uniting the two kingdoms. The result was the Act of Union of 1707.

ARTICLE I.

That the two kingdoms of England and Scotland shall upon the first day of May, which shall be in the year one thousand seven hundred and seven, and for ever after, be united into one kingdom by the name of Great Britain; and that the ensigns armorial of the said united kingdom be such as her Majesty shall appoint, and the crosses of St. George and St. Andrew be conjoined in such manner as her Majesty shall think fit, and used in all flags, banners, standards, and ensigns, both at sea and land.

ARTICLE II.

That the succession of the monarchy to the united kingdom of Great Britain, and of the dominions thereto belonging, after her most sacred Majesty, and in default of issue of her Majesty, be, remain, and continue to the most excellent princess Sophia, electoress and dutchess dowager of Hanover, and the heirs of her body being Protestants . . . and that all papists, and persons marrying papists, shall be excluded from, and forever incapable to inherit, possess, or enjoy the imperial crown of Great Britain. . . .

ARTICLE III.

That the united kingdom of Great Britain be represented by one and the same parliament, to be stiled The Parliament of Great Britain.

ARTICLE IV.

That all the subjects of the united kingdom of Great Britain shall, from and after the union, have full freedom and intercourse of trade and navigation to or from any port or place within the said united kingdom, and the dominions and plantations thereunto belonging. . . .

ARTICLE XVI.

That from and after the union, the coin shall be of the same standard and value throughout the united kingdom, as now in England. . . .

ARTICLE XVII.

That from and after the union, the same weights and measures shall be used throughout the united kingdom, as are now established in England. . . .

ARTICLE XXII.

That by virtue of this treaty, of the peers of Scotland, at the time of the union, sixteen shall be the number to sit and vote in the house of lords, and forty five the number of the representative of Scotland in the house of commons of the parliament of Great Britain. . . .

The Act also preserved for the Scots their Protestant Church and Presbyterian government, and for the English the security of the Church of England.

176. QUALIFICATIONS FOR SITTING IN THE HOUSE OF COMMONS (1710)

For the better preserving the constitution and freedom of parliament, be it enacted . . . That from and after the determination of this present parliament, no person shall be capable to sit or vote as a member of the house of commons, for any county, city, borough, or cinque port, within that part of Great Britain called England, the dominion of Wales, and town of Berwick upon Tweed, who shall not have an estate, freehold or copyhold, for his own life, or for some greater estate, either in law or equity, to and for his own use and benefit, of or in lands, tenements, or hereditaments, over and above what will satisfy and clear all incumbrances that may affect the same, lying or being within that part of Great Britain called England, the dominion of Wales, and town of Berwick upon Tweed, of the respective annual value hereafter limited, *videlicet,* The annual value of six hundred pounds, above reprizes, for every knight of a shire; and the annual value of three hundred pounds, above reprizes, for every citizen, burgess, or baron of the cinque ports. . . .

177. THE NAVIGATION ACTS (1660; 1696)

While the seventeenth century did not produce in England anything that can be clearly identified as a trade *policy,* trading activity increased steadily and laws were passed to advance English shipping by lessening the competition of the Dutch and other Europeans in the carrying trade. This part of what is called mercantilism took the form of the following parliamentary Acts:

A. *Navigation Act of 1660*

For the increase of shipping and encouragement of the navigation of this nation, wherein, under the good providence and protection of God, the wealth, safety and strength of this kingdom is so much concerned; (2) be it enacted by the King's most excellent majesty, and by the lords and commons in this present parliament assembled, and by the authority thereof, That from and after the first day of December one thousand six hundred and sixty, and from thenceforward, no goods or commodities whatsoever shall be imported into or exported out of any lands, islands, plantations or

territories to his Majesty belonging or in his possession, or which may hereafter belong unto or be in the possession of his Majesty, his heirs and successors, in Africa, Asia or America, in any other ship or ships, vessel or vessels whatsoever, but in such ships or vessels as do truly and without fraud
belong only to the people of England or Ireland, dominion of Wales or town
of Berwick upon Tweed, or are of the built of and belonging to any the said
lands, islands, plantations or territories, as the proprietors and right owners
thereof, and whereof the master and three fourths of the mariners at least are
English; (3) under the penalty of the forfeiture and loss of all the goods
and commodities which shall be imported into or exported out of any of the
aforesaid places in any other ship or vessel. . . .

And it is further enacted by the authority aforesaid, That no goods or
commodities that are of foreign growth, production or manufacture, and
which are to be brought into England, Ireland, Wales, the islands of Guern-
sey and Jersey, or town of Berwick upon Tweed, in English-built shipping,
or other shipping belonging to some of the aforesaid places, and navigated
by English mariners, as aforesaid, shall be shipped or brought from any
other place or places, country or countries, but only from those of the said
growth, production or manufacture, or from those ports where the said
goods and commodities can only, or are, or usually have been, first shipped
for transportation, and from none other places or countries; (2) under the
penalty of the forfeiture of all such of the aforesaid goods as shall be imported from any other place or country contrary to the true intent and meaning hereof, as also of the ship in which they were imported, with all her
guns, furniture, ammunition, tackle and apparel; one moiety to his Majesty,
his heirs and successors and the other moiety to him or them that shall seize,
inform or sue for the same in any court of record, to be recovered as is before
exprest. . . .

B. *Act for Preventing Frauds, and Regulating Abuses in the Plantation Trade* (*1696*)

Be it enacted, and it is hereby enacted and ordained by the King's most
excellent majesty, by and with the advice and consent of the lords spiritual
and temporal, and commons, in parliament assembled, and by the authority
of the same, That after the five and twentieth day of March, one thousand
six hundred ninety eight, no goods or merchandizes whatsoever shall be imported into, or exported out of, any colony or plantation to his Majesty, in
Asia, Africa or America, belonging, or in his possession, or which may hereafter belong unto, or be in the possession of his Majesty, his heirs or suc-

cessors, or shall be laden in, or carried from any one port or place in the said colonies or plantations to any other port or place in the same, the kingdom of England, dominion of Wales, or town of Berwick upon Tweed, any ship or bottom, but what is or shall be of the built of England, or of the built of Ireland, or the said colonies or plantations, and wholly owned by the people thereof, or any of them, and navigated with the masters and three fourths of the mariners of the said places only (except such ships only as are or shall be taken as prize, and condemnation thereof made in one of the courts of admiralty in England, Ireland, or the said colonies or plantations, to be navigated by the master and three fourths of the mariners English, or of the said plantations as aforesaid, and whereof the property doth belong to English men; and also except for the space of three years, such foreign built ships as shall be employed by the commissioners of his Majesty's navy for the time being, or upon contract with them, in bringing only masts, timber, and other naval stores for the King's service from his Majesty's colonies or plantations to this kingdom, to be navigated as aforesaid, and whereof the property doth belong to English men) under pain of forfeiture of ship and goods; one third part whereof to be to the use of his Majesty, his heirs and successors, one third part to the governor of the said colonies or plantations, and the other third part to the person who shall inform and sue for the same, by bill, plaint or information, in any of his Majesty's courts of record at Westminster, or in any court in his Majesty's plantations, where such offence shall be committed. . . .

> By means of these Navigation Acts the government had given to the shipping interest the protection from competition believed necessary for its growth and development. It also made an effort to aid and to regulate domestic industries.

178. AN ACT TOUCHING THE MAKING OF FELT AND HATS (1604)

And be it further enacted by the authority aforesaid, That no person or persons from and after the said forty days shall make, or cause to be made, any felt or hat, of or with any wool or stuff whatsoever, unless he or they shall have first served as apprentices in the foresaid trade or art of felt-making during the space of seven years at the least; neither shall they retain and set to work in the said art any other person or persons than journeymen that have lawfully served in that art, and apprentices lawfully bound in the said trade or art, nor above the number of two apprentices at one time, nor those for any less term than seven years; (2) upon pain to forfeit five pound for every month that he shall continue offending contrary to the true meaning of this act, and to be recovered to the uses and in manner and form aforesaid. . . .

179. AN ACT AGAINST EXPORTING SHEEP, WOOL, WOOL-FELLS, WOOL YARN (1662)

Whereas against the laws of this kingdom great number of sheep, and great quantities of wool, wool-fells, mortlings, shorlings, yarn made of wool, wool-flocks, fullers-earth or fulling-clay, are secretly exported, transported, carried and conveyed out of the kingdom of England, dominion of Wales, the town of Berwick upon Tweed, and kingdom of Ireland, into the kingdom of Scotland, and into foreign parts, to the great decay of the woolen manufactures, the ruin of many families, and the destruction of the navigation and commerce of the kingdoms, town, and dominion aforesaid, which is like daily to increase, if some further remedy be not provided, and further penalties imposed upon the offenders therein:

II. Be it therefore enacted That if any person or persons shall from . . . the first day of August one thousand six hundred sixty and two, directly or indirectly export, transport, carry or convey, or shall cause to be exported, transported, carried or conveyed out of or from the kingdom of England, dominion of Wales, or town of Berwick upon Tweed, or after the first day of January . . . [1662] out of . . . Ireland, into any parts or places out of the kingdoms or dominion aforesaid, or into the kingdom of Scotland, any sheep or wool whatsoever, of the breed or growth of the kingdoms or dominion aforesaid, or any wool-fells, mortlings, shorlings, yarn made of wool, wool-flocks, or any fullers-earth or fulling-clay whatsoever, or shall directly or indirectly pack or load, or cause to be packed or loaden upon any horse, cart or other carriage, or shall load or lay on board, or cause to be loaden or laid on board, in any ship or other vessel, in any place within the kingdoms of England or Ireland, dominion of Wales or town of Berwick upon Tweed aforesaid, any such sheep . . . [and so forth] to the intent or purpose to export . . . out of the kingdoms of England or Ireland, the dominion of Wales or town of Berwick . . . into . . . Scotland or into any foreign parts; that then every such offence shall be adjudged felony, and the offender . . . convicted, shall suffer and forfeit as in case of felony. . . .

180. AN ACT FOR BURYING IN WOOLENS (1677)

And it is hereby enacted by the authority aforesaid, That from and after the first day of August one thousand six hundred and seventy-eight, no corpse of any person or persons shall be buried in any shirt, shift, sheet or shroud, or any thing whatsoever made or mingled with flax, hemp, silk, hair, gold or silver, or in any stuff or thing, other than what is made of sheeps wool only, or be put in any coffin lined or faced with any sort of cloth or stuff, or any other thing whatsoever, that is made of any material but sheeps wool only: (2) upon pain of the forfeiture of five pounds of lawful money of England, to be recovered and divided as is hereafter in this act expressed and directed. . . .

181. AN ACT TO PREVENT THE EXPORTATION OF WOOL AND TO ENCOURAGE ITS MANUFACTURE IN ENGLAND (1688)

Be it enacted . . . That all and every owner of wooll, or their agent or agents, that shall at any time carry, or cause to be carried any wooll to any port or place on the sea coasts, with an intention to convey the same to any other port or place on the sea coasts within the kingdom of England, dominion of Wales, or from the town of Berwick upon Tweed, from whence the same may be shipped off, or otherwise transported . . . into foreign parts, that the said owner or owners shall in the first place cause a due entry to be made of the said wooll, at the port from whence the same shall be so intended to be conveyed, containing the exact weight, marks, and numbers of the same, before he or they presume to load or carry away any of the said wooll, within five miles of any such port or place on the sea coasts from whence the same is so to be conveyed. And if any wooll shall be carrying towards the sea without being first entred in manner aforesaid, the wooll so found, as also the horse or horses, cart, waggon, or other beasts, or carriages conveying the same, shall be forfeited and lost: And the person or persons carrying, driving, aiding, or abetting the same, shall suffer and forfeit in such manner as by the laws and statutes now in force against the exportation of wooll is provided. . . .

In the seventeenth century England experienced a power struggle between king and Parliament, a civil war, the execution of a king, a many-sided experiment in liberty, a restoration of a limited monarchy, and a revolution. It was therefore natural for the century to be productive of a great deal of political thought. The following readings reveal the wide range of political ideas that flourished in that exciting century.

182. APOLOGY OF THE COMMONS (1604)

What cause we your poor Commons have to watch over our privileges is manifest in itself to all men. The prerogatives of princes may easily, and do daily grow: the privileges of the subject are for the most part at an everlasting stand. They may be by good providence and care preserved, but being once lost are not recovered but with much disquiet.

The rights and liberties of the Commons of England consisteth chiefly in these three things: first, that the shires, cities and boroughs of England, by representation to be present, have free choice of such persons as they shall put in trust to represent them: secondly, that the persons chosen, during the time of the parliament, as also of their access and recess, be free from restraint, arrest and imprisonment: thirdly, that in parliament they may speak freely their consciences without check and controlment, doing the same with due reverence to the sovereign court of parliament, that is, to your Majesty and both the Houses, who all in this case make but one politic body, whereof your Highness is the head. . . .

183. JAMES I'S SPEECH ON THE GRIEVANCES OF PARLIAMENT (1609)

In this speech the king admonished Parliament to be careful to avoid three subjects in their discussion of grievances.

First, that you doe not meddle with the maine points of Gouernment; that is my craft . . . ; to meddle with that, were to lesson me: I am now an old King; for sixe and thirtie yeeres haue I gouerned in Scotland personally, and now haue I accomplished my apprenticeship of seuen yeeres heere; and seven yeeres is a great time for a Kings experience in Gouernment: Therefore there would not bee too many Phormios to teach Hannibal: I must not be taught my Office.

Secondly, I would not haue you meedle with such ancient Rights of mine, as I haue receiued from my Predecessors, possessing them, *More Maiorum:* such things I would bee sorie should bee accounted for Grieuances. All nouelties are dangerous as well in a politique as in a naturall Body: And therefore I would be loth to be quarrelled in my ancient Rights and possessions; for that were to iudge mee vnworthly of that which my Predecessors had and left me.

And lastly, I pray you beware to exhibit for Grieuance any thing that is established by a setled Law, and whereunto (as you haue already had a proofe) you know I will neuer giue a plausible answere: For it is an vndutifull part in Subiects to presse their King, wherein they know beforehand he will refuse them. . . .

184. JAMES I'S SPEECH ON THE ROYAL MIRROR (1614)

It is the sayeing of the wyseste king that evere was, "That the harte of kings weare inscrutable;" but in the laste parleamente, I muste calle to your remembrance the comparisone I used, whearin I presented myselfe unto you as a mirrore, whearin you mighte cleereley see the integretye of my purpos for our lengtheninge that parleamente for the generall good and benefyte of the commonwelthe; but as I then sayd of the nature of mirrore, that it mighte be deffyled by the eyes of the behoulders, so did some of the lowere house looke uppon me with poluted eyes, and as I may saye, deffyled my mirrore; I canne saye no more nowe then I did then, but to offere you the same mirrore to looke to protestyng as I shall answere it to Almyghty God, that my integretye is like the whitness of my roabe, my purety like the mettle of golde in my crowne, my firmness and clearness like the presious stones I weare, and my affectyones naturalle like the rednes of my harte. . . .

185. THOMAS HOBBES' GREAT "LEVIATHAN" (1651)

Hobbes, who was born in 1588 and died in 1679, insisted that man in a state of nature would be constantly at war with his fellowmen and that government was instituted precisely for the purpose of limiting this state of anarchy. Therefore the government should have absolute control over civil, moral, and ecclesiastical affairs.

The only way to erect such a Common Power, as may be able to defend them from the invasion of Forraigners, and the injuries of one another, and thereby to secure them in such sort, as that by their owne industrie, and by the fruites of the Earth, they may nourish themselves and live contentedly; is, to conferre all their power and strength upon one Man, or upon one Assembly of men, that may reduce all their Wills, by plurality of voices, unto one Will; which is as much as to say, to appoint one Man, or Assembly of men, to beare their Person; and every one to owne, and acknowledge himselfe to be Author of whatsoever he that so beareth their Person, shall Act, or cause to be Acted, in those things which concerne the Common Peace and Safetie; and therein to submit their Wills, every one to his Will, and their

Judgements, to his Judgment. This is more than Consent, or Concord; it is a reall Unitie of them all, in one and the same Person, made by Covenant of every man with every man, in such manner, as if every man should say to every man, I Authorise and give up my Right of Governing my selfe, to this Man, or to this Assembly of men on this condition, that thou give up thy Right to him, and Authorise all his Actions in like manner. This done, the Multitude so united in one Person, is called a COMMON-WEALTH, in latine CIVITAS. This is the Generation of that great LEVIATHAN, or rather (to speake more reverently) of that Mortall God, to which wee owe under the Immortall God, our peace and defence. For by this Authoritie, given him by every particular man in the Common-Wealth, he hath the use of so much Power and Strength conferred on him, that by terror thereof, he is inabled to forme the wills of them all, to Peace at home, and mutuall ayd against their enemies abroad. And in him consisteth the Essence of the Common-wealth; which (to define it,) is One Person, of whose Acts a great Multitude, by mutuall Covenants one with another, have made themselves every one the Author, to the end he may use the strength and means of them all, as he shall think expedient, for their Peace and Common Defence.

And he that carryeth this Person, is called SOVERAIGNE, and said to have Soveraigne Power; and every one, besides his SUBJECT.

The attaining to this Soveraigne Power, is by two wayes. One, by Naturall force; as when a man maketh his children, to submit themselves, and their children to his government, as being able to destroy them if they refuse; or by Warre subdueth his enemies to his will, giving them their lives on that condition. The other, is when men agree amongst themselves, to submit to some Man, or Assembly of men, voluntarily, on confidence to be protected by him against all others. This latter, may be called a Politicall Common-wealth, or Common-wealth by Institution: and the former, a Common-wealth by Acquisition. . . .

186. THE LEVELLERS: LILBURNE'S SPEECH IN HIS OWN DEFENSE (1653)

John Lilburne is the best known of the Levellers, a group (about 10,000 in London) who were Independents (Congregationalists) in religion. Artisans, common soldiers, tradesmen, and farmers, they became the political "radicals" of the time. They believed in natural rights, natural justice, and political equality without regard to property-holding. They also believed that the people were sovereign and that Parliament was their servant. Lilburne was arrested, tried, and acquitted for publishing a pamphlet, *The*

Just Defence of John Lilburne, Against Such as Charge him with Turbu-
lency of Spirit, from which the following excerpt is taken:

As for instance, the first fundamental right I contended for in the late
Kings and Bishops times, was for the freedom of mens persons, against arbitrary and illegal imprisonments, it being a thing expresly contrary to the law
of the land, which requireth, That no man be attached, imprisoned, &c. (as
in Magna Charta, cap. 29) But by lawful judgement of a Jury, a law so just
and preservative, as without which intirely observed, every mans person is
continually liable to be imprisoned at pleasure, and either to be kept there for
moneths or yeers, or to be starved there, at the wills of those that in any time
are in power, as hath since been seen and felt abundantly, and had been
more, had not some men strove against it; but it being my lot so to be imprisoned in those times, I conceive I did but my duty to manifest the injustice thereof, and claime and cry out for my right, and in so doing was serv-
iceable to the liberties of my country, and no wayes deserved to be accounted
turbulent in so doing.

Another fundemental right I then contended for, was, that no mans
conscience ought to be racked by oaths imposed, to answer to questions concerning himself in matters criminal, or pretended to be so.

187. POLITICAL OPINIONS AND SCHEMES (1658–1660)

In the years between the death of Oliver Cromwell and the Restoration of
1660 a great many ideas on political'plans were discussed, as the following
excerpt from *Ludlow's Memoirs* illustrates.

At this time the opinions of men were much divided concerning a form
of government to be established amongst us. The great officers of the army,
as I said before, were for a select standing senate to be joined to the representative of the people. Others laboured to have the supream authority to
consist of an assembly chosen by the people, and a council of state chosen by
that assembly to be vested with the executive power, and accountable to that
which should next succeed, at which time the power of the said council
should determine. Some were desirous to have a representative of the people
constantly sitting, but changed by a perpetual rotation. Others proposed that
there might be joined to the popular assembly, a select number of men in the
nature of the Lacedemonian Ephori, who should have a negative in things,
wherein the essentials of the government should be concerned, such as the
exclusion of a single person, touching liberty of conscience, alteration of the
constitution, and other things of the last importance to the state. Some were

of opinion that it would be most conducing to the publick happiness, if there
might be two councils chosen by the people, the one to consist of about three
hundred, and to have the power only of debating and proposing laws; the
other to be in number about one thousand, and to have the power finally to
resolve and determine: every year a third part of each council to go out, and
others to be chosen in their places. For my own part, if I may be permitted
to declare my opinion, I could willingly have approved either of the two latter propositions, presuming them to be most likely to preserve our just liberties, and to render us a happy people.

188. JOHN LOCKE'S "TWO TREATISES OF GOVERNMENT" (1689)

John Locke, the great English philosopher, wrote in the early 1680's what
became the justification of the Revolutionary Settlement of 1688–1689. His
first treatise is an able refutation of the divine origin of government; the
second, from which the following excerpts are taken, is a classic statement
of the contract theory of government.

And thus every man, by consenting with others to make one body
politic under one government, puts himself under an obligation, to every one
of that society to submit to the determination of the majority, and to be concluded by it; or else this original compact, whereby he with others incorporate into one society would signify nothing and be no compact. . . .

Whosoever therefore out of a state of nature unite into a community,
must be understood to give up all the power, necessary to the ends for which
they unite into society, to the majority of the community, unless they expressly agreed in any number greater than the majority. And this is done by
barely agreeing to unite into one political society, which is all the compact
that is, or needs be, between the individuals, that enter into, or make up a
commonwealth. And thus that, which begins and actually constitutes any
political society, is nothing, but the consent of any number of freemen capable of a majority, to unite and incorporate into such a society. And that is
that, and that only, which did, or could give beginning to any lawful government in the world. . . .

If man in the state of nature be so free, as has been said; if he be absolute lord of his own person and possessions, equal to the greatest, and subject
to nobody, why will he part with his freedom? why will he give up his empire, and subject himself to the dominion and control of any other power?
To which it is obvious to answer, that though in the state of nature he hath
such a right, yet the enjoyment of it is very uncertain and constantly exposed
to the invasion of others . . . [and] the enjoyment of the property he has in

this state is very unsafe, very insecure. This makes him willing to quit a condition which, however free, is full of fears and continual dangers: and it is not without reason, that he seeks out, and is willing to join in society with others, who are already united, or have a mind to unite, for the mutual preservation of their lives, liberties and estates which I call by the general name, property. . . .

But though men, when they enter into society, give up the equality, liberty, and executive power they had in the state of nature, into the hands of the society, to be so far disposed of by the legislative, as the good of society shall require; yet it being only with an intention in every one the better to preserve himself, his liberty and property; (for no rational creature can be supposed to change his condition with an intention to be worse), the power of the society, or legislative constituted by them, can never be supposed to extend farther, than the common good, but is obliged to secure every one's property. . . . And so whoever has the legislative or supreme power of any commonwealth, is bound to govern by established standing laws, promulgated and known to the people. . . .

To understand political power right, and derive it from its original, we must consider what state all men are naturally in, and that is, a state of perfect freedom to order their actions and dispose of their possessions and persons as they think fit, within the bounds of the law of nature; without asking leave, or depending upon the will of any other man.

A state also of equality (exists), wherein all the power and jurisdiction is reciprocal, no one having more than another. . . .

But though this be a state of liberty, yet it is not a state of license: though man in that state have an uncontrollable liberty to dispose of his person or possessions, yet he has not liberty to destroy himself, or so much as any creature in his possession, but where some nobler use than its bare preservation calls for it. The state of nature has a law of nature to govern it, which obliges every one: and reason, which is that law, teaches all mankind, who will but consult it, that being all equal and independent, no one ought to harm another in his life, health, liberty, or possessions. . . .

The natural liberty of man is to be free from any superior power on earth, and not to be under the will or legislative authority of man, but to have only the law of nature for his rule. The liberty of man in society is to be under no other legislative power, but that established, by consent, in the commonwealth; nor under the dominion of any will, or restraint of any law, but what that legislative shall enact according to the trust put in it. Freedom, then, is . . . to have a standing rule to live by, common to every one of that society and made by the legislative power erected in it; a liberty to follow my own will in all things, where the rule prescribes not; and not to be subject to the inconstant, uncertain, unknown, arbitrary will of another man: as freedom of nature is, to be under no other restraint but the law of nature.

This freedom from absolute, arbitrary power, is so necessary to, and closely joined with a man's preservation, that he cannot part with it but by what forfeits his preservation and life together. . . .

Men being, as has been said, by nature all free, equal, and independent, no one can be put out of this estate, and subjected to the political power of another, without his own consent. The only way, whereby one divests himself of his natural liberty, and puts on the bonds of civil society, is by agreeing with other men to join and unite into a community, for their comfortable, safe, and peaceable living one amongst another in a secure enjoyment of their properties and a greater security against any that are not of it. This any number of men may do, because it injures not the freedom of the rest; they are left as they were in the liberty of the state of nature. When any number of men have so consented to make one community or government, they are thereby presently incorporated and make one body politic wherein the majority have a right to act and conclude the rest. . . .

189. THE WHIGS CURRY FAVOR WITH QUEEN ANNE (1702)

During the last years of the seventeenth century there developed two political factions—the Whigs and Tories. Both sought to influence Queen Anne in their favor. On March 21, 1702, Sir John Perceval wrote to Thomas Knatchbull:

The Queen happening to blush very much when she spoke her speech from the throne, some compared her to the sign of the Rose and Crown. You cannot imagine how assiduous the Whigs are to curry favour with her. The Bishop of Salisbury, it is said, lay all night in St. James' Court that he might be the first should wish her joy; but though that is false, so much is certain, he was the very first that told the news of the King's death, but she would not believe him till the Marquis of Normanby affirmed it. The last believes himself much in her favour; attending her the day she was proclaimed, she happened to say it was a very fair day. "Yes, Madame," replied he instantly, "this is the most glorious day I ever saw." He is so solicitous about her health, that I am told he goes every morning to the back stairs to enquire how her Majesty rested last night.

Seventeenth-century Englishmen were generally deeply religious, particularly those who professed one or another of the forms of Puritanism. They had frequently associated religious beliefs with political opposition to the crown; a large number of parliamentary critics of James I and Charles I had been Puritans. The number and variety of sects increased throughout the country as the century wore on, as did their suspicion of Roman Catholics. It was the pro-Catholic policies of James II that, along with his unconstitutional actions, were largely responsible for the Revolution of 1688. The Bill of Rights (1689) and the Act of Settlement (1701) included provisions that debarred forever a Roman Catholic from succeeding to the English throne. The following readings will provide some evidence of religious thought during the century.

190. ARCHBISHOP LAUD (1573–1645)

William Laud, appointed Archbishop of Canterbury in 1633, and a close adviser to Charles I, was the outstanding foe of Puritanism before the civil war. His zeal for reform is indicated in James I's comments, and in Parliament's imprisonment and execution of him in 1641 and 1645, respectively.

A. *James I on Laud*

"You press well," says the king, "and I hear you with patience; neither will I revive a trespass any more which repentance hath mortified and buried. And because I see I shall not be rid of you, unless I tell you my unpublished cogitations, the plain truth is, that I keep Laud back from all place of rule and authority, because I find he hath a restless spirit, and cannot see when matters are well, but loves to toss and change, and to bring things to a pitch of reformation floating in his own brain, which may endanger the steadfastness of that which is in a good pass, God be praised."

B. *Charges by Parliament Against Laud (1641?)*

The archbishop was again brought to his trial, and proofs produced against him, touching his endeavours to set up popery, his removing the communion tables, and setting up altars in their places; his causing superstitious pictures, images, and crucifixes to be set up in many churches; and in the king's chapel causing a popish crucifix to be hung up over the altar upon every Good Friday, which had not been there before since the reign of queen Mary.

Other pictures were shewed to the lords, which were found in the archbishop's study and chambers; as, the inspiring of divers popes and cardinals by the Holy Ghost, resembled in the form of a dove: another was of our Saviour bleeding upon the cross, and Pilate crying out, *Ecce homo!* and his consecrating of churches, tapers, candlesticks, organs, and particular prayers for those purposes, were urged against him.

The commons ordered the taking away of all such pictures, images, and crucifixes in the king's chapel at Whitehall.

191. THE INSTRUMENT OF GOVERNMENT: SECTIONS ON RELIGION (1653)

The Instrument of Government, the only written constitution England has ever had, instituted the Protectorate form of government headed by Oliver Cromwell, Lord Protector. Four articles in the document pertained to religion.

XXXV. That the Christian Religion, as contained in the Scriptures, be held forth and recommended as the public Profession of these nations; and that, as soon as may be, a provision, less subject to scruple and contention, and more certain than the present, be made for the encouragement and maintenance of able and painful Teachers, for instructing the people, and for Discovery and Confutation of Error, Heresy, and whatever is contrary to sound Doctrine: and that until such provision be made, the present Maintenance shall not be taken away nor impeached.

XXXVI. That to the public Profession held forth none shall be compelled by penalties or otherwise; but that endeavours be used to win them by sound doctrine, and the example of a good conversation.

XXXVII. That such as profess Faith in God by Jesus Christ (though differing in judgement from the doctrine, worship, or discipline publicly held forth) shall not be restrained from, but shall be protected in the profession of the faith, and exercise of their Religion; so as they abuse not this liberty to the civil injury of others, and to the actual disturbance of the public peace on their parts: provided this liberty be not extended to Popery nor Prelacy, nor to such as, under the profession of Christ, hold forth and practice licentiousness.

XXXVIII. That all laws, statutes and ordinances, and clauses in any law, statute or ordinance to the contrary of the aforesaid Liberty, shall be esteemed as null and void.

192. CROMWELL'S PROCLAMATION ON PREACHING AND TEACHING (1655)

25th December, 1655. There was no more notice taken of Christmas-day in churches [John Evelyn noted in his Diary].

I went to London, where Dr. Wild preached the funeral sermon of

Preaching, this being the last day; after which Cromwell's proclamation was to take place, that none of the Church of England should dare either to preach, or administer Sacraments, teach schools, etc., on pain of imprisonment, or exile. So this was the most mournful day that in my life I had seen, or the Church of England herself, since the Reformation; to the great rejoicing of both Papist and Presbyter. So pathetic was his discourse, that it drew many tears from the auditory. Myself, wife, and some of our family, received the Communion, God make me thankful, who hath hitherto provided for us the food of our souls as well as bodies! The Lord Jesus pity our distressed Church, and bring back the captivity of Zion!

193. THE QUAKERS

George Fox founded the Society of Friends (Quakers), a Christian freethought association. He and his followers were often persecuted because they preached against war and reliance on force. They possessed a democratic scorn of pomp and worldly authority and dressed drably. In their meeting-house services they did not use any formal service or ritual, nor did they observe the rites of Baptism and Communion. They had no ordained ministry. As a result of these views and practices, says G. M. Trevelyan, "The Presbyterians hated Quakerism because it threatened to take away their tithes; the Baptists because it actually took away their congregations; and the Episcopalians because it was further removed than any other sect from the ideas of ritual and Church government."

A. *Evelyn's Description of Quakers* (1656)

I had the curiosity to visit some Quakers here in prison; a new fanatic sect, of dangerous principles, who show no respect to any man, magistrate, or other, and seem a melancholy, proud sort of people, and exceedingly ignorant. One of these was said to have fasted twenty days; but another, endeavoring to do the like, perished on the 10th, when he would have eaten, but could not.

B. *Quakers and Others Tolerated* (1696)

The Quakers were befriended by Cromwell, who liked them, and by Charles II, who was indifferent toward them. By the end of the seventeenth century the belief was growing that religion, so long as it be some form of Protestantism, should not be forced on people's minds. This belief is reflected in this statute passed during the reign of William III, who was a latitudinarian.

An act that the solemn affirmation and declaration of the people called Quakers, shall be accepted instead of an oath in the usual form [they refused to take oaths].

Whereas divers dissenters, commonly called quakers, refusing to take an oath in court of justice and other places, are frequently imprisoned, and their estates sequestred, by process of contempt issuing out of such courts, to the ruin of themselves and families: for remedy thereof be it enacted . . . That from and after the fourth day of May, which shall be in the year of our Lord, one thousand six hundred ninety six, every quaker within this kingdom of England, dominion of Wales, or town of Berwick upon Tweed, who shall be required upon any lawful occasion to take an oath, in any case where by law an oath is required, shall, instead of the usual form, be permitted to make his or her solemn affirmation or declaration in these words following,

I A.B. do declare in the presence of Almighty God, the witness of the truth of what I say.

Which said solemn affirmation or declaration shall be adjudged and taken, and is hereby enacted and declared to be, of the same force and effect, to all intents and purposes, in all courts of justice and other places where by law an oath is required within this kingdom of England, dominion of Wales, or town of Berwick upon Tweed, as if such quaker had taken an oath in the usual form. . . .

194. THE FIVE MILE ACT AGAINST DISSENTERS (1665)

This Act, part of the Clarendon Code (1661–1665) which reestablished the supremacy of the Church of England following the Restoration of Charles II, was designed by the Anglican-dominated Cavalier Parliament to discourage the spread of Dissenter sects that had thrived during the Interregnum.

And all such person and persons as shall take upon them to preach in any unlawful assembly, conventicle or meeting, under colour or pretence of any exercise of religion, contrary to the laws and statutes of this kingdom; (2) shall not at any time from and after the four and twentieth day of March which shall be in this present year of our Lord God one thousand six hundred sixty and five, unless only in passing upon the road, come or be within five miles of any city or town corporate, or borough that sends burgesses to the parliament, within his Majesty's kingdom of England, principality of Wales, or of the town of Berwick upon Tweed; (3) or within five miles of any parish, town or place, wherein he or they have since the act of oblivion been parson, vicar, curate, stipendiary or lecturer, or taken upon them to preach in any unlawful assembly, conventicle or meeting, under colour or pretence of any exercise of religion, contrary to the laws and statutes of this kingdom; (4) before he or they have taken and subscribed the oath afore-said [renouncing the Solemn League and Covenant and accepting the principle of non-resistance], before the justices of the peace at their quarter-sessions to be holden for the county, riding or division next unto the said corporation, city or borough, parish, place or town, in open court (which said oath the said justices are hereby impowered there to administer); (5) upon forfeiture for every such offence the sum of forty pounds of lawful English money; the one third part thereof to his Majesty and his successors; the other third part to the use of the poor of the parish where the offence shall be committed; and the other third part thereof to the person or persons as shall or will sue for the same by action of debt, plaint, bill or information in any court of record. . . .

195. CATHOLICISM ENCOURAGED BY JAMES II (1685-1688)

One of the principal grievances against King James was his effort to enhance the interests of Roman Catholicism in England. Although he had promised Parliament at the opening of his reign that he would uphold Anglicanism and the law, almost immediately he restored Catholic worship throughout the country and appointed numerous Catholics to public offices.

A. John Evelyn on Catholic Practices at Court (1686)

I went to hear the music of the Italians in the new chapel, now first opened publicly at Whitehall for the Popish Service. Nothing can be finer than the magnificent marble work and architecture at the end, where are four statues, representing St. John, St. Peter, St. Paul, and the Church, in white marble, the work of Mr. Gibbons, with all the carving and pillars of exquisite art and great cost. The altar piece is the Salutation; the volto in fresco, the Assumption of the blessed Virgin, according to their tradition, with our blessed Savior, and a world of figures painted by Verrio. The throne where the King and Queen sit is very glorious, in a closet above, just opposite to the altar. Here we saw the Bishop in his mitre and rich copes, with six or seven Jesuits and others in rich copes, sumptuously habited, often taking off and putting on the Bishop's mitre, who sat in a chair with arms pontifically, was adored and censed by three Jesuits in their copes; then he went to the altar and made divers cringes, then censing the images and glorious tabernacle placed on the altar, and now and then changing place;

the crosier, which was of silver, was put into his hand with a world of mysterious ceremony, the music playing, with singing. I could not have believed I should ever have seen such things in the King of England's palace, after it had pleased God to enlighten this nation; but our great sin has, for the present, eclipsed the blessing, which I hope he will in mercy and his good time restore to its purity.

B. James II's Toleration of Catholics

In January 1687, Princess Anne, James' younger daughter who was a Protestant, wrote to her sister, Mary:

I am sorry the King encourages the Papists so much; and I think it is very much to be feared, that the desire the King has to take off the Test [Act] and all other laws against them, is only a pretence to bring in Popery.

I am sorry the King relies so much upon Lord Sunderland and Lord Godolphin; for every body knows, that once they were as great enemies as any he had, and their own hearts can only tell what converts they are. As for the first of them, by all outward appearance, he must be a great knave (if I may use that expression of a minister) for he goes on fiercely for the interests of the Papists, and yet goes to no church, and has made no public declaration of his religion, whatever it is. I fear he has not much of any. All we can do in these matters, is to pray to God to open the King's eyes, and to order all things for the best, that this poor nation may not be overthrown by Popery.

196. THE SEVEN BISHOPS CASE (1688)

In 1687 King James II had issued a Declaration of Indulgence that suspended all the penal laws against Roman Catholics and Dissenters, and gave to all men the privilege of worshipping publicly and freely as they wished. The Catholics at once made use of this freedom, but the Dissenters, most of whom were Whigs, refused to accept freedom at the cost of a breech of the law. The next year James issued a second Declaration of Indulgence and ordered that it should be read in all the churches of the realm on two successive Sundays. Many clergymen refused to read it. The Archbishop of Canterbury and six other bishops petitioned the king that the clergy in their dioceses not be compelled to read the Declaration.

A. The Bishops' Petition

Humbly sheweth:

That the great averseness they find in themselves to the distributing, and publishing in all their churches your Majesty's late Declaration for liberty of conscience proceedeth—neither from any want of duty and obedience to your Majesty; or Holy Mother, the Church of England, being both in her principles and constant practice, unquestionably loyal; and having (to her great honour) been more than once publickly acknowledged to be so by your gracious Majesty:—nor yet from any want of due tenderness to Dissenters; in relation to whom they are willing to come to such a temper, as shall be thought fit, when that matter shall be considered and settled in Parliament and Convocation:—but among many other considerations, from this especially, because that Declaration is founded upon such a dispensing power, as hath often been declared illegal in Parliament; and particularly in the years 1662 and 1672, and in the beginning of your Majesty's reign; and is a matter of so great moment and consequence to the whole Nation, both in Church and State, that your Petitioners cannot in prudence, honour, or conscience so far make themselves parties to it, as the distribution of it all over the Nation, and the solemn publication of it once, and again, even in God's house, and in the time of his divine service, must amount to in common and reasonable constructions.

Your Petitioners therefore most humbly and earnestly beseech your Majesty, that you will be graciously pleased not to insist upon their distributing and reading your Majesty's said Declaration:

And your Petitioners shall ever pray, etc.,

W. Cant.	Tho. Bath and Wells.
W. Asaph.	Tho. Petriburgens
Jo. Cicester.	Jon. Bristol
Fran. Ely.	

B. *The Bishops Exonerated*

The king unwisely chose to regard this petition as a libel which tended to sedition, and as a standard of rebellion. The bishops were all dismissed from their positions, arrested, and on June 29 and 30, tried for libel and sedition. A chronicler records the court's decision:

Then the Court broke up, the Jury went together, and the Bishops with all the privacy they could, to their respective abodes; but wherever the people met with them, they husza'd and humm'd them in great abundance. There was a prodigious full Court and Hall, a very great many of the Peers and Nobility present; and also the Bishop of Chester, of whom they took no kind of notice: The Bishop of Rochester did not meet with much better regard.

The Jury sate up all night, though they were very soon unanimous in their verdict, which they prudently resolved to give in open Court; and accordingly next day about nine or ten they brought them in

Not Guilty.

> The seventeenth century was one of revolt against authority. In the political arena, there was defiance of royal despotism; in the ecclesiastical, a breaking down of authoritarianism and a growth of toleration; in the world of science, a rejection of old modes of thought and an increasing interest in new discoveries. Advances were made in medicine and sanitation, and in art and literature.

197. STUDENT LIFE AT CAMBRIDGE AND OXFORD

> On October 22, 1674, Robert Perceval wrote from Cambridge to Sir Robert Southwell:

To let you understand what I do in particular would but trouble you too much to read. I shall only say that in the morning, prayers being ended at seven of the clock, my tutor comes to me in my chamber (which indeed proves but a smoky one), and we first take Euclid, and go over six or seven propositions, which being done, we, like honest clients, render a good morrow to our patron Caesar, which ceremony being ended, and the clock striking nine, summons us to our lectures in logic, which do not end till the bell hurries us away to our commons, *anima quamvis invite,* these lie all in Latin, is the scheme of our forenoon's work. Dinner being ended, we return to my chamber and repeat what we read of logic in the morning, which disputations lasts some time; then the other part of the day, for want of maps, I make the balls fly as if I would be something in the Court. . . .

> Apparently the balls (tennis) flew at Oxford also, for on September 18, 1677, Sir Philip Perceval, who was in France, wrote to his son at Christ Church:

I would have you learn to play at tennis as well because it is healthy as because it is a genteel recreation, and to that end I would have you go to Mr. Wood's tennis court, over against Merton College, who will order his marker to teach you to play. I would have you go there thrice a week, and toss half a dozen of balls every time you go. You must go by six or seven o'clock in the morning, and have a care you do not catch cold, but be sure you learn. You may give the marker that tosses with you 2d. or 3d. every third time you go there.

198. SIR ISAAC NEWTON AT TRINITY COLLEGE, CAMBRIDGE (1694)

A diarist gives the following account of a haunted house supposed to contain a "devilish disturber."

On Monday night likewise there being a great number of people at the door there chanced to come by Mr. Newton fellow of Trinity College; a very learned man and perceiving our fellows to have gone in and seeing several scholars about the door "Oh! yee fools" says he, "will you never have any witt, know yee not that all such things are meer cheats and impostures? Fy, fy! go home for shame" so he left them scorning to go in.

I and my companions yester night try'd again what we could do but nothing would appear.

199. CHARTER OF THE ROYAL SOCIETY OF LONDON (1662)

Charles the Second, by the grace of God King of England, Scotland, France, and Ireland, Defender of the Faith, &c., to all to whom these present Letters shall come, greeting.

We have long and fully resolved with Ourself to extend not only the boundaries of the Empire, but also the very arts and sciences. Therefore we look with favour upon all forms of learning, but with particular grace we encourage philosophical studies, especially those which by actual experiments attempt either to shape out a new philosophy or to perfect the old. In order, therefore, that such studies, which have not hitherto been sufficiently brilliant in any part of the world, may shine conspicuously amongst our people, and that at length the whole world of letters may always recognize us not only as the Defender of the Faith, but also as the universal lover and patron of every kind of truth:

Know ye that we, of our special grace and of our certain knowledge and mere motion, have ordained, established, granted, and declared, and by these presents for us, our heirs, and successors do ordain, establish, grant, and declare, that from henceforth for ever there shall be a Society, consisting of a President, Council, and Fellows, which shall be called and named The Royal Society. . . .

And that our royal intention may obtain the better effect, and for the good rule and government of the aforesaid Royal Society from time to time, we will, and by these presents for us, our heirs, and successors do grant to the same President, Council, and Fellows of the Royal Society aforesaid, and

to their successors, that henceforth for ever the Council aforesaid shall be
and consist of twenty-one persons (of whom we will the President to be
always one); And that all and singular other persons who within one
month next following after the date of these presents shall be received and
admitted by the President and Council, and in all time following by the
President, Council, and Fellows, into the same Society, as Members of the
Royal Society, aforesaid, and shall have been noted in the Register by them
to be kept, shall be and shall be called and named Fellows of the Royal Society aforesaid: whom, the more eminently they are distinguished for the
study of every kind of learning and good letters, the more ardently they
desire to promote the honour, studies, and advantage of this Society, the
more they are noted for integrity of life, uprightness of character, and piety,
and excel in fidelity and affection of mind towards us, our Crown, and dignity, the more we wish them to be especially deemed fitting and worthy of
being admitted into the number of the Fellows of the same Society.

200. OBLIGATIONS OF MEMBERS OF THE ROYAL SOCIETY (1663)

Every Fellow of the Society, and every person elected a Fellow thereof, shall
subscribe the Obligation in these words following:

We, who have hereunto subscribed, do hereby promise each for himself,
that we will endeavour to promote the good of the Royal Society of London
for improving natural knowledge, and to pursue the ends for which the
same was founded; that we will be present at the Meetings of the Society as
often as conveniently we can, especially at the Anniversary Elections, and
upon extraordinary occasions; and that we will observe the Statutes and
Orders of the said Society. Provided, that whensoever any of us shall signify
to the President, under his hand, that he desireth to withdraw from the
Society, he shall be free from this Obligation for the future.

And if any Fellow shall refuse to subscribe the said Obligation, he shall
be ejected out of the Society. And if any person elected shall refuse to subscribe the same, the election of the said person shall be void; neither shall
any person refusing to subscribe be admitted, or registered among the Fellows of the Society.

201. TRIAL OF WILLIAM PRYNNE (1637)

The middle years of the seventeenth century witnessed the publication of
many polemical pamphlets and books, some of which were regarded by the
government as dangerous. Prynne, a Puritan lawyer, was tried before the
Court of Star Chamber for printing a libelous volume, *Histriomastix,*

against plays, masques and dancing. The following was the charge against him:

And although he knew well that his Majestie's royal Queen, Lords of the Council, etc., were in their publick festivals and other times present spectators of some masques and dances and many recreations that were tolerable and in themselves sinless, and so published to be by a book printed in the time of his Majestie's royal father; yet Mr. Prynn in his book hath railed, not only against Stage plays, comedies, dancings, and all other exercises of the people, and against all such as behold them; but farther in particular against hunting, publique festivals, Christmas keeping, bonfires, and maypoles; nay, against the dressing up of a house with green ivy. . . .

After a trial of three days, a judge pronounced the following verdict:

I do in the first place begin censure with his book; I condemn it to be burnt, in the most publick manner that can be . . . by the hand of the hang-man.

If it may agree with the court, I do adjudge Mr. Prynn to be put from the barr, and to be for ever uncapable of his profession. I do adjudge him, my lords, that the Society of Lincolns Inn do put him out of the Society; and because he had his offspring from Oxford . . . there to be degraded. And I do condemn Mr. Prynn to stand in the pillory in two places, in Westminster and Cheapside, and that he shall lose both his ears, one in each place, and with a paper on his head declaring how foul an offense it is, viz. that it is for an infamous libel against both their Majestie's state and government. And lastly, nay not lastly, I do condemn him in £5000 fine to the king. And lastly, perpetual imprisonment.

202. JOHN MILTON AND CENSORSHIP OF THE PRESS (1644)

Milton's *Areopagitica,* a spirited defense of freedom of the press, was an attack on a censorship law of 1643 which decreed that no book or pamphlet could be printed before it had been licensed.

I deny not, but that it is of greatest concernment in the church and commonwealth, to have a vigilant eye how books demean themselves as well as men; and thereafter to confine, imprison, and do sharpest justice on them as malefactors. For books are not absolutely dead things, but do contain a potency of life in them to be as active as that soul was whose progeny they are; nay, they do preserve as in a phial the purest efficacy and extraction of that living intellect that bred them. I know they are as lively, and as vigorously productive as those fabulous dragon's teeth, and being sown up and down, may chance to spring up armed men. And yet on the other hand, unless wariness be used, as good almost kill a man as kill a good book. Who kills a man, kills a reasonable creature, God's image; but he who destroys a good book, kills reason itself, kills the image of God, as it were in the eye. Many a man lives a burden to the earth; but a good book is the precious lifeblood of a masterspirit, imbalmed and treasured up on purpose to a life beyond life. It is true no age can restore a life, whereof perhaps there is no great loss; and revolutions of ages do not oft recover the loss of a rejected truth, for the want of which whole nations fare the worse. We should be wary, therefore, what persecution we raise against the living labors of public men, how we spill that seasoned life of man, preserved and stored up in books; since we see a kind of homicide may be thus committed, sometimes a martyrdom, and if it extend to the whole impression, a kind of massacre, whereof the execution ends not in the slaying of an elemental life, but strikes at the ethereal and fifth essence, the breath of reason itself, slays an immortality rather than a life. But lest I should be condemned of introducing license, while I oppose licensing, I refuse not the pains to be so much historical, as will serve to show what hath been done by ancient and famous commonwealths against this disorder, till the very time that this project of licensing crept out of the Inquisition, was catched up by our prelates, and hath caught some of our presbyters. . . .

203. AN ACT FOR REGULATING THE PRESS (1665)

This Act extended the Act of 1662, which required the licensing of all printed matter by these means:

Be it enacted . . . That an act made in the fourteenth year of the reign of our sovereign lord the King that now is, intituled, An act for preventing abuses in printing seditious, treasonable and unlicenced books and pamphlets, and for regulating of printing and printing presses; shall be continued with the alterations and additions made in and by this act, and shall remain in force until the end of the first session of the next parliament.

II. And be it further enacted, That from and after the six and twentieth day of December one thousand six hundred sixty-five, every printer within the city of London or in any other place, except the two universities, shall reserve three printed copies of the best and largest paper of every book, new printed or reprinted by him with additions; and shall, before any publick vending of the said book, bring them to the master of the company of stationers, and deliver them to him; one whereof shall by the said master of the said company of stationers, within ten days after he hath so received the same, be delivered to the keeper of his Majesty's library, and the other two within the said ten days to be sent to the vice-chancellors of the two universities respectively, for the use of the publick libraries of the said universities.

III. And it is further enacted, That the printers in the said universities, and every of them respectively, from and after the said six and twentieth day of December shall deliver one such printed copy as aforesaid, of every book so new printed or reprinted in the said universities, or in either of them, to the keeper of his Majesty's library as aforesaid, as also to the vice-chancellor of either of the said universities for the time being, two other such printed copies for the use of the publick libraries of the said universities respectively. (2) And if any of the printers aforesaid, or the said master of the company of stationers, shall not observe the direction of this act therein, that then he and they so making default in not delivering the said printed copies as aforesaid, shall severally forfeit, besides the value of the said printed copies, the sum of five pounds for every copy not so delivered. . . .

204. AN ACT TO RESTRAIN THE ABUSES OF PLAYERS (1605)

The multiplication of theaters in London in the late Elizabethan period was a matter of concern to some critics, particularly the Puritans. They were particularly incensed over the frequent use of profanity which playwrights often used to amuse the coarse persons who frequented the theaters. The following statute was aimed at discouraging profanity in plays.

For the preventing and avoiding of the great abuse of the holy name of God in stage-plays, enterludes, may-games, shews, and such like; (2) be it enacted . . . That if at any time or times after the end of this present session of parliament, any person or persons do or shall in any stage-play, enterlude, shew, may-game or pageant, jestingly or profanely speak or use the holy name of God, or of Christ Jesus, or of the Holy Ghost, or of the Trinity, which are not to be spoken but with fear and reverence, shall forfeit for every such offence by him or them committed ten pounds: (3) the one moiety thereof to the King's majesty, his heirs and successors, the other moiety thereof to him or them that will sue for the same in any court of record at Westminster, wherein no essoin, protection or wager of law shall be allowed.

205. RESTORATION AMUSEMENTS

Theaters were for the most part closed during the Cromwellian regime, but were opened again during the Restoration. Pepys describes an experience at the theater in his *Diary* for January 23, 1667.

A. *The Theater*

Here, in a box above, we spied Mrs. Pierce; and, going out, they called us, and so we staid for them; and Knipp took us all in, and brought to us Nelly [Nell Gwynn, a famous actress and a mistress of Charles II], a most pretty woman, who acted the great part of Coelia to-day very fine, and did it pretty well: I kissed her, and so did my wife; and a might pretty soul she is . . . . Knipp made us stay in a box and see the dancing preparatory to to-morrow for "The Goblins", a play of Suckling's, not acted these twenty-five years; which was pretty; and so away thence, pleased with this sight also, and especially kissing of Nell.

B. *Sporting Games*

A wide variety of other forms of entertainment amused Englishmen in the Restoration period. The "butcherly sports" described by Evelyn were very popular.

16th June, 1670. I went with some friends to the Bear Garden, where was cock-fighting, dog-fighting, bear and bull-baiting, it being a famous day for all these butcherly sports, or rather barbarous cruelties. The bulls did exceedingly well, but the Irish wolf dog exceeded, which was a tall greyhound, a stately creature indeed, who beat a cruel mastiff. One of the bulls tossed a dog full into a lady's lap as she sat in one of the boxes at a considerable height from the arena. Two poor dogs were killed, and so all ended with the ape on horseback and I most heartily weary of the rude and dirty pastime, which I had not seen, I think, in twenty years before.

206. ACT FOR THE EXECUTION OF LAWS AGAINST ROGUES, VAGABONDS, BEGGARS AND IDLE PERSONS (1609)

The government, concerned at the vast increase in the amount of brigandage, begging, and idleness, and disturbed because the laws against these evils had not been enforced by the local authorities, passed the following statute:

For remedy whereof, be it enacted and established by our sovereign lord the King's majesty, and by the lords spiritual and temporal, and by the commons, in this present parliament assembled, and by the authority of the same, That all laws and statutes now in force, made for the erecting and building of houses of correction, and for punishing of rogues, vagabonds, and other wandering and idle persons, shall be put in due execution.

And be it further enacted and established by the authority aforesaid, That before the feast of Saint Michael the archangel, which shall be in the year of our Lord God one thousand six hundred and eleven, there shall be erected, built or otherwise provided, within every county of this realm of England and Wales, where there is not one house of correction already built, purchased, provided or continued, one or more fit and convenient house or houses of correction, with convenient backside thereunto adjoining, together with mills, turns, cards and such like necessary implements, to set the said rogues or such other idle persons on work; the same houses to be built, erected or provided in some convenient place or town in every county: (2) which houses shall be purchased, conveyed or assured unto such person or persons as by the justices of peace or the more part of them, in their quarter sessions of the peace to be holden within every county of this realm of England and Wales, upon trust, to the intent the same shall be used and imployed for the keeping, correcting and setting to work of the said rogues, vagabonds, sturdy beggars and other idle and disorderly persons. . . .

207. JAMES I ON WOMEN'S DRESS (1620)

Yesterday, the bishop of London called together all his clergie about this towne, and told them he had expresse commandment from the King to will them to inveigh vehemently against the insolencie of our women, and theyre wearing of brode brimed hats, pointed dublets, theyre haire cut short or shorne, and some of them stilettoes or poniards, and such other trinckets of like moment; adding withall that if pulpit admonitions will not reforme them he wold proceed by another course; the truth is the world is very much out of order, but whether this will mende it God knowes.

208. LIFE AT THE COURT OF CHARLES II

The following excerpts from the diaries of Pepys and Evelyn reveal the nature of some activities at the court of Charles II and help to explain why the Restoration period has often been characterized as one of moral laxity.

A. *The Roguish Behavior of Courtiers*

On April 26, 1667, Pepys wrote:

To White Hall, and there saw the Duke of Albemarle, who is not well, and do go crazy . . . . Met with Ned Pickering, who tells me the ill news of his nephew Gilbert, who is turned a very rogue. Then I took a turn with Mr. Evelyn, with whom I walked two hours, till almost one of the clock: talking of the badness of the Government, where nothing but wickedness, and wicked men and women command the King: that it is not in his nature to gainsay any thing that relates to his pleasures; that much of it arises from the sickness of our Ministers of State, who cannot be about him as the idle companions are, and therefore he gives way to the young rogues; and then, from the negligence of the Clergy, that a Bishop shall never be seen about him, as the King of France hath always: that the King would fain have some of the same gang to be Lord Treasurer, which would be yet worse, for now some delays are put to the getting of gifts of the King, as Lady Byron, who had been, as he called it, the King's seventeenth mistress abroad, did not leave him till she had got him to give her an order for 4000 £. worth of plate to be made for her; but by delays, thanks be to God! she died before she had it . . . .

B. *Revelry by Charles and His Courtiers*

About two weeks before Charles died on February 6, 1685, from a stroke, Evelyn noted:

I can never forget the inexpressible luxury and profaneness, gaming, an all dissoluteness, and as it were total forgetfulness of God (it being Sunday evening), which this day se'nnight I was witness of, the King sitting and toying with his concubines, Portsmouth, Cleveland, and Mazarin, etc., a French boy singing love songs in that glorious gallery, while about twenty of the great courtiers and other dissolute persons were at Basset round a large table, a bank of at least 2,000 in gold before them; upon which two gentlemen, who were with me, made reflections with astonishment. Six days after, was all in the dust.

209. THE GREAT FIRE OF LONDON (1666)

In 1665–1666, London was visited by the twin catastrophes of plague and fire. The plague (mentioned later) was a severe visitation of the bubonic plague that had caused thousands of deaths during the century. The fire, which began in the city's east end and was blown westward through the oldest section of the city, destroyed dozens of public buildings and private residences. Although it was an awful experience, it was also a mixed blessing in that it levelled slums and thereby enforced the rebuilding of that part of London. The following eye-witness account is from *Pepys' Diary* for September 2, 1666.

2d. (Lord's day.) Some of our maids sitting up late last night to get things ready against our feast to-day, Jane called us up about three in the morning, to tell us of a great fire they saw in the City. So I rose, and slipped on my nightgown, and went to her window; and thought it to be on the back-side of Marke-lane at the farthest; but, being unused to such fires as followed, I thought it far enough off; and so went to bed again, and to sleep. About seven rose again to dress myself, and there looked out at the window, and saw the fire not so much as it was, and further off. So to my closet to set things to rights, after yesterday's cleaning. By and by Jane comes and tells me that she hears that above 300 houses have been burned down to-night by the fire we saw, and that it is now burning down all Fish Street, by London Bridge. So I made myself ready presently, and walked to the Tower; and there got up upon one of the high places, Sir J. Robinson's little son going up with me; and there I did see the houses at that end of the bridge all on fire, and an infinite great fire on this and the other side the end of the bridge; which, among other people, did trouble me for poor little Michell and our Sarah on the bridge. So down, with my heart full of trouble, to the Lieutenant of the Tower, who tells me that it begun this morning in the King's baker's house in Pudding-lane, and that it hath burned down St. Magnus's Church and most part of Fish Street already. So I down to the water-side, and there got a boat, and through bridge, and there saw a lamentable fire. Poor Michell's house, as far as the Old Swan, already burned that way, and people carried away in beds. Extraordinary good goods carried in carts and on backs . . . . The houses, too, so very thick thereabouts, and full of matter for burning, as pitch and tar, in Thames Street; and ware-houses of oyle, and wines, and brandy, and other things . . . . By this time, it was about twelve o'clock; and so home . . . . Soon as dined, I and Moone away, and walked through the City, the streets full of nothing but people; and horses and carts loaden with goods, ready to run over one another, and removing goods from one burned house to another . . . . Met with the King and Duke of York in their barge, and with them to Queenhithe, and there called Sir Richard Browne to them. Their order was only to pull down houses apace, and so below bridge at the water-side; but little was or could be done, the fire coming upon them so fast. Good hopes there was of stopping it at the Three Cranes above, and at Buttulph's Wharf below bridge, if care be used; but the wind carries it into the City, so as we know not, by the water-side, what it do there . . . . Having seen as much as I could now, I away to White Hall by appointment, and there walked to St. James's Park; and there met my wife, and Creed, and Wood, and his wife, and walked to my boat; and there upon the water again, and to the fire up and down, it still increasing, and the wind great. So near the fire as we could for smoke; and all over the Thames, with one's faces in the wind, you were almost burned with a shower of fire-drops. This is very true: so as houses were burned by these drops and flakes of fire, three or four, nay, five or six houses, one from another. When we could endure no more upon the water, we to a little ale-house on the Bank-side, over against the Three Cranes, and there staid till it was dark almost, and saw the fire grow; and, as it grew darker, appeared more and more; and in corners and upon steeples, and between churches and houses, as far as we could see up the hill of the City, in a most horrid, malicious, bloody flame, not like the fine flame of an ordinary fire. Barbary and her husband away before us. We staid till, it being darkish, we saw the fire as only one entire arch of fire from this to the other side the bridge, and in a bow up the hill for an arch of above a mile long: it made me weep to see it. The churches, houses, and all on fire, and flaming at once; and a horrid noise the flames made, and the cracking of houses at their ruine. So home with a sad heart, and there find every body discoursing and lamenting the fire; and poor Tom Hater come with some few of his goods saved out of his house, which was burned upon Fish Street Hill. I invited him to lie at my house, and did receive his goods; but was deceived in his lying there, the news coming every moment of the growth of the fire; so as we were forced to begin to pack up our own goods, and prepare for their removal; and did by moonshine, it being brave, dry, and moonshine and warm weather, carry much of my goods into the garden; and Mr. Hater and I did remove my money and iron chests into my cellar, as thinking that the safest place. And got my bags of gold into my office, ready to carry away, and my chief papers of accounts also there, and my tallies into a box by themselves.

210. AN ACT FOR THE REBUILDING OF LONDON (1666)

The following are only a few sections from the Act to indicate the kind of provisions that Parliament hoped would prevent another destruction of London such as had occurred that year in the Great Fire.

Forasmuch as the city of London . . . by reason of a most dreadful fire lately happening therein, was for the most part thereof burnt down and destroyed within the compass of a few days, and now lies buried in its own ruins: for the speedy restauration whereof, and for the better regulation, uniformity and gracefulness of such new buildings as shall be erected for habitations in order thereunto; and to the end that great outragious fires . . . so far forth as human providence . . . can foresee, may be reasonably prevented or obviated for the time to come, both by the matter and form of such building: and further, to the intent that all encouragement and expedition may be given unto, and all impediments and obstructions that may retard or protract the undertaking or carrying on a work so necessary, and of so great honour and importance to his Majesty and this kingdom, and to the rest of his Majesty's kingdoms and dominions, may be removed;

II. Be it therefore enacted . . . That the rules and directions hereafter in this act prescribed, be duly observed by all persons therein concerned.

III. And first, That no building or house for habitation whatsoever, be hereafter erected within the limits of the said city and liberties thereof, but such as shall be pursuant to such rules and orders of building, and with such materials, as are herein after particularly appointed, and according to such scantlings as are set down and prescribed in a table in this present act hereafter specified: (2) and if any person or persons shall presume to build contrary thereunto, and be convicted of the same by the oaths of two or more credible witnesses, to be taken before the lord mayor for the time being, or any two or more of the justices of the peace for the said city, who are hereby impowered to administer the same oaths; That then and in such case, the said house so irregularly built as aforesaid, shall be deemed as a common nuisance . . . .

IV. And that the said irregular buildings [built contrary to the act and liable to be demolished by order of the court of aldermen] may be the better prevented, . . . (2) be it further enacted . . . That the lord mayor, aldermen and common council of the said city, shall and may at their will and pleasure elect, nominate and appoint one or more discreet and intelligent person or persons in the art of building, to be the surveyors or supervisors to see the said rules and scantlings well and truly observed . . . .

V. And to the end that all builders may the better know how to provide and fit their materials for their several buildings; (2) be it enacted, that there shall be only four sorts of buildings, and no more; and that all manner of houses so to be erected, shall be of one of these four sorts . . . ; (that is to say) the first and least sort of houses fronting by-lanes; the second sort of housing fronting streets and lanes of note; the third sort of houses fronting high and principal streets; the fourth and largest sort, of mansion-houses, for citizens, or other persons of extraordinary quality, not fronting either of the three former ways: and the roofs of each of the said first three sorts of houses respectively, shall be uniform . . . .

VII. And in regard the building with brick is not only more comely and durable, but also more safe against future perils of fire; (2) be it further enacted . . . That all the outsides of all buildings in and about the said city be henceforth made of brick or stone, or of brick and stone together, except door-cafes and window-frames, . . . and other parts of the first story to the front . . . .

211. ACT FOR THE RELIEF OF PRISONERS FOR DEBT (1670)

For hundreds of years, the law had provided that persons unable to pay their debts, whether through their own fault or not, could be imprisoned until they did so. Hence thousands of persons were thrown into prison, where they often resided with their families for want of other quarters for them. The Great Fire had ruined hundreds of families, some of whom had been imprisoned by cruel creditors for indebtedness. This Act was designed to assist them in particular, as well as other honest debtors.

. . . be it therefore enacted . . . That it shall and may be lawful to and for any justice of the peace of any county, city, town or liberty within the kingdom of England, dominion of Wales, or town of Berwick upon Tweed, . . . to require the sheriff, gaoler, or keeper of any prison within his respective jurisdiction, to bring without delay, the body of any person being in prison for debt, on . . . [April 14, 1671], or damages (and petitioning such justice to be discharged) to some convenient place within the distance of one mile from the said prison; (3) and shall certify the cause and causes of the imprisonment, before the same justice; which warrant every such sheriff, gaoler and keeper is hereby commanded to obey.

II. And in case such prisoner coming before such justice shall take an oath to this effect, viz. I A.B. do upon my corporal oath solemnly profess and declare before Almighty God, That I have not any estate real or personal, in possession, reversion or remainder, of the value of ten pounds in the whole, or sufficient to pay the debt or damages for which I am imprisoned; (2) and that I have not directly or indirectly sold, leased, or otherwise conveyed, disposed of, or entrusted all or any part of my estate, thereby to secure the same, to receive or expect any profit or advantage thereof, or defraud or deceive any creditor or creditors whatsoever to whom I stand indebted:

III. Then after the taking of such oath, that said justice shall remand the prisoner to prison, and shall give a certificate thereof in writing under his hand and seal, to the same prisoner, to be served upon such person or persons, his or her executors or administrators, or to be left at the place of the usual abode of such person or persons at whose suit the prisoner standeth charged and imprisoned, thereby appointing as well the said person or persons, as the said prisoner to appear before the justices at the next general quarter-sessions of the peace to be holden for the same county, city, town, or liberty . . . . [If the oath of the prisoner for debt be not contradicted by testimony under oath, the prisoner shall be freed.]

212. THE USE AND ABUSE OF TOBACCO

In the seventeenth century the use of tobacco, introduced into England in the early years of Elizabeth's reign, was a subject of great interest and divided opinions, just as it is at present. The next two readings relate to this topic from Tudor times to the end of the seventeenth century.

A. *The Benefits of Smoking* (*temp. Elizabeth I*)

There is an herbe which is sowed apart by it selfe, and is called by the inhabitants Uppowoc: in the West Indies it hath divers names, according to the severall places and countreys where it groweth and is used: The Spanyards generally call it Tabacco. The leaves thereof being dried and brought into pouder, they use to take the fume or smoake thereof, by sucking it thorow pipes made of clay, into their stomacke and head; from whence it purgeth superfluous fleame and other grosse humours, and openeth all the pores and passages of the body: by which meanes the use thereof not onely preserveth the body from obstructions, but also (if any be, so that they have not bene of too long continuance) in short time breaketh them: whereby their bodies are notably preserved in health, and know not many grievous diseases, wherewithall we in England are often times afflicted.

This Uppowoc is of so precious estimation amongst them, that they thinke their gods are marvellously delighted therewith: whereupon sometime they make hallowed fires, and cast some of the pouder therein for a sacrifice: being in a storme upon the waters, to pacifie their gods, they cast some up into the aire and into the water: so a weare for fish being newly set up, they cast some therein and into the aire: also after an escape of danger, they cast some into the aire likewise: but all done with strange gestures, stamping, sometime dancing, clapping of hands, holding up of hands, and staring up into the heavens uttering therewithall, and chattering strange words and noises.

We our selves, during the time we were there, used to sucke it after their maner, as also since our returne, and have found many rare and woonderfull experiments of the vertues thereof: of which the relation would require a volume by it selfe: the use of it by so many of late, men and women of great calling, as els, and some learned Physicians also, is of sufficient witnesse.

B. *Another Use for Tobacco* (*1679*)

This is an extract from a letter by Sir William Temple to a friend with eye trouble.

I am mightily sorry to hear that you have an illness fallen upon your eyes, which was an affliction I met with in my employments abroad, and so am the more sensible of it upon your occasion. You must spare them from reading and writing whilst it lasts, and by no means tamper with them. I never found anything do mine so much good as putting a leaf of tobacco into each nostril as soon as you wake, and keep it for an hour either sitting up in your bed or dressing yourself. It will make you a little sick, perhaps, at first, but, when it does, pull it out, and 'tis presently past; then you may put new in, and 'twill grow easier with custom. You should not be cold when you use it.

213. THE GREAT PLAGUE OF 1665–1666

Plagues of various kinds had often descended upon England. Three serious epidemics, each probably of bubonic plague, occurred in the seventeenth century—in 1603; a more serious one in 1625; and the well-known plague of 1665–1666, on which Samuel Pepys has these comments:

August 22, 1665:

I went away, and walked to Greenwich, in my way seeing a coffin with a dead body therein, dead of the plague, lying in an open close belonging to Coome farme, which was carried out last night, and the parish have not appointed any body to bury it; but only set a watch there all day and night, that nobody should go thither or come thence: this disease making us more cruel to one another than we are to dogs . . . .

October 16, 1665:

I walked to the Tower; but, Lord! how empty the streets are, and melancholy, so many poor, sick people in the streets full of sores; and so many sad stories overheard as I walk, every body talking of this dead, and that man sick, and so many in this place, and so many in that. And they tell me that, in Westminster, there is never a physician and but one apothecary left, all being dead; but that there are great hopes of a great decrease this week: God send it!

September 3, 1665:

Up, and put on my coloured silk suit very fine, and new periwigg, bought a good while since, but durst not wear, because the plague was in Westminster when I bought it; and it is a wonder what will be the fashion after the plague is done, as to periwiggs, for nobody will dare to buy any haire, for fear of the infection, that it had been cut off the heads of people dead of the plague.

214. MEDICAL KNOWLEDGE
IN SEVENTEENTH-CENTURY ENGLAND

Although William Harvey and Richard Lower had made great strides in the study of anatomy, and Thomas Sydenham a decided contribution in the area of clinical observation, medical studies in the universities were not very fruitful. In *England Under the Stuarts,* G. M. Trevelyan writes: "Medicine, as commonly practised, was a formulated superstition rather than a science; rules of health were little understood; sanitary habits were free and filthy among rich as well as poor."

A. *A Cure for Spindlelegs*

In 1619, John Chamberlain accounted for James I's frequent hunting excursions:

On 26 June we learn that the King's legs and feet "are come prettelie well to him, having found out a very good expedient of late to bath them in every buck's and stagg's bellie in the place where he kills them, which is counted an excellent remedie to strengthen and restore the sinewes."

B. *Other Prescriptions*

Fifteen years later John Perceval wrote to Sir Robert Southwell from Christ Church, Oxford:

The receipts my mother has sent me are these:—Gather a quantity of woodlice, keep them in a glass bottle with a little earth, take seven of them alive, and wash them in clean water from the earth, then pound them and strain them into a small draught of beer, so take it fasting for your morning's draught. Another, is to take as much powder of pimpernal . . . as will lie upon a groat in a morning fasting, in anything that I would drink, three times in the week. Another was, take a daisy root or two, half a dozen leaves of "oculos cristi" or more, and something more of woodbine leaves, and about twelve loops of woodlice, bruise all together with a stone or a wooden rolling pin, upon a clean board, or in a marble mortar, then put them all into a closed mouth jug or bottle with a dozen stoned raisins of the sun and then fill into it some good beer or ale which is not bitter, of which you may drink a small draught night and morning. This, Sir, with the cutting of my hair was the advice my mother gave me . . . .

SOURCE REFERENCES   Chapter Five

142. Aikin, Lucy, *Memoirs of the Court of James the First,* I, 97–98. London: Longman, Hurst, Rees, Orme and Brown, 1822.
143. A. *Selection from the Harleian Miscellany,* p. 253.
    B. Aikin, *Memoirs of James the First,* I, 267–268.
    C. *Statutes at Large,* 3 James I, CAP. 1.
144. Aikin, *Memoirs of James the First,* I, 388–389.
145. Aikin, *Memoirs of James the First,* II, 214–215.
146. Aikin, *Memoirs of James the First,* II, 139.
147. A. *Collectanea Curiosa or Miscellaneous Tracts and Antiquities of England and Ireland, the Universities of Oxford and Cambridge,* I, 180. Oxford: Clarendon Press, 1781.
    B. Hansard, *Parliamentary History,* I, 1326–1327.
    C. *Miscellaneous State Papers from 1501 to 1726,* ed. by Philip Yorke, I, 451. London: W. Strahan and T. Cadell, 1778.
    D. *Miscellaneous State Papers,* I, 421.
148. Birch, Thomas, *The Court and Times of Charles the First,* I, 30–31. London: Henry Colburn, 1848.
149. A. *Miscellaneous State Papers,* I, 571.
    B. Birch, *Court and Times of Charles the First,* I, 99.
    C. Ellis, *Original Letters,* III, 252.
    D. Wotton, Sir Henry, "A Short View of the Life and Death of George Villiers, Duke of Buckingham," in *Selection from the Harleian Miscellany,* p. 285.
150. *Parliamentary History,* II, 376–377.
151. Whitelocke, Bulstrode, *Memorials of the English Affairs from the Beginning of the Reign of Charles the First to the Happy Restoration of King Charles the Second,* new edition, I, 71. Oxford: University Press, 1853.
152. *Collectanea Curiosa,* I, 234–236.
153. *The Memoirs of Edmund Ludlow . . . ,* ed. by C. H. Firth, I, 25–27. Oxford: Clarendon Press, 1894.
154. Carlyle, Thomas, ed., *Oliver Cromwell's Letters and Speeches with Elucidations,* I, 183–184. Boston: Dana Estes and Charles Lauriat, 1884.
155. Ellis, *Original Letters,* III, 305–307.
156. Ellis, *Original Letters,* 3rd ser., IV, 234–236.
157. Rushworth, John, *Historical Collections The Fourth and Last Part, containing the Principal Matters which happened From the Beginning of the Year 1645, to the Death of King Charles the First 1648 . . . ,* 2nd ed., VII, 1415–1416. London: n. p., 1721.
158. *England's Black Tribunal. Set forth in the Tryal of King Charles the I, By the Pretended High Court of Justice in Westminster-Hall, Jan. 20. 1648 . . . ,* 4th ed., pp. 13–14, 41–42. London: n. p., 1703.
159. *Ludlow's Memoirs,* I, 233–234.
160. A. Hansard, *Parliamentary History,* III, 1383–1384.
    B. *Ludlow's Memoirs,* I, 353.

161. *The Diary of John Evelyn*, ed. by William Bray, I, 326. Akron: M. Walter Dunn, 1901.

162. *Evelyn's Diary*, I, 332.

163. *Statutes at Large*, 12 Charles II, CAP. 11.

164. *Statutes at Large*, 13 Charles II, CAP. 1.

165. *Statutes at Large*, 16 Charles II, CAP. 1.

166. Dalrymple, Sir John, *Memoirs of Great Britain and Ireland* . . . , 2nd ed., II, 126–127. London: W. Strahan and T. Cadell, 1773.

167. *Evelyn's Diary*, II, 227–228.

168. Dalrymple, *Memoirs*, I, 178.

169. *Evelyn's Diary*, II, 278.

170. *Evelyn's Diary*, II, 289–290.

171. Dalrymple, *Memoirs*, I, 351–352.

172. A. *Statutes at Large*, 1 William and Mary, CAP. 2.
    B. *Statutes at Large*, 6 William and Mary, CAP. 2.
    C. *Statutes at Large*, 7 William III, CAP. 3.
    D. *Statutes at Large*, 13 William III, CAP. 6.

173. Jesse, John H., *Memoirs of the Court of England From the Revolution in 1688 to the Death of George The Second*, I, 208–209. Philadelphia: Lea and Blanchard, 1843.

174. *Evelyn's Diary*, II, 360.

175. *Statutes at Large*, 5 Anne, CAP. 8.

176. *Statutes at Large*, 9 Anne, CAP. 5.

177. A. *Statutes at Large*, 12 Charles II, CAP. 18.
    B. *Statutes at Large*, 7 William III, CAP. 22.

178. *Statutes at Large*, 2 James I, CAP. 17.

179. *Statutes at Large*, 13 and 14 Charles II, CAP. 18.

180. *Statutes at Large*, 30 Charles II, CAP. 3.

181. *Statutes at Large*, 1 William III, CAP. 32.

182. From Prothero, G. W., ed., *Select Statutes and Other Constitutional Documents Illustrative of the Reigns of Elizabeth and James I*, p. 289. Oxford: Clarendon Press, 1898.

183. *The Political Works of James I, With an Introduction By Charles Howard McIlwain*, p. 315. Cambridge: Harvard University Press, 1918.

184. Hansard, *Parliamentary History*, I, 1149–1150.

185. Hobbes, Thomas, *Leviathan or The Matter, Forme, and Power of a Commonwealth Ecclesiastical and Civill*, part 2, p. 87. London: Andrew Crooke, 1651.

186. *The Leveller Tracts 1647–1653*, ed. by William Haller and Godfrey Davies, p. 454. New York: Columbia University Press, 1944.

187. *Ludlow's Memoirs*, II, 98–99.

188. *The Works of John Locke*, 11th ed., V, 395–415, *passim*. London: n. p., 1812.

189. Historical Manuscripts Commission, *Report on the Manuscripts of the Earl of Egmont*, II, 208. Dublin: H. M. Stationery Office, 1909.

190. A. Aikin, *Memoirs of the Court of James the First*, II, 256–257.
    B. Whitelocke, *Memorials*, I, 259.

191. Hansard, *Parliamentary History*, III, 1425.

192. *Evelyn's Diary*, I, 307–308.
193. A. *Evelyn's Diary*, I, 311.
    B. *Statutes at Large*, 7 and 8 William III, CAP. 34.
194. *Statutes at Large*, 17 Charles II, CAP. 2.
195. A. *Evelyn's Diary*, II, 258.
    B. Dalrymple, *Memoirs*, II, pt. 1, app., 298–299.
196. A. *Collectanea Curiosa*, I, 336–337.
    B. *Collectanea Curiosa*, I, 381–382.
197. Historical Manuscripts Commission, *Egmont MSS.*, II, 34 and 68.
198. Ponsonby, *English Diaries*, p. 141.
199. *The Record of The Royal Society of London For the Promotion of Natural Knowledge*, 4th ed., pp. 226–228. Edinburgh: Morrison and Gibb, 1940.
200. *The Record of The Royal Society of London*, pp. 287–288.
201. Cheyney, *Readings in English History*, pp. 463–464.
202. Milton, John, *Areopagitica: A Speech for the Liberty of Unlicensed Printing, to the Parliament of England*, in *English Prose Works of John Milton*, II, 21–22. Boston: Bowles and Dearborn, 1826.
203. *Statutes at Large*, 17 Charles II, CAP. 4.
204. *Statutes at Large*, 2 James I, CAP. 21.
205. A. *Diary and Correspondence of Samuel Pepys, F. R. S. Secretary to the Admiralty in the Reigns of Charles II. and James II., With a Life and Notes by Richard Lord Braybrooke*, III, 49. Philadelphia: J. B. Lippincott & Co., 1856.
    B. *Evelyn's Diary*, II, 53–54.
206. *Statutes at Large*, 7 James I, CAP. 4.
207. Statham, Edward P., *A Jacobean Letter-Writer, The Life and Times of John Chamberlain*, p. 182. London: Kegan Paul, Trench, Trubner and Co., 1920.
208. A. *Pepys' Diary*, III, 111–112.
    B. *Evelyn's Diary*, II, 210.
209. *Pepys' Diary*, II, 439–443.
210. *Statutes at Large*, 19 Charles II, CAP. 3.
211. *Statutes at Large*, 22 and 23 Charles II, CAP. 20.
212. A. Tawney and Power, *Tudor Economic Documents*, II, 74–75.
    B. Sidney, Henry, *Diary of the Times of Charles the Second . . .* , I, 294. London: Henry Colburn, 1843.
213. *Pepys' Diary*, II, 286, 314, 289–290.
214. A. Statham, *A Jacobean Letter-Writer*, p. 181.
    B. Historical Manuscripts Commission, *Egmont MSS.*, II, 55.

CHAPTER SIX

The Eighteenth Century
(1714-1815)

In the eighteenth century, England's interest shifted from the constitutional conflicts that had agitated the country in the previous century to economic development, foreign trade, colonial wars, and the expansion of the Empire. For most of the century Englishmen were satisfied with their political system and were content to let it alone. Meanwhile England's flourishing industry and commerce, particularly after mid-century, led to competition with other powers for control of foreign and colonial markets. Except for the dismal decades from 1763 to 1783, when it lost the American Colonies, England was successful in its colonial and European wars against France and Spain. By 1815, England was the world's leading power.

In the realm of domestic politics, the most significant development of the century was the evolution of the Cabinet system. The single most important factor contributing to its growth was the accession of the House of Hanover. In accordance with the provisions of the Act of Settlement (1701), George I became the king of England in 1714. He spoke little English and made no effort to learn more. He brought with him two German mistresses and a host of German friends who annoyed the English politicians. He thought more of Hanover than he did of England. "Partly for that reason," says Professor M. M. Knappen, "and partly because his throne depended on his acceptance of parliamentary supremacy, he accepted the newly developed limitations on royal power and permitted his ministers to formulate governmental policy on nearly all domestic matters." But, although the classes which were represented in Parliament held the ultimate power in the country, the monarchs still exercised considerable authority, and no chief minister in the eighteenth century, even those as strong as Sir Robert Walpole and William Pitt, Earl of Chatham, dared to implement policy without the king's approval.

215. KING GEORGE I (1714–1727)

In his *Memoirs of the Court of England,* John H. Jesse describes George I in most uncomplimentary but accurate terms.

A foreigner as he was, in all his tastes and habits; ignorant, debauched, and illiterate; inelegant in his person and ungraceful in his manners, he had never condescended to acquaint himself with the laws or customs of the English, and was, indeed, utterly unacquainted with their language. In addition to these drawbacks, though he was now in his fifty-fifth year, he had the folly and wickedness to encumber himself with a seraglio of hideous German prostitutes, who rendered him equally ludicrous by their absurdities, and unpopular by their rapacity. . . . It may be remarked . . . that, with the single exceptions of social pleasantry and constitutional good-humour, he seems to have been possessed of no redeeming quality which reflected dignity on him as a monarch, or rendered him amiable as a man. Profligate in his youth and libidinous in old age, he figures through life as a bad husband, a bad father, and, in as far as England is concerned, a bad king. He wanted even those graceful qualifications of the Stuarts, a love for polite literature and the fine arts; he possessed no taste for the one, and extended no patronage to the other. The only thing he seems to have had a regard for was his own ease; the only being he hated heartily was, probably, his own son. Many of these unamiable characteristics were unquestionably owing to his indifferent education; for, notwithstanding his wrong-headedness, he is said to have meant well.

216. KING GEORGE II (1727–1760)

As Prince of Wales, George had quarrelled with his father, and as king, he quarrelled with his son. He was more English-oriented than George I, but remained strongly Hanoverian in his interests.

A. *Description of the King*

William Coxe, in his *Memoirs of Sir Robert Walpole,* has this perceptive description of George II:

George the Second was, at the time of his accession, in the 45th year of his age; and bore the character of a prince of high integrity, honour, and veracity. His countenance was pleasing, dignified, and expressive, with prominent eyes, and a Roman nose . . . . He was naturally reserved, except to those who belonged to his household, or were admitted to his familiar

society, fond of business, and of great application whenever application was
necessary; well acquainted with the state of foreign affairs; and his observations, and replies to the notes of his ministers, dictated by the occasion, prove
good sense, judgment, and rectitude of intentions. His temper was warm,
vehement, and irritable; prone to sudden emotions of anger, and not easily
appeased. He was slow in deliberation, cautious in decision; but his opinion
once formed, he became inflexible, and impatient of remonstrance. He was
strictly economical, punctual in the discharge of his expences; so peculiarly
methodical in all his actions and occupations, that, to use the expression of a
nobleman much about his person, "he seemed to think his having done a
thing to-day, an unanswerable reason for his doing it to-morrow." He was
rigidly attached to etiquette and punctilious forms, and fond of military
parade; without the smallest taste for the arts, or love of science, like his father, he gave no patronage to literature, unless from the suggestions of his
queen, or the intercession of his ministers. Cold and phlegmatic in his general appearance, he at the same time possessed a high degree of sensibility; of
which he gave many proofs, particularly on the death of his queen, and the
resignation of Sir Robert Walpole, which would appear incredible to those
who are not acquainted with his domestic character. The love of women was
his predominant weakness; but it did not lead him into any excesses which
affected his public character, or interfered with the interests of his kingdom.
He had seen, and lamented, that his father had been governed by his mistresses; and was so extremely cautious to avoid a similar error, that the
countess of Yarmouth, the only one among them who possessed any real influence over him, could seldom venture to exert her interest in public con-
cerns.

B. *George II's Preoccupation with Hanoverian Affairs*

The king's frequent and prolonged stays in Hanover caused a great deal of
discontent and adverse criticism in England. Lord Hervey records in his
Memoirs that:

An old lean, lame, blind horse was turned into the streets, with a broken
saddle on his back and a pillion behind it, and on the horse's forehead this
inscription was fixed:—

"Let nobody stop me—I am the King's Hanover Equipage, going to
fetch his Majesty and his . . . to England."

At the Royal Exchange, a paper with these words was stuck up:—

"It is reported that his Hanoverian Majesty designs to visit his British
dominions for three months in the spring."

On St. James's gate this advertisement was pasted:—

"Lost or strayed out of this house, a man who has left a wife and six children on the parish; whoever will give any tidings of him to the church-wardens of St. James's Parish, so as he may be got again, shall receive *four shillings and sixpence* reward.

N.B. This reward will not be increased, nobody judging him to deserve a Crown."

217. KING GEORGE III (1760–1820)

When George III (grandson of George II) came to the throne in 1760, he was twenty-two years of age and the first of the Hanoverians to have been born in England. He loved England and the English, was a dutiful son, and a faithful husband. His sincere piety led him to oppose the worst of the social customs of his time and endeared him to the middle class. His early popularity, however, waned as his narrow-mindedness, prejudices, and obstinacy became generally known. While not possessing the abilities to be a great ruler, he worked hard at being king, had a keen sense of duty, and was determined to rule for himself instead of leaving the chief responsibility to others. He was never the tyrant he is pictured as being in the American Declaration of Independence. Lady Anne Hamilton wrote of him:

We must here do justice to the character of George the Third from all intentional tyranny. Many a time has this monarch advocated the cause of the productive classes, and as frequently have his ministers, urged on by the queen, defeated his most sanguine wishes, until he found himself a mere cipher in the affairs of state. The king's simplicity of style and unaffected respect for the people would have induced him to despise the gorgeous pageantry of state; he had been happy, indeed, to have been "the real father of his subjects." His Majesty well knew that the public good ought to be the sole aim of all governments, and that for this purpose a prince is invested with the regal crown. A king is not to employ his authority, patronage, and riches, merely to gratify his own lusts and ambition; but, if need require it, he ought even to sacrifice his own ease and pleasure for the benefit of his country. We give George the Third credit for holding these sentiments, which however, only increased his regrets, as he really had no power to act, —that power being in the possession of his queen and other crafty and designing persons, to whose opinions and determinations he had become a perfect slave. It is to be regretted that he had not sufficient nerve to eject such characters from his councils; for assuredly the nation would have been, to a man, willing to protect him from their vile machinations; but once subdued, he was subdued forever.

Hanoverian England was indeed fortunate in having had a great number of unusually able statesmen. Of these perhaps the best known are Sir Robert Walpole, William Pitt (Earl of Chatham), William Pitt the Younger, Charles James Fox, and Warren Hastings.

218. SIR ROBERT WALPOLE (1676–1745)

Robert Walpole, son of a Norfolk squire who owned a rich estate, was early in life taught estate management and sound business methods. He entered Parliament in 1700 as a member of the Whig faction. He had invested profitably in the South Sea Company, and, having gained a reputation for business acumen, he was given the task of salvaging the wreck when the South Sea Company collapsed. He was put in charge of the Exchequer, and soon got control of the Cabinet, and for two decades headed the government. He was not so much a leader as a manager of men, and did much to improve the Cabinet system of government. When the election of 1741 went against him, Walpole resigned and went to the Lords as Lord Orford.

A. *Lord Chesterfield's Evaluation of Walpole*
Chesterfield, who was well acquainted with Walpole both in his public and private life, speaks highly of his character and talents.

In private life he was good-natured, cheerful, social; inelegant in his manners, loose in his morals. He had a coarse, strong wit, which he was too free of for a man in his station, as it is always inconsistent with dignity. He was very able as a Minister, but without a certain elevation of mind necessary for great good, or great mischief. Profuse and appetent, his ambition was subservient to his desire of making a great fortune. He had more of the Mazarin than of the Richelieu. He would do mean things for profit, and never thought of doing great ones for glory.

He was both the best Parliament-man, and the ablest manager of Parliament, that I believe ever lived. An artful rather than an eloquent speaker; he saw, as by intuition, the disposition of the House, and pressed or receded accordingly. So clear in stating the most intricate matters, especially in the finances, that, whilst he was speaking, the most ignorant thought that they understood what they really did not. Money, not prerogative, was the chief engine of his administration; and he employed it with a success which in a manner disgraced humanity. He was not, it is true, the inventor of that shameful method of governing which had been gaining ground insensibly ever since Charles II., but with uncommon skill and unbounded profusion he brought it to that perfection, which at this time dishonours and distresses this country, and which (if not checked, and God knows how it can be now checked) must ruin it.

Besides this powerful engine of government, he had a most extraordinary talent of persuading and working men up to his purpose. A hearty kind of frankness, which sometimes seemed impudence, made people think that he let them into his secrets, whilst the impoliteness of his manners seemed to attest his sincerity. When he found anybody proof against pecuniary temptations, which, alas! was but seldom, he had recourse to a still worse art; for he laughed at and ridiculed all notions of public virtue, and the love of one's country, calling them "the chimerical school-boy flights of classical learning"; declaring himself at the same time, "no saint, no Spartan, no reformer." He would frequently ask young fellows, at their first appearance in the world, while their honest hearts were yet untainted, "Well, are you to be an old Roman? a patriot? You will soon come off of that, and grow wiser." And thus he was more dangerous to the morals than to the liberties of his country, to which I am persuaded he meant no ill in his heart.

He was the easy and profuse dupe of women, and in some instances indecently so. He was excessively open to flattery, even of the grossest kind, and from the coarsest bunglers of that vile profession; which engaged him to pass most of his leisure and jovial hours with people whose blasted characters reflected upon his own. He was loved by many, but respected by none; his familiar and illiberal mirth and raillery leaving him no dignity. He was not vindictive, but on the contrary very placable to those who had injured him the most. His good-humour, good-nature, and beneficence, in the several relations of father, husband, master, and friend, gained him the warmest affections of all within that circle.

His name will not be recorded in history among the "best men," or the "best Ministers"; but much less ought it to be ranked amongst the worst.

B. *Walpole's Summary of His Career* (*1741*)

Walpole pursued a policy of peace in foreign affairs. Even though he knew that Great Britain's interests were opposed to those of France and Spain, he sought their friendship because peace seemed to him necessary for England's internal economic development. As a result, his years of power were a time of increasingly prosperous industry and commerce. On the political side, the Cabinet, while still partly dependent on the king, gradually became primarily dependent upon the House of Commons. This being the case, Walpole decided to choose an entirely Whig Cabinet, instead of one partly Whig and partly Tory as had previously been the practice. He insisted that all the members support publicly any general policy the Cabinet decided to adopt. Those who refused had to remain silent or resign. Then, by skillful management of the House and by a well-planned system of corruption, he was able to command a majority in the Commons. His insistence on unanimity in the Cabinet caused opposition to develop in his own party, and by 1741 such Whigs as John Carteret, William Pulteney, George Granville, and William Pitt joined the Tory opposition. They accused him of corruption, avarice, political tyranny, of being pro-Hanoverian in foreign affairs, and of pursuing a policy of peace-at-any-price. The election of 1741 went against him, leaving his majority so small that he resigned. Earlier, an address by Parliament to the king, asking him to remove Walpole, had been defeated. In speaking on the proposal, Walpole summarized his career:

If my whole administration is to be scrutinised and arraigned, why are the most favourable parts to be omitted? If facts are to be accumulated on one side, why not on the other? And why may not I be permitted to speak in my own favour? Was I not called by the voice of the king and the nation to remedy the fatal effects of the South Sea project, and to support declining credit? Was I not placed at the head of the treasury, when the revenues were in the greatest confusion? Is it not at an incredible height, and if so, to whom must that circumstance be attributed? Has not tranquillity been preserved both at home and abroad, notwithstanding a most unreasonable and violent opposition? Has the true interest of the nation been pursued, or has trade flourished? Have gentlemen produced one instance of this exorbitant power, of the influence which I extend to all parts of the nation, of the tyranny with which I oppress those who oppose, and the liberality with which I reward those who support me? But having first invested me with a kind of mock dignity, and styled me a prime minister, they impute to me an unpardonable abuse of that chimerical authority which they only have created and conferred. If they are really persuaded that the army is annually established by me, that I have the sole disposal of posts and honours, that I employ this power in the destruction of liberty, and the diminution of commerce, let me awaken them from their delusion. Let me expose to their view the real condition of the public weal; let me shew them that the crown has made no encroachments, that all supplies have been granted by parliament, that all questions have been debated with the same freedom as before the fatal period, in which my counsels are said to have gained the ascendancy: An ascendancy from which they deduce the loss of trade, the approach of slavery, the preponderance of prerogative, and the extension of influence.
. . .
What is this unbounded sole power which is imputed to me? How has it discovered itself, or how has it been proved?

What have been the effects of the corruption, ambition, and avarice, with which I am so abundantly charged?

Have I ever been suspected of being corrupted? A strange phaenomenon, a corrupter himself not corrupt! Is ambition imputed to me? Why then do I still continue a commoner? I, who refused a white staff and a peerage, I had, indeed like to have forgotten the little ornament about my shoulders, which gentlemen have so repeatedly mentioned in terms of sarcastic obloquy. But surely, though this may be regarded with envy or indignation in another place, it cannot be supposed to raise any resentment in this house, where many may be pleased to see those honours which their ancestors have worn, restored again to the commons.

Have I given any symptoms of an avaricious disposition? Have I obtained any grants from the crown since I have been placed at the head of the treasury? Has my conduct been different from that which others in the same station would have followed? Have I acted wrong in giving the place of auditor to my son, and in providing for my own family? I trust that their advancement will not be imputed to me as a crime, unless it shall be proved that I placed them in offices of trust and responsibility for which they were unfit.

But while I unequivocally deny that I am sole and prime minister, and that to my influence and direction all the measures of government must be attributed, yet I will not shrink from the responsibility which attaches to the post I have the honour to hold; and should, during the long period in which I have sat upon this bench, any one step taken by government be proved to be either disgraceful or disadvantageous to the nation, I am ready to hold myself accountable. . . .

219. WILLIAM PITT, EARL OF CHATHAM (1708–1778)

William Pitt was a grandson of "Diamond Pitt," the governor of Madras who had purchased Old Sarum, the famous "rotten borough" through which William entered the Commons. He at once established himself as one of the greatest orators of all time, helped (as we have seen) to oust Walpole in 1741, and in 1756 became the chief member of Devonshire's Cabinet. England had just entered the Seven Years' War (1756–1763), and it was largely owing to Pitt's brilliant planning, his insistence on giving military command to vigorous young men, and his successful appeals to national pride and patriotism that the war was eventually won.

A. A Contemporary Evaluation of Pitt (1758)

James, Earl Waldegrave, an adviser to George II and a friend of Pitt's, wrote of him:

Mr. Pitt has the finest genius, improved by study and all the ornamental part of classical learning.

He came early into the House of Commons, where he soon distinguished himself; lost a cornetcy of horse, which was then his only subsistence; and in less than twenty years has raised himself to be first minister, and the most powerful subject in this country.

He has a peculiar clearness and facility of expression; and has an eye as significant as his words. He is not always a fair or conclusive reasoner, but commands the passions with sovereign authority; and to inflame or captivate a popular assembly is a consummate orator. He has courage of every sort, cool or impetuous, active or deliberate.

At present he is the guide and champion of the people: whether he will long continue their friend seems somewhat doubtful. But if we may judge from his natural disposition, as it has hitherto shewn itself, his popularity and zeal for public liberty will have the same period: for he is imperious, violent, and implacable; impatient even of the slightest contradiction; and, under the mask of patriotism, has the despotic spirit of a tyrant.

However, though his political sins are black and dangerous, his private character is irreproachable; he is incapable of a treacherous or ungenerous action; and in the common offices of life is justly esteemed a man of veracity and a man of honor.

He mixes little in company, confining his society to a small juncto of his relations, with a few obsequious friends, who consult him as an oracle, admire his superior understanding, and never presume to have an opinion of their own.

This separation from the world is not entirely owing to pride, or an unsociable temper; as it proceeds partly from bad health and a weak constitution. But he may find it an impassable barrier in the road of ambition; for though the mob can sometimes raise a minister, he must be supported by persons of higher rank, who may be mean enough in some particulars, yet will not be the patient followers of any man who despises their homage and avoids their solicitations.

Besides, it is a common observation, that men of plain sense and cool resolution have more useful talents, and are better qualified for public business, than the man of the finest parts, who wants temper, judgement, and knowledge of mankind. Even parliamentary abilities may be too highly rated; for between the man of eloquence and the sagacious statesman there is a wide interval.

However, if Mr. Pitt should maintain his power a few years, observation and experience may correct many faults, and supply many deficiencies: in the mean time, even his enemies must allow that he has the firmness and activity of a great minister; that he has hitherto conducted the war with spirit, vigor, and tolerable success; and though some favorite schemes may have been visionary and impracticable, they have at least been more honorable and less dangerous than the passive, unperforming pusillanimity of the late administration.

B. Lord John Russell on Pitt

This session of Parliament [1778] was rendered for ever memorable by the death of Lord Chatham. Factious in the commencement of his career, and impracticable at the close, he was yet a great man, and the only great man of England during his period. His flashes of eloquence scattered his opponents; and his war measures swept the enemies of his country before them. He loved and venerated liberty; was free from all personal corruption, and, with a sagacity and boldness seldom equalled, raised the glory and greatness of his country.

220. WILLIAM PITT THE YOUNGER (1759–1806) AND CHARLES JAMES FOX (1749–1806)

William Pitt the Younger, second son of the Earl of Chatham, entered Parliament when twenty years of age. He was self-confident, politically courageous, and while not the orator his father had been, spoke clearly and vigorously. Like Walpole he was an astute manager of men, and on becoming prime minister in 1783, re-organized and strengthened the Tory party. He unsuccessfully sought to reform Parliament in 1784, but thereafter abandoned the project. He resigned his office in 1801, and died five years later.

Charles James Fox, second son of the wealthy Lord Holland, was a spendthrift, and lived a wild and reckless life. He gambled to excess, wasted his father's vast fortune, and borrowed heavily from his friends. Affectionate and lovable, he was one of the most popular men of his time. He was a liberal, but, loyally clinging to liberalism after the French Revolution had made it unpopular, he had few political followers. His hatred of George III was reciprocated. In 1781, Horace Walpole said he was "the hero in parliament, at the gaming table, at Newmarket [the race-track]. Last week he passed twenty-four hours without interruption at all three, and ill the whole time."

A. Pitt and Fox Compared

It was these notorious irregularities, as has already been pointed out, which, on Pitt's making his appearance in public life, gave the latter so great an

advantage over his elder rival. The world, in discussing their several characters and claims to public confidence, naturally drew a comparison unfavourable to Fox. They beheld in him a man of broken fortunes and ruined
reputation, associating with the "most dissolute characters," and, by his im-
moralities, openly setting public opinion at defiance. Pitt, on the other hand,
stood before them, not only himself a model of youthful purity, but attract-
ing to his standard the sober and rising young politicians of the day, who
almost worshipped him on account of his genius and his virtues. Fox, no less
than Pitt, was undoubtedly actuated in his public conduct by an honourable
ambition; but with Pitt ambition was an all-absorbing passion, while with
Fox it was made subservient to the pursuit of pleasure. Pitt was all industry
and application; while Fox, on the other hand, trusted partly to his natural
abilities, and partly to the stock of knowledge which he had already stored
up, to procure him victory over his opponents. Thus it was, then, that Pitt
raised himself to a power which he succeeded in retaining for seventeen
years, while Fox, during the whole of his political career, held office scarcely
more than as many months. George Selwyn wittily compared them to the
industrious and idle apprentices in Hogarth's prints. "Charles," said his
friend Boothby, at a later period, "has three passions—women, play, and
politics. Yet he never formed a creditable connection with a woman in his
life; he has squandered all his means at the gaming-table; and, with the exception of eleven months, he has invariably been in opposition."

B. *Sir Walter Scott's Epitaph on Pitt and Fox*
Fox's remains were solemnly interred in Westminster Abbey within eighteen inches of the grave of Pitt. Scott's well-known lines are there inscribed:

> Genius, and taste, and talent gone,
> For ever tombed beneath the stone,
> Where—taming thought to human pride—
> The mighty chiefs sleep side by side.
> Drop upon Fox's grave the tear,
> 'Twill trickle to his rival's bier.
> O'er Pitt's the mournful requiem sound,
> And Fox's shall the notes rebound.
>
> The solemn echo seems to cry—
> "Here let their discord with them die.
> Speak not for those a separate doom
> Whom Fate made brothers in the tomb;

But search the land of living men,
Where wilt thou find their like again?"

221. WARREN HASTINGS (1732–1818)

During the Seven Years' War the English had driven the French out of India, and at its conclusion the East India Company was empowered to collect the revenues of Bengal and adjacent provinces, pay a stated amount to the nabob, maintain the native military establishment, and pocket the surplus. As a consequence the Company acquired power over the natives of Bengal without any legal responsibility for their government. Agents of the Company at once entered upon careers of plunder. The British government, on the passage of the Regulating Act (1773), by which it hoped to restore order and proper administration in India, sent out Warren Hastings as governor of the presidency of Calcutta. As governor from 1773 to 1785, Hastings, by a series of extensions of the influence of the East India Company, brought a large part of northern and central India under Company control. His despotic and oppressive actions against the native princes, in which he forced some of the weaker princes to provide him with treasure, led to his impeachment by the House of Commons, but he was finally acquitted by the Lords.

A. *Edmund Burke's Impeachment Speech*

This speech ends in these stirring words:

—Therefore it is with confidence ordered by the commons, that I impeach Warren Hastings, esq. of high crimes and misdemeanors;

I impeach him in the name of the commons of Great Britain in parliament assembled, whose parliamentary trust he has betrayed.

I impeach him in the name of all the commons of Great Britain, whose national character he has dishonoured.

I impeach him in the name of the people of India, whose laws, rights, and liberties, he has subverted, whose properties he has destroyed, whose country he has laid waste and desolate.

I impeach him in the name of human nature itself, which he has cruelly outraged, injured, and oppressed in both sexes, in every age, rank, situation, and condition of life.

B. *Hastings' Own Defense*

In successfully defending himself against these charges, Warren Hastings declared:

To the Commons of England, in whose name I am arraigned, for desolating the provinces of their dominion in India, I dare to reply that they are, and their representatives annually persist in telling them so, the most flourishing of all the states of India— It was I who made them so. The valour of others acquired, I enlarged, and gave shape and consistency to the dominion which you hold there: I preserved it: I sent forth its armies with an effectual but economical hand through unknown and hostile regions, to the support of your other possessions, to the retrieval of one from degradation and dishonour, and of the other from utter loss and subjection. I maintained the wars which were of your formation, or that of others, not of mine: I won one member of the great Indian confederacy from it by an act of seasonable restitution: with another I maintained a secret intercourse, and converted him into a friend: a third I drew off by diversion and negotiation, and employed him as the instrument of peace. When you cried out for peace, and your cries were heard by those who were the object of it, I resisted this and every other species of counteraction, by rising in my demands; and accomplished a peace, a lasting, and I hope an everlasting one, with one great state; and I at least afforded the efficient means by which a peace, if not so durable, more seasonable at least, was accomplished with another. I gave you all; and you have rewarded me with confiscation, disgrace, and a life of impeachment.

The Treaty of Utrecht, ending the War of the Spanish Succession (1702–1713), gave to England greater advantages than to any other European country. Its gains were primarily in the direction of that extension of her colonial empire which was the most marked characteristic of English growth during the eighteenth century. On the Continent it retained Gibraltar and Minorca; in America it obtained recognition of its claims to Newfoundland, Nova Scotia, the lands around Hudson's Bay, and one of the West Indian Islands. It also received valuable commercial concessions from Spain known as the "Asiento." The latter gave Britain not only permission to take Negro slaves to the Spanish West Indies, but an actual (and legal) monopoly of the slave trade with the Spanish colonies for thirty years. Furthermore, the right to send to Porto Bello annually one ship of six hundred tons burden, loaded with goods to sell to the Spanish colonists, proved an entering wedge into Spanish colonial trade of which Britain quickly took full advantage.

This broadening of commercial interests and advantages, the increasing wealth of the country, and its naval supremacy, led to the formation of numerous trading companies to exploit the new opportunities. One of these companies, the South Sea Company, was formed in 1711 to exploit the trade with the Spanish-American colonies and other parts of America and Asia. It was favored by the Cabinet, given great commercial privileges, and treated like a part of the government. Holders of the national debt were encouraged to exchange their bonds for South Sea Company stock. In 1720 the government authorized the Company to take over the management of the entire national debt on payment of an immense sum to the government. As it was then necessary for the Company to expand its trade and money-making, vast projects were announced, profits were promised investors, and speculation therefore set in on an unheard of scale. The value of the Company's stock skyrocketed, but it was carried too far, and in 1721 the bubble burst resulting in the Company's failure.

222. THE SOUTH SEA BUBBLE (1721)

The collapse of everything, when all the bubbles burst at once, and the South Sea stock, which had reached 1100, sunk to 135, was overwhelming. A great national disaster, it was discovered, had been brought about by the madness of that summer. Ruin and bankruptcy were universal. Then came the inevitable cry against the Directors. One does not understand how far they were simply borne along with the stream. Did they by any false representations or needless promises create the rush? Did they by any words of caution try to diminish the madness? No reproaches, however, were too bad for the Directors. Lord Molesworth said in the House that they ought to be tied in a sack and thrown into the sea. Two of them, Jacob Sawbridge and Theodore Janssen, were expelled the House and committed to the Tower, while their firm—Janssen and Sawbridge—had to disgorge a quarter of a million. The Earl of Sunderland, First Commissioner of the Treasury, resigned on being charged with receiving £50,000 in stock without any consideration. Craggs, Secretary of State, and Aislabie, Chancellor of the Exchequer, were convicted of taking bribes. Craggs died of smallpox during the inquiry, but his estate was confiscated. Aislabie was sent to the Tower. Gibbon's grandfather, one of the Directors, had to give up £50,000 out of an estate worth no more than £60,000. The final collapse of the South Sea scheme was really brought about, or hastened, by the action of the Directors themselves in calling for the prosecution of other bubbles. The smaller bubbles burst as soon as they were pricked; with them burst, to their dismay, the great bubble itself. The Directors fell into poverty and obscurity; some of them into absolute poverty. John Law himself, the great leader of Rainbow Finance, died in want a few years later. Some of them found themselves, after all their grandeur, in a debtor's prison. . . . Some, of course, were fortunate in their dealings. Among them was Guy, the bookseller, at the corner of Lombard

Street and Cornhill. A part, not all, of his fortune was made by lucky speculation in this stock. Among those who lost were Gay, the poet, who had
£1000 in South Sea stock, which rose to £20,000; he was advised to sell out,
but would not, in consequence of which he lost the whole. The Duke of
Chandos had £300,000; he, too, lost the whole. Eustace Budgell lost; Prior
lost; and "Tom of Ten Thousand" lost not only his shares but also his reason.

> The South Sea Bubble did not arrest interest in colonial trade and expan-
> sion. Until 1763 England extended its possessions in the colonial world by a
> series of successful wars which culminated in the Treaty of Paris (1763). By
> it, England acquired Florida from Spain, and from France it gained
> Canada, the Old Northwest, some West Indian islands, and defortification
> of the French posts in India.

223. THE STAMP ACT (1765)

> To protect its new possessions in America, the English government pro-
> posed to establish a resident army of 10,000 men and to increase the number
> of crown officials. The extra cost being heavy, it was decided to enforce the
> Navigation Acts and to raise one-half the funds for paying the soldiers and
> officials through higher taxes on colonial importations. One of these unpop-
> ular taxes was the stamp tax.

Whereas by an act made in the last session of parliament, several duties were
granted, continued, and appropriated, towards defraying the expences of defending, protecting, and securing, the British colonies . . . we, . . . the
commons of Great Britain in parliament assembled, have therefore resolved
to give and grant unto your Majesty the several rates and duties herein after
mentioned; and do most humbly beseech your Majesty that it may be enacted . . . that from and after [November 1, 1765] . . . there shall be
raised, levied, collected, and paid unto his Majesty, his heirs, and successors,
throughout the colonies and plantations in America . . . .

For every skin or piece of vellum or parchment, or sheet or piece of
paper, on which shall be ingrossed, written or printed, any declaration, plea,
replication, rejoinder, demurrer, or other pleading, or any copy thereof, in
any court of law within the British colonies and plantations in America, a
stamp duty of three pence.

For every skin or piece of vellum or parchment, or sheet or piece of
paper, on which shall be ingrossed, written or printed, any special bail and
appearance upon such bail . . . a stamp duty of two shillings. . . .

224. REPEAL OF THE STAMP ACT AND THE
DECLARATORY ACT (1766)

As the Stamp Act produced very little revenue because of the violence of colonial opposition, Parliament felt compelled to pass the following Repeal Act, accompanying it with a declaration that the colonies were subordinate to England:

A. *Repeal of the Stamp Act*

Whereas an act was passed in the last session of parliament, intituled, An act for granting and applying certain stamp duties, and other duties, in the British colonies and plantations in America, towards further defraying the expences of defending, protecting, and securing the same; and for amending such parts of the several acts of parliament relating to the trade and revenues of the said colonies and plantations, as direct the manner of determining and recovering the penalties and forfeitures therein mentioned: and whereas the continuance of the said act would be attended with many inconveniencies, and may be productive of consequences greatly detrimental to the commercial interests of these kingdoms; may it therefore please your most excellent Majesty, that it may be enacted . . . That from and after [May 1, 1766] . . . the above-mentioned act, and the several matters and things therein contained, shall be, and is and are hereby repealed and made void to all intents and purposes whatsoever.

B. *Declaratory Act*

Whereas several of the houses of representatives in his Majesty's colonies and plantations in America, have of late, against law, claimed to themselves, or to the general assemblies of the same, the sole and exclusive right of imposing duties and taxes upon his Majesty's subjects in the said colonies and plantations; and have, in pursuance of such claim, passed certain votes, resolutions, and orders, derogatory to the legislative authority of parliament, and inconsistent with the dependency of the said colonies and plantations upon the crown of Great Britain: may it therefore please your most excellent Majesty, that it may be declared; and be it declared . . . That the said colonies . . . have been, are, and of right ought to be, subordinate unto, and dependent upon the imperial crown and parliament of Great Britain; and that the King's majesty, by and with the advice and consent of the lords spiritual and temporal, and commons of Great Britain, in parliament assembled, had, hath, and of right ought to have, full power and authority to make laws and statutes of sufficient force and validity to bind the colonies and people of America, subjects of the crown of Great Britain, in all cases whatsoever.

II. And be it further declared and enacted by the authority aforesaid, That all resolutions, votes, orders, and proceedings in any of the said colonies or plantations, whereby the power and authority of the parliament of Great Britain, to make laws and statutes as aforesaid, is denied, or drawn into question, are and are hereby declared to be, utterly null and void to all intents and purposes whatsoever.

225. CHARLES JAMES FOX'S SPEECH ON THE STAMP ACT

Upon the whole, I will beg leave to tell the House what is precisely my opinion. It is that the Stamp Act be repealed, absolutely, totally, and immediately. That the reason for the repeal be assigned, that it was founded on an erroneous principle. At the same time, let the sovereign authority of this country over the colonies be asserted in as strong terms as can be devised, and made to extend to every kind of legislation whatsoever. That we may bind their trade, confine their manufactures, and exercise every power whatsoever, except only that of taking their money from their pockets without their own consent.

226. SOME BRITISH COMMENTS ON THE WAR FOR AMERICAN INDEPENDENCE (1775–1783)

Partly because of the incredible weakness and folly of a succession of prime ministers, and the growing intransigence of the American Colonies, the latter declared their independence of the mother country in 1776, some months after fighting had already erupted. The following readings reveal with great clarity the opinions of many leading Englishmen, and that of the king, on the revolution.

A. *John Wesley*

Wesley, leader of the Methodists, wrote to Lord North, the prime minister, on June 15, 1775:

I do not intend to enter upon the question, whether the Americans are in the right or in the wrong?—Here all my prejudices are against the Americans, for I am a High Churchman, the son of a High Churchman, bred up from my childhood in the highest notions of passive obedience and non-resistance; and yet, in spite of all my long-rooted prejudices, I cannot avoid thinking, if I think at all, these, an oppressed people, asked for nothing more than their legal rights, and that in the most modest and inoffensive manner that the nature of the thing would allow.

B. *Horace Walpole*

In the same vein, Walpole wrote to H. S. Conway:

The Americans at least have acted like men, gone to the bottom at once, and set the whole upon the whole. Our conduct has been that of pert children: we have thrown a pebble at a mastiff, and are surprised it was not frightened. Now we must be worried by it, or must kill the guardian of the house, which will be plundered the moment little master has nothing but the old nurse to defend it. But I have done with reflections; you will be fuller of them than I.

C. *Earl of Chatham*

The chief opponent of North's policies was Chatham, who made the following eloquent plea for conciliation with America:

When your lordships, he said, look at the papers transmitted to us from America; when you consider their decency, firmness, and wisdom, you cannot but respect their cause, and wish to make it your own. For myself, I must declare and avow that in all my reading and observation of history, and it has been my favourite study,—I have read Thucydides, and have admired the master-states of the world,—that for solidity of reasoning, force of sagacity, and wisdom of conclusion, under such a complication of difficult circumstances, no nation or body of men can stand in preference to the General Congress at Philadelphia. I trust it is obvious to your lordships that all attempts to impose servitude upon such men, to establish despotism over such a mighty continental nation, must be vain, must be fatal. We shall be forced ultimately to retract. Let us retract while we can, not when we must. I say we must necessarily undo these violent oppressive acts. They must be repealed. You will repeal them. I pledge myself for it that you will in the end repeal them. I stake my reputation on it. I will consent to be taken for an idiot if they are not finally repealed. And then this humiliating necessity! With a dignity becoming your exalted situation, make the first advances to concord, to peace and happiness; for that is your true dignity, to act with prudence and justice.

D. *George III*

King George, however, remained adamant in his determination to prevent the independence of the colonies. When, in 1779, Lord North wished to resign as prime minister in favor of Lord Gower, the king wrote to him:

It is no compliment when I say that Lord Gower would be a poor sub-stitute for Lord North. What I said yesterday was the dictates of frequent and severe self-examination. I can never depart from it. Before I will hear of any man's readiness to come into office, I will expect to see it signed under his own hand, that he is resolved to keep the Empire entire, and that no troops shall consequently be withdrawn from thence, nor independence ever allowed. I can never suppose this country so lost to all ideas of self-importance, as to be willing to grant American independence. If that word be ever universally adopted, I shall despair of this country being preserved from a state of inferiority. I hope never to see that day, for however I am treated, I must love this country.

227. THE NAVAL VICTORY AT TRAFALGAR (1805)

Within a few years of the conclusion of the American War for Indepen-dence (1783), England became involved in war first with the French Revolutionary Government and then with Napoleon. The Duke of Well-ington was the architect of the final military victory at Waterloo (1815), while Admiral Horatio Nelson, England's greatest naval hero, won the great naval victory at Trafalgar at the cost of his life. The *Annual Register* for 1805 summarized the battle of Trafalgar thusly:

About noon the dreadful contest began, by the leading ships of the columns breaking through the enemy's line: which was first effected by ad-miral Collingwood, in the Royal Sovereign, . . . about the twelfth ship from the rear of the enemy, leaving his van unoccupied; the succeeding ships breaking through in all parts a-stern of their leaders, and engaging the enemy at the muzzles of their guns. At twenty minutes past twelve the ac-tion became general—It had been the intention of lord Nelson to have pene-trated the adversary's line, between the tenth and eleventh of his ships in the van; but finding it so close, that there was not room to pass, he ordered the Victory, which bore his flag, to be run on board the ship opposed to him, and the Temeraire, his second, also ran on board of the next ship in the enemy's line, so that these four ships formed one mass, and were so close, that every gun fired from the Victory set the Redoubtable, to which she was opposed, on fire; whilst the British sailors were employed, at intervals, in the midst of the hottest action, in pouring buckets of water on the flames in the enemy's vessels, lest their spreading should involve both ships in destruction! An instance of cool and deliberate bravery not to be paralleled in ancient or modern history.

The action was equally severe around the Royal Sovereign, and in several other quarters; the enemy's ships being fought with the greatest gallantry; but the attack upon them was irresistible, and a great and glorious victory was its reward. About three in the afternoon admiral Gravina, with ten sail of the line, joining the enemy's frigates to leeward, bore away to Cadiz; five more of their headmost ships in the van, under admiral Dumanoir, about ten minutes after, tacked and stood to the southward, to windward of the British line; they were engaged, and the sternmost taken; the four others got off, leaving a noble prey to the British fleet of nineteen ships of the line, of which two were first-rates, and none under 74 guns, with three flag officers, namely admiral Villeneuve, the commander-in-chief, and the Spanish admirals d'Aliva and Cisneros. General Contamin, who commanded the land forces, was also taken on board the Bucentaure. At forty minutes after four all firing ceased, and a complete victory was reported to lord Nelson, who, having been wounded early in the action, survived just long enough to hear the joyful tidings . . . , and then died, . . . a few minutes before five. . . .

Thus ended the battle of Trafalgar, the most glorious, whether in respect to the science and judgment with which it was conducted, the bravery and spirit with which it was fought, or its fortunate and brilliant result to the conquerors, ever recorded in the naval annals of Great Britain. . . .

228. SLAVERY AND THE SLAVE TRADE

The expansion of colonial trade along with the growth of the British Empire had resulted in a marked increase of the slave trade. Merchants, particularly in western England, made much money on this nefarious traffic between Africa and America. As its horrors became generally known, agitation for putting an end to it increased sharply. The Quakers petitioned Parliament against it, and benevolent reformers such as Thomas Clarkson, William Wilberforce, and John Cartwright became active abolitionists.

A. *Cartwright on Slavery*

The most ancient inheritance cannot strengthen this right, the want of inheritance cannot impair it. The child of a slave is as free-born according to the law of nature, as he who could trace a free ancestry up to the creation. Slavery in all its forms, in all its degrees, is an outrageous violation of the rights of mankind; an odious degradation of human nature. It is utterly impossible that any human being can be without a title to liberty, except he himself have forfeited it by crimes which make him dangerous to society.

B. *Regulation of the Slave Trade*

Although the effort of Pitt to secure the abolition of the slave trade in 1788 was unsuccessful, a regulative Act was passed. John Aikin, in his *Annals of the Reign of George the Third,* describes it in these words:

At length, Sir William Dolben, after observing that some of the greatest evils of the trade arose from the sufferings of the negroes in their passage, for which an immediate remedy might be applied, moved for a bill to regulate the transportation of the natives of Africa, to the British colonies in the West Indies, the provisions of which should go to the limiting of their number in proportion to the tonnage of the vessel conveying them, and also to other points for their health and comfort. This proposal was generally approved; the bill was brought in and carried, notwithstanding a petition from Liverpool praying that no alteration in the slave-trade might take place, and the examination of witnesses to prove that the evil which the bill was to remedy did not exist. It afterwards went through the House of Lords with some amendments, and passed into a law.

C. *Abolition of the Slave Trade*

In 1806, when Fox was prime minister, the following statute was passed providing that the slave trade should cease on May 1, 1807.

. . . That from and after the First Day of May One thousand eight hundred and seven, the African Slave Trade, and all and all manner of dealing and trading in the Purchase, Sale, Barter, or Transfer of Slaves, or of Persons intended to be sold, transferred, used, or dealt with as Slaves, practised or carried on, in, at, to or from any Part of the Coast or Countries of Africa, shall be, and the same is hereby utterly abolished, prohibited, and declared to be unlawful; and also that all and all manner of dealing, either by way of Purchase, Sale, Barter, or Transfer, or by means of any other Contract or Agreement whatever, relating to any Slaves, or to any Persons intended to be used or dealt with as Slaves, for the Purpose of such Slaves or Persons being removed or transported either immediately or by Transhipment at Sea or otherwise, directly or indirectly from Africa, or from any Island, Country, Territory, or Place whatever, in the West Indies, or in any other Part of America, not being in the Dominion, Possession, or Occupation of His Majesty, to any other Island, Country, Territory or Place whatever, is hereby in like Manner utterly abolished, prohibited, and declared to be unlawful; and if any of His Majesty's Subjects, or any Person or Persons resident within this United Kingdom, or any of the Islands, Colonies, Dominions, or

Territories thereto belonging, or in His Majesty's Occupation or Possession, shall from and after the Day aforesaid, by him or themselves, or by his or their Factors or Agents or otherwise howsoever, deal or trade in, purchase, sell, barter, or transfer, or contract or agree for the dealing or trading in, purchasing, selling, bartering, or transferring of any Slave or Slaves, or any Person or Persons intended to be sold, transferred, used, or dealt with as a Slave or Slaves contrary to the Prohibitions of this Act, he or they so offending shall forfeit and pay for every such Offence the Sum of One Hundred Pounds of lawful Money of Great Britain for each and every Slave so purchased, sold, bartered, or transferred, or contracted or agreed for as aforesaid, the One Moiety thereof to the Use of His Majesty . . . and the other Moiety to the Use of any Person who shall inform, sue, and prosecute for the same. . . .

> A statute passed in 1811 put teeth into the Act of 1807 by declaring anyone who participated in any way in the slave trade guilty of a felony and punishable by transportation to a penal colony for fourteen years, or by hard labor for terms of from three to five years.

229. THE RIOT ACT (1715)

> The Whigs, having won the election of 1715, at once began to impeach the leading Tories. As a result some Tories threw in their lot with the Jacobites (supporters of the Catholic Stuart Pretender James III) who rebelled in 1715 against George I. Riots and demonstrations on behalf of James provoked the Whig Government to pass the famous Riot Act. The following are the main provisions of this Act:

. . . be it enacted . . . That if any persons to the number of twelve or more, being unlawfully, riotously, and tumultuously assembled together, to the disturbance of the publick peace, at any time after the last day of July 1715 . . . , and being required or commanded by any one or more justice or justices of the peace, or by the sheriff of the county, or his under-sheriff, or by the mayor, bailiff or bailiffs, or other head-officer, or justice of the peace of any city or town corporate, where such assembly shall be, by proclamation to be made in the King's name, in the form herein after directed, to disperse themselves, and peaceably to depart to their habitations, or to their lawful business, shall, to the number of twelve or more . . . unlawfully, riotously, and tumultuously remain or continue together by the space of one hour after such command . . . , that then such continuing together . . . shall be adjudged felony without benefit of clergy, and the offenders therein shall be adjudged felons, and shall suffer death as in case of felony without benefit of clergy.

II. And be it further enacted by the authority aforesaid, That the order and form of the proclamation that shall be made . . . shall be as hereafter followeth (that is to say) the justice of the peace, or other person authorized by this act to make the said proclamation shall, among the said rioters, or as near to them as he can safely come, with a loud voice command, or cause to be commanded silence to be, while proclamation is making, and after that, shall openly and with loud voice make or cause to be made proclamation in these words, or like in effect:

Our sovereign Lord the King chargeth and commandeth all persons, being assembled, immediately to disperse themselves, and peaceably to depart to their habitations, or to their lawful business, upon the pains contained in the act made in the first year of King George, for preventing tumults and riotous assemblies. God save the King. . . .

230. THE SCOTTISH REBELLION OF 1745

In 1745 a second attempt to restore the Stuart family in the person of Charles Edward—the Young Pretender—was made in Scotland. The Scottish force which he collected in the Highlands defeated the English at Preston Pans, but were utterly routed by the Duke of Cumberland's troops at Culloden Moor in April of 1746. A Mr. Stone described the battle in this letter to the Duke of Bedford:

I have the honour to acquaint your Grace, that a messenger arrived this day with letters from his Royal Highness the Duke of Cumberland, dated at Inverness the 18th instant, and containing further particulars of the victory obtained by his Majesty's troops over the rebels; which appears to have been more considerable, as to the number of men lost by them, than was at first imagined. The account sent by his Royal Highness makes the number of the rebels killed, on the field of battle, and in the pursuit, to amount to 2000: other letters, by this messenger, say 2500; and they all agree that the rebels themselves acknowledge that they have lost from 3000 to 4000 men. Many of their chiefs are killed; amongst whom are Lord Strathallan, Lord Balmerino, (and, it is strongly reported, the Duke of Perth, though that is not so certain,) Cameron of Lochiel, Appen, Kinloch, and many others of the rank of Colonel; and it is supposed by the rebel prisoners that many of their chiefs are killed who are not yet known. There is a long list of prisoners, many of which are of considerable rank; but I do not find Murray of Broughton's name amongst them. All their cannon, all their baggage, and

twelve colours are taken; in short, there never was known a more total defeat. The Pretender's son fled very early, and was seen to pass Fort Augustus,
with only eight men in his company. He lay that night at Lord Lovat's.
Brigadier Mordaunt was sent the next day by his Royal Highness into that
country, and went to Lord Lovat's house; but found it empty, and left it in
flames. The rebels are supposed to be, in a manner, totally dispersed; his
Royal Highness not having been able to learn that there was any considerable number of them any where together, so that he was at a loss which way
to pursue them.

231. SCOTLAND AND THE SCOTS IN THE MID-EIGHTEENTH CENTURY

In 1759, Tom Lyttleton, son of Lord Lyttleton, an English statesman who
had been on a tour of Scotland, wrote to Mrs. Elizabeth Montague:

The characteristical virtues of the Scotch are courage, temperance,
prudence, economy and hospitality. This last is not only peculiar to the nobility, but is universally practised by all kinds of people. *Good breeding,*
though it cannot be properly styled a virtue, is of the greatest *consequence* to
Society. This the Scotch universally possess, and there is not in the North
such a character as that of an English country Squire, whose whole life is
spent in the laudable customs of hunting, drinking, swearing and sleeping. . . . Scotch ladies are very handsome and very sweet-tempered. It is
their general character to be rather too free of their favours before marriage;
however that may be, they are very chaste after that ceremony. They breed
up their children in a particular manner, for they are accustomed from their
infancy to go without shoes or stockings, nor in the coldest weather do their
parents permit them to wear a great-coat; if they are of a puny constitution
they die, if not, they are the better for it all their life.

He further commented on religious fervor in Scotland: "few of the nobility
omit going to Church on Sunday, and what is of more importance, when
they are there they do not trifle, but seem seriously to reflect upon the duty
they owe their maker." The author of the letter was a boy of 15!

232. IRELAND AND THE IRISH

The following letter by Bishop Nicolson, written in 1718 from London-
derry, Ireland, to Archbishop Wake, reveals not only the attitude of an
Anglican bishop, but also the sordid conditions in Ireland. What he wrote
of that blighted land in that year would have been equally true had it been
composed in the last part of the century.

My very good Lord,

I had the honour of your Grace's letter of the 10th. just as I was leaving Dublin this day se'n-night, and about an hour after I had sent to the post my last letter for Lambeth. The Archbishop of Dublin did not come home whilst I staid in town, which bereft me of the opportunity of getting his particular informations concerning the state of his quondam diocese of Derry, which his singular courtesy would not have suffered him to withhold. I was also forced to come away without personal assent to my licence of return to my family, and of continuing in England till May next; which favour I readily obtained from the other two Lords Justices.

They were also pleased to grant me a guard of dragoons, with whom I travelled in great security through a country said to be much infested with a set of barbarous and pilfering Tories. I saw no danger of losing the little money I had; but was under some apprehensions of being starved: having never beheld even in Picardy, Westphalia, or Scotland, such dismal marks of hunger and want as appeared in the countenances of most of the poor creatures that I met with on the road. The wretches lie in reeky sod-hovels; and have generally no more than a rag of coarse blanket to cover a small part of their nakedness. Upon the strictest inquiry, I could not find that they are better-clad or lodged in the winter season. These sorry slaves plough the ground to the very top of their mountains, for the service of their lords; who spend truly rack rents, as somebody supposed those of this diocese would be spent, in London. A ridge or two of potatoes is all the poor tenant has for the support of himself, a wife, and commonly ten or twelve bare-legged children. To complete their misery, these animals are bigoted Papists; and we frequently met them trudging to some ruined church or chapel, either to mass, a funeral, or a wedding, with a priest in the same habit with themselves.

233. THE ACT OF UNION (1800)

In the eighteenth century, Ireland was made completely subservient to England, and was in every way treated as a conquered country. Anglicanism was the Established Church in Ireland and Roman Catholic worship was illegal, although it could not be effectively suppressed. Nor could a Roman Catholic attend the university, be a schoolmaster, or send his children to a Catholic school at home or abroad. The Parliament at Dublin was composed of Protestants, and Roman Catholics could neither hold public office nor serve in any position of honor or trust. Economically, also, Ireland was subservient to England, which forbade the importation into England of any cattle, meat, butter, or cheese from Ireland. This provoked growing discontent and increasing hostility toward the English.

One of the effects of the French Revolutionary War, which England entered in 1793, was an attempt in 1789 by the "United Irishmen" led by Wolfe Tone to establish an Irish republic. Atrocities were committed by both Englishmen and Irishmen before the insurrection was put down. The result was that the English government decided that the only hope for peace and order in Ireland was to unite its Parliament with that of England and rule the two countries as one. This was the background to the Act of Union, the first four articles of which are as follows:

That it be the first article of the union of the kingdoms of Great Britain and Ireland, that the said kingdoms of Great Britain and Ireland shall, upon the first day of January . . . [1801], and for ever after, be united into one kingdom, by the name of the United Kingdom of Great Britain and Ireland; and that the royal stile and titles appertaining to the imperial crown of the said united kingdom and its dependencies; and also the ensigns, armorial flags and banners thereof, shall be such as his Majesty, by his royal proclamation under the great seal of the united kingdom, shall be pleased to appoint.

That it be the second article . . . that the succession to the imperial crown of the said united kingdom, and of the dominions thereunto belonging, shall continue limited and settled in the same manner as the succession to the imperial crown of the said kingdoms of Great Britain and Ireland now stands limited and settled, according to the existing laws, and to the terms of union between England and Scotland.

That it be the third article of union, that the said united kingdom be represented in one and the same parliament, to be stiled The Parliament of the United Kingdom of Great Britain and Ireland.

That it be the fourth article of union, that four lords spiritual of Ireland by rotation of sessions, and twenty-eight lords temporal of Ireland elected for life by the peers of Ireland, shall be the number to sit and vote on the part of Ireland in the house of lords of the parliament of the united kingdom; and one hundred commoners (two for each county of Ireland, two for the city of Dublin, two for the city of Cork, one for the university of Trinity College, and one for each of the thirty-one most considerable cities, towns, and boroughs), be the number to sit and vote on the part of Ireland in the house of commons of the parliament of the united kingdom:

That such act as shall be passed in the parliament of Ireland previous to the union, to regulate the mode by which the lords spiritual and temporal, and the commons, to serve in the parliament of the united kingdom on the part of Ireland, shall be summoned and returned to the said parliament, shall be considered as forming part of the treaty of union. . . .

234. THE COAL INDUSTRY

England remained primarily an agricultural country in the eighteenth century, and during the second half of the century many improvements were made in agricultural methods by wealthy landlords who could afford to experiment. Equally great, if not greater, were the changes in industry associated with the Industrial Revolution, which resulted partly in a spectacular growth of the cotton industry. A consequence of the increasing use of machinery in industry was the growing consumption of coal, which reached its peak more than a century later. The nature of this industry is revealed in the following selections:

A. *Growth of Coal Mining*

In 1758, Mrs. Elizabeth Montague wrote from the north of England to Dr. Stillingfleet:

Pan, Ceres, and Pomona, seem to neglect us; we are under the domination of the god of mines. There is a great deal of rich land in this country, but agriculture is ill understood. The great gain made by several branches of the coal trade has turned all attention that way. Every gentleman in the country, from the least to the greatest, is as solicitous in the pursuit of gain as a tradesman. The conversation always turns upon money; the moment you name a man, you are told what he is worth, the losses he has had, or the profit he has made by coal mines. As my mind is not naturally set to this tune, I should often be glad to change it for a song from one of your Welsh Bards.

B. *The Hardships of Colliers*

Coal mining had previously been done in the south of England, but, in the last half of the eighteenth century, the center of this extractive industry shifted to the north, principally in and around the county of Durham. Although most mines were shallow, colliers labored under harsh conditions. Professor Thomas S. Ashton quotes an anonymous pamphleteer as saying:

"Labourers in the south are obliged to endure wet and cold in a very great variety of their work, and when they come home at night, poor victuals and a cool chimney corner is their general fare; they have neither time nor fire enough to dry their stockings, cloaths, etc., before the next morning, when they put them on again damp as they are; and the repetition of this hardship chills their blood, and throws them into agues". The incidence of this complaint, it was said, was eight times as heavy in Dorset as in

Durham. The shortage of fuel outside the areas of coal-mining became accentuated as population increased. . . .

And Ashton goes on to say of colliers:

Generally the miners lived in villages where the whole community was concerned with the one occupation of getting and carrying coal. Apart from a grocer, a butcher, and one or two publicans, there were no shopkeepers and no members of the middle class. In an area of twenty square miles occupied by the Kingswood colliers there was no Established church and only one small Nonconformist chapel. Kingswood was only three or four miles from Bristol, Bedworth about the same from Coventry, yet the miners had no part in the lives of these cities. To the traders and shopkeepers the colliers appeared in the same light as the barbarian tribes to the townfolk of a Roman garrison on the outskirts of the Empire, and when the colliers came to town they bolted their doors and barricaded their windows.

C. *Women in the Mines*

Although conditions of labor in the mines were not as bad for the women as they were to become early in the nineteenth century, they were bad enough. Professor Ashton quotes R. Bald as saying that a man generally went to work at about eleven o'clock at night, and:

"In about three hours after, his wife (attended by her daughters, if she has any sufficiently grown) sets out for the pit, having previously wrapped her infant child in a blanket, and left it to the care of an old woman, who for a small gratuity, keeps three or four children at a time, and who, in their mother's absence, feeds them with ale or whisky, mixed with water. . . . The mother . . . descends the pit with her older daughters, when each, having a basket of a suitable form, lays down, and into it the large coals are rolled; and such is the weight carried, that it frequently takes two men to lift the burden upon their backs: the girls are loaded according to their strength. The mother sets out first, carrying a lighted candle in her teeth; the girls follow, and in this manner they proceed to the pit bottom, and with weary steps and slow, ascend the stairs, halting occasionally to draw breath, till they arrive at the hill or pit top, where the coals are laid down for sale; and in this manner they go for eight or ten hours almost without resting. It is no uncommon thing to see them, when ascending the pit, weeping most bitterly, from the excessive severity of their labour; but the instant they have laid down their burden on the hill, they resume their cheerfulness, and return down the pit, singing."

Further, on women in the mines, Ashton notes:

The creel or basket had a supporting strap that passed round the forehead. It would hold as much as 170 lb. of coal, and a woman might bear such a load a distance of 150 yards underground, then ascend with it 117 feet to the surface, and finally carry it 20 yards farther to the pit hill. And this she might do as often as twenty-four times in the course of the day. When the hewers had no female relatives, they would secure from the overman of the pit the services of women, known as fremd bearers, who were unattached to any coal-miner's family. These unfortunates had not even the protection which the self-interest of the slave-owner ensures to the slave, for they were transferred from one hewer to another and might find themselves in the service of a new master each day. Their story will form one of the most sombre chapters in that history of the working classes that has yet to be written.

235. THE STAFFORDSHIRE POTTERIES AND IRONWORKS

After a six-month tour of northern England, Arthur Young, a careful and astute observer, wrote the following descriptions of the potteries and ironworks:

A. *Potteries*

From Newcastle-under-lime I had the pleasure of viewing the Staffordshire potteries at Burslem, and the neighbouring villages, which have of late been carried on with such amazing success. . . .

It dates its great demand from Mr. Wedgwood (the principal manufacturer) introducing, about four years ago, the cream-coloured ware, and since that the increase has been very rapid. Large quantities are exported to Germany, Ireland, Holland, Russia, Spain, the East Indies, and much to America: Some of the finest sorts to France. . . .

The common clay of the country is used for the ordinary sorts; the finer kinds are made of clay from Devonshire and Dorsetshire, chiefly from Biddeford; but the flints from the Thames are all brought rough by sea, either to Liverpool or Hull, and so by Burton. There is no conjecture formed of the original reason of fixing the manufacture in this spot, except for the convenience of plenty of coals, which abound under all the country.

The flints are first ground in mills, and the clay prepared by breaking, washing, and sifting, and then they are mixed in the requisite proportions.

The flints are bought first by the people about the country; and by them burnt and ground, and sold to the manufacturer by the peck.

It is then laid in large quantities, on kilns, to evaporate the moisture; this is a nice work, as it must not be too dry: Next it is beat with large wooden hammers, and then is in order for throwing, and is moulded into the forms in which it is to remain: This is the most difficult work in the whole manufacture. A boy turns a perpendicular wheel, which, by means of thongs, turns a small horizontal one, just before the thrower, with such velocity, that it twirls round the lump of clay he lays on it, into any form he directs it with his fingers.

B. *Ironworks*

Rotherham is famous for its iron works, of which it contains one very large one, belonging to Mr. Walker, and one or two smaller. Near the town are two collieries, out of which the iron ore is dug, as well as the coals to work it with; these collieries and works employ together near 500 hands. The ore is here worked into metal and then into bar iron, and the bars sent in Sheffield to be worked, and to all parts of the country; this is one branch of their business. Another is the foundery, to which they run the ore into metal, pigs, and then cast it into all sorts of boilers, pans, plough-shares, etc. etc. etc. The forgemen work by weight, and earn from 8s. to 20s. a week, but 12s. or 14s. the average; the foundery men are paid by the week, from 7s. to 10s. No boys are employed younger than 14, such from 3s. to 4s. a week. In the collieries, the men earn from 7s. to 9s. a week. There are few women employed; and only in piling old bits of scrap iron . . . into the form of small pyramids, upon round pieces of stone, after which they are set into the furnace till they become of a malleable heat, and are then worked over again.

Besides the iron manufactory, they have a pottery, in which is made the white, cream-coloured (Staffordshire) and tortoise-shell earthen-ware: It employs about two or three and twenty men and 40 boys; the men are paid 9s. a week for day-work, but much is done by the piece, in which case they all earn more, up to 15s. a week. Boys of nine or ten years old have 2s. and 2s. 6d. a week. There is also a very large quantity of lime burnt in this town, which constantly employs about 20 hands, that earn at a medium of 9s. a week.

C. *Industries in Sheffield, Yorkshire*

Young was greatly impressed by the various industries in Sheffield, which he described as follows:

Sheffield contains about 30,000 inhabitants, the chief of which are employed in the manufacture of hardware. The great branches are the plating-work, the cutlery, the lead works, and the silk mill. . . .

In the plated work some hundreds of hands are employed; the men's pay extends from 9s. a week to 60 £ a year: in works of curiosities it must be supposed that dexterous hands are paid very great wages. Girls earn 4s. 6d. and 5s. a week; some even to 9s. No men are employed that earn less than 9s. Their day's work, including the hours of cessation, is thirteen.

In the cutlery branch are several subdivisions, such as razor, knife, scissar, lancets, stems, etc. etc. Among these the grinders make the greatest earnings; 18s. 19s. and 20s. a week, are common among them; but this height of wages is owing in a great measure to the danger of the employment. . . .

Simultaneously with the Industrial Revolution there occurred a revolution in agriculture led by men like Jethro Tull, Robert Bakewell, and Charles Townshend. Their work was later publicized by Arthur Young in his famous *Tours of England*. Young visited all parts of the country, including Wales, and described the agricultural methods in use, the crops produced, and experiments conducted to increase agricultural productivity. Tull (1674–1741) began to drill seeds (which he carefully selected) in rows some distance apart, and to hoe between the rows. In 1701 he invented a drill for planting, and in 1714 a horse-hoe. Townshend, on his Norfolk estate, worked out a crop-rotation system of wheat, turnips, barley and clover, hence producing crops for human consumption and for animal fodder in alternate years. He also fertilized his land with marl (soil of lime, clay, and calcium carbonate) and as a result made his estate a profitable one. Bakewell developed the art of scientific cattle breeding and thereby more than doubled the weight of cattle. This agricultural revolution resulted in more land under cultivation and an increase in the amount and variety of foodstuffs.

236. SCIENTIFIC CATTLE BREEDING BY ROBERT BAKEWELL (1723–1795)

Having remarked that domestic animals, in general, produce others possessing qualities nearly similar to their own, he conceived he had only to select from the most valuable breeds such as promised to return the greatest possible emolument to the breeder; and that he should then be able, by careful attention to progressive improvements, to produce a race of sheep, or other animals, possessing a maximum of advantage. Under the influence of this excellent notion, Mr. B. made excursions into different parts of England, to inspect the various breeds, and to ascertain those which were the best adapted to his purposes, and the most valuable of their kinds. His next step was to select and purchase the best of all the sorts wherever they could be found; and this selection . . . was the original stock from which he afterward propagated his own. . . . Some time afterward [after 1760], he began to let out some of his rams, and for a few seasons received only 15s. and a guinea [21s.] apiece for them. . . . Since that time . . . single rams have been let for the season for the enormous sum of 400 guineas and upwards . . . . He directed his attention, however, the most successfully to the improvement of the sheep known by the name of "The Dishley," or "New Leicestershire"; to long-horned cattle; and to strong horses of the black breed, suitable for the harness and the army. . . . The race of Dishley Sheep are known by the fineness of their bones and flesh, the lightness of offal, the disposition to quietness, and, consequently, to mature and fatten with less food than other sheep of equal weight and value. . . .

237. THE MARQUIS OF ROCKINGHAM'S EXPERIMENTS IN DRAINAGE OF LAND (1730–1782)

Arthur Young described the drainage system perfected by the Marquis of Rockingham on his lands between Rotherham and Barnsley in these words:

Throughout this extensive tract of land, I found very deep fosses cut, or old ditches sunk so deep as to give in every field the command of a sufficient descent. These are kept open. Into them run the covered drains, which are cut in number proportioned to the wetness of the land, but in general but a small distance from each other.

Of these, there are three sorts, the leading or main ones of two kinds, and the branches or secondary ones. The first . . . are two feet wide at top and bottom, and four or five feet deep, walled on each side and covered at top with large broad stones. . . . The second are a yard deep, two feet wide at top, and 10 inches at bottom . . . the tops of the stones joining; then they are filled up with bits of stone, within seven or eight inches of the top; and, lastly, the molds thrown over.

The branches are three quarters of a yard deep, 18 inches wide at top, and nine at bottom; they are then filled up in the same manner as the other. . . .

The improvement of these drains . . . is almost immediately manifest; the summer succeeding the first winter totally eradicates in grass lands all those weeds which proceed from too much water, and leaves the surface in the depth of winter perfectly dry and sound. . . . In arable lands, the effect is equally striking, for the corn in winter and spring upon land that used to be flowed with rain, and quite poisoned by it, now lies perfectly dry throughout the year, and in the tillage of it, a prodigious benefit accrues from this excellent practice, for the drained fields are ready in the spring for the plough, before the others can be touched. . . .

238. FERTILIZATION OF THE SOIL

In his *Six Weeks Tour Through the Southern Counties of England and Wales,* Arthur Young writes of the country between Holkam and Houghton:

All the country . . . was a wild sheep-walk before the spirit of improvement seized the inhabitants; and this glorious spirit has wrought amazing effects; for instead of boundless wilds, and uncultivated wastes, inhabited by scarcely anything but sheep; the country is all cut into inclosures, cultivated in a most husband-like manner, richly manured, well peopled, and yielding an hundred times the produce that it did in its former state. What has wrought these vast improvements is the marling; for under the whole country run veins of a very rich soapy kind, which they dig up, and spread upon the old sheep-walks, and then by means of inclosing they throw their farms into a regular course of crops, and gain immensely by the improvement. . . .

The culture of turnips is here carried on in a most extensive manner; Norfolk being more famous for this vegetable than any county in the kingdom. . . . The use to which they apply their vast field of turnips, is the feeding of their flocks, and expending the surplus in fatting Scotch cattle. . . . When the marl begins to wear out the soil, many of the great farmers have latterly got into a method of manuring with oil-cakes for their winter corn, which they import from Holland, and spread on their fields at the expense of about 15s. per acre. . . .

239. SOURCES OF THE NATIONAL INCOME IN 1771

When he had concluded his survey of England, Young showed how important agriculture was by drawing up the following rough estimate of the sources of England's national income:

The Soil	£ 66,000,000
Manufactures	27,000,000
Commerce	10,000,000
Publick Revenue	9,000,000
Sums at Interest	5,000,000
Law, Physic, etc	5,000,000
Total Income of England	£ 122,000,000

240. THE TRADING COMPANIES OF LONDON

London, with its large population, was naturally a center of activity of tradesmen and artisans who supplied the city with a wide variety of consumer goods. The next reading enumerates the trading companies and explains their organization:

The Traders of London are divided into Companies, or Corporations, and are so many Bodies Politick: Of these there are 12, called the chief Companies; and he that is chosen Lord-Mayor, must be free of one of these Companies; which are,

1. Mercers,	5. Goldsmiths,	9. Salters,
2. Grocers,	6. Skinners,	10. Ironmongers,
3. Drapers,	7. Merchant-Taylors,	11. Vintners,
4. Fishmongers,	8. Haberdashers,	12. Clothworkers

All these 12 Companies have stately Halls.

And if it happen that the Lord-Mayor Elect is of any other Company, he presently removes to one of the Twelve. It hath been the Custom of some of our Kings to honour some of these Companies, by taking their Freedom thereof; as his late Majesty King William was pleased to be made free of the Drapers Company, one of his Predecessors of the Grocers, &c. Each Company, or Mystery, hath a Master annually chosen from among themselves, and hath other subordinate Governors, called Wardens, or Assistants: These do exactly correspond to the general Government of the City, by a Lord-Mayor and Common-Council, who are selected out of these several Companies; so excellent an Harmony there is in that Government.

There are besides 74 other Companies, or Corporations, all enjoying large Privileges, by Royal Charters granted unto them, and most of them fair Halls to meet in.

Mercantilism continued to be the dominant economic system in the eighteenth century, as it had been in the seventeenth. The principal purpose of mercantilism was to strengthen the state by enriching it through trade, industry, and colonial expansion. It was believed that the acquisition of colonies, whose trade and industry were closely regulated by the mother country, would create a favorable balance of trade, ruin European competitors, and bind more closely the ties of Empire. While mercantilism was primarily intended to benefit the mother country, it likewise often helped the colonies. Although the population of the mother country as a whole was to reap the rewards of the system, very often particular groups of merchants and large landowners gained the greatest benefit because of numerous regulations passed by Parliament in favor of special interest groups. The following statutes illustrate the advantages acquired by some of these groups:

241. AN ACT TO ENCOURAGE WOOLEN AND SILK MANUFACTURING (1720)

. . . be it enacted . . . That from and after [December 25, 1722] . . . it shall not be lawful for any person whatsoever to use or wear in Great Britain, in any garment or apparel whatsoever, any printed, painted, stained or dyed callico, under the penalty of forfeiting to the informer the sum of five pounds of lawful money . . . for every such offence, being lawfully convicted thereof by the oath or oaths of one or more credible witness or witnesses before any one or more justice or justices of the peace. . . .

II. And be it further enacted . . . That if any mercer, draper, upholder, or any other person or persons or corporation whatsoever, shall at any time or times after [December 25, 1722] . . . sell, utter or expose to sale any printed, painted, stained or dyed callico, or any bed, chair, cushion, window-curtain or other household stuff or furniture whatsoever, made up of or mixed with . . . callico, unless for exportation thereof, and unless the same shall be cleared outwards accordingly, as is usual in case of sale for exportation, every such person or corporation so offending shall for every offence, being lawfully convicted thereof, forfeit and pay the sum of twenty pounds of lawful money . . . to be recovered as is . . . directed; and every steward or other officer of such corporation, or his deputy, offending herein, and being lawfully convicted of such offence, shall, over and besides the forfeiture or penalty aforesaid, forfeit and lose his office and employment and be incapable to hold the same. . . .

242. AN ACT TO PREVENT THE EXPORTATION OF HATS OUT OF ANY AMERICAN COLONIES (1732)

. . . be it enacted . . . That from and after the twenty ninth day of September [1732] . . . , no hats or felts whatsoever, dyed or undyed, finished or unfinished, shall be shipt, loaden or put on board any ship or vessel in any place or parts within any of the British plantations, . . . by any person or persons whatsoever, and also that no hats or felts, either dyed or undyed, finished or unfinished, shall be loaden upon any horse, cart or other carriage, to the intent or purpose to be exported, transported, shipped off, carried or conveyed out of any of the said British plantations to any other of the British plantations, or to any other place whatsoever, by any person or persons whatsoever. . . .

III. And be it further enacted . . . That it shall and may be lawful to and for any person or persons to seize, take, secure and convey to his Majesty's next warehouse all such hats and felts . . . as he or they shall happen to see, find, know, or discover to be laid on board in any ship . . . or to be brought, carried or laid on shore, at or near the sea, or in any navigable river or water, to the intent . . . to be exported or conveyed out of the said plantations. . . .

243. THE SUGAR ACT (1733)

Whereas the welfare and prosperity of your Majesty's sugar colonies in America are of the greatest consequence and importance to the trade, navigation and strength of this kingdom: and whereas the planters of the said sugar colonies have of late years faire under such great discouragements, that they are unable to improve or carry on the sugar trade upon an equal footing with the foreign sugar colonies, without some advantage and relief be given to them from Great Britain: for remedy whereof, and for the good and welfare of your Majesty's subjects, we . . . the commons of Great Britain . . . have given and granted unto your Majesty the several and respective rates and duties herein after mentioned, and in such manner and form as is herein after expressed, and do most humbly beseech your Majesty that it may be enacted, and be it enacted . . . That from and after [December 25, 1733] . . . there shall be raised, levied, collected and paid, unto and for the use of his Majesty, . . . upon all rum or spirits of the produce or manufacture of any of the colonies or plantations in America, not in the possession or under the dominion of his Majesty, . . . which at any time or times within or during the continuance of this act, shall be imported or brought into any of the colonies . . . in America . . . the sum of nine pence, money of Great Britain, to be paid according to the proportion and value of five shillings and six pence the ounce in silver, for every gallon thereof, and after that rate for any greater or lesser quantity; and upon all molasses or syrups of such foreign produce or manufacture as aforesaid, which shall be imported or brought into any of the said colonies or plantations of or belonging to his Majesty, the sum of six pence of like money for every gallon thereof, and after that rate for any greater or lesser quantity; and upon all sugars and paneles of such foreign growth, produce or manufacture as aforesaid, which shall be imported into any of the said colonies or plantations of or belonging to his Majesty, a duty after the rate of five shillings of like money, for every hundred weight Avoirdupoize, of the said sugar and paneles, and after that rate for a greater or lesser quantity. . . .

> In addition to the regulation and encouragement of trade and industry, Parliament passed laws to protect manufacturers against the destruction of machinery by disgruntled workers who believed it led to unemployment and lower wages, and against agitation by combinations of workers (unions) for higher wages and better working conditions.

244. AN ACT TO PUNISH PERSONS WHO SHALL DESTROY OR PULL DOWN MILLS, OR ENGINES FOR DRAINING COLLIERIES AND MINES, OR BRIDGES, WAGON WAYS, ETC. (1768)

Be it enacted . . . That if any person or persons unlawfully, riotously, and tumultuously assembled together, to the disturbance of the public peace, shall, at any time after [July 1, 1769] . . . unlawfully and with force demolish or pull down, or begin to demolish . . . any wind saw mill, or other wind mill, or any water mill, or other mill which shall have been or shall be erected, or any of the works thereto respectively belonging; that then every such demolishing or pulling down, or beginning to demolish or pull down, shall be adjudged felony without benefit of clergy, and the offenders therein shall be adjudged felons, and shall suffer death as in case of felony without benefit of clergy.

II. And whereas no effectual provision hath heretofore been made for preventing the burning of mills, be it therefore enacted . . . That if any person or persons shall from and after [July 1, 1769] . . . wilfully or maliciously burn, or set fire to, any wind saw mill, or other wind mill, or any water mill, or other mill; such person so offending, being lawfully convicted thereof, shall be adjudged guilty of felony . . . and shall suffer death. . . .

III. And for more effectually preventing the destroying of engines for
draining collieries, coal mines, and other mines, and bridges and waggon
ways used in conveying coals, lead, and other minerals from thence; and also
fences made or to be made for inclosing lands by virtue of acts of parliament; be it further enacted . . . That if any person or persons shall at any
time after [July 1, 1769] . . . wilfully or maliciously set fire to, burn, demolish, pull down, or otherwise destroy or damage, any fire engine or other engine erected, or to be erected, for draining water from collieries or coal
mines; or for drawing coals out of the same; or for draining water from any
mine of lead, tin, copper, or other mineral; or any bridge, waggon way, or
trunk erected, or to be erected, for conveying coals from any colliery or coal
mine, or staith for depositing the same . . . ; or any fence or fences that are
or shall be erected, set up, provided, or made, for dividing or inclosing any
common waste or other lands or grounds . . . ; every such person, being
lawfully convicted of any or either of the said offences, or of causing or
procuring the same to be done, shall be adjudged guilty of felony, and shall
be subject to the like pains and penalties as in cases of felony. . . .

245. AN ACT TO PREVENT UNLAWFUL COMBINATIONS OF WORKMEN (1798)

Whereas great numbers of journeymen manufacturers and workmen in
various parts of this kingdom, have, by unlawful meetings and combinations, endeavoured to obtain advance of their wages, and to effectuate other
illegal purposes; and the laws at present in force against such unlawful conduct have been found to be inadequate to the suppression thereof, whereby it
is become necessary that more effectual provision should be made against
such unlawful combinations; and for preventing such unlawful practices in
future, and for bringing such offenders to more speedy and exemplary justice: . . . be it enacted . . . That, from and after the passing of this act, all
contracts, covenants, and agreements whatsoever, in writing, or not in writing, at any time or times heretofore made or entered into by or between any
journeymen manufacturers or other workmen, or other persons within this
kingdom, for obtaining an advance of wages of them, or any of them, or any
other journeymen manufacturers or workmen, or other persons in any
manufacture, trade, or business, or for lessening or altering their or any of
their usual hours of time of working, or for decreasing the quantity of work,
or for preventing or hindering any person or persons from employing

whomsoever he, she, or they shall think proper to employ in his, her, or their manufacture, trade, or business, or for controlling or anyway affecting any person or persons carrying on any manufacture, trade, or business, in the conduct or management thereof, shall be . . . illegal, null, and void, to all intents and purposes whatsoever.

II. And be it further enacted, That . . . every journeyman, workman, or other person who, after the passing of this act, shall be guilty of any of the said offences, being thereof lawfully convicted, upon his own confession, or the oath or oaths of one or more credible witness or witnesses, before any one or more justice or justices of the peace for the county, riding, division, city, liberty, town, or place, where such offence shall be committed . . . within three calendar months next after the offence shall have been committed, shall, on order of such justice or justices, be committed to and confined in the common gaol within his or their jurisdiction, for any time not exceeding three calendar months, or, at the discretion of such justice or justices, shall be committed to some house of correction, there to remain and be kept to hard labour for any time not exceeding two calendar months. . . .

246. REGULATION OF CHIMNEY SWEEPERS AND THEIR APPRENTICES (1788)

Whereas the laws now in being respecting masters and apprentices do not provide sufficient regulations, so as to prevent various complicated miseries, to which boys employed in climbing and cleansing of chimneys are liable, beyond any other employment whatsoever, in which boys of tender years are engaged: and whereas the misery of the said boys might be much alleviated, if some legal powers and authorities were given for the regulation of chimney sweepers, and their apprentices: may it therefore please your Majesty that it may be enacted; and be it enacted . . . That, from and after [July 5, 1788] . . . it shall and may be lawful to and for the churchwardens and overseers of the poor, for the time being, of the several and respective parishes, townships, or places, within the kingdom of Great Britain, by and with the consent and approbation of two or more of his Majesty's justices of the peace, acting in and for any county, riding, city, town corporate, borough, or division, within Great Britain . . . to bind or put out any boy, or boys, who is, are, or shall be of the age of eight years, or upward; and who is, are, or shall be chargeable, or whose parents are or shall become chargeable to the parish or parishes, or places, where they shall so be; or who shall beg for alms; or by and with the consent of the parent or parents . . .

to be apprentice and apprentices to any person or persons using or exercising the trade, business, or mystery of a chimney sweeper, for so long time, and until such boy or boys shall attain or come to the age of sixteen years; and such binding out any such apprentice and apprentices, shall be as effectual in the law, to all intents and purposes, as if such boy or boys was or were of full age, and by indenture had bound himself or themselves an apprentice or apprentices. . . .

> The Act also provided for the punishment of any persons taking apprentices under eight years of age.

247. THE FACTORY ACT (1802)

Whereas it hath of late become a practice in cotton and woollen mills, and in cotton and woollen factories, to employ a great number of male and female apprentices, and other persons, in the same building; in consequence of which certain regulations are become necessary to preserve the health and morals of such apprentices and other persons; be it therefore enacted . . . That from and after [December 2, 1802] . . . all such mills and factories . . . wherein three or more apprentices, or twenty or more other persons, shall at any time be employed, shall be subject to the several rules and regulations contained in this act. . . .

II. And be it further enacted, That all and every the rooms and apartments in or belonging to any such mill or factory shall, twice at least in every year, be well and sufficiently washed with quick lime and water over every part of the walls and ceiling thereof; and that due care and attention shall be paid by the master and mistress of such mills or factories, to provide a sufficient number of windows and openings in such rooms or apartments, to insure a proper supply of fresh air in and through the same.

III. And be it further enacted, That every such master or mistress shall constantly supply every apprentice, during the term of his or her apprenticeship, with two whole and complete suits of clothing, with suitable linen, stockings, hats, and shoes; one new complete suit being delivered to such apprentice once at least in every year.

IV. And be it further enacted, That no apprentice that now is or hereafter shall be bound to any such master or mistress, shall be employed or compelled to work for more than twelve hours in any one day, (reckoning from six of the clock in the morning to nine of the clock at night), exclusive of the time that may be occupied by such apprentice in eating the necessary meals: provided always, that, from and after [June 1, 1803] . . . , no apprentice shall be employed or compelled to work upon any occasion whatever, between the hours of nine of the clock at night and six of the clock in the morning. . . .

VI. And be it further enacted, That every such apprentice shall be instructed, in some part of every working day, for the first four years at least of his or her apprenticeship . . . in reading, writing, and arithmetick, or either of them, according to the age and abilities of such apprentice, by some discreet and proper person, to be provided and paid by the master or mistress of such apprentice, in some room or place in such mill or factory to be set apart for that purpose. . . .

VII. And be it further enacted, That the room or apartment in which any male apprentice shall sleep, shall be entirely separate and distinct from the room or apartment in which any female apprentice shall sleep; and that not more than two apprentices shall in any case sleep in the same bed. . . .

Eighteenth-century England (particularly the first half) was still dominated politically and socially by the landowners and characterized by small agricultural villages. But society was rapidly changing: alongside the wealthy landholders there had arisen a prosperous industrial bourgeoisie centered in towns, which became more numerous and populous. London remained the center of the national government, but it also became the center of economic and social activity as increasing numbers drifted into the city to seek their fortunes. As will be seen from the following readings, by the end of the century, London was a city of the very rich and the very poor, of fine houses and filthy slums, of genteel society and rioting, and of elegant and inelegant vice.

248. A LONDON COMMON LODGING HOUSE (1788)

He himself holds twenty houses by lease, which are let out, ready furnished. Matters are conducted in a manner so perfectly economical, that though there is no more than one bed in each room, there are usually two or three, and sometimes even four, occupiers of that one room and bed. That the furniture is of an expensive and luxurious kind no one can say, as it consists only of a stump bedstead, a flock bed, a pair of sheets (frequently only one sheet), a blanket or two, a chair or two (generally without backs), and a grate, but mostly without shovel, tongs, and poker. The sheets are usually marked with the name of the owner, and the words "stop thief" are added, for private reasons.

In two adjoining alleys are forty more houses, let out in like sort to inhabitants, in number 400, consisting of whores, pickpockets, footpads, housebreakers, and thieves of every description, from all quarters of the town. But what then? They must have lodgings as well as other people, and if they were to be in the street all night it would be dangerous for the rest of His Majesty's subjects to pass. To avoid suspicion the houses are continually lighted, and kept open all night; and to show that hypocrisy has no place there, what used to be practiced only in private at midnight is now practiced in public at midday.

To accomodate the poor, there are two-penny lodging-houses. One man, in particular, makes up every night thirty-five beds, and takes in men and women, at twopence or threepence a night; but if a man and woman come in together, he receives one shilling a night for the two.

No society can be under better regulations than this is. Thus, for instance, when a prostitute has decoyed a man, and robbed him, the mistress of the house has half the pay and plunder; and if one of these ladies intrude upon that beat and walk which another regards as her exclusive right, the matter is determined, as much greater matters are, by a battle.

Nor can there be reason to fear that this society should ever become so numerous as to be any annoyance to the public; since care is taken that a sufficient number is hanged every session to maintain a balance; and some rooms are always reserved for the reception of the dead bodies, which are brought back after execution to their old lodgings, till they can be otherwise disposed of.

249. NEWGATE PRISON (LONDON, 1754)

It is a large prison and made very strong, the better to secure such sort of criminals which too much fill it. It is a dismal place within. The prisoners are sometimes packed so close together, and the air so corrupted by their stench and nastiness, that it occasions a disease called the Jail Distemper, of which they die by dozens, and cartloads of them are carried out and thrown into a pit in the churchyard of Christ's Church, without ceremony; and so infectious is this distemper, that several judges, jurymen, and lawyers, etc., have taken it off the prisoners when they have been brought to the Old Bailey to be tried, and died soon after. . . . And to this wretched place innocent people are sometimes sent, and loaded with irons before their trial, not to secure them, but to extort money from them by a merciless jailor; for, if they have money to bribe him, they may have the irons as light as they please. The City [of London] have been so good lately as to introduce a ventilator on the top of Newgate, to expel the foul air and to introduce fresh, to preserve the prisoners' health, and the prisoners are many of them kept in distant and more airy prisons, till within a few days of their trials. Sweet herbs, also, are strewed in the court and passages of it, to prevent infection; and the snuffing up vinegar, it is said, is the most likely way to preserve the healths of those that are obliged to attend such trials.

250. SOCIAL ACTIVITIES OF LADIES AND YOUNG MEN OF FASHION

Although the following readings do not illustrate the pastimes of all members of the aristocracy, since many worked hard and contributed significantly to the life of the century, these readings do throw light on some aspects of aristocratic life:

A. *Ladies*

Ladies, chiefly without the company of gentlemen, played cards every evening. The lives of ladies, indeed, were so monotonous and dull that the excitement of cards became necessary for them. A great lady had none of her husband's company except perhaps at dinner: he had his own pursuits, his own friends, often his mistresses as well; he was drunk most nights. The lady, for her part, had no intellectual resources whatever: she read no books; she knew nothing that went on, and cared nothing; her maid dressed her; she had a carriage and four horses—her running footmen before, her hanging footmen behind; she had her town and her country house; her nurse looked after the children; her life was that portentously dull kind of life in which everything is provided and there is nothing left to desire.

Certain sets of ladies met every evening to gamble. They began by putting a shilling for every player under the candlesticks. This offering was not a kind of gift to Lady Fortune, but to the servants; it was supposed to pay for the cards; and as it was renewed every game, there was always a handsome sum at the close of the evening. Some ladies were accused of appropriating the card-money to themselves, an act of meanness strongly denounced.

B. *Fashionable Young Men*

Roughly speaking, a fine gentleman of the Georgian era ordinarily began the day about ten o'clock in the forenoon by a general reception of visitors in his dressing chamber, having first fortified himself for that arduous task by swallowing a cogue of Nantsey. When the last batch of callers had taken their departure he rose and placed himself under the superintendence of his valet for about two hours. Now was brought into requisition his ex-

tensive assortment of perfumery—oil of Venus, spirit of lavender, atar of
roses, spirit of cinnamon or eau-de-luce—among others—with which the
various articles of attire were severally and carefully sprinkled. Then, as
now, there were in vogue certain sweetly-scented soaps which were largely
patronised by fashionable beaux, and with a cake of one of these he freely
lathered his hands and face. He next dabbed his face with scented powder
till it was as white as that of a miller, and plastered his hair with scented
pomatum, and having perfumed his pocket-handkerchief with rose or
jessamine water, tied his cravat and adjusted his periwig, he finally sat down
to dine about three, either alone or in company with his friends. The repast
concluded, he buckled on his sword, brushed his hat with great care, gave it
the 'cock,' placed it with much ceremony on his head, and for a brief space
surveyed himself in the mirror. When quite satisfied with his appearance the
beau took up his cane, ordered a sedan-chair, and proceeded in state to some
coffee-house in the neighbourhood of St. James's (generally White's),
where for about an hour he aired his political views, or tickled the ears of the
company with choice samples of his wit and pleasantry, intermingled with
jests from the newest play or the gist of the latest scandalous story that had
been circulated. Then this 'killing creature,' having first smeared his upper
lip with snuff, hailed a chair and was borne along to the door of the play-
house, where, instead of attending to the performance (his mind would
have recoiled with horror at the thought!), he wandered from pillar to post,
now laughing and chatting with his friends, and then pulling out by turns
his watch and pocket-handkerchief. When the play concluded the beau usually repaired either to the coffee-house or to the residence of some boon companions, with whom he spent the remainder of the night, lending a hand at
crimp, ombre, loo, or whist, over bowls of punch and bottles of claret, until
the small hours of the following morning—not unfrequently being conducted reeling home by a friendly watchman, bribed with sixpence for the
purpose. The sketch here presented is of course open to slight modification,
for absolute likeness in individuals it is impossible to find anywhere, but that
this was the mode of the age in its main outlines is incontestable.

251. LONDON CLUBS AND CLUB LIFE

Political activity in Hanoverian England centered in the clubs and coffee-
houses of London. Although the Whigs were more active clubmen than the
Tories, politicians of all party factions gathered in their clubs to dine, drink,
gamble, develop political strategy, discuss public affairs, or while away their
time in gossip over the latest events at court or in Parliament.

A. *Coffee-Houses*

Sir Walter Besant quotes the following passage from *A Brief and Merry History of Great Britain* on coffee-houses.

There's a prodigious Number of Coffee-Houses in London, after the manner I have seen some in Constantinople. The Outsides have nothing remarkable or worth describing, so that I'll speak only of their Customs, which deserve some Notice, because most of the Men resort to them to pass away the Time. These Coffee-Houses are the constant Rendezvous for Men of Business, as well as the idle People, so that a Man is sooner asked about his Coffee-House than his Lodgings. Besides Coffee, there are many other Liquors, which People cannot well relish at first. They smoak Tobacco, game, and read Papers of Intelligence; here they treat Matters of State, make Leagues with Foreign Princes, break them again, and transact Affairs of the last Consequence to the whole World. In a word, 'tis here the *English* discourse freely of everything, and where they may in a very little time be known; their character likewise may be partly discovered, even by People that are Strangers to the Language, if they appear cool in their Discourses, and attentive to what they hear. They represent these Coffee-Houses as the most agreeable things in *London,* and they are, in my Opinion, very proper Places to find People that a Man has Business with, or to pass away the Time a little more agreeably than he can do at home; but in other respects they are loathsome, full of smoak, like a Guard-Room, and as much crowded. I believe 'tis these Places that furnish the Inhabitants with Slander, for there one hears exact Accounts of everything done in Town, as if it were but a village. . . .

B. *Clubs*

White's Club, . . . a chocolate-house originally, was founded in 1692 . . . and was from the outset a house of high play. Innumerable are the gambling stories connected with the club. Chesterfield, Bubb Dodington, Colley Cibber, Horace Walpole, Charles James Fox, and Selwyn are among the names of the bygone members. No one could be a member unless he was a man of fortune as well as family. Apparently the club was expensive in its charges, for we find that in 1780 the house dinner cost 12s., and in 1797, 10s. 6d. a head without wine; Also that hot suppers could be had at 8s. or cold meat at 4s. Hazard was played all night long and every night. Whist was also played.

Boodle's Club, like White's and Brooke's, was a club for gentlemen—

that is, for men of rank and good family only. Its traditions are less picturesque than those of White's, and the play is not reported to have been so ruinous. Its distinctive points were its entertainments.

C. *Clubs and Politics*

In 1750 Erasmus Mumford, a pamphleteer, alarmed at the politically influential position of White's Club, wrote the following letter to the Club officials:

The Pertinency of my Address to You, my Lords and Gentlemen, on this Occasion, must be evident to every one that knows any thing of your history; as that you are a Club of about Five Hundred, much the greatest Part of you P[ee]rs and M[em]b[e]rs of P[ar]l[iame]nt, who meet every Day at a celebrated Chocolate House near St. James's, with much greater Assiduity than you meet in the Court of Requests; and there, all Party Quarrels being laid aside, all State Questions dropp'd, Whigs and Tories, Placemen and Patroits, Courtiers and Country-Gentlemen, you all agree for the Good of the Public, in the salutary Measures of Ex[cessi]ve G[a]m[bl]ing.

252. NEWCASTLE IN 1758

Mrs. Elizabeth Montague wrote to her sister from the north country town of Newcastle:

The town of Newcastle is horrible, like the ways of thrift it is narrow, dark and dirty, some of the streets so steep one is forced to put a dragchain on the wheels: the night I came I thought I was going to the center. The streets are some of them so narrow, that if the tallow chandler ostentatiously hangs forth his candles, you have a chance to sweep them into your lap as you drive by, and I do not know how it has happened that I have not yet caught a coach full of red herrings, for we scrape the Citty wall on which they hang in great abundance. There are some wide streets and good houses. Sir Walter Blackett's seems a noble habitation.

253. EIGHTEENTH-CENTURY ROADS

For the greater part of the century the roads in England were very bad. Sometimes those in the immediate vicinity of a trading center such as London, Salisbury, and Bristol were quite adequate, but in other parts of the country they were often mere trails. Most roads had no surfacing or foundation and were frequently ungraded. Consequently the weather turned them into quagmires or pitted them with chuckholes so that in some seasons of the year they were impassable.

A. *Young's Description of Roads in Southern England*

The inveterate traveler and *raconteur,* Arthur Young, who seems to have had something to say about almost everything in the eighteenth century, describes some of the roads on which he had traveled during his tours of England. Of the roads in southern England, he says:

Of all the cursed roads that ever disgraced this kingdom, in the very ages of barbarism, none ever equalled that from Billericay to the King's-head at Tilbury. It is for near 12 miles so narrow, that a mouse cannot pass by any carriage; I saw a fellow creep under his waggon to assist me to lift, if possible, my chaise over a hedge. The rutts are of incredible depth—and a pavement of diamonds might as well be sought for as a quarter. The trees everywhere over-grow the road, so that it is totally impervious to the sun, except at a few places: And to add to all the infamous circumstances, which concur to plague a traveller, I must not forget the eternally meeting with chalk-waggons; themselves frequently stuck fast, till a collection of them are in the same situation, that twenty or thirty horses may be tacked to each, to draw them out one by one.

B. *A Good Road*

On the other hand, Young discovered at least one good road in England between Salisbury and Romney.

The road from Salisbury to Romney, and the first four miles from thence to Winchester, I found so remarkably good, that I made particular inquiries concerning their making and mending it. They first lay a foundation of large stones, which they level with smaller ones; then make a layer of chalk on that gravel, and, lastly, another of sifted gravel, exceeding fine; and in some places tending towards a sand. There are many miles as level, as firm, and as free from loose stones as any the finest garden walk I ever beheld; and yet the traffic on it is very great by waggons. But scarcely the print of a wheel is to be seen on it for miles; and I really believe there was not a loose stone to make a horse stumble, nineteen miles from Salisbury.

254. REGULATION OF LAND TRANSPORTATION

The main problem in the improvement of roads (necessitated by the wider market area created by the Industrial Revolution and the growth of towns) was the question of who would bear the cost. Since Elizabethan times, each village, parish, and town was obliged to keep its roads in good repair, but the local community rarely lived up to the letter of the law. Nor, as we have seen, were county roads cared for any better. A solution was found finally in the construction of toll roads by the turnpike trusts. Parliament would authorize a private company to charge tolls on roads it had built on condition that it maintained them as well. The foremost road engineers of the century were John Macadam and Thomas Telford. Their improvement of roads resulted in such an increase in passenger traffic that Parliament passed an Act to regulate the conduct of drivers, and to require guards on stage-coaches and carriages to protect the passengers from highwaymen. The following is an abstract of the Act:

From the 29th day of September, 1790, if the driver of any coach, or other such carriage, drawn by three or more horses, and going for hire, permit more than one person on the coach-box besides himself, and four on the roof; and, if such carriage shall be drawn by less than three horses, more than one person on the coach-box and three persons on the roof (except the driver of a carriage drawn by less than three horses, which shall not go a greater distance than twenty-five miles from the Post-Office in London, nor carry more than one person on the coach-box and four persons on the roof), to be conveyed thereby, he shall pay to the collector of the tolls, at every turnpike-gate thro' which the carriage shall pass, five shillings for each person above the limited number: and if any passenger, above the limited number, be set down, or taken up, whereby the payment of five shillings may be evaded, the driver, on conviction, by his own confession, the view of a Justice, or oath of a credible witness, to be committed to gaol, or the house of correction, for not more than one month, and not less than fourteen days. The five shillings per head beyond the limited number to be levied in the same manner as the tolls.

After the same day, to be painted on the outside of each door of every stage-coach (except mail-coaches) in legible characters, the proprietor's name, and, when different ones, the name of that which shall live within the Bills of Mortality to be used. If the coachman suffer any other person to drive his coach, without consent of passengers, or quit the box without reasonable occasion, or by misconduct overturn the carriage, or endanger the person or property of passengers, to forfeit not more than five pounds, nor less than forty shillings. . . .

255. THE OPENING OF A SESSION OF PARLIAMENT
IN THE EIGHTEENTH CENTURY

The Commons sit in their House promiscuously, only the Speaker hath a Chair, or Seat, fixed towards the upper End thereof; and the Clerk, with his Assistant, sits near him at the Table, just below the Speaker's Chair. The Members of the House of Commons never had any Robes, as the Lords ever had, except the Speaker and Clerks, who always in the House wear Gowns, as Professors of the Law in Term-time do; and the four Members of the City of London, the first Day of every new Parliament wear Scarlet-Gowns, and sit altogether on the Right-hand of the Chair, next to the Speaker.

The Time of Sitting in Parliament is upon any Day in the Morning; only upon some high Festivals, or Fast-Days, and Sundays, it hath not been usual to assemble, but upon the most urgent Occasions. The Speaker always adjourns the House at Nine of the Clock in the Morning of such Day as the House agrees to adjourn to; though the House seldom meets 'till Twelve.

Upon the Day prefix'd by the King in the Writ of Summons, the King comes in Person; if to Westminister, where Parliaments of late Years have constantly been held, at his Arrival there, twenty-one Great Guns on the other Side of the River of Thames are discharged, as they are again at his Majesty's Return from the House of Lords; in the Room next to which, called the Prince's Chamber, the King puts on his Crown and Robes, and from thence is conducted into the House of Lords by the Lord Great Chamberlain; where being seated with his Crown on his Head, and cloathed in his Royal Robes, he sends for the Commons by the Gentleman-Usher of the Black-Rod, who at the Bar of the House makes a Bow, and advancing a few Steps, a Second and a Third, saying, Gentlemen of the House of Commons, the King commands this Honourable House to attend him immediately in the House of Peers; and then retiring backwards, bowing, withdraws; and the Commons forthwith attending his Majesty in the House of Lords, are, in the King's Name, by the Lord-Chancellor, or Keeper, commanded to choose them a Speaker. Whereupon they returning to their own House, make Choice of one of their own Members, whom afterwards, upon another Day appointed, they present to the King and if approved of by his Majesty sitting on the Throne, all the Lords Spiritual and Temporal being in their Robes of Scarlet, he petitions his Majesty, That the Commons may have, during their Sitting, free Access to his Majesty, Freedom of Speech in their own House, and Freedom from Arrests. After which

the King makes his Speech in both Houses, the whole House of Commons
being presumed to be at the Bar of the House of Lords.

256. CORRUPTION AND BRIBERY IN PARLIAMENTARY ELECTIONS

A great deal of corruption and bribery attended the elections of members of
Parliament, as the following excerpts fully illustrate.

A. Bribery

The case made out for Viscount Grimston and Joshua Lomax against William Clayton and William Gore, "the sitting" M.P.s, in St. Albans in 1721 is
typical.

To prove the riotous behaviour of the agents of the sitting members before and at the election. That the cry was "Down with the Roundheads! No
King George's justices!" That the petitioners' persons were assaulted out of
the houses of the late mayor and present mayor; the windows of several of
the inhabitants were broken, and the mob was encouraged by Mr. Gape,
junior, who, with his drawn sword, begun the riot on the election day, and
caused the music to play "The King shall enjoy his own again," and the
meeting-houses were threatened to be pulled down, and many outrages
committed. [Eleven Witnesses are to prove these things].

[Details as to the poll here follow, which show a majority of legal votes
in favour of the petitioners].

"There being so considerable a majority already proved for the petitioners, the said petitioners are willing to decline at present any further disqualification of votes which they can prove by threats, and bribes were procured
against them; but if the sitting members' councel refuse to confine their defence to the before-mentioned list, then the case as to bribery is as follows,
viz.:—

"The sitting members, or their agents, perceiving they had very much
disobliged the inhabitants by making foreign freemen and threatening them
that they should never more have votes, and apprehending the parliament
would set aside their pretended freemen, came to a resolution of bribing
every inhabitant and legal freeman that would receive the same and promise
to vote for the sitting members, and a public office of bribery was fixed at the
town clerk's house, and as agents abroad fixed the prices, the party agreeing
went to the said office and received the same, signing a note in the following
or like words:—'Received, March 14th, 1721, of Thomas Gape, esquire, ten
pounds ten shillings, upon the consideration that I am to vote for William
Gore and William Clayton, esquires, at the next election of burgesses in par-

liament for the burrough of St. Albans, and I do promise to repay the same again if I do not vote as aforesaid. Witness my hand.' Which notes were usually witnessed by the town clerk and his servant. The number of notes so given and electors who thereupon were influenced and did vote for the sitting members were upwards of 150, as the said town clerk hath acknowledged; which being deducted from their poll reduced them to less than 100, and, indeed, so notorious and public was the bribery which the agents of the sitting members carried on that the particular sums the electors received, and at whose hands, was matter of public conversation, insomuch that the bribed made no scruple to give as a reason why they could not vote for the petitioners, viz.: That they were listed by such an one for such a sum to vote for the sitting members. . . .

B. *Manipulation of Elections*

Vast sums were spent by candidates on parliamentary elections. Horace Walpole says he was told that £55,000 would not cover the expenses of an Oxfordshire candidate. In the election of 1753 the total costs of the general election came to £240,000. The manner in which seats in Parliament were "managed," and families "taken care of" is revealed in a letter written to the Duke of Bedford by Alderman Thomas Beckford in May, 1754.

I hope your Grace will excuse the liberty I take in troubling you with the following relation. As I look on myself tolerably zealous for the liberty of this country, and used my utmost endeavours to get as many friends elected into the new Parliament as I well could, with prudence in respect to my fortune; and I think I have no reason to complain of want of success, having carried three cities and two boroughs. Four seats were originally intended for the four brothers, and the fifth for a good friend and patriot. Here were my original intentions; but I was prevented having my younger brother chosen by an old relation, Mr. Thomas Beckford of Ashted, on whom my brothers have great dependence; as he was unwilling to have my youngest brother, Francis, elected, I gave a promise to Sir John Phillips that he should be the man to succeed me at Petersfield, and thus matters stood when I received a letter from my brother Richard, member for Bristol, wherein he does most earnestly desire that I will use my utmost endeavours to get all four brothers returned, notwithstanding the opposition of Mr. Thomas Beckford to my original plan. The favour I have to ask of your Grace is that, in case you should have a vacancy in any of your boroughs, to think of this brother of mine, and I will venture to say there are not four men in the kingdom more zealously attached to the Protestant Succession, and to the liberties of the people; more desirous of joining in every attempt to place the administration of public affairs in abler hands than we are.

C. *Violence Attending Elections*

Violence frequently occurred in these elections, and it increased in intensity as the century went on. Emily Climenson describes the election in Windsor in 1757 in this letter to Mrs. Montague:

I know you will be curious to hear how the famous election has been carried at Windsor, and the greatest pleasure I can have is to impart any to you. Mr. Fox [Henry Fox] had a majority of 52, the Mayor, who is Mr. Bowles' friend, owns he had a legal majority of nine. The boxers and the bruisers Mr. Fox had on his side beat the Windsor mob out of the Field, but they had once the courage to attack Mr. Fox's person, and pulled off his wig, and threw it in his face. In short the affair has been very tumultuous. The town is quiet, none are actually dead, but four or five are dangerously ill, and the Doctors and Apothecarys had a great harvest of bruises and fractures. . . . The ladies wore party gowns, Fox's is partly yellow and green, and the others blue; our sex have a wise way of expressing their political principles.

D. *John Wilkes Stands for Parliament (1768)*

A part of the rioting that accompanied the election in which John Wilkes was a candidate was attributable to the reprehensible character of his public life. In the *Memoirs of George III,* John Jesse describes the most publicized of his activities as follows:

But, whatever agreeable or redeeming qualities Wilkes may have possessed, they were completely thrown into the shade by the unblushing licentiousness of his private life. His profligacy shocked even the profligate. He was one of that debauched fraternity, consisting of men of wit and fashion, who, having restored and fitted up the ruins of Medmenham Abbey, near Marlow, adopted the monastic garb at their convivial meetings, and instituted the most immodest rites and ribald mysteries within its sacred walls. The ruins of the old abbey, formerly a convent of Cistercian monks, still stands, surrounded by rich meadows, by hanging woods, and venerable elms, in a beautiful and secluded spot on the banks of the Thames. . . . In the pleasure-grounds, the temples, statues, and inscriptions all savoured of the impure tastes and irreverent wit of the modern denizens of the abbey. The members of the new order styled themselves Franciscans, in honour of their father abbot, Sir Francis Dashwood.

> Dashwood shall pour from a Communion cup
> Libations to the Goddess without eyes,
> And hob and nob in cider and excise.

Each monk had his cell and appropriate name. In the chapel—the embellishments of which were of so immodest a character that none but the initiated were permitted access to it—the monks not only adapted the sacred rites of the Roman Catholic Church to the profane worship of Bacchus and Venus, but are said to have carried their blasphemy to such a pitch as to administer the Eucharist to an ape. . . .

257. REPEAL OF THE LAWS AGAINST WITCHCRAFT (1736)

The softening of human relationships in the eighteenth century was reflected in a fresh attitude toward witchcraft. In the last part of the seventeenth century judges became less willing to send accused witches for trial at the Assizes, and the last judicial execution for witchcraft came in 1712. In 1736, the following statute repealed the English and Scottish laws against witchcraft:

Be it enacted . . . That the statute made in the first year of the reign of King James the First, intituled, An act against conjuration, witchcraft, and dealing with evil and wicked spirits, shall, from the twenty fourth day of June next, be repealed and utterly void and of none effect. . . .

II. And be it further enacted . . . That from and after the said twenty fourth day of June, the act passed in the parliament of Scotland in the ninth parliament of Queen Mary . . . shall be . . . repealed.

III. And be it further enacted, That from and after the said twenty fourth day of June, no prosecution, suit, or proceeding, shall be commenced or carried on against any person or persons for witchcraft, sorcery, inchantment, or conjuration, or for charging another with any such offence, in any court whatsoever in Great Britain. . . .

258. THE CHURCH OF ENGLAND IN THE EIGHTEENTH CENTURY

The general religious milieu of the age was cold, unspiritual, and formal. This condition had resulted partly from the reaction against the intense theological controversies that had characterized the seventeenth century, partly from the effects of the Enlightenment on the Continent, and partly from the weakening of religious zeal and lack of adequate training among some of the clergy. By mid-century, according to Bishop Butler of Bristol, author of the *Analogy of Religion* (1736), the influence of religion was "wearing out of the mind of men," and the generality of folk practically disregarded it. This attitude was also reflected in all ranks of the clergy from bishops to curates.

A. *Poverty of the Parochial Clergy*

Lord Macaulay could just as properly have been describing the eighteenth- as well as the late seventeenth-century parochial priesthood when he wrote:

In general the divine who quitted his chaplainship for a benefice and a wife found that he had only exchanged one class of vexations for another. Not one living in fifty enable the incumbent to bring up a family comfortably. As children multiplied and grew, the household of the priest became more and more beggarly. Holes appeared more and more plainly in the thatch of his parsonage and in his single cassock. Often it was only by toiling on his glebe, by feeding swine, and by loading dung-carts, that he could obtain daily bread; nor did his utmost exertions always prevent the bailiffs from taking his concordance and his inkstand in execution. It was a white day on which he was admitted into the kitchen of a great house, and regaled by the servants with cold meat and ale. His children were brought up like the children of the neighboring peasantry. His boys followed the plough; and his girls went out to service. Study he found impossible; for the advowson of his living would hardly have sold for a sum sufficient to purchase a good theological library; and he might be considered as unusually lucky if he had ten or twelve dog-eared volumes among the pots and pans on his shelves. Even a keen and strong intellect might be expected to rust in so unfavourable a situation.

B. *Affluence and Apathy of Some Bishops*

John Wilson Cooker, editor of Lord Hervey's *Memoirs*, gives the following account of a discussion Hervey had with the royal family relating to a bishop:

At his return to the Queen's side the Queen used often to send for Lord Hervey to entertain them till they retired, which was generally at eleven. One evening among the rest, as soon as Lord Hervey came into the room, the Queen, who was knitting whilst the King walked backwards and forwards, began jocosely to attack Lord Hervey upon an answer just published to a book of his friend Bishop Hoadley's on the Sacrament, in which the Bishop was very ill treated; but before she had uttered half what she had a mind to say, the King interrupted her, and told her she always loved talking

of such nonsense and things she knew nothing of; adding, that, if it were
not for such foolish people loving to talk of those things when they were
written, the fools who wrote upon them would never think of publishing
their nonsense, and disturbing the Government with impertinent disputes
that nobody of any sense ever troubled himself about. The Queen bowed,
and said, "Sir, I only did it to let Lord Hervey know that his friend's book
had not met with that general approbation he had pretended." "A pretty fellow for a friend!" said the King, turning to Lord Hervey. "Pray what is it
that charms you in him? His pretty limping gait" (and then he acted the
Bishop's lameness), "or his nasty stinking breath?—phaugh!—or his silly
laugh, when he grins in your face for nothing, and shows his nasty rotten
teeth? Or is it his great honesty that charms your Lordship?—his asking a
thing of me for one man, and, when he came to have it in his own power to
bestow, refusing the Queen to give it to the very man for whom he had
asked it? Or do you admire his conscience that makes him now put out a
book that, till he was Bishop of Winchester, for fear his conscience might
hurt his preferment, he kept locked up in his chest? Is his conscience so
much improved beyond what it was when he was Bishop of Bangor, or
Hereford, or Salisbury (for this book, I hear, was written so long ago)?
or was it that he would not risk losing a shilling a-year more whilst there
was anything better to be got than what he had? My Lord, I am very sorry
you choose your friends so ill; but I cannot help saying, if the Bishop of
Winchester is your friend, you have a great puppy and a very dull fellow
and a great rascal for your friend. It is a very pretty thing for such
scoundrels, when they are raised by favour so much above their desert, to be
talking and writing their stuff, to give trouble to the Government that has
showed them that favour; and very modest in a canting hypocritical knave
to be crying, 'The kingdom of Christ is not of this world,' at the same time
that he, as Christ's ambassador, receives 6000*l.* or 7000*l.* a-year. But he is just
the same thing in the Church that he is in the Government, and as ready to
receive the best pay for preaching the Bible, though he does not believe a
word of it, as he is to take favours from the Crown, though, by his republi-
can spirit and doctrine, he would be glad to abolish its power.

259. THE RISE OF METHODISM

After 1729, a small group of students at Oxford protested against the spiritual apathy of the Anglican Church, and, because of their methodical
manner of life, were dubbed "Methodists." They fasted regularly, discussed

the Bible together, visited hospitals and prisons, and lived exemplary lives. The best known leaders of this group were George Whitefield and John and Charles Wesley (the latter becoming famous for the numerous hymns which he wrote).

John Wesley was born in 1703, educated at Lincoln College, Oxford, and ordained to the ministry in 1725. He was deeply attached to the Established Church, and sought to imbue it with evangelical zeal. At first the Methodists were treated with contempt, but by the end of the century they were a well-established and numerous sect. The following selections from John Wesley's letters are explanatory of the man and the movement.

To the King's Most Excellent Majesty (George II.)

The humble Address of the Societies in England and Wales in derision called Methodists.

[LONDON, *March* 5, 1744.]

MOST GRACIOUS SOVEREIGN,—So inconsiderable as we are, 'a people scattered and peeled, and trodden underfoot from the beginning hitherto,' we should in nowise have presumed, even on this great occasion, to open our lips to your Majesty, had we not been induced, indeed constrained to do so, by two considerations: the one, that in spite of all our remonstrances on that head, we are continually represented as a peculiar sect of men, separating ourselves from the Established Church; the other, that we are still traduced as inclined to Popery, and consequently as disaffected to your Majesty.

Upon these considerations we think it incumbent upon us, if we must stand as a distinct body from our brothers, to tender for ourselves our most dutiful regards to your sacred Majesty: and to declare, in the presence of Him we serve, the King of kings and Lord of lords, that we are a part (however mean) of that Protestant Church, established in these kingdoms: That we unite together for this, and no other end—to promote, so far as we may be capable, justice, mercy, and truth; the glory of God, and peace and good-will among men: That we detest and abhor the fundamental doctrines of the Church of Rome, and are steadily attached to your Majesty's royal person and illustrious House.

We cannot, indeed, say or do either more or less than we apprehend consistent with the written word of God; but we are ready to obey your Majesty to the uttermost, in all things which we conceive agreeable thereto. And we earnestly exhort all with whom we converse, as they fear God, to honour the King. . . .

To a Friend.

PENRYN, CORNWALL, *September* 20, 1757.

DEAR SIR,—The longer I am absent from London, and the more I attend the service of the Church in other places, the more I am convinced of the unspeakable advantage which the people called Methodists enjoy. I mean with regard to public worship, particularly on the Lord's Day. The church where they assemble is not gay or splendid, which might have been a hindrance on the one hand; nor sordid or dirty, which might give distaste on the other; but plain as well as clean. The persons who assemble there are not a giddy crowd who come chiefly to see and be seen; nor a company of goodly, formal, outside Christians whose religion lies in a dull round of duties; but a people most of whom do, and the rest earnestly seek to, worship God in spirit and in truth. Accordingly they do not spend their time there in bowing and curtsying, or in staring about them; but in looking upward and looking inward, in hearkening to the voice of God, and pouring out their hearts before Him.

It is also no small advantage that the person who reads prayers (though not always the same, yet) is always one who may be supposed to speak from his heart, one whose life is no reproach to his profession; and one who performs that solemn part of divine service, not in a careless, hurrying, slovenly manner, but seriously and slowly, as becomes him who is transacting so high an affair between God and man.

Nor are their solemn addresses to God interrupted either by the formal drawl of a parish clerk or the screaming of boys, who bawl out what they neither feel nor understand, or the unseasonable and unmeaning impertinence of a voluntary on the organ. When it is seasonable to sing praise to God, they do it with the spirit, and with the understanding also; not in the miserable, scandalous doggerel of Hopkins and Sternhold, but in psalms and hymns which are both sense and poetry: such as would sooner provoke a critic to turn Christian than a Christian to turn critic. What they sing is therefore a proper continuation of the spiritual and reasonable service, being selected for that end (not by a poor humdrum wretch who can scarce read what he drones out with such an air of importance, but) by one who knows what he is about, and how to connect the preceding with the following part of the service. Nor does he take just 'two staves,' but more or less, as may best raise the soul to God; especially when sung in well-composed and well-adapted tunes, not by a handful of wild, unawakened striplings, but by a whole serious congregation; and these, not lolling at ease or in the indecent posture of sitting, drawling out one word after another, but all standing before God and praising Him lustily, and with a good courage.

Nor is it a little advantage as to the next part of the service, to hear a preacher whom you know to live as he speaks, speaking the genuine gospel of present salvation through faith, wrought in the heart by the Holy Ghost; declaring present, free, full justification, and enforcing every branch of inward and outward holiness. And this you hear done in the most clear, plain, simple, unaffected language; yet with an earnestness becoming the importance of the subject, and with the demonstration of the Spirit.

With regard to the last and most awful part of divine service, the celebration of the Lord's Supper, although we cannot say that either the unworthiness of the minister or the unholiness of some of the communicants deprives the rest of a blessing from God, yet do they greatly lessen the comfort of receiving. But these discouragements are removed from you: you have proof that he who administers fears God: and you have no reason to believe that any of your fellow-communicants walk unworthy of their profession. Add to this that the whole service is performed in a decent and solemn manner, is enlivened by hymns suitable to the occasion, and concluded with prayer that comes not out of feigned lips. . . .

260. THE LORD GEORGE GORDON RIOTS (1780)

The riots of 1780 [occurred] when Lord George Gordon raised a no-popery cry, and assembled many thousand persons in St. George's Fields, to accompany him to the House of Commons, with a petition for the repeal of the act passed for the relief of the Roman Catholics in the preceding session. The petition was, of course, rejected; which being communicated to the mob by Lord George, they dispersed for a while, but on that evening commenced their work of mischief, destroying two Catholic chapels in Duke-street and Warwick-street: Newgate and all the other prisons were likewise fired; the Bank was attempted; and the riot was not quelled until 210 persons were killed and 248 wounded, of whom seventy-five died in the hospitals. Lord George was committed to the Tower; and many of the ringleaders, after being tried by special commissioners, suffered the extreme penalty of the law.

261. THE NUMERICAL STRENGTH OF CHURCHES (1811)

Returns of the Archbishops and Bishops of the number of Churches and Chapels of the Church of England in every parish of 1000 persons and upwards; also of the number of other places of worship NOT of the establishment. (Ordered to be printed by the House of Lords, April 5, 1811.)

DIOCESE.	Churches and Chapels of the Establishment.	Chapels and Meeting-Houses NOT of the Establishment, besides many private houses used for religious worship, not enumerated.
1 Bath and Wells	78	103
2 Bangor	52	99
3 Bristol	59	71
4 Canterbury	84	113
5 Carlisle	49	39
6 Chester	352	439
7 Chichester	47	58
8 Durham	116	175
9 Ely	22	32
10 Exeter	180	245
11 Gloucester	46	76
12 Hereford	51	42
13 Llandaff	21	45
14 Lincoln	165	269
15 Lichfield and Coventry	190	288
16 London	187	265
17 Norwich	78	114
18 Oxford	50	39
19 Peterborough	20	36
20 Rochester	36	44
21 Salisbury	135	142
22 St. Asaph	49	95
23 Winchester	193	164
24 Worcester	66	60
25 York	221	404
Total	2547	3457

N.B. The smaller parishes, not amounting to 1000 inhabitants, were not returned.

262. THE STATE OF MEDICINE AND MEDICAL PRACTICE IN THE EIGHTEENTH CENTURY

The population of England increased slowly from 1710 to 1780, an increase attributable more to the declining death rate than to the higher birth rate. The death rate declined for several reasons. Greater attention was paid to cleanliness and more persons could afford to purchase soap, which, comparatively speaking, was quite expensive. There were increased efforts by municipal authorities to keep streets clear of garbage and refuse. Food was cheaper and more plentiful. Midwives, physicians, and surgeons grew more skilled. Inoculation against certain diseases, notably smallpox, although not widely trusted in the eighteenth century, helped to allay deaths from contagious disease.

A. *Principal Causes and the Number of Deaths in London*

The following is a digest of a list of the principal diseases and the number of deaths in London for the year 1770 as recorded by Sir Walter Besant:

Convulsions	6156
Consumption	4809
Fever, malignant fever, scarlet fever, spotted fever, and purples	2273
Small-pox	1660
Aged	1512
Dropsy	1024
Abortive and stillborn	696
Asthma and Phthisic	590
Teeth	809
Apoplexy and suddenly	223
Childbed	172
Cough and whooping-cough	249
Jaundice	156
Measles	115
Inflamation	79
Gout	91

B. *The Universal "Cure": Bleeding*

For each of these diseases there were, of course, a multitude of "cures." The most common cure for fever, convulsions, and melancholy was bleeding, which was done in this fashion:

First of all, if it was done in the presence of a physician, it must be done by a surgeon. Poor people, however, were content to go to an apothecary, or even to a barber. Sometimes it was performed on the neck; in the case of a woman, however, this was seldom the place chosen, because even the slight puncture of a lancet might make a disfiguring mark. The arm was therefore chosen.

They began by throwing a handkerchief over the patient's head, so that she should see nothing of the blood. Then the physician placed a ball of worsted in the patient's hand. When she pressed it, the veins of the arm swelled. The physician then took the basin. By long practice he knew exactly how far the fountain of blood would spring forth; the surgeon just touched with his lancet a blue vein; the jet of blood leaped out; the physician caught it dexterously, so that not a single drop was spilled. His task was to order the stop of the blood-letting when the proper amount had been taken. In cases of fever they took eight ounces—two and a half for health and five and a half for fever; this was called bleeding *ad defectionem,* because the patient generally fainted from loss of blood; or *ad plenum rivuum*—a full bleeding. Taraxacum was then administered, with Rhenish wine, or broth in which porage had been steeped.

C. *Two Prescriptions for Ague*

In 1743 Mrs. Delaney wrote to Mrs. Dewes of two "infallible receipts" for ague:

1. Pounded ginger, made into a paste with brandy, spread on sheep's leather, and a plaster of it laid over the stomach. 2. A spider put into a goose-quill, well sealed and secured, and hung about the child's neck as low as the pit of the stomach. Either of these I am assured will ease. . . .

D. *Mental Illness*

Mental disorders were understandably the most difficult of all ailments to diagnose and to treat. The Earl of Chatham, suffering from what was perhaps manic depression, had gone to take the baths at Tunbridge Wells. From there, on May 27, 1753, a Mr. West wrote to Mrs. Montague:

Your kind letter . . . came very seasonably to relieve my spirits which were much sunk by the extreme dejection which appears to-day in Mr. Pitt, from a night passed entirely without sleep, notwithstanding all the precautions which were taken within doors to make it still and quiet, and the accidental tranquillity arising from the present emptiness and desolation of this place, to which no other invalids, except ourselves are yet arrived, or even expected to arrive as yet. He began to drink the waters to-day, but as they are sometimes very slow in their operations, I much fear that both he and those friends who cannot help sympathizing with him, will suffer a great deal before the wished-for effect will take place, for this *Insomnium* his Physicians have prescribed Opiates, a medicine which, in this case, though they may procure a temporary ease, yet often after recoil upon the spirits. He seems inclined to take Musk, and intends to talk with Molly about it. I think his Physicians have been to blame in giving all their attention to the disorder in his bowels, and not sufficiently regarding the Distemperature of his spirits, a Disease much more to be apprehended than the other; while he continues under this Oppression, I am afraid it will be impossible for me to leave him, as he fancies me of the greatest use to him as a friend, and a comforter, but I hope in God he will soon find some alteration for the better, of which I shall be glad to give you the earliest information . . . .

E. *The Medical Profession in 1792*

Medical men were not highly respected and were often made the butt of ridicule. In an article, "Friendly Hints to the Modern Practice of Physicians," an anonymous author wrote:

Men are never such dupes as when they are ill, or fancy themselves so. Physicians need not possess talents, or have much knowledge of their profession; it is sufficient if they have skill and address to captivate the understanding of a few fashionable but weak women, or if they write in quantity to satisfy the avarice of apothecaries.

Ladies of the bon ton must have tonish physicians; and tonish physicians are useful to give advice in more things than one.

Women, especially old ones, are quacks. These must be humoured; by no means contradicted, at least abruptly. Partly by gratifying their vanity, partly by surprising them, by divulging some nostrums as wonderful arcana, those physicians who have the most knowledge of the world, and the best talents for pleasing, will ingratiate themselves into the good opinion of females, when men of profound learning, but awkward manners, will be neglected. On these occasions the nurses are entitled to their share of adulation. The fact is, that a case that requires great penetration, does not occur once in a hundred instances; and Nature being left to herself, a physician often acquires credit where no credit is due.

The recommendation of a brother physician is the most suspicious thing imaginable, either for a consultation, or to prescribe in the absence of the family doctor. In the first instance, it is meant only as a cloke or a pretence to enlarge fees. In the second, a man recommends one who in his turn will recommend him; in like manner as the master of the Black Bear in one town will recommend the publican of the White Bear in another. . . .

263. EIGHTEENTH-CENTURY UNIVERSITIES

The University of Oxford contributed very little to the life of eighteenth-century England. In fact, it was at a much lower ebb scholastically than it had been in the seventeenth century. Most of the students came from aristocratic families and preferred gambling, drinking, and wenching to study. They received degrees simply by fulfilling residency requirements and without taking examinations.

A. *Regulation of Students' Personal Conduct*
(*Described by an Anonymous Author*)

The Discipline of these Colleges and Halls is very exact. First, All that intend to take their first Degree, that of Bachelor of Arts, are to take their Diet and Lodging, and have a Tutor constantly in some College or Hall; then they are to perform all exercises, to be subject to all Statutes, and to the Head of the House. They are never to be seen abroad out of their Chambers, much less out of their Colleges, without their Caps and Gowns; an excellent Order, and no where observed in foreign Parts but in Salamancha, Alcala de Henares, called in Latin, *Complutum,* and the rest of the Universities of Spain, and in Conimbra and Evora in Portugal. Their Gowns are all to be black, only the Sons of the higher Nobility are herein indulged; for they may wear rich flowered Silk Gowns, and all Doctors Scarlet Robes.

B. *An Oxford Education*

Among others, Charles James Fox, Edward Gibbon, and Jonathan Swift have testified to the inadequacy of an Oxford education. On August 6, 1767, Fox wrote to a friend:

In the last letter I received from you, before that I have now before me, you were so good as to enquire what studies I had pursued at Oxford. To tell you the truth, I have read a great deal since you left England, and have learnt nothing. I employed almost my whole time at Oxford in the mathematical and classical knowledge, but more particularly in the latter, so that I understand Latin and Greek tolerably well. I am totally ignorant in every part of useful knowledge. I am more convinced every day how little advantage there is in being what at school and the university is called a good scholar: one receives a good deal of amusement from it, but that is all. . . .

C. *Gibbon at Oxford*

In Gibbons' *Autobiography,* he writes of the years (1752–1753) he spent at Oxford as follows:

The stately buildings of Oxford, and especially of Magdalen College, excite the admiration of a stranger; the apparent decencies of habit and order solicit his reverence: and the cloysters, the walks, and the libraries are appropriated to the use of a studious and contemplative life. I was delighted with the novelty of the scene; my dress and rank of a gentleman-commoner, a competent allowance, and a spacious apartment elated my childish vanity with the idea of manly independence. But I must blush for myself or for my teachers, when I declare that, of all the years of my life, the fourteen months which I spent at Oxford were most compleately lost for every purpose of improvement; and the University will not be ambitious of a son who disclaims all sense of filial piety and gratitude. I am willing to make every reasonable abatement for my tender age, insufficient preparation, and short residence. Yet I must confess the presumptuous belief that neither my temper nor my talents were averse to the lessons of science; that the discipline of well-regulated studies might have inflamed the ardour and restrained the wanderings of youth; and that some share of reproach will adhere to the Academical institution which could damp every spark of industry in a curious and active mind. . . .

D. *Jonathan Swift on the Universities*

It is true, I have known an academical education to have been exploded in public assemblies; and have heard more than one or two persons of high rank declare, they could learn nothing more at Oxford and Cambridge, than to drink ale and smoke tobacco; wherein I firmly believed them, and could have added some hundred examples from my own observation in one of those universities; but they all were of young heirs sent thither only for form; either from schools, where they were not suffered by their careful parents to stay above three months in the year; or from under the management of French family tutors, who yet often attended them to their college, to prevent all possibility of their improvement; but I never yet knew any one person of quality, who followed his studies at the university, and carried away his just proportion of learning, that was not ready upon all occasions to celebrate and defend that course of education, and to prove a patron of learned men.

264. EIGHTEENTH-CENTURY CAMBRIDGE

According to the poet, Thomas Gray, the same situation existed at Cambridge as at Oxford. He wrote of it:

Surely it was of this place, now Cambridge, but formerly known by the name of Babylon, that the prophet spoke when he said "the wild beasts of the desert shall dwell there, and their houses shall be full of doleful creatures, and owls shall build there, and satyrs shall dance there; their forts and towers shall be a den for ever, a joy of wild asses," etc., etc. You must know that I do not take degrees, and after this term shall have nothing more of college impertinences to undergo. I have endured lectures daily and hourly since I came last. Must I plunge into metaphysics? Alas! I cannot see in the dark; nature has not furnished me with the optics of a cat. Must I pore upon mathematics? Alas! I cannot be in too much light; I am no eagle. It is very possible that two and two make four, but I would not give four farthings to demonstrate this ever so clearly.

265. THE THEATER IN THE EIGHTEENTH CENTURY

Much has been written about the immorality of the stage in the Restoration period, but it grew worse in the eighteenth century.

A. *Censorship of the Theater*

In his *Memoirs of Walpole,* William Coxe explains the reasons for this change as arising from the fact that the Lord Chancellor's authority as the official censor was not clearly defined. Coxe writes:

But as this exercise of his power had been always attended with much unpopularity, it was seldom exerted. Numerous theatres were erected in different parts of the metropolis, in which the actors performed without licence or authority. To prevent this, several attempts were made to enforce the laws then existing. An actor, who performed on the theatre of the Haymarket, without licence, was taken from the stage, by the warrant of a justice of peace, and committed to Bridewell, as coming under the penalty of the vagrant act. The legality of the committment was disputed; a trial ensued; it was decided, that the comedian being a house-keeper, and having a vote for electing members of parliament, did not come within the description of the said act; and he was discharged amidst the loud acclamations of the populace. The issue of this trial gave full scope to the licentiousness of the stage, and took away all hopes of restraining the number of playhouses. . . .

The attempt of Sir John Barnard [an M. P.] having thus failed [to restrain by Parliamentary statute the number of houses for playing of interludes, and for regulating the players] the immorality of the drama increased, and the most indecent, seditious, and blasphemous pieces were performed, and resorted to with incredible eagerness. Among those who principally supported this low ribaldry was the celebrated Henry Fielding, who, though he never shone in the higher line of perfect comedy, wrote these dramatic satires in a style agreeable to the populace. One of his pieces, called Pasquin, which was acted in the theatre at the Haymarket, ridiculed, in the grossest terms, the three professions of divinity, law, and physic, and gave offence to persons of morality. . . .

B. *Rioting at the Theater*

In the absence of an effective censorship in the early and middle years of the century, the immorality of the drama increased along with its popularity. The audiences grew restless and often first-rate riots occurred. Horace Walpole describes one such affair in a letter to Sir Horace Mann (1744):

The town [London] has been trying all this winter to beat pantomimes off the stage, very boisterously; for it is the way here to make even an affair of taste and sense a matter of riot and arms. Fleetwood, the master of Drury-Lane, has omitted nothing to support them, as they supported his house. About ten days ago, he let into the pit great numbers of Bear-garden bruisers (that is the term), to knock down everybody that hissed. The pit rallied their forces, and drove them out: I was sitting very quietly in the side-boxes, contemplating all this. On a sudden the curtain flew up, and discovered the whole stage filled with blackguards, armed with bludgeons and clubs, to menace the audience. . . .

C. *A Frenchman's View of the English Theater*

Two decades later, the number of theaters in London and in the other principal cities having greatly increased, the Frenchman M. G. Dourx wrote an article, "An Animadversion on the Principal Follies of the English," which was reprinted as follows in the *Annual Register:*

Some of our nation consider the English stage, which affords that people so much delight, as a proof of their barbarity. Their tragedies, it is true, though interesting and replete with beauties, are nevertheless dramatic monsters, half butchery and half farce. Grotesque character, and extravagant pleasantry, constitute the chief part of their comedies: in one of these the devil enters sneezing, and somebody says to the devil, God bless you. They are not however all of this stamp: they have even some in a very good taste; but there are hardly any which give us an advantageous idea of the English nation; though it is from the theatre that a stranger forms his opinion of the manners of a people. The English comic poets do not endeavour to paint their countrymen such as they are: for they are said to possess as much humanity as reason. . . .

D. *Popular Plays in the 1780's*

In the 1780's the theater was very popular, and although the quality of many of the plays was far from ideal, they were improving. William C. Sydney, contemplating the prevailing taste in plays, provides a list of them

staged in a one month period at the Drury Lane, Covent Garden, and Haymarket theaters in London.

Thus an examination of the theatrical registers for the month of January
1782 shows that at Drury Lane 'The Beggar's Opera' was represented once,
'The Fair Circassian' four times, 'The Carnival of Venice' five times, 'The
Way of the World' once, 'The Clandestine Marriage' once, 'Hamlet' once,
'The Maid of the Oaks' four times. In the same month, at Covent Garden
Theatre, 'The Fair Penitent,' 'The Gamester,' 'Macbeth,' 'As You Like It,'
and 'Henry IV,' were each performed once; 'Jane Shore' was represented
thrice, and 'The Merry Wives of Windsor' once. In June of the same year
'The Beggar's Opera' was performed at the Haymarket Theatre no fewer
than six times, 'The Suicide' four times, 'Jason and Medea' seven times, 'The
Separate Maintenance' three times, and the 'Agreeable Surprise' six times.
With regard to the character of the plays, this much only needs be said, that,
although Garrick and others worked hard during the second half of the century to eliminate the coarse, obscene, and scandalous elements which entered
only too largely into the composition of many of them, the state of the stage
was very far from satisfactory even in the closing decades of the century, although by that time the stream of public opinion was being fairly directed
against the coarseness by which it had been so long disfigured. Foote and
other playwrights had introduced a class of dramatic compositions which,
although often of a humble and unpretending character, exercised great influence in developing a taste for more natural portraiture and language, and
these in turn led the way to those higher productions which are now venerated as the legitimate comedies of England. . . .

266. THE ALIEN ACT (1793)

Fearful lest French Revolutionary ideas be brought to England—especially
after the onset of the Reign of Terror in Paris in 1793—Parliament passed
the Alien Act, excerpts of which point up the fear of radicalism by allegedly
seditious foreigners.

Be it . . . enacted . . . That, during the continuance of this act, the
master or commander of every ship . . . which shall arrive in any port or
place of this kingdom, shall, immediately on his arrival, declare in writing to
the collector and comptroller, or other chief officer of the customs, at or near
such port or place, whether there are, to the best of his knowledge, any foreigners on board the said vessel; and shall, in his said declaration, specify the
number of foreigners, if any, on board . . . and also specify their names and

respective rank, occupation, or description as far as he shall be informed thereof.

II. And be it further enacted by the authority aforesaid, That the master or commander of every ship or vessel, so arriving as aforesaid, who shall neglect or refuse to make such declaration as aforesaid, shall, for every such offence, forfeit and pay the sum of ten pounds, for each and every foreigner who shall have been on board at the time of the arrival of such ship. . . .

III. And be it further enacted by the authority aforesaid, That every alien who shall arrive in any port or place of this kingdom on or after the tenth day of January one thousand seven hundred and ninety-three, shall, immediately after such arrival, declare in writing to the collector, comptroller, or other chief officer of the customs, at or near such port or place, his or her name and rank, occupation or description, or if a domestick servant, then also the name, rank, occupation, or description of his or her master or mistress, or shall verbally make to such officer as aforesaid such declaration, to be by him reduced to writing; and shall also in like manner declare the country or countries, place or places where he or she shall have principally resided for six calendar months next immediately preceding such arrival: and that every such alien who shall neglect to make declaration of the aforesaid particulars, or who shall wilfully make any false declaration thereof, shall, for every such offence, on conviction thereof in his Majesty's court of king's bench, or in any court of oyer and terminer, gaol delivery, or great sessions, or justiciary court in Scotland, be adjudged to depart out of this realm, and all other his Majesty's dominions, within a time to be limited in such judgement; and if he or she shall be found therein after such time . . . without lawful cause . . . he or she shall, being duly convicted thereof, be transported [to a penal colony] for life.

SOURCE REFERENCES   *Chapter Six*

215. Jesse, John H., *Memoirs of the Court of England From the Revolution of 1688 to the Death of George the Second,* III, 138; 161–162. Boston: Francis A. Nicholls, n.d.

216. A. Coxe, William, *Memoirs of the Life and Administration of Sir Robert Walpole, Earl of Orford,* II, 2–4. London: Cadell and Davis, 1800.

    B. Hervey, John, Lord, *Memoirs of the Reign of George the Second,* II, 191. London: John Murray, 1848.

217. Hamilton, Lady Anne, *Secret History of the Court of England from the Accession of George the Third to the Death of George the Fourth,* I, 20–21. Boston: L. C. Page, 1901.

218. A. Bradshaw, John, ed., *The Letters of Philip Dormer Stanhope Earl of Chester-field with the Characters*, III, 1417–1418. London: George Allen and Unwin, 1892.

B. Coxe, *Memoirs of Sir Robert Walpole*, III, 197–200.

219. A. Waldegrave, James, Earl, *Memoirs From 1754 to 1758*, pp. 15–17. London: John Murray, 1821.

B. Russell, Lord John, ed., *Memorials and Correspondence of Charles James Fox*, I, 198–199. London: Richard Bentley, 1853.

220. A. Jesse, John H., *Memoirs of King George the Third, His Life and Reign*, IV, 46–47. Boston: L. C. Page, 1902.

B. Lines by Sir Walter Scott, in Jesse, *Memoirs of King George the Third*, V, 333–334.

221. A. *Annual Register, Or a View of the History, Politics, and Literature For the Year* (1788), pp. 164–165. London: various publishers, 1790.

B. Aikin, John, *Annals of the Reign of King George the Third from its Com-mencement in the Year 1760, to the Death of His Majesty in the Year 1820*, 2nd ed., I, 436. London: Longman, Hurst, *et al.*, 1820.

222. Besant, Sir Walter, *London in the Eighteenth Century*, pp. 8–9. London: Adam and Charles Black, 1902.

223. *Statutes at Large*, 5 George III, CAP. 12.

224. A. *Statutes at Large*, 6 George III, CAP. 11.

B. *Statutes at Large*, 6 George III, CAP. 12.

225. Russell, *Memorials and Correspondence of Charles James Fox*, I, 110–111.

226. A. Eayrs, George, ed., *Letters of John Wesley, A Selection of Important and New Letters with Introductions and Biographical Notes by George Eayrs*, p. 474. Lon-don: Hodder and Stoughton, 1915.

B. *The Letters of Horace Walpole, Earl of Orford*, V, 398.

C. Quoted in Jesse, *Memoirs of King George the Third*, II, 331–332.

D. Russell, *Memorials and Correspondence of Charles James Fox*, I, 236–237; 244.

227. *Annual Register* (1805), pp. 235–236.

228. A. Cartwright, F. D., ed., *The Life and Correspondence of Major Cartwright*, I, 65–66. London: Henry Colburn, 1826.

B. Aikin, *Annals of the Reign of George the Third*, I, 390–391.

C. *Statutes at Large*, 47 George III, CAP. 36.

229. *Statutes at Large*, 1 George I, CAP. 5.

230. Russell, Lord John, *Correspondence of John, Fourth Duke of Bedford*, I, 75–76. London: Longman, Brown, Green, and Longmans, 1842.

231. Climenson, Emily J., *Elizabeth Montague the Queen of the Blue-Stockings Her Correspondence from 1720 to 1761*, pp. 168–169. London: John Murray, 1906.

232. Ellis, *Original Letters*, 2nd series, IV, 317–319.

233. *Statutes at Large*, 40 George III, CAP. 67.

234. A. Climenson, *Elizabeth Montague*, p. 149.

B. Ashton, Thomas S., and Sykes, Joseph, *The Coal Industry of the Eighteenth Century*, pp. 149–150. Manchester: Manchester University Press, 1929.

C. Bald, R., *General View of the Coal Trade*, in Ashton and Sykes, *Coal Industry*, pp. 24–25.

235. A. Young, Arthur, *A Six Months Tour Through the North of England,* III, 306–
308. London: W. Strahan, W. Nicoll, and T. Cadell, 1770.
B. Young, *A Six Months Tour,* I, 123–124.
C. Young, *A Six Months Tour,* I, 132.
236. *The Gentleman's Magazine: and Historical Chronicle, for the Year 1795,* LVX,
Part 2, 969–970. London: John Nichols, 1795.
237. Young, *A Six Months Tour,* I, 275–277.
238. Young, Arthur, *A Six Weeks Tour Through the Southern Counties of England
and Wales,* 2nd ed., pp. 21–26. London: W. Strahan *et al.,* 1769.
239. Young, *A Six Months Tour,* IV, 393.
240. *A Description of Great Britain; and First of The Southern Part of it, Called England,* Part 1, pp. 210–211. No place, publisher, or date.
241. *Statutes at Large,* 7 George I, CAP. 7.
242. *Statutes at Large,* 5 George II, CAP. 22.
243. *Statutes at Large,* 6 George II, CAP. 13.
244. *Statutes at Large,* 8 George III, CAP. 29.
245. *Statutes at Large,* 39 George III, CAP. 81.
246. *Statutes at Large,* 28 George III, CAP. 48.
247. *Statutes at Large,* 42 George III, CAP. 73.
248. Percy's *London,* cited in Besant, *London in the Eighteenth Century,* pp. 140–141.
249. Strype's *Chronicle,* cited in Besant, *London in the Eighteenth Century,* pp. 538–
539.
250. A. Besant, *London in the Eighteenth Century,* pp. 280–281.
B. Sydney, William C., *England and the English in the Eighteenth Century,* I,
44–45. New York: Macmillan, 1891.
251. A. Cited in Besant, *London in the Eighteenth Century,* p. 311.
B. Besant, *London in the Eighteenth Century,* p. 324.
C. Cited in Allen, Robert J., *The Clubs of Augustan London,* p. 150. Cambridge:
Harvard University Press, 1933.
252. Climenson, *Elizabeth Montague,* p. 138.
253. A. Young, *A Six Weeks Tour,* p. 88.
B. Young, *A Six Weeks Tour,* p. 207.
254. *Annual Register* (1790), pp. 274–275 of Appendix to Chronicle.
255. *Present State of Great Britain,* Part I, pp. 88–89.
256. A. Historical Manuscripts Commission, *Report on The Manuscripts of the Earl of
Verulam preserved at Gorhambury,* p. 119. London: Stationery Office, 1906.
B. Russell, *Correspondence of the Duke of Bedford,* II, 145–146.
C. Climenson, *Elizabeth Montague,* p. 103.
D. Jesse, *Memoirs of the Reign of George III,* I, 256–257.
257. *Statutes at Large,* 9 George II, CAP. 5.
258. A. Macaulay, Thomas Babington, *The History of England from the Accession of
James II,* I, 257. Boston: Phillips, Sampson, and Co., 1855.
B. Hervey, *Memoirs of the Reign of George the Second,* II, 45–48.
259. Eayrs, *Letters of John Wesley,* pp. 463; 113–115.
260. *The Letters of Horace Walpole, Earl of Orford,* VI, 87.

261. *Annual Register* (1811), p. 268 of Appendix to Chronicle.
262. A. Besant, *London in the Eighteenth Century,* Appendix V, p. 637.
    B. Besant, *London in the Eighteenth Century,* p. 367.
    C. *Autobiography and Correspondence of the Duchess of Portland,* 1st series, I, 185, in Sydney, *England and the English in the Eighteenth Century,* I, 276.
    D. Climenson, *Elizabeth Montague,* p. 31.
    E. *Annual Register* (1792), pp. 448–449 of Chronicle.
263. A. *Present State of Great Britain,* Part 1, pp. 266–267.
    B. Russell, *Memorials and Correspondence of Charles James Fox,* I, 41.
    C. Murray, John, ed., *The Autobiography of Edward Gibbon,* pp. 224–225. London: John Murray, 1896.
    D. Scott, Walter, *The Works of Jonathan Swift, D.D. with Notes and a Life of the Author,* IX, 373–374. Edinburgh: Archibald Constable, 1814.
264. Cited in Sydney, *England and the English in the Eighteenth Century,* II, 98–99.
265. A. Coxe, *Memoirs of Sir Robert Walpole,* II, 433–436.
    B. *The Letters of Horace Walpole, Earl of Orford,* II, 5.
    C. *Annual Register* (1766), pp. 36–37 of Chronicle.
    D. Sydney, *England and the English in the Eighteenth Century,* I, 165.
266. *Statutes at Large,* 33 George III, CAP. 4.

CHAPTER SEVEN

The Nineteenth Century
(1815-1901)

The conclusion of the Napoleonic War in 1815 left England the strongest power on earth. By mid-century it held first place in the production of coal and iron, in the manufacture and sale of pottery and textiles, and in banking and insurance. England's carrying trade expanded steadily, and the power of its navy was awesome. The stability of the Cabinet system of government with its principle of ministerial responsibility was the envy of the civilized world. It had vast colonial possessions which added to its economic and military strength. For these reasons it sought to maintain a balance of power in Europe and to pursue a policy of world peace. After 1846, due to Sir Robert Peel's repeal of the Corn Laws, the Empire operated on a principle of free trade. England also assumed to a degree the moral leadership of the world and attempted to spread parliamentary government. And, content with its colonial possessions, it generally abjured imperialism until the last three decades of the century.

Profound changes at home altered the character and some of the institutions of the country. The growth of the factory system transformed England from an essentially rural and agricultural nation into a predominantly industrial and urban nation. Consequently the pressures to reform its social and political institutions could not be effectively resisted by the ruling aristocratic oligarchy that had dominated them since the seventeenth century. Parliament reformed local and national government; political parties were formed with clearly defined leadership and programs. In religion, the Roman Catholics and Jews were freed from previous restrictions, Dissenting Churches significantly increased their membership and influence, and the Established Church lost much of its power and privileges. In the area of finance, the old mercantile system was ended by the repeal of the Navigation Acts and the adoption of free trade. Simultaneously the government became increasingly active in enacting regulative statutes that affected al-

most all segments of the economy. Parliament also reformed England's legal
and judicial system, and, to a lesser extent, the educational systems. Finally,
as one would expect, the social changes accompanying the industrialization
and urbanization of the country were reflected in its art and literature.

267. KING GEORGE IV (1820–1830)

During the ten years (1810–1820) in which George III had been insane,
George IV, then Prince of Wales, had acted as Regent. He had developed
thoroughly unwholesome characteristics which became worse when he
ascended the throne in 1820. He was untrustworthy, in many ways uncouth,
and his debaucheries and laziness made him so fat that his critics dubbed
him "The Prince of Whales." Five years after his death a writer described
him and his friends.

George the Fourth always appeared to us nothing more than a man of
pleasure, whom the accident of birth had made a king. His means of indulgence were ample, and he did not spare them. At first he affected
Whiggism; but this might arise from his favourite companions in horse-
racing, drinking, and intriguing being of that persuasion. . . .

In the choice of his ministers, as in other things, the king considered his
personal ease. At the commencement of the Regency, a slight effort was
made to bring into the administration his early friends; but, finding them
fastidious, pragmatical, and disposed to meddle in his household establishment, the design was abandoned, and never again seriously resumed.
Castlereagh, Canning, Huskisson, and Sidmouth were the most appropriate
servants for a voluptuous monarch. These men held no principles that could
interfere with his most lavish desires; their objects were limited to the enjoyment of power and its emoluments: how little they cared about the general
weal may be instanced in the fact that, though they managed the affairs of
the empire during a long period of profound peace, they never set about reforming the most glaring and admitted abuses in its public administration. . . . The persecution by the King, of the unfortunate Caroline, and all
who supported her, was mean, ungenerous, and unrelenting. His love of
dress and etiquette was coxcomical, and detracted from the regal dignity.
. . . George IV. was a spoiled child, who, through life, had been accustomed
only to do what ministered to his own gratification. . . .

268. KING WILLIAM IV (1830–1837)

Charles Greville, the celebrated diarist of the nineteenth century, thought
King William was only a slight improvement on George IV.

William IV. was a man who, coming to the throne at the mature age of sixty-five, was so excited by the exaltation, that he nearly went mad, and distinguished himself by a thousand extravagances of language and conduct, to the alarm or amusement of all who witnessed his strange freaks; and though he was shortly afterward sobered down into more becoming habits, he always continued to be something of a blackguard and something more of a buffoon. It is but fair to his memory at the same time to say that he was a good-natured, kind-hearted, and well-meaning man, and he always acted an honorable and straightforward, if not always a sound and discreet, part. The two principal Ministers of his reign, the Duke of Wellington and Lord Grey (though the former was only his Minister for a few months), have both spoken of him to me with strong expressions of personal regard and esteem. . . .

269. QUEEN VICTORIA (1837–1901)

> Victoria, coming to the throne when she was eighteen years of age, so dominated the period of her reign that it is called the "Victorian Age." Her sturdy moral virtues and the purity of her family life gave a much-needed dignity to the crown. Queen Alexandra, her daughter-in-law, perceptively described the early years of her married life as follows:

From her marriage in 1840 to the death of the Prince Consort in 1861, the Court of Queen Victoria was the most brilliant in Europe. . . .

During the life-time of the Prince Consort the English Court was the scene of many splendid functions. Most of the European sovereigns paid state visits to England, and on each occasion were received with great pomp. The Court ceremonies generally were conducted on a scale of great magnificence. At Court banquets, which were frequent, covers were laid for from five to six hundred persons, and the famous gold plate was always used. The Queen also gave several garden-parties and balls during the season at Buckingham Palace and Windsor. The balls were fancy dress affairs. . . .

She found great enjoyment in these balls, in which she and her husband impersonated the great personages of the past. . . . In those days, young, happy, and in love with a husband who adored her, life was like the realisation of some wonderful dream to Victoria. She was a fine horse-woman, and was fond of riding in Windsor Forest accompanied by thirty or forty people. Mounted on her superb bay Emperor, she was the life and soul of these equestrian jaunts. Pleasure appealed to her. She was constantly seen at the opera and the play. . . .

With the death of the Prince Consort [1861] all this was suddenly changed. A simplicity of the most monotonous description took the place of the former splendour. . . .

For five years she lived in the strictest seclusion. When she emerged from it her Court was the mere skeleton of what it had been. The atmosphere of the grave in which she had buried her happiness and youth enveloped it. She was always dressed in mourning and surrounded by elderly ladies and gentlemen similarly attired. . . . As pleasure reminded her too bitterly of all she had lost, she banished it from the routine of the Court. There were no longer balls, concerts, and dramatic performances as of yore. . . . Gone were the gay cavalcades in Windsor Forest in which she had once delighted. No fiery Emperor now did she ride; instead, a little pony drew her about the grounds of her castles in a chaise. . . .

Always a stickler for etiquette and propriety, she became more exacting in regard to their rigid enforcement. . . . To the innovations of fashion she had a rooted objection. . . . Divorcées she positively refused to countenance. No woman could be presented to her whose conduct was not irreproachable. Avoiding London as much as possible, and passing her secluded existence between Windsor, Balmoral, and Osborne, the Court of Queen Victoria practically ceased to function with the death of the Prince Consort.

> The century produced its full quota of famous statesmen. Chief among them were such men as Sir Robert Peel, Lord Palmerston, Benjamin Disraeli, and William E. Gladstone. While Lord Melbourne does not rank as one of the great leaders of the century, he exercised a profound influence on the young queen, and contributed mightily to her political education.

270. LORD MELBOURNE (1779–1848)

On Melbourne's death, Greville wrote of him:

November 29, 1848: . . . It was upon the accession of the Queen that his post suddenly grew into one of immense importance and interest, for he found himself placed in the most curious and delicate position which any statesman ever occupied. Victoria was transferred at once from the nursery to the throne—ignorant, inexperienced, and without one human being about her on whom she could rely for counsel and aid. She found in her Prime Minister and constitutional adviser a man of mature age, who instantly captivated her feelings and her fancy by his deferential solicitude, and by a shrewd, sagacious, and entertaining conversation, which were equally new and delightful to her. She at once cast herself with implicit confidence upon Melbourne, and, from the first day of her reign, their relations assumed a peculiar character, and were marked by an intimacy which he never abused; on the contrary, he only availed himself of his great influence to impress upon her mind sound maxims of constitutional government, and truths of every description that it behoved her to learn. It is impossible to imagine anything more interesting than the situation which had thus devolved upon him, or one more calculated to excite all the latent sensibility of his nature. His loyal devotion soon warmed into a parental affection, which she repaid by unbounded manifestations of confidence and regard. He set himself wisely, and with perfect disinterestedness, to form her mind and character, and to cure the defects and eradicate the prejudices from which the mistakes and faults of her education had not left her entirely free. In all that Melbourne said or did, he appears to have been guided by a regard to justice and truth. He never scrupled to tell her what none other would have dared to say; and in the midst of that atmosphere of flattery and deceit which kings and queens are almost always destined to breathe, and by which their minds are so often perverted, he never scrupled to declare boldly and frankly his real opinions, strange as they sometimes sounded, and unpalatable as they often were, and to wage war with her prejudices and false impressions with regard to people or things whenever he saw that she was led astray by them. He acted in all things an affectionate, conscientious, and patriotic part, endeavouring to make her happy as a woman and popular as a queen.

271. BENJAMIN DISRAELI (1804–1881)

This young novelist and lawyer was a Jew whose family had become nominal Christians, which made it possible for him to stand for Parliament in 1837. He was one of the most colorful personalities of the century. Disappointed that Peel did not give him a position in his great ministry of 1841–1846, Disraeli broke with Peel on the question of Corn Law repeal in 1846 and became the leader in the Commons of the Protectionist Tories for a few years. After Lord Derby's death in 1869, he led the Conservative party. Lord George Hamilton, a friendly Tory, wrote of him:

He [Disraeli] liked the young men of the party to come and talk with him in the lobby during divisions [voting]. He nearly always stood with his back to a fireplace, and he was interested in any little piece of gossip or rumor relating to current events, as he wished to know what was going on outside Parliament. Many were the terse and witty replies he would make to our communications. . . .

Disraeli was so complex a personality that only those who knew him and whom he liked came in contact with the fine and fascinating traits of his inner self. He was much more sensitive than was generally believed; his immovable and sphinx-like callousness in debate was originally a pose, but it gradually became second nature. He was profoundly conscious of his unpopularity in certain quarters, and especially amongst those with whom he was most anxious to establish kindly relations. To those whom he liked and who were intimate with him, he revealed an extraordinarily kind and magnanimous disposition. He was the staunchest of friends and most brilliant and entertaining of hosts. When I knew him, he was advanced in years, and his health was indifferent, and he suffered from a kind of gouty asthma which was very difficult to relieve or counteract. It was only when he was excited or spurred up that he would exhibit his superlative conversational charms. . . .

To me Disraeli was not only a leader and adviser, but in many ways he behaved more like an elderly relative than a political chief, ever ready to listen to what one had to say, and, no matter how occupied, ever ready to give his advice to the matter placed before him. His mannerisms and gait were, to a large extent, foibles, and they disappeared with the generation to which he belonged; but the proofs of his prescience, resource, sound judgment, and patriotism remain, and his name and policy as years roll on, will be more and more esteemed by the present generation and those that are to come.

272. WILLIAM EWART GLADSTONE (1809–1898)

Gladstone began his long political career in 1835 as Undersecretary for War and the Colonies. He was then a High-Church Tory, but in succeeding years, although always a worthy disciple of Anglicanism, he became a Conservative, then a Peelite, and finally the leader of the Liberal party on the death of Palmerston in 1865. His chief interest and abilities lay in finance and domestic reform. He represented the solid, middle-class interests, and his entire career was characterized by a moral fervor—outwardly, at least—that was typical of Victorian society.

A. *An Opponent's Description of Gladstone* (ca. *1890*)

His [Disraeli's] great rival, Gladstone, was just as interesting a study. I doubt if there has ever been a man in politics during the last two centuries who combined such extraordinary physical and mental gifts. His knowledge was varied and great. His power of work and assimilation was amazing; his capacity to stand fatigue and long hours equally remarkable; he was endowed with unusual physical courage and unlimited assurance. For Parliamentary purposes he was unquestionably the most efficient and eloquent speaker of his generation, his voice, elocution, and gestures being almost

faultless. Others might occasionally strike a finer note or give a higher intellectual flavour to a speech after careful preparation; but with or without
preparation Gladstone always spoke superbly well so far as the technique of
speaking was concerned, and with an apparent conviction and a histrionic
power that were most impressive. Without an effort he could always assume
the attitude which most appealed to the sympathies of his audience, and his
general pose was that of a very good man struggling with wickedly minded
opponents. When I first got into the House of Commons, I was immensely
struck by his personality, and though I did not agree with him it was a
physical pleasure to me to hear him speak and argue; but, little by little, a
suspicion was awakened, which grew and developed, as to how far all these
protestations had their origin in high motives or principles, or were merely a
part of his political baggage. As his Government became weaker his passion-
ate appeals became stronger and more exalted, and then the conviction was
slowly forced upon me that the main inspiration of his transcendental atti-
tudes was to keep a majority in his lobby. His power of twisting the plain
meaning of words and explaining away obvious facts was so extraordinary
as to create the belief that whatever he wished he really did believe. . . .

No statesman in my time possessed anything approaching his marvellous histrionic power. It is true that the pose was always the same . . . [a
grave and pious man]; but the wonderful adaptation of this pose to every
Parliamentary difficulty and contingency was an exhibition of the highest
art, and this pose so grew upon him that it became to him second nature. . . .

If you believed in him, he became to you a Parliamentary Superman; if
you suspected him or detected him in what you believed to be tricks, then
dislike rapidly hardened into repulsion and wholesale distrust. So it came to
pass that no statesman had as supporters a more devoted clientele, or as
antagonists more irreconcilable opponents. . . .

B. *Gladstone as Orator*

Richard Cobden, one of the Anti-Corn Law League leaders, described
Gladstone's public speaking in the following letter to William Forster:

Gladstone's speeches have the effect on my mind of a beautiful strain of
music. I can rarely remember any clear unqualified expression of opinion on
any subject outside his political, economical, and financial statements. I remember on the occasion when he left Sir Robert Peel's Government on account of the Maynooth grants, and when the House met in unusual num-

bers to hear his explanation, I sat beside Villiers and Ricardo for an hour, listening with real pleasure to his beautiful rhetorical involutions and evolutions, and at the close, turning to one of my neighbors and exclaiming, "What a marvellous talent that is! Here have I been listening with pleasure for an hour to his explanation, and I know no more why he left the Government than before he commenced." It is, however, a talent of questionable value for public leadership.

C. Salisbury's Evaluation of Gladstone (1898)

Perhaps the best evaluation of Gladstone is that of the Conservative leader, Lord Salisbury:

What is the cause of this unanimous feeling? Of course, he had qualities that distinguished him from all other men; and you may say that it was his transcendent intellect, his astonishing power of attaching men to him, and the great influence he was able to exert upon the thought and convictions of his contemporaries. But these things, which explain the attachment, the adoration of those whose ideas he represented, would not explain why it is that sentiments almost as fervent are felt and expressed by those whose ideas were not carried out by his policy. My Lords, I do not think the reason is to be found in anything so far removed from the common feelings of mankind as the abstruse and controversial questions of the policy of the day. They had nothing to do with it. Whether he was right, or whether he was wrong, in all the measures, or in most of the measures which he proposed—those are matters of which the discussion has passed by, and would certainly be singularly inappropriate here; they are really remitted to the judgment of future generations, who will securely judge from experience what we can only decide by forecast. It was on account of considerations more common to the masses of human beings, to the general working of the human mind, than any controversial questions of policy that men recognized in him a man guided—whether under mistaken impressions or not, it matters not—but guided in all the steps he took, in all the efforts that he made, by a high moral ideal. What he sought were the attainments of great ideals, and, whether they were based on sound convictions or not, they could have issued from nothing but the greatest and the purest moral aspirations; and he is honoured by his countrymen, because through so many years, across so many vicissitudes and conflicts, they had recognised this one characteristic of his action, which has never ceased to be felt. He will leave behind him . . . the memory of a great Christian statesman.

273. THE SOCIAL STRUCTURE IN 1815

The following table needs no explanation except to say that it indicates quite clearly the nature of English society and the relative wealth and prestige of the several classes which existed at that time.

	Number of Persons, including their Families & Domestics	Total Income of each class
NOBILITY AND GENTRY:—Peers, Baronets, Knights, Country Gentlemen, and others, having large income	416,535	£58,433,590
CLERGY:—Eminent Clergymen	9,000	1,080,000
Lesser Ditto	87,000	3,500,000
Dissenting Clergy, including Itinerant Preachers	20,000	500,000
STATE AND REVENUE, including all Persons employed under Government	114,500	6,830,000
LAW:—Judges, Barristers, Attorneys, Clerks, &c.	95,000	7,600,000
PHYSIC:—Physicians, Surgeons, Apothecaries, &c.	90,000	5,400,000
AGRICULTURE:—Freeholders of the better sort	385,000	19,250,000
Lesser Freeholders	1,050,000	21,000,000
Farmers	1,540,000	33,600,000
TRADE:—Eminent Merchants	35,000	9,100,000
Shopkeepers, and Tradesmen retailing goods	700,000	28,000,000
Innkeepers and Publicans, licensed to sell ale, beer, and spirituous liquors	437,000	8,750,000
WORKING CLASSES:—Agricultural labourers, Mechanics, Artizans, Handicrafts, and all Labourers employed in Manufactures, Mines, and Minerals	7,497,531	82,451,547

Here then the subject is clearly exposed;—we see now how matters really stand, and who are the *pillars of the state*. We see the total number and income of each class; consequently, their relative power, dependence, and importance in the community. The facts too are unquestionable; it cannot be said they are founded on the exaggerated data of some Jacobin, drawn up for Jacobinical purposes; they are the data of PATRICK COLQU-

HOUN, Receiver of the Thames Police Office, a most loyal man, and who, partly for his loyalty, receives out of the public purse more than £6000 per annum.

The inferences to be drawn from the above statement are many and important, and we shall enumerate them in order.

1. Peers, baronets, knights, country gentlemen, and persons of that description, including their families, amount to more than 400,000, and their total income to more than 58 millions, which is exactly £145 a year to each individual. The working classes, including their families, amount to seven millions and a half, and their total income to 82 millions, which is about £10 a year for each individual.

274. CONDITIONS IN ENGLAND AFTER THE WAR WITH NAPOLEON (1815)

The long years of war with France (1793–1815) had left England with an exorbitant debt, widespread unemployment, and a hostility to reform on the part of the governing classes. The situation in 1815–1816 is described in the *Annual Register:*

The discontents among the inferior ranks of people, occasioned by the want of regular employment, and by reduced wages, first began to assume a menacing appearance in the counties of Norfolk, Suffolk, Huntingdon, and Cambridge; where nightly assemblages were held, threatening letters were sent, and houses, barns, and rick-yards were set on fire, displaying melancholy proofs of the degradation of national character produced by long distress, and an interruption of the usual habits of industry. . . .

The distresses arising from the stagnation of manufactures were no where more severely felt than in those districts which had been rendered populous and flourishing by the numerous branches of the iron trade, several of which derived a large share of their demand from the consumption of war. Many great works of this class were suddenly put to a stop, with the effect of throwing entirely out of employment the labourers of different kinds, who had been engaged in them. The southern part of Staffordshire was particularly affected by this melancholy change; and the most lamentable accounts were transmitted of the state to which the working people of the populous village of Bilston were reduced, being rendered totally dependent on parochial relief, the funds of which were inadequate to preserve them from absolute famine. A body of men intimately connected with the iron factories, were the colliers, whose labours were nearly suspended from

the same cause. Some of these resorted to a mode of obtaining relief from the
public, occasionally practised in hard times—that of drawing loaded waggons of coals to distant towns, for the purpose of exciting commiseration. A
division of these wandering petitioners approached the metropolis; but their
advance was properly intercepted by the police, through the apprehension
that their appearance might be attended by tumults, and they were sent back
with admonition, and a gratuity. The same reception was given them on
their march to other capitals; for although they preserved due decorum of
behaviour, their mendicity came within the notice of the vagrant laws.

For the most part the sufferers in the iron manufactories bore their
hardships with due resignation, and were grateful for the charitable exertions made for their relief. In the great works of South Wales, however,
especially those in the vicinity of that new creation of art and industry,
Merthyr Tydvil, large bodies of discarded workmen assembled in a tumultuous manner; and were not restored to order without military interference,
joined with such concilliatory measures as prevented any considerable mischief. In the other districts of the kingdom which partook, some of them
largely, of the declension of manufactures, the public tranquillity was rarely
disturbed. The hand of charity was liberally extended to the relief of distress; and plans were adopted in many places, for supplying the want of
usual employment by new undertakings of public utility. In the metropolis,
large subscriptions were entered into for relieving the numerous poor, who
were reduced to the most urgent necessity by the failure of demand for the
silk manufactures in Spitalfields, as well as by the loss of various other
sources of employment; and in almost every parish contributions were raised
for enlarging donations without additional burthens upon the poor-rates. . . .

275. THE PETERLOO MASSACRE (1819)

Continued unemployment, crop failures, and high food prices led to rioting
and demonstrations by the working classes. The Peterloo Massacre, a name
obviously coined in criticism of the government, is a good example of governmental measures against those who sought to ameliorate economic conditions.

A little before noon on the 16th of August, the first body of reformers
began to arrive on the scene of action, which was a piece of ground called St.
Peter's field, adjoining a church of that name in the town of Manchester.
These persons bore two banners, surmounted with caps of liberty, and bear-
ing the inscriptions—"No Corn Laws," "Annual Parliaments," "Universal
Suffrage," "Vote by Ballot." Some of these flags, after being paraded round

the field, were planted in the cart on which the speakers stood; but others remained in different parts of the crowd. Numerous large bodies of reformers continued to arrive from the towns in the neighbourhood of Manchester till about one o'clock, all preceded by flags, and many of them in regular marching order, five deep. . . . A band of special constables assumed a position on the field without resistance. The congregated multitude now amounted to a number roundly computed at 80,000, and the arrival of the hero of the day was impatiently expected. At length Mr. [Orator] Hunt made his appearance, and after a rapturous greeting, was invited to preside; he signified his assent, and mounting a scaffolding, began to harangue his admirers. He had not proceeded far, when the appearance of the yeomanry cavalry advancing towards the area in a brisk trot, excited a panic in the outskirts of the meeting. They entered the inclosure, and after pausing a moment to recover their disordered ranks, and breathe their horses, they drew their swords, and brandished them fiercely in the air. The multitude, by the direction of their leaders, gave three cheers, to show that they were undaunted by this intrusion, and the orator had just resumed his speech to assure the people that this was only a trick to disturb the meeting, and to exhort them to stand firm, when the cavalry dashed into the crowd, making for the cart on which the speakers were placed. The multitude offered no resistance; they fell back on all sides. The commanding officer then approaching Mr. Hunt, and brandishing his sword, told him that he was his prisoner. Mr. Hunt, after enjoining the people to tranquillity, said, that he would readily surrender to any civil officer on showing his warrant, and Mr. Nadin, the principal police officer, received him in charge. . . . A cry now arose among the military of, "Have at their flags," and they dashed down not only those in the cart, but the others dispersed in the field; cutting to right and left to get at them. The people began running in all directions; and from this moment the yeomanry lost all command of temper: numbers were trampled under the feet of men and horses; many, both men and women were cut down by sabres and a peace officer and a female in the number, slain on the spot. The whole number of persons injured amounted to between three and four hundred. The populace threw a few stones and brick bats in their retreat; but in less than ten minutes the ground was entirely cleared of its former occupants, and filled by various bodies of military, both horse and foot. Mr. Hunt was led to prison, not without incurring considerable danger, and some injury on his way from the swords of yeomanry and the bludgeons of police officers; the broken staves of two of his banners were carried in mock procession before him. The magistrates directed him to be locked up in a solitary cell, and the other prisoners were confined with the same precaution. The town was brought into a tolerably quiet state before night, military patroles [sic] being stationed at the end of almost every street. . . .

276. THE CATO STREET CONSPIRACY (1820)

If England was in distress, there arose a question what was the remedy. Impatient men had attempted sheer violence:

February 24, 1820: The Plot which has been detected had for its object the destruction of the Cabinet Ministers, and the chief actor in the conspiracy was Arthur Thistlewood. I was at Lady Harrowby's last night, and about half-past one o'clock Lord Harrowby came in and told us the following particulars: A plot has been in agitation for some time past, of the existence of which, the names and numbers of the men concerned, and of all particulars concerning their plans, Government has been perfectly well informed. The conspirators had intended to execute their design about last Christmas at a Cabinet dinner at Lord Westmoreland's, but for some reason they were unable to do so and deferred it. At length Government received information that they were to assemble to the number of from twenty to thirty at a house in Cato Street, Edgware Road, and that they had resolved to execute their purpose last night, when the Cabinet would be at dinner at Lord Harrowby's. Dinner was ordered as usual. Men had been observed watching the house, both in front and rear, during the whole afternoon. It was believed that nine o'clock was the hour fixed upon, for the assault to be made. The Ministers who were expected at dinner remained at Fife House, and at eight o'clock Mr. Birnie with twelve constables was despatched to Cato Street to apprehend the conspirators. Thirty-five foot guards were ordered to support the police force. The constables arrived upon the spot a few moments before the soldiers, and suspecting that the conspirators had received intimation of the discovery of their plot, and were in consequence preparing to escape, they did not wait for the soldiers, but went immediately to the house. A man armed with a musket was standing sentry, whom they secured. They then ascended a narrow staircase which led to the room in which the gang were assembled, and burst the door open. The first man who entered was shot . . . but was only wounded; he who followed was stabbed by Thistlewood and killed. The conspirators then with their swords put out the lights and attempted to escape. By this time the soldiers had arrived. Nine men were taken prisoners; Thistlewood and the rest escaped. . . .

277. CONDITIONS IN AGRICULTURE (1815–1846)

In 1815 a landlord-dominated Parliament passed the celebrated Corn Law, the purpose of which was to protect the interests of important large landowners by maintaining the high price level of grain attained during the Napoleonic War. The law forbade the importation of foreign-grown grain until the price of home-grown grain reached eighty shillings a quarter (eight bushels). Because the Corn Law kept the price of bread high, the working classes interpreted the law as a measure of class legislation in the interest of landlords, but in its operation it actually did little to benefit the landlord or to harm the consumer. In any event, it did nothing to aid farm laborers, whose wages remained low, or to those who were unemployed because of several market depressions during this period.

A. *Agricultural Productivity*

In 1830 William Cobbett, a pamphleteer and journalist, made a tour through much of England, which he described in his famous *Rural Rides*. Of the Parish of Milton in the Avon valley he wrote:

The parish of Milton does . . . produce food, drink, clothing, and all other things, enough for 502 families, or 2510 persons . . . , which is a great deal more than three times the present allowance, because the present allowance includes clothing, fuel, tools and every thing. Now, then, according to the "Population Return," laid before Parliament, this parish contains 500 persons, or, according to my division, one hundred families. So that here are about one hundred families to raise food and drink enough, and to raise wool and other things to pay for all other necessaries, for five hundred and two families! Aye, and five hundred and two families fed and lodged, too, on my liberal scale. Fed and lodged according to the present scale, this one hundred families raise enough to supply more, and many more, than fifteen hundred families; or seven thousand five hundred persons! And yet those who do the work are half-starved! In the 100 families there are, we will suppose, 80 able working men, and as many boys, sometimes assisted by the women and stout girls. What a handful of people to raise such a quantity of food! What injustice, what a hellish system it must be, to make those who raise it skin and bone and nakedness, while the food and drink and wool are almost all carried away to be heaped on the fund-holders, pensioners, soldiers, dead-weight, and other swarms of tax-eaters! If such an operation do not need putting an end to, then the devil himself is a saint.

And of Alnwick, Northumberland, he wrote:

Here we get amongst the mischief. Here the farms are enormous; the stack-yards containing from fifty to a hundred stacks each, and each stack containing from five to ten large southern wagon-loads of sheaves. Here the thrashing-machines are turned by STEAM-ENGINES; here the labourers live in a sort of barracks: that is to say, long sheds with stone walls, and covered with what are called pantiles. They have neither gardens nor privies nor back-doors, and seem altogether to be kept in the same way as if they were under military discipline. There are no villages; no scattered cottages; no up-stairs; one little window, and one door-way to each dwelling in the shed or barrack. A large farm-house, and large buildings for the cattle and the im-plements; one farmer drawing to one spot the produce of the whole country all around; a sort of manufactory of corn and of meat, the proceeds of which go, with very little deduction, into the pocket of the big landlord, there being no such thing as a small proprietor to be seen, though the land is exceedingly fine and produces the most abundant crops: the good part of the produce all sent away; and those who make it all, compelled to feed upon those things . . . which we in the South give to horses and to hogs. This . . . is the scene, chopsticks of Kent, Sussex, Hampshire, Wiltshire, and Berkshire; this is the scene, and these the "country people". . . .

B. *Women and Children in Agriculture*

In 1843 the Assistant Poor Law Commissioners investigated the employ-ment of women and children in agriculture. While in Wiltshire, one of the Commissioners questioned a surgeon by the name of Blandford, who said:

I am of opinion that, generally speaking, boys above 12 years of age are the better for employment in agricultural labour: it tends to develop their persons and strength. Generally they are strong and hearty, and better in health from the employment. I have known, however, cases of boys having inflammation of the knee-joint, . . . and rheumatism, from being over-fatigued, and working exposed to cold and wet in the open air. I have at the present time, under my care, a boy with knee inflamed, from being too much on his legs all day, from over-walking at an early age. It is like over-working a young horse, which produces diseases. . . . These things happen suffi-ciently often to make it necessary that care should be taken in working boys. Sometimes their work is very hard—too fatiguing for their years. Scrofula is frequently developed by exposure to cold and wet; it appears in such cases in the form of consumption, glandular enlargements, and diseases of the bones and joints. Boys of a scrofulous habit are occasionally exposed to a degree of wet and cold injurious to them which would not produce any ill consequences in a healthy boy. . . .

Generally the cottages are too small for the families living in them, and tend to produce and aggravate disease from the inmates living so closely together. Two years ago typhus fever occurred in a neighbouring parish, which I attend. There was one cottage I attended, which consisted of one room on the ground-floor, and two small bed-rooms up stairs. In this cottage lived an old man, with his wife, his two daughters, middle-aged women, and his son and wife, with their children—in all, ten individuals. The whole family had the fever, some of them very severely. The son's wife, with two of her children, were on a bed in an out-house. In the out-house was a well, and a large tub containing pig's victuals, and was the general receptacle for everything. The floor was earthen, with no ceiling but the thatch of the roof. In the same village there were more than 40 cases of typhus, and the spread of the disease must be attributed to the people living so closely packed together. . . .

C. *Poverty Breeds Discontent*

In Devonshire . . . the wages of the [farm] labourers were from seven to nine shillings a week; . . . they seldom saw meat or tasted milk; and . . . their chief food was a compost of ground barley and potatoes. It was little wonder that in a county where such was the condition of labour, the lecturer was privately asked by poor men at the roadside if he could tell them where the fighting was to be. Nor need we doubt that, . . . though ignorant of Chartism as a political question, the great mass of the population of Devon were just as ready for pikes and pistols, as the most excitable people of the factory towns. In Somersetshire the budget of a labourer, his wife, and five children under ten years of age, was as follows. Half a bushel of wheat cost four shillings; for grinding, baking, and barm, sixpence; firing, sixpence; rent, eighteen pence; leaving, out of the total earnings of seven shillings, a balance of sixpence, out of which to provide the family with clothing, potatoes, and all the other necessaries and luxuries of human existence.

278. THE ANTI-CORN LAW LEAGUE (1836-1846)

Agrarian discontent, fanned by the agitation of factory owners who insisted that factory wages were high enough if the price of food was reduced, resulted in the formation of the Anti-Corn Law League, whose activities are thus summarized by Leone Levi:

The Anti-Corn Law agitation was one of those movements which, being founded on right principles, and in harmony with the interest of the masses, was sure to gather fresh strength by any event affecting the supply of food. It was popular to attempt to reverse a policy which aimed almost exclusively to benefit one class of society. It was well known that the League wanted to outset an economic fallacy, and that they wished to relieve the people from a great burden. And as time elapsed and the soundness of the principles propounded by the League at their public meetings was more and more appreciated, their triumph became certain, and Her Majesty's government itself began to see that it was no longer possible to treat the agitation either by a silent passiveness, or by expressed contempt. The economic theorists had the mass of the people with them. Their gatherings were becoming more and more enthusiastic. And even amidst conservative landowners there were not a few enlightened and liberal minds who had already, silently at least, espoused the new ideas. No change certainly could have been expected so long as bread was cheap and labour abundant. But when a deficient harvest and a blight in the potato crop crippled the resources of the people and raised grain to famine prices, the voice of the League acquired greater power and influence. Hitherto they had received hundreds of pounds. Now, thousands were sent in to support the agitation. A quarter of a million was readily contributed. Nor were the contributors Lancashire mill owners exclusively. Among them were merchants and bankers, men of heart and men of mind, the poor labourer, and the peer of the realm. The fervid oratory of Bright, the demonstrative and argumentative reasoning of Cobden, the more popular appeals of Fox, Rawlins, and other platform speakers, filled the newspaper press and were eagerly read. And when parliament dissolved in August 1845, even Sir Robert Peel showed some slight symptoms of a conviction that the days of the corn laws were numbered. Every day, in truth, brought home to his mind a stronger need for action, and as the ravages of the potato disease progressed, he saw that all further resistance would be absolutely dangerous.

279. THE FAILURE OF THE POTATO CROP IN IRELAND (1845–1846)

Anti-Corn Law agitation became irresistible when the Irish potato crop failed, and the Irish were faced with starvation. A political economist thus summarized the importance of the potato to the Irish and the dangers in relying on one crop:

Ireland has often grievously suffered from social and political wrongs, from absenteeism and repeal cries, from Protestant and Roman Catholic bigotry, from orangeism and ribbonism, from threatening notices and mid-day assassinations, but seldom has her cup of adversity been so brimfull as in 1845 and 1846 from the failure of the potato crop. Though comparatively of recent importation, the first potato root having been imported by Sir Walter Raleigh in 1610, potatoes had for years constituted a large proportion of the food of the people of Ireland. A considerable acreage of land was devoted to that culture, and an acre of potatoes would feed more than double the num-ber of individuals that can be fed from an acre of wheat. Such cultivation was, moreover, very attractive to small holders of land. It cost little labour. It entailed scarcely any expense, and little or no care was bestowed on it, since the people were quite satisfied with the coarsest and most prolific kind, called lumpers or horse potatoes. Nor was it the food of the people only in Ireland. Pigs and poultry shared the potatoes with the peasant's family, and often became the inmates of his cabin also. One great evil connected with potato culture is, that whilst the crop is precarious and uncertain, it cannot be stored up. The surplus of one abundant year is quite unfit to use in the next, and owing to its great bulk it cannot even be transported from place to place. Moreover, once used to a description of food so extremely cheap no retrenchment is possible, and when blight comes and the crop is destroyed the people seem doomed to absolute starvation. This unfortunately was the case in 1822 and 1831. In those years public subscriptions were got up, king's letters issued, balls and bazaars held, and public money granted. But in 1845 and 1846 the calamity was greater than any previously experienced.

280. REPEAL OF THE CORN LAWS (1846)

While the Irish famine exercised an important effect in convincing the prime minister, Peel, that the Corn Laws must go, he and others in the Cabinet—especially Sir James Graham, Sidney Herbert, and Lord Aberdeen —had in previous years been moving in the direction of free trade. The famine afforded them the opportunity they needed to justify in Parliament the repeal of the Corn Laws. Aided by Lord John Russell and his Whig followers, and supported by many in his own party, Peel accomplished his goal in 1846.

A cabinet council was held on October 31 to consult as to what to be done, and at an adjourned meeting on November 5 Sir Robert Peel intimated his intention to issue an order in council remitting the duty on grain in bond to one shilling, and opening the ports for the admission of all species of grain at a smaller rate of duty until a day to be named in the order; to call parliament together on the 27th inst. to ask for an indemnity, and a sanction of the order by law; and to submit to parliament immediately after the recess a modification of the existing law, including the admission at a nominal duty of Indian corn and of British colonial corn. A serious difference of opinion, however, was found to exist in the cabinet on the question brought before them, the only ministers supporting such measures being the Earl of Aberdeen, Sir James Graham, and Mr. Sidney Herbert. Nor was it easy to induce the other members to listen to reason. And though at a subsequent meeting, held on November 28, Sir Robert Peel so far secured a majority, it was evident that the cabinet was too divided to justify him in bringing forward his measures. And he decided upon resigning office.

This resolution having been communicated to the Queen, Her Majesty summoned Lord John Russell to form a cabinet, and, to smooth his path, Sir Robert Peel, with characteristic frankness, sent a memorandum to Her Majesty embodying a promise to give him his support. But Lord John Russell failed in his efforts, and the Queen had no alternative but to recall Sir Robert Peel, and give him full power to carry out his measures. . . .

281. THE MACCLESFIELD RIOTS (1824)

From 1815 to mid-century, England was distressed by serious fluctuations in the business cycle. There were several periods of widespread and devastating depression. Returning servicemen glutted a labor market depressed by the cancellation of war contracts, which caused unemployment and falling wages. Times were very bad from 1815 to 1823, and in 1824 a riot occurred among the silk weavers in Macclesfield (Cheshire), who complained of long hours of work and low wages.

Riot.—The custom among the silk weavers at Macclesfield has been to work eleven hours a day, but the masters determined lately to commence working twelve hours daily, paying extra for the additional hour. This the workmen determined to resist; and at six o'clock p.m. after having been idle and turbulent all day, they met opposite the Macclesfield Arms, and in the Market place, to about the number of 6,000. The yeomanry began to assemble about seven, and the Riot Act was read by the mayor, and the Yeomanry were ordered to clear the streets. This they performed with great steadiness under a shower of stones, but a party of about 400 of the mob got into the church-yard, and there, protected by a strong wall and iron gates, which the cavalry could not force, they defended themselves till half-past nine, and repulsed the Yeomanry twice. In this service Lieut. Grimsditch received five or six desperate contusions, and a severe wound in the face. Cornet Daintry was severely wounded in the head, and carried into the Macclesfield Arms. Several of the corps were also wounded. At length the mob was dislodged by an attack on their rear, by the constables forcing their way through a side wall into the church-yard.

282. OVERSPECULATION (1824–1825)

In 1824 business quickly picked up, an air of confidence pervaded the land, and, as often happens, it led to overspeculation.

In all these speculations, only a small investment, seldom exceeding five per cent, was paid at first: so that a very moderate rise in the price of the shares produced a large profit on the sum actually invested. If, for instance, shares of 100£, on which 5£ had been paid, rose to a premium of 40£, this yielded on every share a profit equal to eight times the amount of the money which had been paid. This possibility of enormous profit by risking a small sum, was a bait too tempting to be resisted: all the gambling propensities of human nature were constantly solicited into action: and crowds of individuals of every description—the credulous and the suspicious—the crafty and the bold—the raw and the experienced—the intelligent and the ignorant—princes, nobles, politicians, placemen, patriots, lawyers, physicians, divines, philosophers, poets, intermingled with women of all ranks and degrees—spinsters, wives, and widows—hastened to venture some portion of their property in schemes, of which scarcely any thing was known except the name. . . .

283. LANCASHIRE RIOTS (1826)

The business failures resulting from this overspeculation, which was the principal cause of the financial panic of 1825, led to unemployment and rioting. Disorder often took the form of destruction of machinery, which workers believed to be the chief cause of their miseries. The riots in Lancashire were typical.

On Monday forenoon, a large assembly of weavers took place on a hill at Henfield, a place where the four roads leading to Blackburn, Burnley, Whalley, and Haslingden meet. After remaining some time in discussion, they left the ground, and a very large body of them proceeded to Accrington, where some indications of riot occurred a week before, and where considerable alarm had been excited in the morning by about an hundred armed men passing through the village on their way to Henfield. Amongst the mob there assembled, no fewer, it is asserted, than 500 were armed with knives and pieces of iron ground sharp fastened to the end of sticks; some carried scythes; others had large sledge-hammers; and a few had pistols and guns. The messenger, who had been despatched to Blackburn for military aid, had not returned, when, about 12 o'clock, the mob proceeded to Messrs. Sykes's new mill, which they immediately broke open. In the course of 15 or 20 minutes they completely demolished the power-looms, 60 in number, with the whole apparatus, and the warps and cloths in the looms; besides doing much injury to the throstles and the steam-engine. The shops of the provision dealers were almost cleared of their contents. They next proceeded to a place called Wood Nook, where there were about 20 looms; these likewise they destroyed. They then went to Mr. B. Walmsley's, at Rough Hey, where also they broke 20 looms, and did considerable other damage; they did not however do any wilful injury to the spinning part of the machinery. . . .

284. CONDITIONS OF LABOR IN FACTORIES

Long hours of labor at wages often below what was necessary for mere existence caused widespread suffering. William Cobbett describes the plight of factory workers in the midland town of Preston.

The situation of Preston is deplorable. To so low a state has the trade come, that some, or, at least, one (one was named to me) of the manufacturers who have hitherto used power-looms, now employ hand weavers instead of the power-looms, being able to get the work done at a *lower price* in that way. Let any one judge, then, what are the wages that the poor creatures must receive who do the work now! Indeed, when I look at the body of good and sincere men, industrious and ingenious men, who stood before me at Preston; when I beheld the rags that covered them, unworthy of the name of clothing; when I beheld their pale and thin faces, their sunk eyes, and their anxious and miserable looks, the picture presented by my own group of men and boys at Barn Elm, rushed into my mind, I could not forbear cursing the horrible system which had reduced so many meritorious men to such a state. The coverings of the bodies of these people of "proud Preston" (in which borough, observe, Lord Derby has a mansion) were far inferior to the coverings of many a shoy-hoy that I have seen in many of the fields in Surrey and in Hampshire. Yes, the stakes put up in the fields, twisted round with straw, and then covered over with garments to frighten away the birds, I have never seen covered with such miserable rags as the people of "proud Preston" are now covered with. There might be a couple or three thousand standing before me, and leaving out the garments of the insolent and tyrannical masters, I verily believe that the covering of the whole, with the exception of the wooden clogs upon their feet, was not worth forty shillings. I remember that my father used to buy tons of rags to chop up for manure for his hop garden. Scores of garments have I seen amongst those rags far more valuable, far better looking, than the things which covered, or in part covered, the nakedness of this shivering and ill-treated group.

285. THE FACTORY ACT OF 1833

The employment of women and children (often at ages of eight and nine, and sometimes as young as five and six), and at dangerous occupations in factories, aroused the greatest public concern. Led by men like Anthony Ashley Cooper (later Lord Shaftesbury), who described the evils of the factory system in unforgettable speeches, reformers convinced Parliament to pass the Factory Act of 1833, the main sections of which are:

Whereas it is necessary that the Hours of Labour of Children and young Persons employed in Mills and Factories should be regulated, . . . be it therefore enacted . . . That from and after [January 1, 1834] . . . no Person under Eighteen Years of Age shall be allowed to work in the Night, . . . between the Hours of Half past Eight o'Clock in the Evening and Half past Five o'Clock in the Morning, except as herein-after provided, in or about any Cotton, Woollen, Worsted, Hemp, Flax, Tow, Linen, or Silk Mill or Factory wherein Steam or Water or any other mechanical Power is or shall be used to propel or work the Machinery in such Mill or Factory, either in scutching, carding, roving, spinning, piecing, twisting, winding, throwing, doubling netting, making Thread, dressing or weaving of Cotton, Wool, Worsted, Hemp, Flax, Tow, or Silk, either separately or mixed, in any such Mill or Factory situate in any Part of the United Kingdom of Great Britain and Ireland. . . .

II. And be it further enacted, That no Person under the Age of Eighteen Years shall be employed in any such Mill or Factory in such Description of Work as aforesaid more than Twelve Hours in any One Day, nor more than Sixty-nine Hours in any One Week, except as herein-after provided. . . .

VI. And be it further enacted, That there shall be allowed in the Course of every Day not less than One and a Half Hours for Meals to every such Person restricted as herein-before provided to the Performance of Twelve Hours Work daily.

VII. And be it enacted, That from and after [January 1, 1834] . . . it shall not be lawful for any Person whatsoever to employ in any Factory or

Mill . . . except in Mills for the Manufacture of Silk, any Child who shall not have completed his or her Ninth Year of Age.

VIII. And be it further enacted, That from and after the Expiration of Six Months after the passing of this Act it shall not be lawful for any Person whatsoever to employ, keep, or allow to remain in any Factory or Mill as aforesaid for a longer Time than Forty-eight Hours in any One Week, nor for a longer Time than Nine Hours in any One Day . . . any Child who shall not have completed his or her Eleventh Year of Age. . . .

XI. And be it further enacted, That from and after the Expiration of Six Months after the passing of this Act it shall not be lawful for any Person to employ, keep, or allow to remain in any Factory or Mill any Child who shall not have completed his or her Eleventh Year of Age without such Certificate . . . certifying such Child to be of the ordinary Strength and Appearance of a Child of the Age of Nine Years. . . .

XIV. And be it further enacted, That from and after the Commencement of the . . . Periods . . . for restricting the Employment of Children . . . it shall not be lawful to employ . . . any Person between the said Ages [at first eleven, afterward twelve, and still later, fourteen years, as defined in a schedule earlier in this Act] . . . and the Age of Eighteen for more than Nine Hours in any Day. . . . That upon the passing of this Act it shall be lawful for His Majesty by Warrant . . . to appoint . . . Four Persons to be Inspectors of Factories and Places where the Labour of Children and young Persons under Eighteen Years of Age is employed . . . and such Inspectors . . . are hereby empowered to enter any Factory or Mill, and any School attached or belonging thereto, at all Times and Seasons, by Day or by Night, when such Mills or Factories are at work, and . . . to examine therein the Children and any other Person . . . employed therein, and to make Inquiry respecting their Condition, Employment, and Education. . . .

XX. And be it further enacted, That from and after the Expiration of Six Months from the passing of this Act every Child herein-before restricted to the Performance of Forty-eight Hours of Labour in any One Week shall, so long as such Child shall be within the said restricted Age, attend some School to be chosen by the Parents or Guardians of such Child. . . .

XXXI. And be it further enacted, That if any Employer of Children in any Factory or Mill shall . . . offend against any of the Provisions of this Act, . . . such Offender shall for such Offence . . . forfeit and pay any Sum not exceeding Twenty Pounds, nor less than One Pound, at the Discretion of the Inspector or Justice before whom such Offender shall be convicted.
. . .

286. THE FACTORY ACT OF 1844

As many had predicted, the passage of the Factory Act of 1833 proved to be an entering wedge, and many Acts limiting and regulating hours of work since then have been passed. The second such Act came in 1844. The first sections of this Act relate to the appointment of sub-inspectors to see that the law was being enforced, and made provision for surgeons to check the health of workers. Its principal provisions are:

XIX. And be it enacted, That after the Expiration of Six Months from the Date of this Act coming into operation no Child or young Person shall be employed in any Part of a Factory in which the wet-spinning of Flax, Hemp, Jute, or Tow is carried on, unless sufficient Means shall be employed and continued for protecting the Workers from being wetted, and, where hot Water is used, for preventing the Escape of Steam into the Room occupied by the Workers.

XX. And be it enacted, That no Child or young Person shall be allowed to clean any Part of the Mill-gearing in a Factory while the same is in motion for the Purpose of propelling any Part of the manufacturing Machinery. . . .

XXI. And be it enacted, That every Fly-wheel directly connected with the Steam Engine or Water-wheel or other mechanical Power, whether in the Engine House or not, and every part of a Steam Engine and Water-wheel, and every Hoist or Teagle [lift], near to which Children or young Persons are liable to pass or be employed, and all Parts of the Mill-gearing in a Factory, shall be securely fenced. . . .

XXVI. And be it enacted, That the Hours of the Work of Children and young Persons in every Factory shall be reckoned from the Time when any Child or young Person shall first begin to work in the Morning in such Factory, and shall be regulated by a public Clock, or by some other Clock open to the public View. . . .

XXVIII. [Abstracts of this Act] . . . shall be fixed on a moveable Board, and be hung up as soon as received by the Occupier of the Factory or his Agent in the Entrance of the Factory. . . .

XXX. And be it enacted, That no Child shall be employed in any Factory more than Six Hours and Thirty Minutes in any One Day . . . unless the Dinner Time of the young Persons in such Factory shall begin at One of the Clock. . . .

XXXII. And be it enacted, That no Female above the Age of Eighteen

Years shall be employed in any Factory save for the same Time and in the same Manner as young Persons. . . .

XXXV. And be it enacted, That no Child or young Person shall be employed in a Factory, either to recover lost Time or for any other Purpose, on any Saturday after Half past Four of the Clock in the Afternoon.

XXXVI. And be it enacted, That . . . no Child or young Person shall be employed more than Five Hours before One of the Clock in the Afternoon of any Day without an Interval for Meal Time of at least Thirty Minutes; and during any Meal Time which shall form any Part of the Hour and a Half allowed for Meals no Child or young Person shall be employed or allowed to remain in any Room in which any manufacturing Process is then carried on. . . .

287. THE TEN HOURS ACT (1847)

Be it enacted . . . That, . . . from the First Day of July One Thousand eight hundred and forty-seven no Person under the Age of Eighteen Years shall be employed in any Mill or Factory . . . for more than Eleven Hours in any One Day, nor for more than Sixty-three Hours in any One Week. . . .

II. And be it enacted, That from the First Day of May . . . [1848] no Person under the Age of Eighteen Years shall be employed in any . . . Mill or Factory for more than Ten Hours in any One Day nor more than Fifty-eight Hours in any One Week. . . .

III. And be it enacted, That the Restrictions respectively by this Act imposed as regards the working of Persons under the Age of Eighteen Years shall extend to Females above the Age of Eighteen Years. . . .

288. ARGUMENTS AGAINST LIMITING HOURS OF LABOR

The Earl of Clarendon . . . objected to the Bill [the Ten Hours Act] because it extended much further than it professed to do: it would affect adults as well as young persons, men as well as women; would limit the hours during which machinery must run; limit the quantity of manufactured produce, and proportionately reduce wages. All this would be done without any of the reasons for legislative interference formerly presented by the excessive labour in factories and the actual torture of children.

The labour was now performed in comfortable buildings, well warmed and well ventilated, and generally more healthy than the houses of the workpeople. The loss in wages would not be the only loss. The Act would reduce the amount of fixed and floating capital, and would affect other trades. There would be less coal consumed, less oil, less tallow, less leather, less flour; less cotton, wool, flax, hemp, silk, indigo, madder, and dyes; there would be less shipping, less labour for the shipping: indeed, all classes would suffer for this apparently humane effort to lessen the hours of labour. The leases of factories were framed on the basis that the machinery was to run twelve hours: the leaseholders would suffer proportionably. Foreign competition already pressed on this country: Russia imported 15,000,000 pounds of cotton yarn; and for the first time last year she imported 55,000 bales of raw cotton. The duty on imports secured their own markets—(Cheers from the Opposition)—and we should lose their markets. . . . The average time of work in Austria, Russia, and France was thirteen hours; in Germany, twelve hours; in the United States, twelve in winter, and fourteen in summer. As to the desire of the operatives, they would not accept the measure except under the notion that they were to receive twelve hours' wages for ten hours' work.

289. LABOR CONDITIONS AMONG CHIMNEY-SWEEPS (1817)

Complaints had been made in Parliament about the mistreatment of boys engaged in sweeping chimneys. It was known that children, including girls, had been employed in that trade at the tender age of five years, and that many had been burned and maimed for life. A committee appointed in 1817 to investigate the situation reported that:

It is in evidence that they are stolen from their parents, and inveigled out of the workhouses; that in order to conquer the natural repugnance of the infants to ascend the narrow and dangerous chimneys, to clean which their labour is required, blows are used; that pins are forced into their feet by the boy that follows them up the chimney, in order to compel them to ascend it; and that lighted straw has been applied for that purpose; that the children are subject to sores and bruises, and wounds and burns on their thighs, knees, and elbows; and that it will require many months before the extremities of the elbows and knees become sufficiently hard to resist the excoriations to which they are at first subject. . . . Your committee are informed that the deformity of the spine, legs, arms, etc. of these boys proceeds generally, if not wholly, from the circumstance of their being obliged to ascend chimneys at an age when their bones are in a soft and growing state; but likewise, by their being compelled to carry bags of soot and cloths, the weight of which sometimes exceed twenty or thirty pounds, not including the soot, the burthen of which they also occasionally bear for a great length of distance and time; the knees and ankle joints become deformed, in the first instance, from the position they are obliged to put them in, in order to support themselves, not only while climbing up the chimney, but more particularly so whilst coming down, when they rest solely on the lower extremities, the arms being used for scraping and sweeping down the soot.

Laws to put an end to this evil were passed in 1840, 1865, and 1870.

290. AN ACCIDENT AT A COLLIERY (1815)

Conditions were every bit as bad in England's coal mines. Women and children were employed (the latter as early as six years of age) in the wet and unhealthy mines, often at tasks that ruined their health. Accidents were frequent, and the ever-present mine gas caused fatal explosions. The accident described below resulted from the bursting of the boiler on a steam engine used to haul up the coal.

On Monday, the 31st of July, another melancholy accident happened at Messrs. Nesham and Co.'s colliery, at Newbottle, in the county of Durham. The proprietors had provided a powerful locomotive steam-engine, for the purpose of drawing 10 or 12 coalwaggons to the staith at one time; and Monday being the day it was to be put in motion, a great number of persons belonging to the colliery had collected to see it; but unfortunately, just as it was going off, the boiler of the machine burst. The engine-man was dashed to pieces, and his mangled remains blown 114 yards; the top of the boiler (nine feet square, weight 19 cwt.) was blown 100 yards: and the two cylinders 90 yards. A little boy was also thrown to a great distance. By this accident 57 persons were killed and wounded, of whom 11 were dead on Sunday night, and several remain dangerously ill. The cause of the accident is accounted for as follows: the engine-man said, "as there were several owners and viewers there, he would make her (the engine) go in grand style," and he had got upon the boiler to loose the screw of the safety valve, but being overheated, it unfortunately exploded. It will be recollected, that at the fatal blast which recently took place at this colliery, the first who arrived at the bank, holding by a rope, was a little boy, about six or seven years of age. The poor little fellow is among the number dead.

291. THE MINES ACT OF 1842

While this Act, of course, did not correct all the evils in the collieries, and could not in any material way prevent explosions, it did remove some of the main abominations.

Whereas it is unfit that Women and Girls should be employed in any Mine or Colliery, and it is expedient to make Regulations regarding the Employment of Boys in Mines and Collieries, and to make Provisions for the Safety of Persons working therein; Be it therefore enacted . . . That from and after the passing of this Act it shall not be lawful for any Owner of any Mine or Colliery whatsoever to employ any Female Person within any Mine or Colliery, or permit any Female Person to work or be therein . . . ; and that from and after Three Calendar Months from the passing of this Act it shall not be lawful for any Owner of any Mine or Colliery to employ any Female Person who at the passing of this Act shall be under the Age of Eighteen Years . . . and from and after the First Day of March . . . [1843] it shall not be lawful for any Owner of any Mine or Colliery to employ any Female Person whatsoever within any Mine or Colliery, or to allow or permit any Female Person to work or be therein. . . .

II. And be it enacted, That from and after the First Day of March . . . [1843] it shall not be lawful for any Owner of any Mine or Colliery to employ any Male Person under the Age of Ten Years within any Mine or Colliery. . . .

III. [Provided for the appointment of mining inspectors.]

292. CANAL BUILDING

Along with the industrial, commercial, and agricultural revolutions of the century after 1750 there went a revolution in the means of transportation. Canal building began in the early eighteenth century and increased rapidly during and immediately after the wars with France (1793–1815). Unfortunately, the canals were not well planned, and the owners made the mistake of using men and mules or horses to pull the barges and boats instead of employing steam power. The development of railways brought an abrupt end to the construction of canals. The extent of canal building in 1822 on the eve of the railway boom can be judged by this account:

The number of navigable canals in the United Kingdom is 103; of which 97 are formed in England alone, not including those of which the length does not exceed 5 miles; five in Scotland; and one only in Ireland. The total extent of these canals is 2682¼ miles; i.e. 2471 miles of English canals, 149¾ miles in Scotland, and 69½ miles in the Dublin and Shannon canal. The sum expended in these constructions is estimated at more than £30,000,000 sterling; and, in some cases, the original shares have risen in a few years to fifteen and even twenty times their original value. In the lines of these canals, forty-eight subterraneous passages occur, the entire length of which is not accurately known; but forty of them, whose lengths are stated, give a total developement of 57,051 yards, or more than thirty-two miles. It is deserving of remark, that, of the total length of the English canals, more than 1400 miles communicate with the grand navigable line between London and Liverpool, the length of this alone being 264 miles; and it is connected in its course with forty-five others, of which the united extent equals 1150 miles. Such is the present state of the English navigable canals; not a yard of which existed before the year 1755.

293. RAILWAYS

By 1830 there were about 4,600 miles of canals, but the development of the railway industry at that time put an effective damper on canal building. Beginning during the last part of the eighteenth century, rails were laid in mine shafts as well as on the surface near the pits to ease the burden of transporting the heavy coal tubs and wagons, which were pulled along the rails, either by people or horses, to canals and rivers. When steam power was applied to locomotion, railways quickly overtook and surpassed canals as the principal means of transportation. Accidents were frequent in the early railroad days of the 1820's and 1830's, largely because of boiler explosions, improperly laid roadbeds, and the like. Despite such problems, the railways offered a decided advantage over the canals and coaches, as the following description in the *Annual Register* for 1832 will attest:

Advantages of Rail-Roads—Before the establishment of the Liverpool and Manchester railway, there were twenty-two regular and about seven occasional extra coaches between those places, which, in full, could only carry per day 688 persons. The railway, from its commencement, carried 700,000 persons in eighteen months being an average of 1,070 per day. It has not been stopped for a single day. There has occurred but one fatal accident on it in eighteen months. The fare by coach was 10s. inside, and 5s. outside —by railway it is 5s. inside and 3s. 6d. outside. The time occupied in making the journey by coach was four hours—by railway it is one hour and three-quarters. All the coaches but one have ceased running, and that chiefly for the conveyance of parcels. The mails all travel by the railway, at a saving to government of two-thirds of the expense. The railway coaches are more commodious than others. The travelling is cheaper, safer, and easier. A great deal of traffic, which used to go by other roads, comes now by railway; both time and money are saved, though the length of the journey may be often increased. . . . A great deal of land on the line has been let for garden ground, at increased rents. Residents on the line find the railway a great convenience, by enabling them to attend to their business in Manchester and Liverpool with ease, at little expense. No inconvenience is felt by residents from smoke or noise; and, on the contrary, great advantage is experienced by means of travelling, to and fro, distances of ten miles in half an hour for 1s. and without any fatigue. . . .

294. THE RAILWAY PASSENGER ACT (1844)

As the railways, privately built and owned, refused to publish train schedules or to take measures for the safety and convenience of passengers, they were, like the mines and factories, subjected to government regulation. The Act of 1844, after stating that any railway which made profits in excess of ten per cent was subject to having its scale of tolls revised by the Treasury, provided that:

All Passenger Railway Companies . . . shall, by means of One Train at the least to travel along their Railway from one End to the other of each Trunk, Branch, or Junction Line, belonging to or leased by them, so long as they shall continue to carry other Passengers over such . . . Line, once at the least each Way on every Week Day, except Christmas Day and Good Friday . . . provide for the Conveyance of Third Class Passengers to and from the terminal and other ordinary Passenger Stations of the Railway, . . . under the following conditions;

Such Train shall start at an Hour to be from Time to Time fixed by the directors . . . :
Such Train shall travel at an average Rate of Speed not less than Twelve Miles an Hour for the whole Distance travelled on the Railway, including Stoppages:
Such Train shall, if required, take up and set down Passengers at every Passenger Station which it shall pass on the line:
The Carriages in which Passengers shall be conveyed by such Train shall be provided with Seats, and shall be protected from the Weather, in a Manner satisfactory to the Lords of the said Committee [Lords Commissioners of the Treasury]:
The Fare or Charge for each Third Class Passenger by such Train shall not exceed One Penny for each Mile travelled:
Each Passenger by such Train shall be allowed to take with him Half a Hundred weight of Luggage . . . .
Children under Three Years of Age accompanying Passengers by such Train shall be taken without any Charge, and Children of Three Years and upwards, but under Twelve Years of Age, at Half the charge for an Adult Passenger . . . .

This Act was but the first of a long series of regulative measures which culminated in the nationalization of transport in the present century.

295. A RAILWAY ACCIDENT (1851)

The Act of 1844 was only the first of many regulative Acts passed by Parliament to improve the service and to require safety devices. Accidents, such as the one described below, focused attention on the perils of railway travel in its early years.

A most disastrous accident occurred at the Bicester Station of the Buckinghamshire Railway, a few minutes before 7 o'clock in the evening, to an excursion train for Oxford, which left the Euston Square Station at half past 4 in the afternoon. The Buckinghamshire Railway branches from the North-Western at Bletchley (half-way between London and Rugby) and runs through Winslow and Bicester to Oxford. The line has a double set of rails between Bletchley and Winslow; but at Winslow one set diverges westward to Buckingham and Banbury, and the other set continues on to Bicester and Oxford. As the line at Bicester is single, a siding is formed on the left hand going from London to Oxford, for the alighting of passengers at the Bicester down-station. For the purpose of diverting into this siding the trains intended to stop at Bicester, there are points in the main line, which in their regular and permanent state face straight for the main line, but which are made to face into the siding on being manipulated by a pointsman. It appears that the driver and the guards having care of the excursion train supposed they were to go straight to Oxford without stopping at Bicester; but the station-master, and some or one of the subordinate officers at the station expected, or intended, that the train would stop at Bicester. Either from this misunderstanding, and from some failure of hand and eye in the pointsman, . . . when the points were reached, the engine went one way and the train another; the train was overturned on itself, and became a mass of ruins, from which it took three or four hours to remove the dead and rescue the wounded. . . . The company have paid nearly £30,000 to the sufferers in the way of compensation.

The industrialization and urbanization of England in the nineteenth century was accompanied by a steady movement toward political democracy. Reform of Parliament, particularly in view of the corruption prevalent in eighteenth-century politics, had been discussed for decades, and bills to accomplish such reform had been introduced on several occasions on the eve of the French Revolutionary War. With the increasing radicalism in France, which the English ruling classes feared might also overtake them, any thought of reform was out of the question; in fact, the liberalizing tendencies inherent in the aims of abolitionists, trade unionists, and social reformers of the 1780's and 1790's in England provoked stern governmental reprisals that continued intermittently until the 1820's. Thereafter, the country having experienced an economic depression and workingmen's riots and demonstrations, the liberal Tories enacted economic and religious reforms that rekindled the zeal for electoral and representative reform of Parliament.

296. A CLASSIFICATION OF MEMBERS OF PARLIAMENT (1830)

John Wade, in his critical volume, *The Black Book; or Corruption Unmasked,* thus classified the membership of the House of Commons:

    1. Relations to Peers 228
    2. Lawyers 25
    3. Officers in the Navy 15
    4. Officers in the Army 80
    5. Placemen and Pensioners 126
    6. Miscellaneous 186
    7. Representatives of the People . . 0

297. THE DUKE OF WELLINGTON ON REFORM (1830)

The death of George IV (1830) necessitated a general election which the Whigs, pledged to reform, won. When Parliament assembled in the autumn, the Whigs began to discuss reform of the Commons. It was then that Wellington bared his ultra-conservative thoughts on reform. He refers first to Earl Grey's proposals on that subject.

The noble Earl had alluded to the propriety of effecting Parliamentary Reform. The noble Earl had, however, been candid enough to acknowledge that he was not prepared with any measure of reform, and he could have no scruple in saying that his Majesty's Government was as totally unprepared with any plan as the noble Lord. Nay, he, on his own part, would go further, and say, that he had never read or heard of any measure up to the present moment which could in any degree satisfy his mind that the state of the representation could be improved, or be rendered more satisfactory to the country at large than at the present moment. He would not, however, at such an unseasonable time, enter upon the subject, or excite discussion, but he should not hesitate to declare unequivocally what were his sentiments upon it. He was fully convinced that the country possessed at the present moment a Legislature which answered all the good purposes of legislation, and this to a greater degree than any Legislature ever had answered in any country whatever. He would go further and say, that the Legislature and the system of representation possessed the full and entire confidence—deservedly possessed that confidence—and the discussions in the Legislature had a very great influence over the opinions of the country. He would go still further and say, that if at the present moment he had imposed upon him the duty of forming a Legislature for any country, and particularly for a country like this, in possession of great property of various descriptions, he did not mean to assert that he could form such a Legislature as they possessed now, for the nature of man was incapable of reaching such excellence at once; but his great endeavour would be, to form some description of legislature which would produce the same results. . . .

298. THE COMMONS PASS THE REFORM BILL (1831)

Wellington's resignation as prime minister in 1830 brought Earl Grey and his Whig followers into power, pledged to introduce a Reform Bill. The Bill, written by a committee composed of Lord John Russell, Sir James Graham, Lord Duncannon, and Lord Durham, was read in the Commons by Russell. It called for transferring the representation in Parliament from many "rotten" and "pocket" boroughs to the new large cities created by the Industrial Revolution, and for a modest extension of the franchise. Although it was a mild Bill indeed, the House of Commons voted it down. Grey advised the king to dissolve Parliament, and the Reform Bill became the main issue in the ensuing elections. The Whigs, having won the election, at once reintroduced the Bill, which this time passed the Commons. Lord Macaulay described the scene in the House during the division in a letter to a friend.

Such a scene as the division of last Tuesday I never saw, and never expect to see again. . . . The crowd overflowed the House in every part. When the strangers were cleared out, and the doors locked, we had six hundred and eight members present—more by fifty-five than ever were in a division before. The ayes and noes were like two volleys of cannon from opposite sides of a field of battle. When the opposition went out into the lobby, an operation which took up twenty minutes or more, we spread ourselves over the benches on both sides of the House; for there were many of us who had not been able to find a seat during the evening. When the doors were shut we began to speculate on our numbers. Every body was desponding. 'We have lost it. We are only two hundred and eighty at most. I do not think we are two hundred and fifty. There are three hundred. Alderman Thompson has counted them. He says they are two hundred and ninety-nine.' This was the talk of our benches. . . . I had no hope, however, of three hundred. . . . We were all breathless with anxiety, when Charles Wood, who stood near the door, jumped up on a bench and cried out, 'They are only three hundred and one.' We set up a shout that you might have heard to Charing Cross, waving our hats, stamping against the floor, and clapping our hands. The tellers scarcely got through the crowd; for the House was thronged up to the table, and all the floor was fluctuating with heads like the pit of a theatre. But you might have heard a pin drop as Duncannon read the numbers. Then again the shouts broke out, and many of us shed tears. I could scarcely refrain. And the jaw of [Sir Robert] Peel fell; and the face of Twiss was as the face of a damned soul; and Herries looked like Judas taking his neck-tie off for the last operation. We shook hands, and clapped each other on the back, and went out laughing, crying, and huzzaing into the lobby. And no sooner were the outer doors opened than another shout answered that within the House. All the passages and the stairs into the waiting-rooms were thronged with people who had waited till four in the morning to know the issue. We passed through a narrow lane between two thick masses of them; and all the way down they were shouting and waving their hats, till we got into the open air. I called a cabriolet, and the first thing the driver asked was, 'Is the bill carried?' 'Yes, by one.' 'Thank God for it, sir!' And away I rode to Gray's Inn—and so ended a scene which will probably never be equalled till the reformed Parliament wants reforming. . . .

299. THE REFORM ACT OF 1832

The House of Lords, although opposed to the Reform Bill, was brought around to voting for it on the threat that the king would appoint a sufficient number of pro-Bill peers to assure its passage. Rather than see an increase in the number of Lords (and, in their view, a pollution of their ranks), the upper House accepted it. The chief provisions of the Act are as follows:

Whereas it is expedient to take effectual Measures for correcting divers Abuses that have long prevailed in the Choice of Members to serve in the Commons House of Parliament, to deprive many inconsiderable Places of the Right of returning Members, to grant such Privileges to large, populous, and wealthy Towns, to increase the Number of Knights of the Shire, to extend the Elective Franchise to many of His Majesty's Subjects who have not heretofore enjoyed the same, and to diminish the Expence of Elections; be it therefore enacted . . . That each of the Boroughs enumerated in the Schedule marked (A) [56 in all] shall from and after the End of this present Parliament cease to return any Member or Members to serve in Parliament.

II. And be it enacted, That each of the Boroughs enumerated in the Schedule marked (B) [30 in all] shall . . . return One Member and no more to serve in Parliament.

III. And be it enacted, That each of the Places named in the Schedule marked (C) [22 in all] . . . shall from and after the End of this present Parliament return Two Members to serve in Parliament.

IV. And be it enacted, That each of the Places named in the Schedule marked (D) [20 in all] . . . shall . . . return One Member to serve in Parliament. . . .

V. [This section and those through section XVII list the boroughs and shires which were to be subdivided; those that were to be given more than two Members; and those that were to have their representation reduced.]

XVIII. And be it enacted, That no Person shall be entitled to vote in the Election of a Knight or Knights of the Shire to serve in any future Parliament, or in the Election of a Member or Members to serve in any future Parliament for any City or Town being a County of itself . . . except such Person shall be in the actual and *bona fide* Occupation of such Lands or Tenements, or except the same shall have come to such Person by Marriage, Marriage Settlement, Devise, or Promotion to any Benefice or to any Office, or except the same shall be of the clear yearly Value of not less than Ten Pounds above all Rents and Charges payable out of or in respect of the same. . . .

XIX. [Copyholders of lands] . . . of the clear yearly value of not less than Ten Pounds over and above all Rents and Charges payable out of or in respect of the same, shall be entitled to vote in the Election of a Knight or Knights of the Shire. . . .

XX. [This section gave the rights of voting in counties to leaseholders and occupiers of premises of the yearly value of not less than fifty pounds.]

XXVI. And be it enacted, That notwithstanding any thing hereinbefore contained no Person shall be entitled to vote in the Election of a Knight or Knights of the Shire to serve in any future Parliament unless he shall have been duly registered according to the Provisions herein-after contained; and that no Person shall be so registered in any Year in respect of his Estate or Interest in any Lands or Tenements, as a Freeholder, Copyholder, Customary Tenant, or Tenant in Ancient Demesne, unless he shall have been in the actual Possession thereof, or in the Receipt of Rents and Profits thereof for his own Use, for Six Calendar Months at least next previous to the last Day of July in such Year . . . and that no Person shall be so registered in any Year . . . unless he shall have been in the actual Possession [of such property] . . . or in the Receipt of the Rents and Profits thereof for his own Use, as the Case may require, for Twelve Calendar Months next previous to the last Day of July in such Year. . . .

XXVII. And be it enacted, That in every City or Borough which shall return a Member or Members to serve in any future Parliament, every Male Person of full age, and not subject to any legal Incapacity, who shall occupy, within such City or Borough, or within any Place sharing in the Election for such City or Borough, as Owner or Tenant, any House, Warehouse, Counting-House, Shop, or other Building, being, either separately or jointly with any Land within such City, Borough, or Place occupied therewith by him as Owner, or occupied therewith by him as Tenant under the same Landlord, of the clear yearly Value of not less than Ten Pounds, shall, if duly registered according to the Provisions herein-after contained, be entitled to vote in the Election of a Member or Members to serve in any future Parliament for such City or Borough. . . . [But no occupier could vote unless rated to the Poor Rate and unless he had paid all his taxes.]

XXXVI. And be it enacted, That no Person shall be entitled to be registered in any Year as a Voter in the Election of a Member . . . for any City or Borough who shall within Twelve Calendar Months next previous to the last Day of July in such Year have received Parochial Relief or other Alms [the Poor Law] which by the Law of Parliament now disqualify from voting in the Election of Members to serve in Parliament. . . .

There follows a number of sections that relate to the registration lists of voters, the duties of overseers in the matter of checking lists, overseeing elections, the handling of cases of disputed registrations, and the publication of voting lists.

LXII. [In elections] . . . the polling shall commence at Nine o'Clock in the Forenoon of the next Day but Two after the Day fixed for the Election, unless such Day but Two shall be Saturday or Sunday, and then on the Monday following, at the principal Place of Election . . . and such polling shall continue for Two Days only, such Two Days being successive Days; (that is to say) for Seven Hours on the First Day of Polling, and for Eight Hours of the Second Day of Polling; and no Poll shall be kept open later than Four o'Clock in the Afternoon of the Second Day. . . .

LXIII and LXIV. [These sections provide for the division of counties into polling districts and for booths for polling places in the counties.]

LXXVIII. Provided always, and be it enacted, That nothing in this Act

contained shall extend to or in anywise affect the Election of Members to
serve in Parliament for the Universities of Oxford or Cambridge, or shall
entitle any Person to vote in the Election of Members to serve in Parliament
for the City of Oxford or Town of Cambridge in respect of the Occupation
of any Chambers or Premises in any of the Colleges or Halls of the Universities of Oxford or Cambridge. . . .

300. THE PEOPLE'S CHARTERS OF 1842 AND 1848

Many workingmen were deeply disappointed with the Reform Act, for it
had given votes only to the upper and middle classes. Therefore, at a meeting of some "radical" M.P.s and leaders of the workingmen in 1837, a
"People's Charter" was drafted. It declared for additional reform in its six
points: (1) universal manhood suffrage; (2) annual Parliaments; (3) vote
by secret ballot; (4) abolition of property qualifications for voting; (5) payment of M.P.s; (6) equal electoral districts.

A. *Charter of 1842*

In 1842, these and other demands were presented in a petition to Parliament. The *Annual Register* describes the scene as follows:

The most striking shape, however, in which the grievances of the working classes presented themselves to the notice of the Legislature during this
Session, was the presentation of a petition, which for bulk and number of
signatures, was unparalleled in the annals of Parliament. The sum total of
names attached was stated to amount to upwards of 3,000,000.—the proportion of bona fide signatures being considerably less—its prayer was for the
enactment of the great constitutional changes which form the "six points"
comprised in the Chartist creed—besides these demands, however, the petition declared the weight of the National Debt too great to be borne, and
pointed in significant language at the abolition of all "Monopolies," including those of paper-money, machinery, land, religion, the public press, and
railway travelling. The conveyance and presentation of this enormous document afforded a curious spectacle, and a task of no small difficulty—it required sixteen men to support it, and was escorted to Palace-yard by a long
procession of working men, who marched in good discipline and with
peaceful demeanour to the Houses of Parliament. Arrived at the door of the
House of Commons, however, it proved too big for admission, and in order
to effect its entrance it became necessary to divide it into sections. Hastily
plucked asunder in many parts each piece formed a load for a troop of the
petitioners, who carried it into the body of the House. . . .

B. *The Charter of 1848*

Nothing having resulted from the petition of 1842, Parliament received another in 1848, under less amicable conditions. Greville records the circumstances in his *Diary* for April 13, 1848.

In the morning (a very fine day) everybody was on the alert; the parks were closed; our office was fortified, a barricade of Council Registers were erected in the accessible room on the ground floor, and all our guns were taken down to be used in defence of the building. However, at about twelve o'clock crowds came streaming along Whitehall, going northward, and it was announced that all was over. The intended tragedy was rapidly changed into a ludicrous farce. The Chartists, about 20,000 in number, assembled on Kensington Common. Presently Mr. Mayne appeared on the ground, and sent one of his inspectors to say he wanted to speak to Feargus O'Connor [owner of the (Leeds) *Morning Star* and a proponent of trade unionism and Chartism]. Feargus thought he was going to be arrested and was in a terrible fright; but he went to Mayne, who merely said he was desired to inform him that the meeting would not be interfered with, but the procession would not be allowed. Feargus insisted on shaking hands with Mayne, swore he was his best of friends, and instantly harangued his rabble, advising them not to provoke a collision, and to go away quietly—advice they instantly obeyed, and with great alacrity and good humour. Thus all evaporated in smoke. Feargus himself then repaired to the Home Office, saw Sir George Grey, and told him it was all over, and thanked the Government for their leniency, assuring him the Convention would not have been so lenient if they had got the upper hand. Grey asked him if he was going back to the meeting. He said No; that he had had his toes trodden on till he was lame, and his pocket picked, and he would have no more to do with it. The petition was brought down piecemeal and presented in the afternoon. Since that there has been an exposure of the petition itself, covering the authors of it with ridicule and disgrace. It turns out to be signed by less than two millions, instead of by six as Feargus stated; and of those, there were no end of fictitious names, together with the insertion of every species of ribaldry, indecency, and impertinence. . . .

301. POLITICAL PARTIES

The political factions, Whig and Tory, underwent a change in the years following the repeal of the Corn Laws in 1846. The Tories who followed Peel on the repeal issue were known as Peelites; those who opposed him, led by Lord Derby and Disraeli, were called Protectionists. When, in 1851, the latter group abandoned protection to all intents and purposes, some of the Peelites after Peel's death (1850) joined them, and under Disraeli's strong leadership, the modern Conservative party evolved. During the same years the Whigs, abandoning the term Whig gradually, were joined by some of the former Peelites and formed the modern Liberal party, first under Lord Palmerston and then under Gladstone. In a very real sense, then, it can be said that the first modern political party was the one formed by Palmerston in 1859.

A. *Principles of the Liberal Party*

Russell, the Whig leader, had defined the objectives or principles of the Whigs as follows, and these, when free trade is added, became the main principles of the new Liberal party:

1. Not to interfere in the internal government of other countries . . . .
3. To promote religious liberty, and to remove the political disabilities affecting Protestant dissenters and Roman Catholics.
4. To favour parliamentary reform and liberty of the press.

B. *The Conservative Party Program (1872)*

In a speech at Manchester, April 3, 1872, Disraeli described the program of the Conservatives (he still used the word "Tory") as follows:

Now I have always been of opinion that the Tory party has three great objects. The first is to maintain the institutions [Crown, Church, and Parliament] of the country—not from any sentiment of political superstition, but because we believe that they embody the principles upon which a community like England can alone safely rest. The principles of liberty, of order, of law, and of religion ought not to be entrusted to individual opinion or to the caprice and passion of multitudes, but should be embodied in a form of permanence and power. We associate with the Monarchy the ideas which it represents—the majesty of the law, the administration of justice, the fountain of mercy and of honour. . . . I think that the nation . . . has arrived at the conclusion which we have always maintained, that it is the first duty of England to maintain its institutions, because to them we principally ascribe the power and prosperity of the country.

Gentlemen, there is another and second great object of the Tory party. If the first is to maintain the institutions of the country, the second is . . . to uphold the Empire of England . . . , and in my opinion no minister in this country will do his duty who neglects any opportunity of reconstructing as much as possible our Colonial Empire. . . .

Gentlemen, another great object of the Tory party, and one not inferior to the maintenance of the Empire, or the upholding of our institutions, is the elevation of the condition of the people. . . . Recently [the working classes in 1867] . . . have obtained . . . a great extension of political rights; and when the people of England see that under the constitution of this country . . . they possess every personal freedom, and, according to the conviction of the whole country, also an adequate concession of political rights, is it at all wonderful that they should wish to elevate and improve their condition, and is it unreasonable that they should ask the Legislature to assist them in that behest as far as it is consistent with the general welfare of the realm . . . ?

302. REFORM ACT OF 1867

The Reform Act of 1832 had enfranchised the middle class, but the working class, which generally did not meet the high property qualification for voting, had not been given the vote. The second great Reform Act of the nineteenth century, passed in 1867, nearly doubled those entitled to vote by extending the franchise to practically all adult male residents of parliamentary boroughs. The Act also redistributed some seats in Parliament without altering its size along roughly the same lines followed in 1832. After 1867, only agricultural laborers without land or whose lodgings were too modest to meet the minimum financial qualification, and the poorest industrial workers and domestics among the male population were overlooked. But the Reform Act of 1884 remedied this situation. The following are the chief provisions of the Act of 1867:

1. This Act shall be cited for all Purposes as The Representation of the People Act, 1867.

2. This Act shall not apply to Scotland or Ireland, nor in anywise affect the Election of Members to serve in Parliament for the Universities of Oxford or Cambridge.

PART I

FRANCHISES

3. Every Man shall, in and after . . . [1868] be entitled to . . . vote for a Member or Members to serve in Parliament for a Borough, who is qualified as follows; (that is to say,)

    1. Is of full Age, and not subject to any legal Incapacity; and

    2. Is on the last Day of July in any Year, and has during the whole of the preceeding Twelve Calendar Months been, an Inhabitant Occupier, as Owner or Tenant, of any Dwelling House within the Borough; and

3. Has during the Time of such Occupation been rated as an ordinary Occupier in respect of the Premises so occupied by him within the Borough to all Rates . . . made for the Relief of the Poor . . . ; and

4. Has on or before the Twentieth Day of July in the same Year bona fide paid an equal Amount in the Pound to that payable by other ordinary Occupiers in respect of all Poor Rates . . . :

Provided that no Man shall under this Section be entitled to be registered as a Voter by reason of his being a joint Occupier of any Dwelling House.

4. Every Man shall, in and after . . . [1868], be entitled . . . to vote for a Member or Members to serve in Parliament for a Borough, who is qualified as follows; (that is to say,)

1. Is of full Age and not subject to any legal Incapacity; and

2. As a Lodger has occupied in the same Borough separately and as sole Tenant for the Twelve Months preceding the last Day of July in any Year the same Lodgings . . . of a clear yearly Value, if let unfurnished, of Ten Pounds or upwards; and

3. Has resided in such Lodgings during the Twelve Months immediately preceding the last Day of July . . . .

5. Every Man shall, in and after . . . [1868], be entitled to . . . vote for a Member or Members to serve in Parliament for a County, who is qualified as follows; (that is to say,)

1. Is of full Age, and not subject to any legal Incapacity, and is seised at Law or in Equity of any Lands or Tenements of Freehold, Copyhold, or any other Tenure whatever, for his own Life, or for the Life of another, or for any Lives whatsoever, or for any larger Estate of the clear yearly Value of not less than Five Pounds over and above all Rents and Charges payable out of or in respect of the same, or who is entitled, either as Lessee or Assignee, to any Lands or Tenements of Freehold or of any other Tenure whatever, for the unexpired Residue . . . of any Term originally created for a Period of not less than Sixty Years . . . of the clear yearly Value of not less than Five Pounds over and above all Rents and Charges . . . :

Provided that no Person shall be registered as a Voter under this Section unless he has complied with the Provisions of the Twenty-sixth Section of the Act of the Second Year of the Reign of His Majesty William the Fourth, Chapter Forty-five.

6. Every Man shall, in and after . . . [1868], be entitled to . . . vote

for a Member or Members to serve in Parliament for a County, who is qualified as follows; (that is to say,)

1. Is of full Age, and not subject to any legal Incapacity; and
2. Is on the last Day of July in any Year, and has during the Twelve Months immediately preceding been, the Occupier, as Owner or Tenant, of Lands or Tenements within the County of the rateable Value of Twelve Pounds or upwards; and
3. Has during the Time of such Occupation been rated in respect to the Premises so occupied by him to all Rates . . . made for the Relief of the Poor in respect of the said Premises; and
4. Has on or before the Twentieth Day of July in the same Year paid all Poor Rates that have become payable by him . . . .

17. From and after the End of this present Parliament, no Borough which had a less Population than Ten thousand at the Census of One Thousand eight hundred and sixty-one shall return more than One Member to serve in Parliament . . . .

18. From and after the End of this present Parliament, the City of Manchester, and the Boroughs of Liverpool, Birmingham, and Leeds, shall each respectively return Three Members to serve in Parliament . . . .

24. In all future Parliaments the University of London shall return One Member to serve in Parliament.

25. Every Man whose Name is for the Time being on the Register of Graduates constituting the Convocation of the University of London shall, if of full Age, and not subject to any legal Incapacity, be entitled to vote in the Election of a Member to serve in any future Parliament for the said University . . . .

30. The following Regulations shall in and after the Year [1868] . . . be observed with respect to the Registration of Voters:

1. The Overseers of every Parish or Township shall make out or cause to be made out a List of all Persons on whom a Right to vote for a County in respect of the Occupation of Premises is conferred by this Act, in the same Manner, and subject to the same Regulations, as nearly as Circumstances admit, in and subject to which the Overseers of Parishes and Townships in Boroughs are required by the Registration Acts to make out or cause to be made out a List of all Persons entitled to vote for a Member or Members for a Borough in respect of the Occupation of Premises of a clear yearly Value of not less than Ten Pounds. . . .

303. THE BALLOT ACT (1872)

Oral voting in parliamentary elections had been practiced since time immemorial. Such a method admitted of evils through coercion, intimidation, or other forms of persuasion by one's social superiors or employer. One of the points in the Chartists' People's Charters was the secret ballot, which became the practice in elections after the passage of this Act.

PART I

PARLIAMENTARY ELECTIONS

1. A candidate for election to serve in Parliament for a county or borough shall be nominated in writing. The writing shall be subscribed by two registered electors of such county or borough as proposer and seconder, and by eight other registered electors of the same county or borough as assenting to the nomination, and shall be delivered during the time appointed for the election to the returning officer by the candidate himself, or his proposer or seconder.

If at the expiration of one hour after the time appointed for the election no more candidates stand nominated than there are vacancies to be filled up, the returning officer shall forthwith declare the candidates who may stand nominated to be elected . . . ; but if at the expiration of such hour more candidates stand nominated than there are vacancies to be filled up, the returning officer shall adjourn the election and shall take a poll in manner in this act mentioned.

A candidate may, during the time appointed for the election, but not afterwards, withdraw from his candidature by giving a notice to that effect, signed by him, to the returning officer. . . .

2. In the case of a poll at an election the votes shall be given by ballot. The ballot of each voter shall consist of a paper . . . showing the names and description of the candidates. Each ballot paper shall have a number printed on the back, and shall have attached a counterfoil with the same number printed on the face. At the time of voting, the ballot paper shall be marked on both sides with an official mark, and delivered to the voter within the polling station, and the number of such voter on the register of voters shall be marked on the counterfoil, and the voter having secretly marked his vote on the paper, and folded it up so as to conceal his vote, shall place it in a closed box in the presence of the officer presiding at the polling station. . . .

Any ballot paper which has not on its back the official mark, or on which votes are given to more candidates than the voter is entitled to vote for, or on which anything, except the said number on the back, is written or marked by which the voter can be identified, shall be void and not counted.

PART II
MUNICIPAL ELECTIONS

20. The poll at every contested municipal election shall, so far as circumstances admit, be conducted in the manner in which the poll is by this Act directed to be conducted at a contested parliamentary election, and, subject to the modifications expressed in the schedules annexed hereto, such provisions of this Act and of the said schedules as relate to or are concerned with a poll at a parliamentary election shall apply to a poll at a contested municipal election. . . .

304. THE REFORM ACT OF 1884

The Reform Act of 1867 had enfranchised practically all the urban workers and tenants in the country, but it had overlooked the farm laborers. The Act of 1884, sponsored and passed by the Liberals, granted the right to vote to farm laborers on the same conditions as had been done for the town workers in 1867, thereby adding some 2,000,000 voters to the existing rolls.

2. A uniform household franchise and a uniform lodger franchise at elections shall be established in all counties and boroughs throughout the United Kingdom, and every man possessed of a household qualification or a lodger qualification shall, if the qualifying premises be situate in a county in England or Scotland, be entitled to be registered as a voter, and when registered to vote at an election for such county, and if the qualifying premises be situate in a county or borough in Ireland, be entitled to be registered as a voter, and when registered to vote at an election for such county or borough.

3. Where a man himself inhabits any dwelling-house by virtue of any office, service, or employment, and the dwelling-house is not inhabited by any person under whom such man serves in such office, service, or employment, he shall be deemed for the purposes of this Act and of the Representation of the People Acts to be an inhabitant occupier of such dwelling-house as a tenant. . . .

305. ABOLITION OF SLAVERY (1833)

The slave trade in British territories had been abolished in 1807, and in 1833 the following statute abolished the institution of slavery itself:

Whereas divers Persons are holden in Slavery within divers of His Majesty's Colonies, and it is just and expedient that all such Persons shall be manumitted and set free, and that a reasonable Compensation should be made to the Persons hitherto entitled to the Services of such Slaves for the Loss which they will incur by being deprived of their Right to such Services . . . ; be it therefore enacted . . . That from and after the First Day of August One thousand eight hundred and thirty-four all Persons who in conformity with the Laws now in force in the said Colonies respectively shall on or before the First Day of August One thousand eight hundred and thirty-four have been duly registered as Slaves in any such Colony, . . . and who shall be actually within any such Colony, and who shall by such Registries appear to be . . . of the full Age of Six Years or upwards, shall by force and virtue of this Act, . . . become and be apprenticed Labourers; provided that . . . every Slave engaged in his ordinary Occupation on the Seas shall be deemed and taken to be within the Colony to which such Slave shall belong. . . .

III. Provided also, and be it further enacted, That all Slaves who may at any Time previous to the passing of this Act have been brought with the Consent of their Possessors, and all apprenticed Labourers who may hereafter with the like Consent be brought into any Part of the United Kingdom of Great Britain and Ireland shall from and after the passing of this Act be absolutely and entirely free, to all Intents and Purposes whatsoever. . . .

XXIV. And whereas, towards compensating the Persons at present entitled to the Services of the Slaves to be manumitted and set free by virtue of this Act for the loss of such Services, His Majesty's most dutiful and loyal Subjects the Commons of Great Britain and Ireland in Parliament assembled have resolved to give and grant to His Majesty the Sum of Twenty Millions Pounds Sterling [for the former slave owners]. . . .

306. THE CRYSTAL PALACE EXHIBITION (1851)

This international exhibition, first suggested by Prince Albert, was designed to show the world how far England had advanced in commerce, manufacturing and agriculture, and to induce other nations to display their wares for purposes of comparison and observation. This first truly world's fair was held in the Crystal Palace, a large iron and glass building erected in Hyde Park, London. Lord Macaulay's vivid description of the opening day testifies to its success:

Thursday, May 1st, 1851.—A fine day for the opening of the Exhibition. A little cloudy in the morning, but generally sunny and pleasant. I was struck by the number of foreigners in the streets. All, however, were respectable and decent people. I saw none of the men of action with whom the Socialists were threatening us. I went to the Park, and along the serpentine. There were immense crowds on both sides of the water. I should think that there must have been near three hundred thousand people in Hyde Park at once. The sight among the green boughs was delightful. The boats and little frigates darting across the lake; the flags; the music; the guns; every thing was exhilarating, and the temper of the multitude the best possible. I fell in with Punch Greville, and walked with him for an hour. He, like me, thought the outside spectacle better worth seeing than the pageant under cover. He showed me a letter from Madame de Lieven, foolish, with an affectation of cleverness and profundity, just like herself. She calls this Exhibition a bold, a rash experiment. She apprehends a horrible explosion: "You may get through it safe; and, if you do, you will give yourselves more airs than ever." And this woman is thought a political oracle in some circles! There is just as much chance of a revolution in England as of the falling of the moon.

I made my way into the building: a most gorgeous sight; vast; graceful; beyond the dreams of the Arabian romances. I can not think that the Caesars ever exhibited a more splendid spectacle. I was quite dazzled, and I felt as I did on entering St. Peter's. I wandered about, and elbowed my way through the crowd which filled the nave, admiring the general effect, but not attending much to details.

307. THE PUBLIC SCHOOLS

In the field of education, nineteenth-century England left much to be desired. Its educational systems were every bit as much in need of reform as its other institutions. Little was done, except for the Act of 1870, and, at the end of the century, opportunities for education were still grossly inadequate. There were, of course, no state educational institutions of any kind; illiteracy was widespread; the practices and curricula in dame and grammar schools were outmoded. And the well-known public schools were designed to make gentlemen of the sons of the well-to-do. Conditions at these schools were hard, and turbulent disturbances frequent, as the following readings show:

A. *Gladstone at Eton*

Doyle tells a story of the boy being flogged for bringing wine into his study. When questioned on this, Mr. Gladstone said, 'I *was* flogged, but not for anything connected in any way with wine, of which, by the by, my father supplied me with a small amount, and insisted upon my drinking it, or some of it, all the time that I was at Eton. The reason why I was flogged was this. I was praepostor of the remove on a certain day, and from kindness or good nature was induced to omit from the list of boys against whom H. [the master] had complained, and who ought to have been flogged next day, the names of three offenders. The three boys in question got round me with a story that their friends were coming down from London to see them, and that if they were put down on the flogging list they could not meet their friends. Next day when I went to school H. roared out in a voice of thunder, "Gladstone, put down your own name on the list of boys to be flogged." ' Mr. Gladstone on this occasion told another tale of this worthy's 'humour.' 'One day H. called out to the praepostor, "Write down Hamilton's name to be flogged for breaking my window." "I never broke your window, sir," exclaimed Hamilton. "Praepostor," retorted H., "write down Hamilton's name for breaking my window and lying." "Upon my soul, sir, I did not do it," ejaculated the boy, with increased emphasis. "Praepostor, write down Hamilton's name for breaking my window, lying, and swearing." Against this final sentence there was no appeal, and, accordingly, Hamilton was flogged (I believe unjustly) next day.'

B. *Salisbury at Eton*

Robert Salisbury gives the following account of his experiences at Eton in a letter to his father on May 13, 1844:

I know you do not like complaints, and I have tried to suppress them and conceal all this, but you are the only person to whom I can safely confide these things. Really now Eton has become insupportable. I am bullied from morning to night without ceasing. Just multiply ten times the bullying I got under C. . . . and you will have some faint idea of what I get at present. I am obliged to hide myself all the evening in some corner to prevent being bullied, and if I dare venture from my room I get it directly. . . . When I come in to dinner they kick and shin me and I am obliged to go out of dinner without eating anything and to avoid it because of that. I have hardly any time to do lessons because I pass so much time in being bullied. I get a punishment regularly every morning because I have no time to learn my lessons.

C. *A Parody on Scholarship Examinations*

Most boys who finished their preparatory work at public schools such as Eton, Harrow, Rugby and Winchester, went to either of the two universities. The types of questions asked in the scholarship examinations for Cambridge were lampooned in the following parody entitled, "Utopia University, Undecember 9657."

1. Give a comparative sketch of the principal English Theatres, with the dates of their erection, and the names of the most eminent Candle-snuffers at each. What were the Stage-boxes? What were the Offices of Prompter—Ballet-master—and Scene-shifter? In what part of the Theatre was the one-shilling Gallery? Distinguish accurately between Operas and Puppet-shews.

2. Where was Downing-street? Who was Prime Minister when Crib defeated Molineux—and where did the battle take place? Explain the terms milling—fibbing—cross-buttock—neck and crop—bang up—and—prime.

3. Give the dates of all the Parliaments from their first institution to the period of the hard frost on the Thames. In what month of the year was Mr. Abbot elected Speaker? Why was he called "The little man in the wig?" When the Speaker was out of the chair, where was the mace put?

4. Enumerate the principal houses of call in and about London, marking those of Tailors, Bricklayers, and Shoemakers, and stating from what Brewery each house was supplied with Brown Stout. Who was the tutelary Saint of the Shoemakers? . . . Who was Saint Swithin? . . .

6. Give characters of Wat Tyler, Jack Cade, and Sir Francis Burdett. Did the latter return from the Tower by water or by land? . . .

17. Scan the following lines—

> But for shaving and tooth-drawing,
> Bleeding, cabbaging and sawing,
> Dicky Gossip, Dicky Gossip is the man!

What is known of the character and history of Dicky Gossip?

308. OXFORD UNIVERSITY (1810–1812)

Speaking on the Irish Colleges Bill in 1839, Sir James Graham said of Christ Church, Oxford:

I now solemnly state that during the two years of my residence at College [Christ Church, Oxford], I was never—with the exception of the required attendance at Chapel—once called upon to attend any lectures either upon theology or divinity. During the whole of that time, I never received any religious instruction whatever independently and apart from that which I derived from enforced attendance upon chapel. I never, during those two years [1810–1812], attended a university sermon; and I am ashamed to say, that whilst I was at Oxford, I never, during the whole period of my residence, heard one single sermon.

309. UNIVERSITY OF LONDON (1825-1836)

Under the leadership of Lord Brougham, Lord John Russell, Joseph Hume, Dr. Birkbeck and others, a new university was established in London (1828) in which the emphasis should be on science, literature, and the arts. Churchmen objected to an entirely secular institution, and, as a result, King's College (London) was founded on Anglican principles as a rival institution. In 1836 the two were incorporated as the University of London. The 1825 prospectus of the proposed University of London reads, in part:

The object of the institution is, to bring the means of a complete scientific and literary education home to the doors of the inhabitants of the metropolis, so that they may be enabled to educate their sons at a very moderate expense, and under their own immediate and constant superintendance. It is known that a young man cannot be maintained and instructed at Oxford or Cambridge under £200 or £250 a year, while the expenses of many very far exceed this sum; and the vacations last about five months in the year. The whole expense of education at the London University will not exceed £25 or £30 a year, including the sums paid to the general fund; and there will not be more than ten weeks of vacation in the year.

A suitable piece of ground for the buildings and walks, and in a central situation, is now in treaty for; and it is expected that the structure will be completed in August, 1826, and the classes opened in October following. . . .

310. UNIVERSITY TESTS

In 1854 and 1856 statutes were passed by which undergraduates at Oxford and Cambridge were relieved of having to take the religious tests that had been designed to keep the universities as Anglican preserves. In 1871 a bill was introduced in Parliament to remove the requirement that all teaching posts be held by Anglicans. One of the most effective speeches in favor of the bill was made by Henry Campbell-Bannerman.

All the arguments addressed to the House (last year and this) have proceeded on the assumption that the University system is nearly perfect. Honourable gentlemen opposite have expressed their fears lest the influx of a large body of students unconnected with the Church of England should impair the present excellent system; while honourable gentlemen on this side have endeavoured to calm those fears. Sir, if I wish to see this measure passed into law, I am almost afraid to say that it is precisely because of what I conceive to be the gross inefficiency of the present system, and because my only hope of its amendment lies in the infusion of fresh blood. Honourable

members look back on the Universities through a mist of pleasant recollections and associations which, to a great extent, blinds their eyes to the real
state of the case. But I am only expressing the opinion of a great many University men when I say that not only do these Universities with a maximum
of endowments educate a minimum number of the young men of the nation, but to those few young men they afford a minimum of education at a
maximum of expense. We used to hear the Universities spoken of as 'places
of sound learning and religious education.' Our belief is that the learning is
not very sound and that the religion is not very learned. Sir, I have no wish
to disparage or depreciate the good which a young man receives from his
residence at a University. He can hardly fail to acquire, in greater or less
degree, that most subtle but most valuable quality which may perhaps best
be termed knowledge of the world. But this benefit is entirely extraneous,
entirely extra-academical; he obtains it from mixing in society with his contemporaries, and not in any sense from the University system. So far as more
solid acquirements are concerned the University and colleges leave him to
his own resources; he is obliged to hire for himself a tutor to conduct his
studies, and for all practical purposes he might every bit as well prepare for
the periodical examinations in London or Paris as at Oxford or Cambridge. . . .

311. THE UNIVERSITY TESTS ACT (1871)

3. From and after the passing of this Act, no person shall be required,
upon taking or to enable him to take any degree (other than a degree in
divinity) within the Universities of Oxford, Cambridge, and Durham, or
any of them, or upon exercising or to enable him to exercise any of the rights
and privileges which may heretofore have been or may hereafter be exercised
by graduates in the said universities or any of them, or in any college subsist-
ing at the time of the passing of this Act in any of the said universities, or
upon taking or holding or to enable him to take or hold any office in any of
the said universities or any such college as aforesaid, or upon teaching or to
enable him to teach within any of the said universities or any such college
. . . or upon opening or to enable him to open a private hall or hostel in any
of the said universities for the reception of students, to subscribe any article
or formulary of faith, or to make any declaration or take any oath respecting
his religious belief or profession, or to conform to any religious observance,
or to attend or abstain from attending any form of public worship, or to belong to any specified church, sect, or denomination; nor shall any person be
compelled, in any of the said universities or any such college as aforesaid, to

attend the public worship of any church, sect, or denomination to which he does not belong. . . .

312. THE EDUCATION ACT (1870)

The Education Act of 1870, excerpts from which are given below, was the most important education legislation of the nineteenth century.

5. There shall be provided for every school district a sufficient amount of accomodation in public elementary schools . . . available for all the children resident in such district for whose elementary education efficient and suitable provision is not otherwise made, and where there is an insufficient amount of such accomodation, . . . the deficiency shall be supplied in manner provided by this Act.

6. Where the Education Department . . . are satisfied . . . that there is an insufficient amount of public school accomodation for any school district, and the deficiency is not supplied as here-in-after required, a school board shall be formed for such district and shall supply such deficiency, and in case of default by the school board the Education Department shall cause the duty of such board to be performed in manner provided by this Act.

7. Every . . . public elementary school shall be conducted in accordance with the following regulations . . . ;

(1.) It shall not be required, as a condition of any child being admitted into or continuing in the school, that he shall attend or abstain from attending any Sunday school, or any place of religious worship, or that he shall attend any religious observance or any instruction in religious subjects in the school or elsewhere. . . .

(2.) The time or times during which any religious observance is practised or instruction in religious subjects is given at any meeting of the school shall be either at the beginning or at the end or at the beginning and the end of such meeting, and shall be inserted in a time table to be approved by the Education Department. . . .

(3.) The school shall be open at all times to the inspection of Her Majesty's inspectors. . . .

10. If after the expiration of a time, not exceeding six months . . . the Education Department are satisfied that all the public school accomodation required . . . has not been so supplied, nor is in the course of being supplied with due despatch, the Education Department shall cause a school board to

be formed for the district as provided in this Act, and shall send a requisition to the school board so formed requiring them to take proceedings forthwith for supplying the public school accomodation. . . .

14. Every school provided by a school board shall be conducted under
the control and management of such board in accordance with the following
regulations:

> (1.) The school shall be a public elementary school within the mean-
> ing of this Act:
> (2.) No religious catechism or religious formulary which is dis-
> tinctive of any particular denomination shall be taught in
> school. . . .

17. Every child attending a school provided by any school board shall
pay such weekly fee as may be prescribed by the school board . . . but the
school board may from time to time . . . remit the whole or any part of
such fee in the case of any child when they are of opinion that the parent
of such child is unable from poverty to pay the same. . . .

26. If a school board satisfy the Education Department that, on the
ground of poverty of the inhabitants of any place in their district, . . . the
Education Department may provide such school, and may admit scholars to
such school without requiring any fee. . . .

313. CHARLES DARWIN (1809–1882)

The scientific discoveries of previous centuries were, in the nineteenth century, applied to problems of everyday life. This meant, among other things,
the rise of the scientific method in the study of social and economic problems. Darwin did so in his famous *Descent of Man and Selection in Relation
to Sex,* the conclusion of which reads:

The main conclusion arrived at in this work, namely, that man is descended from some lowly-organized form, will, I regret to think, be highly
distasteful to many persons. But there can hardly be a doubt that we are
descended from barbarians. The astonishment which I felt on first seeing a
party of Fuegians on a wild and broken shore will never be forgotten by me,
for the reflection at once rushed into my mind—such were our ancestors.
These men were absolutely naked and bedaubed with paint, their long hair
was tangled, their mouths frothed with excitement, and their expression was
wild, startled, and distrustful. They possessed hardly any arts, and, like wild
animals, lived on what they could catch; they had no government, and were
merciless to every one not of their own small tribe. He who has seen a savage

in his native land will not feel much shame, if forced to acknowledge that the blood of some more humble creature flows in his veins. For my own part, I would as soon be descended from that heroic little monkey, who braved his dreaded enemy in order to save the life of his keeper; or from that old baboon, who, descending from the mountains, carried away in triumph his young comrade from a crowd of astonished dogs—as from a savage who delights to torture his enemies, offers up bloody sacrifices, practises infanticide without remorse, treats his wives like slaves, knows no decency, and is haunted by the grossest superstitions.

Man may be excused for feeling some pride at having risen, though not through his own exertions, to the very summit of the organic scale; and the fact of his having thus risen, instead of having been aboriginally placed there, may give him hopes for a still higher destiny in the distant future. But we are not here concerned with hopes or fears, only with the truth as far as our reason allows us to discover it. I have given the evidence to the best of my ability; and we must acknowledge, as it seems to me, that man with all his noble qualities, with sympathy which feels for the most debased, with benevolence which extends not only to other men but to the humblest living creature, with his godlike intellect which has penetrated into the movements and constitution of the solar system—with all these exalted powers—Man still bears in his bodily frame the indelible stamp of his lowly origin.

314. THOMAS MALTHUS (1766–1834)

The scientific method was used by the political economist, Malthus, in his study of population problems. His famous essay, written in 1798, states:

That population has this constant tendency to increase beyond the means of subsistence, and that it is kept to its necessary level by these causes [war, famine, disease, etc.] will sufficiently appear from a review of the different states of society in which man has existed. But, before we proceed to this review, the subject will perhaps be seen in a clearer light, if we endeavour to ascertain what would be the natural increase of population, if left to exert itself with perfect freedom; and what might be expected to be the rate of increase in the productions of the earth, under the most favourable circumstances of human industry. . . .

It may fairly be pronounced, therefore, that, considering the present average state of the earth, the means of subsistence, under circumstances the most favourable to human industry, could not possibly be made to increase faster than in an arithmetical ratio. . . .

Taking the whole earth, instead of this island, emigration would of course be excluded; and, supposing the present population equal to a thousand millions, the human species would increase as the numbers, 1, 2, 4, 8, 16, 32, 64, 128, 256; and subsistence is 1, 2, 3, 4, 5, 6, 7, 8, 9. In two centuries the population would be to the means of subsistence as 256 to 9; in three centuries as 4096 to 13, and in two thousand years the difference would be almost incalculable.

In this supposition no limits whatever are placed to the produce of the earth. It may increase for ever, and be greater than any assignable quantity; yet still the power of population being in every period so much superior, the increase of the human species can only be kept down to the level of the means of subsistence by the constant operation of the strong law of necessity, acting as a check upon the greater power.

315. USE OF CHLOROFORM IN SURGERY (1847)

Physicians and surgeons made significant strides in medicine in the nineteenth century. One of the most important discoveries was the application of chloroform in surgery, which had formerly been an unbearable and frequently fatal experience. Greville describes his observation of surgery performed with chloroform.

I went yesterday to St. George's Hospital to see the chloroform tried. A boy two years and a half old was cut for a stone. He was put to sleep in a minute; the stone was so large and the bladder so contracted, the operator could not get hold of it, and the operation lasted above twenty minutes, with repeated probings by different instruments; the chloroform was applied from time to time, and the child never exhibited the slightest sign of consciousness, and it was exactly the same as operating on a dead body. A curious example was shown of what is called the *étiquette* of the profession. The operator (whose name I forget) could not extract the stone, so at last he handed the instrument to Keate, who is the finest operator possible, and he got hold of the stone. When he announced that he had done so, the first man begged to have the forceps back that he might draw it out, and it was transferred to him; but in taking it he let go the stone, and the whole thing had to be done over again. It was accomplished, but not of course without increasing the local inflammation, and endangering the life of the child. I asked Keate why, when he had got hold of the stone, he did not draw it out. He said the other man's 'dignity' would have been hurt if he had not been allowed to complete what he had begun! I have no words to express my admiration for this invention, which is the greatest blessing ever bestowed on mankind, and the inventor of it the greatest of benefactors, whose memory ought to be venerated by countless millions for ages yet to come. All the great discoveries of science sink into insignificance when compared with this. It is a great privilege to have lived in the times which saw the production of steam, of electricity, and now of ether—that is, of the development and application of them to human purposes, to the multiplication of enjoyments and the mitigation of pain. But wonderful as are the powers and the feats of the steam-engine and the electric telegraph, the chloroform far transcends them all in its beneficent and consolatory operations.

> With almost all other institutions—political, social, educational—undergoing reform, it was not possible for the religious institutions to resist change. Beginning quite early in the nineteenth century, England moved steadily in the direction of religious toleration until, by the end of the century, religious liberty and equality had been recognized for all sects.

316. PROTEST AGAINST RELIGIOUS CEREMONIES IN MARRIAGE (1827)

> One of the earliest indications of the new spirit of religious change is seen in a public protest against the law requiring certain forms in the marriage ceremony.

"Against the present established mode of legalizing marriage, of compelling submission to a religious ceremony, and also against the particular ceremony by law appointed, they hereby offer the following especial grounds of protest:—

> "Because it introduces a religious rite into a merely civil compact.
> "Because it is an interference of human authority in matters of faith.
> "Because it operates as a test of religious opinions.
> "Because it becomes an act of compulsive conformity with the church of England.
> "Because it establishes a rite or ceremony in religion, all such being contrary to the commands of Jesus, and to the spirit of that religion of which he was the divinely-appointed teacher.
> "Because, although marriage be sanctioned, and its duties, like all the social duties, enforced in the Scriptures, it is no where appointed to be entered upon as a religious rite. In no single instance in any age, either in the Antediluvian, in the Patriarchal, or the Jewish, does it appear that such rite was performed. Neither by Moses, nor by the prophets, nor by Jesus nor by his apostles, was such rite instituted.

"Because the marriage ceremony, as contained in The Book of Common Prayer, is a popish rite, rendered compulsory in the church by a corrupt pontiff (in the thirteenth century), and by him raised to 'a sacrament,' together with transubstantiation and auricular confession, as a means of increasing the revenue of the clergy.

"Because, by reason of its origin from the popish mass-book, together with the obsoleteness of certain of its terms, its forms are superstitious, its meaning in many places has frequently become obscure, its assertations false, and its allusions indelicate, offensive, and revolting. . . .

317. REPEAL OF TEST AND CORPORATION ACTS (1828)

The Corporation Act of 1661 had excluded Dissenters from government in the towns, and the Test Act of 1673 had stipulated that no one could hold any official position in the government unless he had received Communion according to the Anglican rite. The effect of these two statutes was to insure that the important positions in the state remained in control of the Anglicans. In 1828, long after the Dissenter Churches had grown strong, Parliament repealed these disabling laws.

Be it therefore enacted . . . That so much and such Parts of the said several Acts passed in the Thirteenth and Twenty-fifth Years of the Reign of King Charles the Second, and of the said Act passed in the Sixteenth Year of the Reign of King George the Second as require the Person or Persons in the said Acts respectively described to take or receive the Sacrament of the Lord's Supper according to the Rites or Usage of the Church of England, for the several Purposes therein expressed, or to deliver a Certificate or make Proof of the Truth of such his or their receiving the said Sacrament in manner aforesaid, or as impose upon any such Person or Persons any Penalty, Forfeiture, Incapacity, or Disability whatsoever for or by reason of any Neglect or Omission to take or receive the said Sacrament, within the respective Periods and in the Manner in the said Acts respectively provided in that Behalf, shall, from and immediately after the passing of this Act, be and the same are hereby repealed.

II. [In lieu of the Sacramental Test] Be it therefore enacted, That every Person who shall hereafter be placed, elected, or chosen in or to the Office of Mayor, Alderman, Recorder, Bailiff, Town Clerk or Common Councilman, or in or to any Office of Magistracy, or Place, Trust, or Employment relating to the Government of any City, Corporation, Borough, or Cinque Port within England and Wales or the Town of Berwick-upon-Tweed, shall, within One Calendar Month next before or upon his Admission into any of the aforesaid Offices or Trusts, make and subscribe the Declaration following:

'I A. B. do solemnly and sincerely, in the Presence of God, profess, testify, and declare, upon the true Faith of a Christian, That I will never exercise any Power, Authority, or Influence which I may possess by virtue of the Office of   to injure or weaken the Protestant Church as it is by Law established in England, or to disturb the said Church, or the Bishops and Clergy of the said Church, in the Possession of any Rights or Privileges to which such Church, or the said Bishops and Clergy, are or may be by Law entitled . . . .

318. THE CATHOLIC EMANCIPATION ACT (1829)

Neither the Test nor Corporation Acts referred to above had been rigorously enforced against Dissenters since an annual Indemnity Act beginning in the reign of George I had been passed to cover those who broke the law. But both Acts had carefully excluded Roman Catholics. In 1829, Parliament passed the Catholic Emancipation Act, given below, that repealed all penal laws subjecting Roman Catholics to civil disabilities, and opened most public offices to them.

Be it enacted . . . That from and after the Commencement of this Act all such Parts of the said Acts as require the said Declarations, or either of them, to be made or subscribed by any of His Majesty's Subjects, as a Qualification for sitting and voting in Parliament, or for the Exercise or Enjoyment of any Office, Franchise, or Civil Right, be and the same are . . . hereby repealed.

II. And be it enacted, That from and after the Commencement of this Act it shall be lawful for any Person professing the Roman Catholic Religion, being a Peer, or who shall after the Commencement of this Act be returned as a Member of the House of Commons, to sit and vote in either House of Parliament respectively, being in all other respects duly qualified to sit and vote therein, upon taking and subscribing the following Oath, instead of the Oaths of Allegiance, Supremacy, and Abjuration:

I A.B. do sincerely promise and swear, That I will be faithful and bear true Allegiance to His Majesty King George the Fourth, and will defend him to the utmost of my Power against all Conspiracies and Attempts whatever, which shall be made against his Person, Crown, or Dignity . . . . And I do further declare, That it is not an Article of my Faith, and that I do renounce, reject, and abjure the Opinion, that Princes excommunicated or deprived by the Pope, or any other Authority of the See of Rome, may be deposed or murdered by their Subjects, or by any Person whatsoever . . . .

And I do hereby disclaim, disavow, and solemnly abjure any Intention to subvert the present Church Establishment, as settled by Law within this Realm: And I do solemnly swear, That I never will exercise any Privilege to which I am or may become entitled, to disturb or weaken the Protestant Religion or Protestant Government in the United Kingdom: And I do solemnly, in the presence of God, profess, testify, and declare, That I do make this Declaration . . . without any Evasion, Equivocation, or mental Reservation whatsoever. So help me God . . . .

IX. And be it further enacted, That no Person in Holy Orders in the Church of Rome shall be capable of being elected to serve in Parliament as a Member of the House of Commons; and if any such Person shall be elected . . . , such Election shall be void; and if any Person, being elected . . . as a Member of the House of Commons, shall, after his Election, take or receive Holy Orders in the Church of Rome, the Seat of such Person shall immediately become void . . . .

XII. Provided also, . . . That nothing herein contained shall extend or be construed to extend to enable any Person or Persons professing the Roman Catholic Religion to hold or exercise the Office of Guardians and Justices of the United Kingdom, or of Regent of the United Kingdom, under whatever Name, Style, or Title such Office may be constituted; nor to enable any Person, otherwise than as he is now by Law enabled, to hold or enjoy the Office of Lord High Chancellor, Lord Keeper or Lord Commissioner of the Great Seal of Great Britain or Ireland; or the Office of Lord Lieutenant, or Lord Deputy, or other Chief Governor or Governors of Ireland; or His Majesty's High Commissioner to the General Assembly of the Church of Scotland. . . .

319. THE JEWISH DISABILITIES QUESTION

By 1829 Dissenters and Roman Catholics had been freed from civil disabilities on account of their religion, but the Jews had not. It was natural that a movement should have begun to extend the same consideration to them. The problem was traceable to the oath that all M.P.s were obliged to swear before being admitted to a seat in Parliament. The oath contained the words "on the true faith of a Christian," which Catholics and Protestants could take, but which Jews obviously could not. The problem is discussed in the following report of a debate in the Commons in 1841:

A question involving very important principles, though it occasioned but little discussion, and slight interest in the public mind, was raised in this session by a bill introduced by . . . one of the members for Exeter, the object of which was to do away with the declaration required by the Municipal Corporations Act from all persons taking corporate offices, by reason of which members of the Jewish persuasion had been debarred from holding civic magistracies . . . . On a division, the second reading of the bill was carried in a thin house by a majority of 113, only 24 members voting in the minority. Some further discussion on the principle of the bill took place on the third reading. Mr. Gladstone renewed the opposition by rising to move that it be read that day six months.

He was satisfied that it was not possible to draw a line between a bill to admit Jews to municipal offices, and one to permit them to hold other offices, including seats in Parliament. He would state his reasons for objecting to the bill. They were these. The Jew's profession was in itself a disqualification for legislative offices in a christian country. Christianity was part and parcel of the law of England. Our laws were modelled on the principles of Christianity. The proceedings in both houses of parliament were commenced by the solemn invocation of the Almighty, and the object set before them was the promotion of true religion and the glory of God. The question, then, really was, would they destroy the distinctive Christianity of the constitution? The test for office was at present a Christian test, and this the bill went to annul. He did not know whether he was not rendering himself liable to the charge of 'sheer intolerance;' but the ground he occupied was precisely the same as if he were discussing a purely civil question. Let him guard himself in speaking of the Jews as a body. Who could doubt there were many honest, zealous-minded men amongst them? The stronger, therefore, was the objection to investing them with the privilege of legislating for Christians. There were many Jews, doubtless, who would discharge those duties well, but still it was the duty of the state to choose those who, as a class, were most competent for the duties to which they were appointed. Now, he did not see how it could be held that the Jews possessed the necessary qualifications. Mr. Gladstone here called attention to the great number of questions, essentially connected with the highest Christian considerations, which had come before the house during the last ten years. For instance, in England the questions of church-rates, church extension, and national education; in Scotland, the appointment of ministers of the established church; in Ireland such questions were always arising. These were the questions the most difficult to adjust, the most impossible to agree upon, and which most agitated the country . . . .

In 1866 a new oath was written that did not contain the words "on the true faith of a Christian," thus enabling Jews to sit in Parliament.

320. PRINCE ALBERT ON THE DUTIES OF BISHOPS (1845)

This letter, written by Queen Victoria's husband to Dr. Wilberforce, Dean of Westminster, is instructive both as to Albert's opinions and the role that bishops of the Anglican Church should play.

A Bishop ought to abstain completely from mixing himself up with the politics of the day, and beyond giving a general support to the Queen's Government, and occasionally voting for it, should take no part in the discussion of State affairs (for instance, Corn Laws, Game Laws, Trade or Financial questions, &c., &c.); but he should come forward whenever the interests of Humanity are at stake, and give boldly and manfully his advice to the House and Country (I mean questions like Negro Emancipation, education of the people, improvement of the health of towns, measures for the recreation of the poor, against cruelty to animals, for regulating factory labour, &c., &c.).

As to religious affairs, he cannot but take an active part in them; but let that always be the part of a *Christian,* not of a mere *Churchman.* Let him never forget the insufficiency of human knowledge and wisdom, and the impossibility for any man, or even Church, to say, "I am right, and I alone am right." Let him, therefore, be meek, and liberal, and tolerant to other confessions; but let him never forget that he is a representative of the Church of the Land, the maintenance of which is as important to the country as that of its Constitution or its Throne. Let him, here, always be conscious that the Church has duties to fulfil, that it does not exist for itself, but for the people, for the country, and that it ought to have no higher aim than to be the Church of the people. Let there be, therefore, no calling for new rights, privileges, grants, &c., but show the zeal and capacity of the Church to stretch her powers and capabilities to the utmost for the fulfilment of her sacred duties to the people, in ministering and teaching. A Bishop ought to be uniformly a peace-maker, and, when he can, it is his duty to lessen political and other animosities, and remind the Peers of their duties as Christians. He ought to be a guardian of public morality, not, like the press, by tediously interfering with every man's private affairs, speaking for applause, or trampling on those that are fallen, but by watching over the morality of the State in acts which expediency or hope for profit many tempt it to commit, as well in home and colonial as in foreign affairs.

He should likewise boldly admonish the public even against its predominant feeling, if this be contrary to the purest standard of morality (reproving, for instance, the recklessness and the wickedness of the Projectors of Railway schemes, who, having no funds themselves, acquire riches at the expense of others, their dupes). Here the nation is in the greatest danger, as every individual gets corrupted, and every sense of shame is lost.

In this way the Bishops would become a powerful force in the Lords, and the country would feel that their presence there supplies a great want, and is a great protection to the people.

I have spoken as thoughts have struck me, and am sure you will be better able than I am to take a comprehensive view of the position. Ever yours truly, ALBERT.

321. FREDERICK TEMPLE ON PATRONAGE (1875)

> Temple, Bishop of Exeter and later Archbishop of Canterbury, believed that the greatest evil in the Church of England was the patronage system under which Church "livings" were sold. In 1875, as Bishop of Exeter, he gave the following "Charge to the Clergy" in his diocese:

The traffic (in the sale of livings) has unquestionably had the effect of inducing all concerned to disregard altogether the undeniable and most important fact that every patron is an officer of the Church, holding a most important office. A patron is an officer of the Church charged with a very serious and a very responsible duty—at present, indeed, responsible to God alone, but nevertheless responsible to Him in the most serious sense. A patron is entrusted with the duty of seeing that a fit man is appointed to take charge of the spiritual interests of a parish. . . . I believe the Church of England is absolutely the only Church in the world in which this hurtful traffic is still tolerated. Perhaps I may go on and say, it is not only the only Church in the world, but the only institution in the world; and in secular things men have already set themselves free from what they had found a very serious mischief. I cannot but hope that the time will come, and come before long, for the entire prohibition of all this traffic. I do not think that until that is done it will be possible to speak of the Church as free from a serious blot. . . . I believe it to be a duty of all who are interested in the welfare of the Church to study the question carefully, and to do their part towards the creating of public opinion of a healthy and high-toned character. And I shall think it my duty to take fitting opportunities of pressing the matter again and again upon the Church, in the hope that by slow degrees something may be effected, even though it be very little at the time, and even though nothing like a great or real improvement be very near. . . . I feel strongly on the matter, and believe it would be well worth while to pay even a very heavy price in order to get rid of what is a most serious scandal and does most serious mischief.

By the end of the century Parliament had passed a number of measures that all but put a complete stop to this practice.

322. DISESTABLISHMENT OF THE CHURCH IN IRELAND (1869)

One of the major grievances in Ireland since the seventeenth century had been the fact that the Irish Catholics and Presbyterians, who comprised the vast majority of the population in mid-Victorian times, were obliged under the law to support the Protestant (Anglican) Church of Ireland. Since they also had to support their own clergy and chapels, this meant that they had to pay double Church rates, often at the cost of great personal sacrifice because of the widespread poverty in the land. In order to remedy this injustice, and despite strong opposition in the House of Lords and from Victoria, Prime Minister Gladstone successfully promoted this Act to disestablish the Church of Ireland. Thereafter it had no connection with government and contributions to all Churches was entirely voluntary.

Whereas it is expedient that the union created by Act of Parliament between the Churches of England and Ireland, as by law established, should be dissolved, and that the Church of Ireland, as so separated, should cease to be established by law, and that after satisfying, so far as possible, upon principles of equality as between the several religious denominations in Ireland, all just and equitable claims, the property of the said Church of Ireland, or the proceeds thereof, should be applied in such manner as Parliament shall hereafter direct [it was used to alleviate poverty and to support education]:

And whereas Her Majesty has been graciously pleased to signify that she has placed at the disposal of Parliament her interest in the several archbishoprics, bishoprics, benefices, cathedral preferments, and other ecclesiastical dignities and offices in Ireland:

Be it therefore enacted by the Queen's most Excellent Majesty, by and with the advice and consent of the Lords Spiritual and Temporal, and Commons, in this present Parliament assembled, and by the authority of the same, as follows:

1. This Act may be cited for all purposes as The Irish Act, 1869.

2. On and after the first day of January one thousand eight hundred and seventy-one the said union created by Act of Parliament between the Churches of England and Ireland shall be dissolved, and the said Church of Ireland, herein-after referred to as "the said Church," shall cease to be established by law. . . .

323. IRELAND AND THE IRISH

Lord John Russell, who, like most nineteenth-century English political leaders, had been forced to deal with "the Irish Problem," concluded that:

In considering the Irish character I have to observe that the Irish have two remarkable virtues, and two prominent defects. The two virtues are, a sincere love of religion, and a strong sense of justice; the two defects are vanity and pugnacity. It has been the mistake of the English rulers of Ireland to check, to curb, and to misguide the sense of religion and the love of justice, and to indulge the vanity and pugnacity of the nation. In the reign of Henry II. titles were granted by Pope Adrian to the King of England. The Roman Catholic religion continued without interruption to be the faith of the nation till the period of the Reformation; but at the period of the Reformation, Elizabeth, without any preparatory steps, decreed that the nation should be Protestant. The Reformation deepened the animosity which the Irish felt towards England. To the animosities of race and the dispossession of the Irish, guilty of rebellion, from their lands, was added the animosity of an oppressed religion. Down to the year 1778 a priest who celebrated the mass according to his own faith and that of the people to whom he administered was liable to imprisonment for his offence. Lord Shelburne, the great-grandfather of the present Marquis of Lansdowne, when Secretary of State, was obliged to implore the mercy of the Crown to save a priest from the legal penalty which he had incurred by saying mass. The Protestant Church had always been a sickly exotic, and had never taken root in the soil.

324. DANIEL O'CONNELL AND REPEAL OF THE ACT OF UNION (1829–1843)

The Catholic Emancipation Act (1829) did not effect an understanding between England and Ireland as the Tories had hoped it might. While it removed the civil disabilities under which Roman Catholics in Great Britain had labored since Elizabethan times, it did nothing to remedy the grave economic and social problems in Ireland. For this reason as well as the religious issue and governmental supremacy exercised by the British, many Irish began to agitate for complete freedom from British control, that is, the repeal of the Act of Union (1800). To this end, beginning shortly after the Catholic Emancipation Act was passed, Daniel O'Connell, the leader of the Irish M.P.s, and others organized mass meetings to voice their opposition to British domination. The agitation came to a crisis in 1843, which the *Annual Register* described in these words:

The assemblage of immense masses of people at meetings held in the open air . . . was the great step in the conspiracy, and some of the proceedings which took place . . . are deserving of particular notice. The first of these was held at Trim, on the 16th of March, at which Mr. O'Connell . . . and about 30,000 persons were present. After this meeting a dinner took place, at which various exciting speeches were made. Mr. O'Connell . . . said, that when he thought of the multitudes that surrounded him . . . he would ask them, would they be slaves? and would they consent to be everlasting slaves? They would answer No, and he would join in the response. . . . He called on young men present to say whether they would be slaves. He said he would be in his grave or he would be free; that idle sentiments would not do; that they must act upon their thoughts; that they had nothing to hope from an English Parliament. . . .

A large gathering met later at Clontarff, where O'Connell told them to obey the government. As a result, they became disillusioned with him and he lost his leadership.

325. PARNELL AND EVICTIONS OF TENANTS IN IRELAND (1870's-1880's)

The efforts by O'Connell and his supporters to gain complete independence for Ireland having failed, other nationalist leaders connected with organizations such as the Fenian Society and the Land League took to acts of violence and governmental obstructionism to win at least Home Rule— domestic self-determination in Ireland. By the late 1870's the outstanding leader in Parliament among the moderate Irish Home Rulers (the Nationalist party) was Charles Stewart Parnell (1846-1891). He was a brilliant, dedicated, and calculating politician whose tender concern for the oppressed and impoverished Irish peasants burned beneath his seemingly inscrutable countenance. The peasants resented most deeply their exploitation by landlords (some of whom were English or Scotch-Irish), who charged exorbitant rents, refused to compensate them for improvements made on their farms, and sometimes evicted them when they could not pay the rent or complained about conditions.

A. Hardships of Evicted Tenants

Katherine O'Shea, Parnell's intimate friend, herein relates the conditions and hardships occasioned by evictions.

During this period the stories of the evictions brought home to me by Parnell himself made my heart sick, and often he sat far into the night at

Eltham speaking in that low, broken monotone, that with him always betokened intense feeling strongly held in check, of the terrible cruelty of some of the things done in the name of justice in unhappy Ireland. How old people, and sometimes those sick beyond recovery, women with the children they had borne but a few hours before, little children naked as they had come into the world, all thrust out from the little squalid cabins which were all they had for home, thrust out on the roadside to perish, or to live as they could. I in my English ignorance used to say: "Why did they not go into the workhouse or to neighbors?" and Parnell would look wonderingly at me as he told me that for the most part such places were few and far between in Ireland, and "neighbors," good as they were to each other, were in the same trouble. There were instances where a wife would beg, and with none effect, that the bailiffs and police should wait but the little half-hour that her dying husband drew his last breath; and where a husband carried his wife from her bed to the "shelter" of the rainswept moor that their child might be born out of the sight of the soldiers deputed to guard the officials who had been sent to pull their home about their ears. And, remembering these and so many other tales of some of the 50,000 evictions that he afterwards calculated had taken place in Ireland [in the late 1870's and 1880's], I have never wondered at the implacable hatred of England that can never really die out of the Irish heart.

B. *The Boycott*

One means of discouraging evictions, Parnell proposed, was to ostracize those who moved onto farms whose previous tenants had been unjustly evicted.

Speaking at Ennis on September 19 [1880] Mr. Parnell enunciated the principle which has since gone by the name of "The Boycott."

"What are you to do," he asked, "to a tenant who bids for a farm from which another tenant has been evicted?"

Several voices cried: "Shoot him!"

"I think," went on Mr. Parnell, "I heard somebody say "Shoot him!" "I wish to point out to you a very much better way—a more Christian and charitable way, which will give the lost man an opportunity of repenting. When a man takes a farm from which another has been unjustly evicted, you must shun him on the roadside when you meet him; you must shun him in the shop; you must shun him on the fair-green and in the market-place, and even in the place of worship, by leaving him alone; by putting him into a sort of moral Coventry; by isolating him from the rest of the country, as if he were a leper of old—you must show him your detestation of the crime he has committed."

The first to be so treated was a man named Boycott, hence the name.

326. THE CONVENTION OF 1818

After the Napoleonic war Britain generally remained at peace for the remainder of the century. It fought the brief Crimean War of 1854–1855 with Russia and was its rival in Persia and Afghanistan for some years before and after that time. Britain also warred with the Maoris in New Zealand (1840's and 1860's), the Zulus and Boers in South Africa (1879–1881) and the Chinese (1839–1842 and 1850's) among others, but these actions were localized and dealt essentially with particular colonial problems which any great power perforce encountered in carving an Empire or spheres of economic influence. Britain often had serious differences with European nations and the United States, but these were settled at the conference table. The next several readings are exemplary of the conduct of British colonial and foreign policy during the nineteenth century.

The Anglo-American Treaty of Ghent (1814), which concluded the War of 1812, provided for future conferences to settle the outstanding differences between the two states. The Convention of 1818, sections II and III of which are given below, opened a long period of negotiation and understanding between Britain and the United States.

II. It is agreed that a line drawn from the most north-western point of the Lake of the Woods, along the 49th parallel of north latitude, or, if the said point shall not be in the 49th parallel of north latitude, then that a line drawn from the said point due north or south, as the case may be, until the said line shall intersect the said parallel of north latitude, and from the point of such intersection due west along and with the said parallel, shall be the line of demarcation between the Territories of His Britannic Majesty and those of The United States, and that the said line shall form the southern boundary of the said Territories of His Britannic Majesty, and the northern boundary of the Territories of The United States, from the Lake of the Woods to the Stony Mountains.

III. It is agreed, that any Country that may be claimed by either Party on the north-west Coast of America, westward of the Stony Mountains, shall, together with its Harbours, Bays, and Creeks, and the navigation of all rivers within the same, be free and open for the term of 10 years from the date of the signature of the present Convention, to the Vessels, Citizens, and Subjects of the 2 Powers: it being well understood, that this Agreement is

not to be construed to the prejudice of any claim which either of the 2 High
Contracting Parties may have to any part of the said Country, nor shall it be
taken to affect the claims of any other Power or State to any part of the
said Country, the only object of the High Contracting Parties, in that respect, being to prevent disputes and differences amongst themselves.

327. THE TREATY OF WAITANGI (1840)

The first meaningful English contact with New Zealand began in the
1820's, when missionaries, whalers, seamen, and a few colonists visited or
settled parts of the islands. Unlike the Australian aborigines, who had generally moved inland when Englishmen came, the Maoris of New Zealand
resented the intrusion of colonials who threatened to confiscate their land
and who imposed an alien political and social system on them. The Treaty
of Waitangi, signed February 6, 1840, between the British government and
the Maori chiefs, made New Zealand a part of the Empire and guaranteed
the Maoris their property and rights. Unfortunately, when both parties violated this treaty, the first Maori War erupted in 1844.

HER Majesty Queen Victoria, of the United Kingdom of Great Britain
and Ireland, regarding with Her Royal favour the native chiefs and tribes of
New Zealand, and anxious to protect their just rights and property, and to
secure to them the enjoyment of peace and good order, has deemed it necessary, (in consequence of the great number of Her Majesty's subjects who
have already settled in New Zealand, and the rapid extension of emigration
both from Europe and Australia, which is still in progress,) to constitute
and appoint a functionary properly authorized to treat with the aborigines of
New Zealand for the recognition of Her Majesty's sovereign authority over
the whole or any part of those islands.

Her Majesty, therefore, being desirous to establish a settled form of civil
government, with a view to avert the evil consequences which must result
from the absence of the necessary laws and institutions, alike to the native
population and to Her subjects, has been graciously pleased to empower and
authorize me, William Hobson, a captain in Her Majesty's Royal Navy,
Consul and Lieutenant-Governor of such parts of New Zealand as may be,
or hereafter shall be, ceded to Her Majesty, to invite the confederated and
independent chiefs of New Zealand to concur in the following articles and
conditions:

ART. I. The chiefs of the confederation of the united tribes of New Zealand, and the separate and independent chiefs who have not become members of the confederation, cede to Her Majesty, the Queen of England,

absolutely, and without reservation, all the rights and powers of sovereignty which the said confederation or individual chiefs respectively exercise or possess, or may be supposed to exercise or to possess, over their respective territories, as the sole sovereigns thereof.

II. Her Majesty the Queen of England confirms and guarantees to the chiefs and tribes of New Zealand, and to the respective families and individuals thereof, the full, exclusive, and undisturbed possession of their lands and estates, forests, fisheries, and other properties which they may collectively or individually possess, so long as it is their wish and desire to retain the same in their possession. But the chiefs of the united tribes, and the individual chiefs, yield to Her Majesty the exclusive right of pre-emption over such lands as the proprietors thereof may be disposed to alienate, at such prices as may be agreed upon between the respective proprietors and persons appointed by Her Majesty to treat with them in that behalf.

III. In consideration thereof, Her Majesty, the Queen of England, extends to the natives of New Zealand Her Royal protection, and imparts to them all the rights and privileges of British subjects.

Waitangi, 5th February, 1840.

W. HOBSON.

Now, therefore, we the chiefs of the confederation of the united tribes of New Zealand, being assembled in congress at Victoria in Waitangi, and we, the separate and independent chiefs of New Zealand, claiming authority over the tribes and territories which are specified after our respective names, having been made fully to understand the provisions of the foregoing Treaty, accept and enter into the same in the full spirit and meaning thereof.

In witness of which, we have attached our signatures or marks at the places and dates respectively specified.

Done at Waitangi, this 6th day of February, in the year of our Lord 1840.

328. PALMERSTON'S OPINIONS ON BRITISH POLICY VIS-À-VIS AUSTRIAN AND FRENCH INTERVENTION IN ITALY (1848)

The year 1848 witnessed a rash of revolutions throughout Europe. Several revolutions erupted in the Italian states. On August 30, 1848, Lord Palmerston, the brilliant and forthright Foreign Secretary, wrote a letter to Prime Minister Lord John Russell, which reflects the author's aggressiveness in foreign affairs.

With regard to Venice it seems to me that we have to choose whether there shall be peace or war between Austria and France, and whether we shall deliberately let France loose to settle the affairs of Italy in her own way or not. If she goes to Venice without our consent and sanction Austria will consider it an act of war, and the next step will be the entrance of the French into Lombardy [both Lombardy and Venetia were part of the Austrian Empire]. If we associate ourselves morally and politically with the move, Austria will not venture to treat it as war, but will deal with it as an element of negotiation. For my own part, thinking that the Austrians are intruders in Italy and that their expulsion would be no real injury to them and a great blessing to the Italians, and believing that if the French were to enter Italy the Austrians would be swept clean out of it, I should on that account be rather glad than sorry to see a French army cross the Alps; but then if it went in on its own account it would settle all matters as the French Government might choose. We would be put upon the shelf and England would cut but a sorry figure in Europe. My own opinion is that, if France is to act anywhere in Italy, she ought to be tied up by a previous agreement with us as to the extent and object of her action. I think such a course is the only safe one for Europe and honourable and secure for England, and that if we shrink from such a course we shall be the cause of much evil.

France now says that if the mediation is declined she must send a garrison to hold Venice, that she will do it without us if we prefer it, but that she prefers doing it with our concurrence. Do we believe what she says or not? If we do not, then let us give her a civil answer, and take the chance of our incredulity being well founded. But if we believe she will go on, and that is my belief, we must say something about it. You propose that we should say that she has a right to do so if she chooses; she will probably reply by asking whether we object or not. What shall we answer? That we have no objection, I presume.

329. THE CRIMEAN WAR (1854–1855)

This brief but costly war had arisen out of Napoleon III's assertion of ancient French rights over the Holy Places of Palestine, and larger Russian counter-claims in Palestine and European Turkey that would have opened the way to complete domination of Turkish domestic and foreign affairs. Britain was drawn into the war on the Franco-Turkish side. The war revealed an incompetence and backwardness, both on the part of the British military and of the government.

A. *Report on Conditions at the Fighting Front*

We have . . . alluded to this painful subject. The unfitness of our military system to cope with the situation in which the army found itself was glaringly exposed. Nothing that was wanted seemed to be forthcoming: everything seemed to be in its wrong place. The troops were perishing from cold, while piles of great coats were lying useless at Balaklava. Porter would have been an invaluable beverage, while rum was pernicious; but nothing but rum was served out to the soldiers, although abundance of porter had been sent out from England. When a particular medicine was urgently required, it was found that the supply was exhausted, and army surgeons were obliged to borrow some of the simplest elements of the pharmacopoeia from the private medicine-chests of officers. The soldiers were not only ill-clad, but ill-fed: the difficulty of getting up provisions to the camp was so great that they were often obliged to be content with scanty rations. Sick men, who were almost too weak to eat, had to support themselves upon hard biscuit instead of bread. The men had often to eat their rations of meat raw, for they had not sufficient fuel to light fires for cooking. The coffee sent from England was green, neither ground nor roasted; and there was no apparatus for preparing it: scurvy was rife amongst the troops, and there was frequently no lime-juice to be got. The wretched horses of the cavalry gnawed each other's tails in the agony of hunger, and dropped down dead from starvation. They had not strength to struggle through the muddy morass which lay between the camp and Balaklava, when sent down for supplies.

In the meantime the harassing fatigue of nightwork in the trenches decimated the ranks. Cold, wet, and shelterless, the weary soldiers stood hour after hour in the ditch, and then returned to their tents with hardly a single comfort to cheer them, or appliance to keep off disease. Young recruits, fresh from England, and utterly unseasoned to the climate, were owing to the diminished numbers of the army, compelled to undertake this destructive duty, and perished by hundreds in consequence. . . .

B. *Florence Nightingale in the Crimea*

Early in 1855 a fund was raised in England to provide materials for Florence Nightingale and her nurses to minister to the needs of the sick and dying. One of Miss Nightingale's relatives described the work of the nurses in this letter to Lord Houghton:

Very good news from Scutari as far as the way in which the expedition is received, and the use it is of. Mr. B. says, "In one week F. [Florence

Nightingale] has gained the confidence of all; the doctors do her will, and the Fund has poured its cornucopia into her lap: tinpots, saucepans, jars, basins, sherry, combs, shirts, socks, sheets, coal, wooden spoons, form its jewels. They all say that the patience and endurance of the soldiers is something more beautiful than one can tell, and the manner in which they behave to the nurses. We had 1,715 sick and wounded in this hospital, and 650 in the other, of which we have charge also, when a message came to prepare for 510 wounded on our side of the hospital. We had but half an hour's notice before they began to land them. Between 1 and 9 o'clock we had the mattresses stuffed, sewn up and laid down—alas! only on matting on the floor—the men washed, put to bed, and all their wounds dressed. The Turks carry these men who are come out to fight for them so carelessly that they arrive in a state of agony; twenty-four died in the process. We have now nearly four miles of beds not 18 inches apart. We have our quarers in one tower, and this fresh influx has been laid down between us and the main guard in two corridors, with a line of beds down each side, and just room for one to pass between. I can truly say it is good for us to be here, even in the midst of this appalling horror. As I went my last round among the newly wounded that first night there was not a murmur, not one groan; the strictest discipline, the most absolute silence and quiet prevailed; only the step of the sentry; and I heard one man say, "I was dreaming of my friends at home," and another said, "And I was thinking of them." These poor fellows bear pain and mutilation with unshrinking heroism, and die without complaint.

330. THE DECLARATION OF PARIS (1856)

> The plenipotentiaries of the Great Powers, meeting at Paris to write the treaty that concluded the Crimean War, issued a Declaration that resolved several long-standing issues among the maritime powers over neutral rights on the high seas and the legality of blockades.

1. Privateering is, and remains, abolished;
2. The neutral flag covers enemy's goods, with the exception of contraband of war;
3. Neutral goods, with the exception of contraband of war, are not liable to capture under enemy's flag;
4. Blockades, in order to be binding, must be effective, that is to say, maintained by a force sufficient really to prevent access to the coast of the enemy.

The Governments of the undersigned Plenipotentiaries engage to bring the present Declaration to the knowledge of the States which have not taken part in the Congress of Paris, and to invite them to accede to it. . . .

331. GOVERNMENT OF INDIA ACT (1858)

The Sepoy Mutiny in 1857 called attention to weaknesses in the government of India and led Parliament to pass an Act to provide a better system of government for India. The chief provisions of the Act are:

I. The Government of the Territories now in the Possession or under the Government of the East India Company, and all Powers in relation to Government vested in or exercised by the said Company in trust for Her Majesty, shall cease to be vested in or exercised by the said Company, and all Territories in the Possession or under the Government of the said Company, and all Rights vested in or which if this Act had not been passed might have been exercised by the said Company in relation to any Territories, shall become vested in Her Majesty, and be exercised in Her Name. . . .

III. Save as herein otherwise provided, One of Her Majesty's Principal Secretaries of State shall have and perform all such or the like Powers and Duties in anywise relating to the Government or Revenues of India, and all such or the like Powers over all Officers appointed or continued under this Act, as might or should have been exercised or performed by the East India Company, or by the Court of Directors or Court of Proprietors of the said Company. . . .

VII. For the Purposes of this Act a Council shall be established, to consist of Fifteen Members, and to be styled the Council of India; and henceforth the Council in India now bearing that Name shall be styled the Council of the Governor General of India. . . .

XIX. The Council shall, under the direction of the Secretary of State, and subject to the Provisions of this Act, conduct the Business transacted in the United Kingdom in relation to the Government of India and the Correspondence with India. . . .

XXIX. The Appointments of Governor General of India, Fourth Ordinary Member of the Council of the Governor General of India, and Governors of Presidencies in India, now made by the Court of Directors with the Approbation of the Commissioners for the Affairs of India, shall be made by Her Majesty by Warrant under Her Royal Sign Manual. . . .

XXXIX. All lands and Hereditaments, Monies, Stores, Goods, Chattels, and other Real and Personal Estate of the said Company, subject to the Debts and Liabilities affecting the same respectively, and the Benefit of all Contracts, Covenants, and Engagements, and all Rights to Fines, Penalties, and Forfeitures, and all other Emoluments which the said Company shall be seised or possessed of, or entitled to at the Time of the Commencement of this Act, except the Capital Stock of the said Company and the Dividend thereon, shall become vested in Her Majesty, to be applied and disposed of, subject to the Provisions of this Act, for the Purposes of the Government of India.

332. THE ROYAL TITLES ACT (1876)

In 1876 Parliament passed the Royal Titles Bill enabling Queen Victoria to assume the title of "Empress of India."

And whereas by the Act for the better Government of India, passed in the session of the twenty-first and twenty-second years of the reign of Her present Majesty, chapter one hundred and six, it was enacted that the Government of India, theretofore vested in the East India Company in trust for Her Majesty, should become vested in Her Majesty, and that India should thenceforth be governed by and in the name of Her Majesty, and it is expedient that there should be a recognition of the transfer of government so made by means of an addition to be made to the style and titles of Her Majesty.

Be it therefore enacted by the Queen's most Excellent Majesty, by and with the advice and consent of the Lords Spiritual and Commons, in this present Parliament assembled, and by the authority of the same, as follows:

It shall be lawful for Her most Gracious Majesty with a view to such recognition as aforesaid of the transfer of the Government of India, by Her Royal Proclamation under the Great Seal of the United Kingdom, to make such addition to the style and titles at present appertaining to the Imperial Crown of the United Kingdom and its dependencies as to Her Majesty may seem meet.

333. IMPERIALISM (*ca.* 1880–1914)

In the last decades of the nineteenth century, the Great Powers became imperialistic and carved out for themselves huge areas, primarily in Africa and Asia. Britain also got into this scramble and acquired valuable territories. Much of this was done under Conservative ministries, which, in doing so, had to face opposition from many of the Liberals. Campbell-Bannerman, a Liberal party leader, reflected their sentiments when, in a speech at Birmingham (November 24, 1899), he said:

You will have observed that every one nowadays appears to cultivate some peculiar species of his own of what is called Imperialism, and to try to get some qualifying adjective of his own before the word. Now I should be sorry to find myself differing from other people, but I also have a species of Imperialism of which I am a votary, and I have my pet word by which to qualify it. Mine is 'Common-sense Imperialism.' I should be much surprised if it were not found that I belong to the largest congregation of all who worship at that shrine. We have in this country an overflowing population, and we are bound to find for their industrial energy ever fresh . . . outlets. We, therefore, cannot do a work more patriotic and more conducive to the happiness of our own people at home than by developing the resources of the Empire, by securing our trade rights, and by cultivating close, cordial and active relations with all the members of the British family scattered throughout the world. There is ample room here for all our activity, and for my part I grudge to see any of that activity diverted to the acquisition—sometimes it may be inevitable—to the acquisition of new dominions which may bring us glory, but which very often is rather a burden than a source of advantage for many years.

SOURCE REFERENCES   *Chapter Seven*

267. Wade, John, ed., *The Black Book: An Exposition of Abuses in Church and State, Courts of Law, Municipal Corporations, and Public Companies*, new ed., pp. 232–234. London: E. Wilson, 1835.

268. Greville, Charles C. G., ed., *The Greville Memoirs. A Journal of the Reigns of King George IV and King William IV*, II, 520–521. New York: D. Appleton, 1875.

269. Trowbridge, W. R. H., *Queen Alexandra, A Study of Royalty*, pp. 175–179. New York: D. Appleton, 1921.

270. Wilson, Philip W., ed., *The Greville Diary, Including Passages Hitherto Withheld from Publication*, II, 35. New York: Doubleday, Page, 1927.

271. Hamilton, Lord George, *Parliamentary Reminiscences and Reflections*, pp. 60–62. New York: E. P. Dutton, 1917.

272. A. Hamilton, *Parliamentary Reminiscences and Reflections*, pp. 62–64.
B. Cited in Reid, T. Wemyss, *The Life of the Right Honourable William Edward Forster*, 4th ed., I, 366. London: Chapman and Hall, 1888.
C. Morley, John, *The Life of William Ewart Gladstone*, III, 529. New York: Macmillan, 1903.

273. Wade, John, *The Black Book; or Corruption Unmasked*, pp. 193–194. London: John Fairburn, 1820.

274. *Annual Register* (1816), pp. 93–94.

275. *Annual Register* (1819), pp. 106–107.

276. Wilson, *The Greville Diary*, I, 306–307.

277. A. Cobbett, William, *Rural Rides in the Southern, Western, and Eastern Counties of England, Together with Tours in Scotland . . . and Letters from Ireland*, ed. by G. D. H. and Margaret Cole, II, 369; III, 748–749. London: Peter Davies, 1930.

B. *Reports of Special Assistant Poor Law Commissioners on the Employment of Women and Children in Agriculture,* pp. 82–83. London: Stationery Office, 1843.

C. Cited in Morley, John, *The Life of Richard Cobden,* I, 156–157. London: Chapman and Hall, 1881.

278. Levi, Leone, *History of British Commerce and of the Economic Progress of the British Nation, 1763–1870,* pp. 292–293. London: John Murray, 1872.

279. Levi, *History of British Commerce,* p. 296.

280. Levi, *History of British Commerce,* pp. 293–294.

281. *Annual Register* (1824), p. 48 of Chronicle.

282. *Annual Register* (1824), p. 3.

283. *Annual Register* (1826), p. 63 of Chronicle.

284. Cobbett, *Rural Rides,* II, 596.

285. *Statutes at Large,* 3 and 4 William IV, CAP. 103.

286. *Statutes at Large,* 7 and 8 Victoria, CAP. 15.

287. *Statutes at Large,* 10 and 11 Victoria, CAP. 24.

288. *Annual Register* (1847), pp. 122–123.

289. *Annual Register* (1817), pp. 303–304 of Chronicle.

290. *Annual Register* (1815), pp. 509–510 of Chronicle.

291. *Statutes at Large,* 5 and 6 Victoria, CAP. 99.

292. *Annual Register* (1822), p. 703 of Chronicle.

293. *Annual Register* (1832), pp. 445–446 of Chronicle.

294. *Statutes at Large,* 7 and 8 Victoria, CAP. 85.

295. *Annual Register* (1851), pp. 144–145.

296. Wade, *The Black Book; or Corruption Unmasked,* p. 445.

297. Hansard, T. C., *Parliamentary Debates,* 3rd series, I, 52–53. London: various publishers and dates.

298. Cited in Trevelyan, G. O., *The Life and Letters of Lord Macaulay,* I, 186–187. New York: Harper and Brothers, 1876.

299. *Statutes at Large,* 2 William IV, CAP. 45.

300. A. *Annual Register* (1842), pp. 152–153.

B. Wilson, *The Greville Diary,* II, 289–290.

301. A. Russell, Earl, *Recollections and Suggestions, 1813–1873,* p. 43. London: Longmans, Green, 1875.

B. Kebbel, T. E., ed., *Selected Speeches of the Late Right Honourable the Earl of Beaconsfield,* II, 525–533, *passim.* London: Longmans, Green, 1882.

302. *Statutes at Large,* 30 and 31 Victoria, CAP. 102.

303. *Public General Statutes,* 35 and 36 Victoria, CAP. 33.

304. *Public General Statutes,* 48 Victoria, CAP. 3.

305. *Statutes at Large,* 3 and 4 William IV, CAP. 73.

306. Trevelyan, *The Life and Letters of Lord Macaulay,* II, 248–249.

307. A. Lawley, F., in the *Daily Telegraph,* May 20, 1898, as given in Morley, *The Life of William Ewart Gladstone,* I, 32–33, f.n. 1.

B. Cecil, Lady Gwendolen, *Life of Robert Marquis of Salisbury,* I, 13. London: Hodder and Stoughton, 1924.

C. *Annual Register* (1816), pp. 608–610 of Chronicle.

308. Hansard, *Parliamentary Debates,* 3rd series, LXXX, 1146.

309. *Annual Register* (1825), p. 82 of Chronicle.

310. Spender, J. A., *The Life of the Right Honourable Sir Henry Campbell-Bannerman,* I, 35–36. London: Hodder and Stoughton, 1923.

311. *Public General Statutes,* 34 Victoria, CAP. 26.

312. *Public General Statutes,* 33 and 34 Victoria, CAP. 75.

313. Darwin, Charles, *The Descent of Man and Selection in Relation to Sex,* II, 386–387. New York: D. Appleton, 1872.

314. Malthus, Thomas, *An Essay on the Principle of Population or A View of Its Past and Present Effects on Human Happiness,* 8th ed., pp. 2–6. London: Reeves and Turner, 1878.

315. Greville, Charles C. F., ed., *The Greville Memoirs. A Journal of the Reign of Queen Victoria from 1837 to 1852,* III, 110–111. London: Longmans, Green, 1895.

316. *Annual Register* (1827), p. 24 of Chronicle.

317. *Statutes at Large,* 9 George IV, CAP. 17.

318. *Statutes at Large,* 10 George IV, CAP. 7.

319. *Annual Register* (1841), pp. 65–66.

320. *Letters of the Prince Consort 1831–1861,* ed. by Kurt Jagow and trans. by E. S. Dugdale, pp. 97–98. New York: E. P. Dutton, 1938.

321. *Memoirs of Archbishop Temple by Seven Friends,* ed. by E. G. Sandford, I, 425. London: Macmillan, 1906.

322. *Statutes of the United Kingdom,* 32 and 33 Victoria, CAP. 42.

323. Russell, *Recollections and Suggestions, 1813–1873,* pp. 313–314.

324. *Annual Register* (1843), pp. 227–228.

325. A. O'Shea, Katherine, *Charles Stewart Parnell His Love Story and Political Life,* I, 151–152. New York: George Doran, 1914.

    B. O'Shea, *Charles Stewart Parnell,* I, 143.

326. *British and Foreign State Papers, 1818 and 1819,* VI, 3ff. London: James Ridgway, 1835.

327. *British and Foreign State Papers, 1840–1841,* XXIX, 1111–1112. London: James Ridgway, 1857.

328. Gooch, G. P., ed., *The Later Correspondence of Lord John Russell, 1840–1878,* I, 340–341. London: Longmans, Green, 1925.

329. A. *Annual Register* (1855), p. 190.

    B. Reid, T. Wemyss, *The Life, Letters, and Friendships of Richard Monckton Milnes First Lord Houghton,* I, 509–510. London: Cassell, 1891.

330. *Annual Register* (1856), p. 322 of Chronicle.

331. *Public General Statutes,* 21 and 22 Victoria, CAP. 106.

332. *Public General Statutes,* 39 Victoria, CAP. 10.

333. Spender, *Life of Campbell-Bannerman,* I, 257–258.

CHAPTER EIGHT

The Twentieth Century

Twentieth-century developments in Britain have been determined largely by the effects of three periods—the two World Wars (1914–1918; 1939–1945) and the great depression from 1929 to 1939. These periods witnessed sweeping economic, political, and social changes as well as major alterations in Britain's colonial and imperial relationships. The nineteenth-century economic philosophy of *laissez-faire* has been supplanted by the nationalization of important industries and services. The movement toward political democracy, which began early in the nineteenth century, has been carried to fruition. Religious freedom and social equality have been achieved and educational institutions greatly modernized and expanded. When the Empire and Commonwealth were re-constituted through the Statute of Westminster (1931), Britain was still a great colonial power. Since then, however, and particularly after 1945, it has steadily declined as a world power as a result of serious economic problems and the maturation of many of its colonies into independent states.

In 1901, when Queen Victoria died, few people could have foreseen that within one lifetime Britain would relinquish world leadership and be faced with a struggle to maintain an adequate standard of living. Britain was then a wealthy and influential nation: as Anthony Wood put it, it seemed to Edwardians "a time of limitless security, peace, and pleasure." During what Esmé Wingfield-Stratford calls "the Victorian aftermath," the tyranny of respectability began to fade, as did the notion that pleasure was wicked and hard labor an unqualified virtue.

334. KING EDWARD VII (1901–1910)

In 1901, Edward was a mellow monarch of sixty, but he had not, as Anthony Wood so aptly characterized him, "lost the art of enjoyment, and during his reign he delighted in the passing show of the *beau monde* at Ascot, Henley, and Cowes. The wealthiest society in the world had at last ceased to be ashamed to display its opulence, and aristocracy and new rich created a scene of extraordinary brilliance, presided over by a King whose name now stands for the whole of that glittering decade." Sir Edward Grey, the Foreign Secretary in 1905–1916, who knew Edward very well, wrote of him:

He took an active interest in high diplomatic appointments, such as those of Ambassadors, but it was from the point of view of their personal qualities, not from that of policy. He wished us to be represented abroad with dignity and personal prestige.

What, then, were the qualities that made him so important to the country? They are not easy to describe, because they were the intangible qualities of a personality peculiar to himself. Let the more commonplace be considered first. He had in a very high degree the gift, proper and valuable in a Sovereign, for ceremonial. No one knew so well as he how ceremony should be arranged, ordered, and carried through in the manner most effective and impressive. By his own person, and by the part he took in it, he added dignity to it. In all this he performed to perfection the function that only the Sovereign can perform for the British Empire. This, however, is expected of the Sovereign, and, however well it is performed, unless there be something else, people are left satisfied but cold; they may even come to resent the pomp and the display. King Edward had a rare, if not a unique, power of combining bonhomie and dignity. The bonhomie was warm and spontaneous, but it never impaired the dignity. His bearing was a perfect example of tact, ease, and dignity, and to this were added good sense and judgment that not only avoided mistakes, but perceived the thing that should be said to suit the occasion or please an individual. These gifts, valuable in any Sovereign, were particularly so in one who was the living centre of an Empire that included the self-governing Dominions and India.

There was, however, something more that gave a spirit and aspect to it all, and this was due to his individual personality. Warm human kindness was of the very substance of the man . . . . There was, in fact, real sympathy and community of feeling between himself and his people.

335. THE ABDICATION OF KING EDWARD VIII IN 1936

In 1936, on the death of King George V, a steady and popular monarch who had reigned since 1910, his eldest son ascended the throne as Edward VIII. His subjects liked him largely because of his genuine interest in, and sympathy for, the poor. But he immediately encountered a sticky constitutional crisis following his decision to marry Mrs. Wallis Simpson, a twice-divorced American commoner. Stanley Baldwin, the Prime Minister, told him that such a marriage would cause scandal and damage the prestige of the crown. Edward then proposed a morganatic marriage, that is, the exclusion of his heirs from the throne. When Baldwin rejected this compromise, Edward, left with the choice of forsaking his intention of marriage or abdicating, decided on the latter. On December 10, 1936, the Prime Minister read the following abdication message from Edward to the House of Commons:

After long and anxious consideration, I have determined to renounce the Throne to which I succeeded on the death of My father, and I am now communicating this, My final and irrevocable decision. Realizing as I do the gravity of this step, I can only hope that I shall have the understanding of My peoples in the decision I have taken and the reasons which have led Me to take it. I will not enter now into My private feelings, but I would beg that it should be remembered that the burden which constantly rests upon the shoulders of a Sovereign is so heavy that it can only be borne in circumstances different from those in which I now find Myself. I conceive that I am not overlooking the duty that rests on Me to place in the forefront the public interest, when I declare that I am conscious that I can no longer discharge this heavy task with efficiency or with satisfaction to Myself.

I have accordingly this morning executed an Instrument of Abdication in the terms following:—

I, Edward VIII, of Great Britain, Ireland, and the British Dominions beyond the seas, King, Emperor of India, do hereby declare My irrevocable determination to renounce the Throne for Myself and for My descendants, and My desire that effect should be given to this Instrument of Abdication immediately. . . .

336. SEX DISQUALIFICATION ACT (1919)

In 1907 Parliament passed an Act enabling women to be elected to county and borough councils, but they could not as yet be elected to Parliament. As a result of the agitation of the militant "Suffragettes," and as a reward for their loyal services during World War I, Parliament passed an Act permitting women who were at least thirty years of age to sit and vote in the House of Commons. (In 1928 the age limit was reduced to twenty-one.) This Act of 1918 also put an end in most cases to plural voting and substituted for all persons entitled to vote a single vote based on a qualification of six months' residence in one parliamentary district, or on a business connection in such a district for the same period of time, but not on both. In 1919 the Sex Disqualification Act, given below, opened to women careers in the professions and in the public service.

Be it enacted . . . as follows:

1. A person shall not be disqualified by sex or marriage from the exercise of any public function, or from being appointed to or holding any civil or judicial office or post, or from entering or assuming or carrying on any civil profession or vocation, or for admission to any incorporated society (whether incorporated by Royal Charter or otherwise), and a person shall not be exempted by sex or marriage from the liability to serve as a juror. . . .

2. A woman shall be entitled to be admitted and enrolled as a solicitor after serving under articles for three years only if either she has taken such a university degree as would have so entitled her had she been a man, or if she has been admitted to and passed the final examination and kept, under the conditions required of women by the university, the period of residence necessary for a man to obtain a degree at any university which did not at the time the examination was passed admit women to degrees.

3. Nothing in the statutes or charter of any university shall be deemed to preclude the authorities of such university from making such provision as they shall think fit for the admission of women to membership thereof, or to any degree, right, or privilege therein or in connection therewith . . . .

337. THE PARLIAMENT ACT OF 1911

The Liberal party, which came into power in 1905, introduced important and revolutionary social legislation over the strong opposition of the Conservatives, particularly in the House of Lords. The most significant of these new measures were old age pensions, unemployment insurance, and national health insurance. The cost of these programs as well as the cost of the naval build-up necessitated by the arms race with Germany put a heavy strain on government finance. Consequently David Lloyd George, Chancellor of the Exchequer, brought into Parliament in 1909 a budget bill that called for both new and increased taxes, particularly on the wealthy, landed class' property and income. The budget passed the Commons, but it was defeated in the Lords. In the general election of 1910, which was fought principally over the issue of the budget, the Liberal party again gained a majority, and again passed the budget bill. The Lords, sensing that further opposition was pointless, grudgingly agreed to it. But the matter did not end there, for the ministry introduced another bill giving the House of Commons almost complete supremacy over the Lords, which had brought this circumstance upon itself by refusing to pass or by holding up major reform bills since 1866, and which had managed to escape any reduction in its power and influence during the reform era of the nineteenth century. When the Lords loaded down the Parliament Bill of 1911 with so many amendments as to change the nature of the Bill, Prime Minister Asquith secured the king's promise to create enough new peers to assure its passage. Faced with this hopeless cause, the Lords passed the Bill exactly as it was sent up from the Commons. The principal provisions of this Parliament Act are:

1.—(1) If a Money Bill, having been passed by the House of Commons, and sent up to the House of Lords at least one month before the end of the session, is not passed by the House of Lords without amendment within one month after it is so sent up to that House, the Bill shall, unless the House of Commons direct to the contrary, be presented to His Majesty and become an Act of Parliament on the Royal Assent being signified, notwithstanding that the House of Lords have not consented to the Bill.

(2) A Money Bill means a Public Bill which in the opinion of the Speaker of the House of Commons contains only provisions dealing with all or any of the following subjects, namely, the imposition, repeal, remission, alteration, or regulation of taxation; the imposition for the payment of debt or other financial purposes of charges on the Consolidated Fund, or on money provided by Parliament, or the variation or repeal of any such charges; supply; the appropriation, receipt, custody, issue or audit of accounts of public money; the raising or guarantee of any loan or the repayment thereof; or subordinate matters incidental to those subjects or any of them. In this subsection the expressions "taxation," "public money," and "loan" respectively do not include any taxation, money, or loan raised by local authorities or bodies for local purposes . . . .

2.—(1) If any Public Bill (other than a Money Bill or a Bill containing any provision to extend the maximum duration of Parliament beyond five years) is passed by the House of Commons in three successive sessions (whether of the same Parliament or not), and, having been sent up to the House of Lords at least one month before the end of the session, is rejected by the House of Lords in each of those sessions, that Bill shall, on its rejection for the third time by the House of Lords, unless the House of Commons direct to the contrary, be presented to His Majesty and become an Act of Parliament on the Royal Assent being signified thereto, notwithstanding that the House of Lords have not consented to the Bill: Provided that this provision shall not take effect unless two years have elapsed between the date of the second reading in the first of those sessions of the Bill in the House of Commons and the date on which it passes the House of Commons in the third of those sessions. . . .

338. THE DECLINE OF THE LIBERAL PARTY AFTER 1914

The Liberals began to lose supporters and influence because of factionalism within their ranks and because the Labour party, which had first been loosely organized in 1892, took the lead in promoting social and economic legislation. The Liberals steadily lost ground to the Conservatives and Labourites, especially during the years 1929 to 1939. E. L. Woodward, author of the brief and delightful *Short Journey*, offers this explanation for the decline of the Liberal party:

The collapse of the liberal party in Great Britain was due mainly to the intellectual and moral failure of the leaders of this party to assimilate new ideas. The liberal party before 1914 had many faults; nevertheless it had attracted young and generous minds. The party organization was in the hands of men who had been anxious to secure this collaboration; the party program had been drawn up not merely to attract voters but to attract the right type of candidate. After 1918 Asquith and Grey and Haldane had little influence within their old party. The liberal party machine was largely in the hands of Mr. Lloyd George. There was no party program. Mr. Lloyd George's program was a handful of amateur notions picked up at random. The effects of his few years of control over a great political party were catastrophic. The way was left open for the MacDonald era, with an opposition lamed and divided by doctrine, and powerless even to overthrow a succession of weak governments.

My generation wanted a new liberal party; we would have served it; in time we might have led it. Few of us could ever be at ease in any other political party. If this party had come into being, the ideas which it would have represented, the program of action which it could have put into effect might have changed the face of England. It is indeed possible that such a party could never have come into existence while Mr. Lloyd George was in the way. Mr. Lloyd George's adroitness, his prestige, his immense parliamentary experience, his sly, malignant oratory would have been difficult obstacles. Yet I am inclined to think that, without the gaps in our ranks, we might have succeeded in creating a new party to meet a new age. Success of this kind has been known in English history. We needed not merely the qualitatively best among those who were lost in the war. We needed also a certain pressure of numbers; a vigorous body of opinion throughout the country as well as a small group in the House of Commons. The survivors who came back from the war were too few.

339. PARLIAMENTARY ELECTION PROCEDURES

A government, to remain in power, must maintain a majority support in the House of Commons. If the government is defeated on a major issue, it generally resigns, and the sovereign invites the leader of the Opposition to form a new government or dissolves Parliament and an election is held. Hence the government is responsible directly to the electorate. A general election, since the Parliament Act of 1911, must take place at least every five years, but a Parliament is often dissolved by the sovereign on the advice of the Prime Minister before the statutory term of Parliament expires. The *British Record,* a publication of the British Information Services, describes the essential features of parliamentary elections as follows:

CONSTITUENCIES

For electoral purposes the United Kingdom is divided into geographical areas known as constituencies, each having separate representation in the House of Commons. There are two types: borough constituencies and county constituencies. All are single-member constituencies.

At the present time [1966] there are 630 constituencies—511 for England, 36 for Wales, 71 for Scotland and 12 for Northern Ireland. Each constituency represents approximately 55,600 potential voters . . . .

THE VOTERS

British subjects and citizens of the Irish Republic are entitled to vote, provided they are 21 years old or over, and are not subject to any legal incapacity to vote. In order to vote a person must be recorded on the register of electors for the constituency as resident in that constituency on a date fixed by statute. The following are not eligible to register as voters and therefore vote: peers (who are members of the House of Lords), persons under 21 years of age, aliens, persons of unsound mind, felons serving a sentence of more than 12 months, and persons convicted within the previous five years of corrupt or illegal practices in connection with an election. . . .

THE CANDIDATES

A candidate need not be resident in the constituency for which he, or she, "stands." All who are qualified to vote are also qualified to stand for election, except undischarged bankrupts, clergy of the Churches of England, Scotland, Ireland and Roman Catholic Church, and certain persons holding offices of profit under the Crown . . . .

A candidate is normally a member of one of the main political parties, although there is nothing to prevent him standing as an independent.

Candidates, other than independent candidates, may be suggested by the local constituency party or by the party's central office. The choice lies . . . solely with the local party which through a selection committee interviews possible candidates and makes the final decision . . . .

Each candidate must be nominated on the prescribed nomination paper. The nomination paper must be "subscribed" by two electors as proposer and seconder, and by eight other electors as assenting to the nomination . . . . The candidate must deposit the sum of $420 with the Returning Officer. If he polls at least one-eighth of the total votes cast, he is entitled to have his deposit returned; if not, his deposit is forfeited . . . . Counting Sundays and excluding public holidays the election campaign lasts 21 days . . . . The Conservative and Labour Parties . . . each have five television broadcasts of fifteen minutes and seven sound broadcasts . . . while the Liberal Party will have three television broadcasts of fifteen minutes and four sound broadcasts . . . .

ELECTION EXPENSES

The maximum expenditure which may be incurred by a candidate is:

In borough constituencies, $1,260 plus 2 cents for each elector on the register;

In county constituencies, $1,260 plus 2.5 cents for each elector.

A candidate is entitled to send to every elector free of postal charge one communication relating to the election weighing not more than two ounces. Each candidate is allowed to spend a sum not exceeding $280 on his personal expenses, including money spent on travel and hotels. He must render an account of such expenses . . . .

THE POLL

Each constituency is divided into a number of polling districts. Each polling station is in the charge of a presiding officer. The hours of poll are 7 a.m. to 9 p.m.

The ballot is secret. Candidates' names appear on the ballot paper without party designation, arranged alphabetically in the order of their surnames. Any marking other than a cross by the name of the candidate of the voter's choice invalidates the ballot . . . .

The Returning Officer must immediately declare the result of the poll.

The declaration is usually made publicly, often from a balcony outside the hall where count is made . . . .

340. THE FABIAN SOCIETY

This society, founded in 1893, became very influential in the early decades of the present century. Its members advocated the gradual democratization and socialization of Britain's land, industry, and public services by peaceful legislative processes. They gained a degree of fame out of all proportion to their numbers because of the leadership of famous persons, such as George Bernard Shaw, Sidney and Beatrice Webb, Herbert G. Wells, and Ramsay MacDonald, the future Labour Prime Minister. The Fabians wrote hundreds of essays and pamphlets in support of their cause—the improvement of conditions among all individuals within the framework of the law and the constitution. In 1919 the society, having been merged by that time for almost twenty years with the Labour party, adopted the following "constitution":

BASIS OF THE FABIAN SOCIETY
(To Be Signed by All Members)
(Adopted May 23rd, 1919)

The Fabian Society consists of Socialists.

It therefore aims at the reorganization of Society by the emancipation of Land and Industrial Capital from individual ownership, and the vesting of them in the community for the general benefit. In this way only can the natural and acquired advantages of the country be equitably shared by the whole people.

The Society accordingly works for the extinction of private property in land, with equitable consideration of established expectations, and due provision as to the tenure of the home and the homestead; for the transfer to the community, by constitutional methods, of all such industries as can be conducted socially; and for the establishment, as the governing consideration in the regulation of production, distribution and service, of the common good instead of private profit.

The Society is a constituent of the Labour Party and of the International Socialist Congress; but it takes part freely in all constitutional movements, social, economic and political, which can be guided towards its own objects. Its direct business is (a) the propaganda of Socialism in its application to current problems; (b) investigation and discovery in social, industrial, political and economic relations; (c) the working out of Socialist principles in legislation and administrative reconstruction; (d) the publication of the results of its investigations and their practical lessons.

The Society, believing in equal citizenship of men and women in the fullest sense, is open to persons irrespective of sex, race or creed, who commit themselves to its aims and purposes as stated above, and undertake to promote its work.

The Society includes:—

I. Members, who must sign the Basis and be elected by the Committee. Their Subscriptions are not fixed; each is expected to subscribe annually according to his means. They control the Society through the Executive Committee (elected annually by ballot through a postal vote), and at its annual and other business meetings.

II. Associates, who sign a form expressing only general sympathy with the objects of the Society and pay not less than 10s. a year. They can attend all except the exclusively members' meetings, but have no control over the Society and its policy.

III. Subscribers, who must pay at least 5s. a year, and who can attend the Society's Ordinary Lectures.

> Since 1846 Britain had pursued an economic policy of free trade. By the end of the century many political leaders had begun to doubt the wisdom of continuing that policy in view of serious competition from aggressive industrial states such as Germany. Consequently agitation for the adoption of protective tariffs mounted in and out of Parliament. A measure of protection was adopted, particularly after World War I when the chief characteristic of economic activity has been increasing government regulation. By the 1960's Britain had taken giant strides toward the nationalization of its major industries and services. The two World Wars contributed greatly to this development, but the process had already begun in earnest before 1914, and would doubtless have continued, although perhaps at a slower pace, had there been no wars.

341. THE LIBERAL PARTY AND FREE TRADE (1903)

At Newport (Isle of Wight), on November 30, 1903, Sir Henry Campbell-Bannerman, then leader of the Liberal party, explained the views of the free-trade Liberals as follows:

Our position is that poverty in a Free Trade country is nothing like the curse which it is in a Protectionist country where every crust of bread is taxed. We are not fanatics. We do not attribute to Free Trade miraculous powers, or claim for it that it can of itself remove the burden of poverty. We leave panaceas to others. But we don't want to see England turned once more into the poor man's purgatory, a place of unalleviated misery for the workman. We don't want another England of the 'thirties and the 'forties. We don't desire the return of the days when the labourer eked out his wages with the help of the Guardians, and when trade and agriculture were carried on by a universal system of out-relief, filched from the earnings of the poor. No, the Liberal Party, if it is worth its salt, will take up the cause of the poor man, will stand by the poor man, and see him through this business. But we do not leave the matter there, and content ourselves with nice sentiments. If there is a mass of poverty in this country co-existing with our ever-increasing collective wealth, we believe that much of it is preventible, and would be prevented if the principles of freedom and Liberalism were properly applied and enforced. Vested interests and the dead hand of the past lie heavy on this country of ours, and the Protectionist Party [Conservatives] are willing and eager to have it so. What have they done in the last eighteen years but oppose all efforts to secure a better distribution of wealth and a fairer apportionment of taxation? Fiscal reform, indeed! Why, these fiscal reformers are the very men who have clamoured for broadening the basis of taxation; who, after squandering the national treasure on their interests and on their friends, and their career of adventure, come to the poor man to pay for it out of his bread and sugar and tea. Is it any wonder that millions of the people are ill-nourished?

342. THE TRADES DISPUTES ACT (1906)

Trade unions had existed in England since the later eighteenth century, but employers and the government generally regarded them as "combinations" organized for the purpose of restraining trade. Hence they were outlawed until 1825, although they continued to exist under the guise of social and benevolent societies. Thereafter trade unionists were often held up to scorn, and, from time to time, were prosecuted in the courts for striking, picketing, and rioting for higher wages and shorter hours. In 1868, the Trades Union Congress was organized to speak for all British unions, but it completely ignored the unskilled workers. In the 1870's a number of Acts were passed which authorized peaceful picketing, defined the circumstances under which the trade unions might be held liable for criminal conspiracy, and recognized the principle of collective bargaining.

The trade unions having grown steadily in membership and influence in the 1880's and 1890's, particularly after their association with the new Labour party, their status was once more jeopardized in 1900, when the Taff

Vale Railway Company in South Wales sued the railway workers union for the financial loss suffered as a result of a strike. The House of Lords, the highest tribunal in the land, heard the case and decided in favor of the railway company. When the Liberals came to power in 1905, at a time when the Labour party was beginning to make its influence felt in national politics for the first time, they secured the passage of new labor legislation, the Trades Disputes Act, which was intended to win the confidence of the unionists by rectifying the setback that they had suffered in consequence of the Taff Vale decision.

Be it enacted . . . as follows . . . :

2.—(1) It shall be lawful for one or more persons, acting on their own behalf or on behalf of a trade union or of an individual employer or firm in contemplation or furtherance of a trade dispute, to attend at or near a house or place where a person resides or works or carries on business or happens to be, if they so attend merely for the purpose of peacefully obtaining or communicating information, or of peacefully persuading any person to work or abstain from working.

(2) Section seven of the Conspiracy and Protection of Property Act, 1875, is hereby repealed from "attending at or near" to the end of the section.

3. An act done by a person in contemplation or furtherance of a trade dispute shall not be actionable on the ground only that it induces some other person to break a contract of employment or that it is an interference with the trade, business, or employment of some other person, or with the right of some other person to dispose of his capital or his labour as he wills.

4.—(1) An action against a trade union, whether of workmen or masters, or against any members or officials thereof on behalf of themselves and all other members of the trade union in respect of any tortious act alleged to have been committed by or on behalf of the trade union, shall not be entertained by any court.

(2) Nothing in this section shall affect the liability of the trustees of a trade union to be sued in the events provided for by the Trades Union Act, 1871, section nine, except in respect of any tortious act committed by or on behalf of the union in contemplation or in furtherance of a trade dispute . . . .

343. WORKMEN'S COMPENSATION ACT (1906)

For a long time after the common employment of machinery in industry, a laborer who was injured while on the job had no recourse other than to sue his employer for damages. As one might expect, few workers could afford to go to court, and those that could rarely won their cases. Legislation passed in 1897 (an early Workmen's Compensation Act) made employers liable in many industries for compensation to injured employees unless the employer could prove that the injury was due to the willful negligence or misconduct of the injured. The burden of proof in court was, therefore, thrown on the employer. The Act of 1906 included many occupational diseases among the "injuries" for which compensation had to be paid, and included in the list additional occupations covered by insurance, such as household services. The Act protected a total of thirteen million workers—six million more than had the Act of 1897. The chief provisions of the 1906 Act are:

1.—(1) If in any employment personal injury by accident arising out of and in the course of the employment is caused to a workman, his employer shall, subject as herein-after mentioned, be liable to pay compensation in accordance with the First Schedule to this Act.

(2) Provided that—

> (a) The employer shall not be liable under this Act in respect of any injury which does not disable the workman for a period of at least one week from earning full wages at the work at which he was employed:

> (b) When the injury was caused by the personal negligence or wilful act of the employer or of some person for whose act or default the employer is responsible, nothing in this Act shall affect any civil liability of the employer, but in that case the workman may, at his option, either claim compensation under this Act or take proceedings independently of this Act; but the employer shall not be liable to pay compensation for injury to a workman by accident arising out of and in the course of the employment both independently of and also under this Act, and shall not be liable to any proceedings independently of this Act, except in case of such personal negligence or wilful act as aforesaid:

> (c) If it is proved that the injury to a workman is attributable to the serious and wilful misconduct of that workman, any compensation claimed in respect of that injury shall, unless the injury results in death or serious and permanent disablement, be disallowed . . . .

(4) If, within the time herein-after in this Act limited for taking pro-

ceedings, an action is brought to recover damages independently of this Act for injury caused by any accident, and it is determined in such action that the injury is one for which the employer is not liable in such action, but that he would have been liable to pay compensation under the provisions of this Act, the action shall be dismissed; but the court in which the action is tried shall, if the plaintiff so choose, proceed to assess such compensation, but may deduct from such compensation all or part of the costs, which, in its judgment, have been caused by the plaintiff bringing the action instead of proceeding under this Act. In any proceeding under this sub-section, when the court assesses the compensation it shall give a certificate of the compensation it has awarded and the directions it has given as to the deduction for costs, and such certificate shall have the force and effect of an award under this Act.

(5) Nothing in this Act shall affect any proceeding for a fine under the enactments relating to mines, factories, or workshops, or the application of any such fine. . . .

344. THE OLD AGE PENSIONS ACT (1908)

Parliament passed the Old Age Pensions Act partly to reduce high parish rates needed to finance parish workhouses under the Poor Law, and partly to give financial aid to the aged. The cost of the pensions was enormous, but, as Professor Goldwin Smith points out, the cost had to be "set against the exodus of thousands of elderly people from the parish workhouses."

Be it enacted . . . as follows . . . :

2. The statutory conditions for the receipt of an old age pension by any person are—

  (1) The person must have attained the age of seventy:
  (2) The person must satisfy the pension authorities that for at least twenty years up to the date of the receipt of any sum on account of a pension he has been a British subject, and has had his residence . . . in the United Kingdom:
  (3) The person must satisfy the pension authorities that his yearly means as calculated under this Act do not exceed thirty-one pounds ten shillings.

3.—(1) A person shall be disqualified for receiving or continuing to receive an old age pension under this Act, notwithstanding the fulfilment of the statutory conditions—

(a) While he is in receipt of any poor relief . . . provided that
     for the purpose of this provision—
       (i) any medical or surgical assistance . . . supplied by or
           on the recommendation of a medical officer; or
      (ii) any relief given to any person by means of the main-
           tenance of any dependant of that person in any luna-
           tic asylum, infirmary, or hospital, or the payment of
           any expenses of the burial of a dependant; or
     (iii) any relief (other than medical or surgical assistance,
           or relief herein-before specifically exempted) which
           by law is expressly declared not to be a disqualifica-
           tion for registration as a parliamentary elector, or a
           reason for depriving any person of any franchise,
           right, or privilege;
shall not be considered as poor relief . . . :

(2) Where a person has been before the passing of this Act, or is after
the passing of this Act, convicted of any offence, and ordered to be imprisoned without the option of a fine or to suffer any greater punishment, he
shall be disqualified for receiving or continuing to receive an old age pension
under this Act while he is detained in prison in consequence of the order,
and for a further period of ten years after the date on which he is released
from prison.

(3) Where a person of sixty years of age or upwards having been convicted before any court is liable to have a detention order made against him
under the Inebriates Act, 1898, and is not necessarily, by virtue of the provisions of this Act, disqualified for receiving or continuing to receive an old
age pension under this Act, the court may, if they think fit, order that the
person convicted be so disqualified for such period, not exceeding ten years,
as the court direct. . . .

5.—(1) An old age pension under this Act, subject to any directions
of the Treasury in special cases, shall be paid weekly in advance in such
manner and subject to such conditions as to identification or otherwise as the
Treasury direct.

(2) A pension shall commence to accrue on the first Friday after the
claim for the pension has been allowed, or, in the case of a claim provision-
ally allowed, on the first Friday after the day on which the claimant becomes
entitled to receive the pension. . . .

SCHEDULE

Means of Pensioner.	Rate of Pension per Week.
Where the yearly means of the pensioner as calculated under this Act—	*s.* *d.*
Do not exceed 21*l.*	5 0
Exceed 21*l.*, but do not exceed 23*l.* 12*s.* 6*d.*	4 0
Exceed 23*l.* 12*s.* 6*d.*, but do not exceed 26*l.* 5*s.*	3 0
Exceed 26*l.* 5*s.*, but do not exceed 28*l.* 17*s.* 6*d.*	2 0
Exceed 28*l.* 17*s.* 6*d.*, but do not exceed 31*l.* 10*s.* ...	1 0
Exceed 31*l.* 10*s.*	No pension.

345. COAL MINES REGULATION ACT (1908)

This Act, an amendment to numerous earlier Acts passed in the nineteenth century, fixed the hours of labor in underground coal mines.

Be it enacted . . . as follows:

1.—(1) Subject to the provisions of this Act a workman shall not be below ground in a mine for the purpose of his work, and of going to and from his work, for more than eight hours during any consecutive twenty-four hours. . . .

(3) The owner, agent, or manager of every mine shall fix for each shift of workmen in the mine the time at which the lowering of the men to the mine is to commence and to be completed, and the time at which the raising of the men from the mine is to commence and to be completed, in such a manner that every workman shall have the opportunity of returning to the surface without contravention of the foregoing provisions of this section, and shall post and keep posted at the pit head a conspicuous notice of the time so fixed, and shall make all arrangements necessary for the observance of those times in lowering and raising the men. . . .

(7) For the purposes of this Act, the expression "workman" means any person employed in a mine below ground, who is not an official of the mine (other than a fireman, examiner, or deputy), or a mechanic or horse-keeper, or a person engaged solely in surveying or measuring; and any number of workmen whose hours for beginning and terminating work in

the mine are approximately the same shall be deemed to be a shift of work-men. . . .

6. For securing compliance with the provisions of this Act, it shall be the duty of the owner, agent, or manager of every mine—

(a) to make regulations for that purpose and publish such regulations by posting them . . . and by supplying a copy thereof gratis to every workman . . . ; and

(b) to provide necessary means for raising the men from the mine within the time limited by this Act. . . .

346. THE COAL MINES ACT (1911)

The main purpose of this Act was to make mining safer. By it the government stipulated that all mines should have licensed managers and that they should be regularly inspected. The government also required all mine owners to provide colliers with safety lamps; forbade the use of "lucifer matches"; ordered safety devices installed on all machinery, provision of "safety holes" as refuges, underground telephonic communication, and sanitary conveniences. The Act also included the following regulations respecting the employment of boys, girls, and women in coal mines.

91. No boy under the age of fourteen years, and no girl or woman of any age, shall be employed in or allowed to be for the purpose of employment in any mine below ground. Nothing in this section shall apply to any boy who has been lawfully employed in any mine below ground before the passing of this Act.

92. With respect to boys, girls, and women employed above ground, in connexion with any mine, the following provisions shall have effect:—

(1) No boy or girl under the age of thirteen years shall be so employed, unless lawfully so employed before the passing of this Act:

(2) No boy or girl of or above the age of thirteen years and no woman shall be so employed for more than fifty-four hours in any one week or more than ten hours in any one day:

(3) No boy, girl, or woman shall be so employed between the hours of nine at night and five on the following morning, nor on Sunday, nor after two o'clock on Saturday afternoon:

(4) There shall be allowed an interval of not less than twelve hours between the termination of employment on one day, and the commencement of the next employment:

(5) A week shall be deemed to begin at midnight on Saturday night and to end at midnight on the succeeding Saturday night:

(6) No boy, girl, or woman shall be employed continuously for more than five hours, without an interval of at least half an hour for a meal, nor for more than eight hours on any one day, without an interval or intervals for meals amounting altogether to not less than one hour and a half:

(7) No boy, girl, or woman shall be employed in moving railway waggons, or in lifting, carrying, or moving any thing so heavy as to be likely to cause injury to the boy, girl, or woman. . . .

347. THE LABOR EXCHANGES ACT (1909)

This Act was designed to help solve the unemployment problem (the most serious domestic issue before World War I) by establishing several hundred public labor exchanges to serve as clearing houses for job information and to aid workers to find employment.

Be it enacted . . . as follows:

1.—(1) The Board of Trade may establish and maintain, in such places as they think fit, labour exchanges, and may assist any labour exchanges maintained by any other authorities or persons, and in the exercise of those powers may, if they think fit, co-operate with any other authorities or persons having powers for the purpose.

(2) The Board of Trade may also, by such other means as they think fit, collect and furnish information as to employers requiring workpeople and workpeople seeking engagement or employment.

(3) The Board of Trade may take over any labour exchange (whether established before or after the passing of this Act) by agreement with the authority or person by whom the labour exchange is maintained, and any such authority or person shall have power to transfer it to the Board of Trade for the purposes of this Act.

(4) The powers of any central body or distress committee, and the powers of any council through a special committee, to establish or maintain, under the Unemployed Workmen Act, 1905, a labour exchange or employment register shall, after the expiration of one year from the commencement of this Act, not be exercised except with the sanction of, and subject to any conditions imposed by, the Local Government Board for England, Scotland, or Ireland, as the case may require, and that sanction shall not be given except after consultation with the Board of Trade.

2.—(1) The Board of Trade may make general regulations with respect to the management of labour exchanges established or assisted under this Act, and otherwise with respect to the exercise of their powers under this Act, and such regulations may, subject to the approval of the Treasury, authorise advances to be made by way of loan towards meeting the expenses of workpeople travelling to places where employment has been found for them through a labour exchange.

(2) The regulations shall provide that no person shall suffer any disqualification or be otherwise prejudiced on account of refusing to accept employment found for him through a labour exchange where the ground of refusal is that a trade dispute which affects his trade exists, or that the wages offered are lower than those current in the trade in the district where the employment is found. . . .

348. THE FINANCE ACT (1910)

This Act (the budget bill proposed by Lloyd George in 1909 and passed in 1910, which led to the passage of the Parliament Act of 1911) provided the necessary revenue to pay for unemployment compensation, sickness benefits, old age pensions, and the new naval building program begun in 1907. Although the earlier Liberal budgets had been commendably frugal, the Budget of 1909 called for expenditures of gargantuan proportions. Hence revenue had to be sharply increased, principally by the institution of an unearned increment tax, increased duties on liquor licenses, new death duties, and a steeply graduated income tax.

PART I.

DUTIES ON LAND VALUES.

Increment Value Duty.

1. Subject to the provisions of this Part of this Act, there shall be charged, levied, and paid on the increment value of any land a duty, called increment value duty, at the rate of one pound for every complete five pounds of that value accruing after the thirtieth day of April nineteen hundred and nine, and—

> (*a*) on the occasion of any transfer on sale of the fee simple of the land or of any interest in the land, in pursuance of any contract made after the commencement of this Act, or the grant, in pursuance of any contract made after the commencement of this Act, of any lease (not being a lease for a term of years not exceeding fourteen years) of the land; and

> (*b*) on the occasion of the death of any person dying after the commencement of this Act, where the fee simple of the land or any interest in the land is comprised in the property passing on

the death of the deceased within the meaning of sections one and two, subsection (1) (*a*), (*b*), and (*c*), and subsection three, of the Finance Act, 1894, as amended by any subsequent enactment; and

(*c*) where the fee simple of the land or any interest in the land is held by any body corporate or by any body unincorporate as defined by section twelve of the Customs and Inland Revenue Act, 1885, in such a manner or on such permanent trusts that the land or interest is not liable to death duties, on such periodical occasions as are provided in this Act,

the duty, or proportionate part of the duty, so far as it has not been paid on any previous occasion, shall be collected in accordance with the provisions of this Act.

2.—(1) For the purposes of this Part of this Act the increment value of any land shall be deemed to be the amount (if any) by which the site value of the land, on the occasion on which increment value duty is to be collected as ascertained in accordance with this section, exceeds the original site value of the land as ascertained in accordance with the general provisions of this Part of this Act as to valuation. . . .

Part II.

Duties on Liquor Licences.

43. There shall be charged, levied, and paid on the licences for the manufacture or sale of intoxicating liquor specified in the First Schedule to this Act, the duties of excise specified in that Schedule, and the provisions expressed in that Schedule to be applicable to any such licences shall have effect with respect to those licences. The said duties shall be charged on any licences which shall have been granted after the first day of July nineteen hundred and nine or may hereafter be granted, but, in the case of any such licences granted before the thirtieth day of September nineteen hundred and nine, the amount of the duty shall be adjusted so as to make the sum payable in respect of the period up to that date such sum only as would have been payable if this Act had not passed. . . .

Part III.

Death Duties.

54. The scale set out in the Second Schedule to this Act shall, in the case of persons dying on or after the thirtieth day of April nineteen hundred and nine, be substituted for the scale set out in the First Schedule to the

Finance Act, 1907, as the scale of rates of estate duty, and two per cent. shall be substituted for one per cent. in section seventeen of the Finance Act, 1894 (in this Part of this Act referred to as the principal Act), as the rate of settlement estate duty. . . .

58.—(1) Any legacy or succession duty which under the Stamp Act, 1815, or the Succession Duty Act, 1853, or any other Act, is payable at the rate of three per cent. shall be payable at the rate of five per cent., and any legacy or succession duty which under the said Acts is payable at the rate of five per cent. or six per cent. shall be payable at the rate of ten per cent. on the amount or value of the legacy or succession. . . .

Part IV.

Income Tax.

65.—(1) Income tax for the year beginning on the sixth day of April nineteen hundred and nine shall be charged at the rate of one shilling and twopence.

(2) All such enactments relating to income tax as were in force on the fifth day of April nineteen hundred and nine shall, subject to the provisions of this Act, have full force and effect with respect to any duties of income tax hereby granted. . . .

66.—(1) In addition to the income tax charged at the rate of one shilling and twopence under this Act, there shall be charged . . . beginning on the sixth day of April nineteen hundred and nine, in respect of the income of any individual, the total of which from all sources exceeds five thousand pounds, an additional duty of income tax (in this Act referred to as a super-tax) at the rate of sixpence for every pound of the amount by which the total income exceeds three thousand pounds.

(2) For the purposes of the super-tax, the total income of any individual from all sources shall be taken to be the total income of that individual from all sources for the previous year, estimated in the same manner as the total income from all sources is estimated for the purposes of exemptions or abatements under the Income Tax Acts. . . . [Of these taxes, that on unearned increment was the least satisfactory. By 1916 it had been proved that it cost as much to administer the tax as the revenue it produced, and was therefore repealed.]

349. THE GENERAL STRIKE OF 1926

As a result of the economic dislocations and hard times following World War I, the increased use of new labor-saving devices, and foreign competition, the volume of exports in iron and steel as well as textiles and coal steadily diminished. The coal-mining industry suffered most in the decade after 1918: over 98,000,000 tons had been exported in 1913; only 44,000,000 in 1920. This situation grew worse as other countries, who could not afford to buy British coal, began to mine their own coal or to use oil or electricity as a substitute for it. Unemployment and grinding poverty therefore stalked the British mining areas, particularly in Wales and Scotland. Faced with reduced markets and falling prices, in 1925 the mine owners informed their workers of the need to cut wages. To prevent a strike resulting from lower wages, the government subsidized the owners so as to enable them to pay the old scale. When the subsidy ceased, on May 1, 1926, and the owners had taken no ameliorative measures to help their employees, they went on strike, and, under the urging of the Trades Union Congress, were soon joined by millions of other workers in industry, transportation and communication, and public services. The following is a description of the General Strike of 1926 which appeared in the *Annual Register*.

The miners' notices not having been removed, at midnight on May 3 the strike orders of the Trades Union Council came into force. The unions which had been ordered to cease work on that date were those of the railway and transport workers and printers, and of the iron and steel and building trades, and all these obeyed the call with remarkable unanimity. Consequently, on the next day the country presented an unwonted appearance. Practically no trains were running, and no trams or buses in the streets of the large towns; the morning papers appeared only in the reduced size which it had been possible to produce before midnight, and the evening papers not at all. The public naturally was gravely inconvenienced in going about its affairs, and business immediately began to suffer severely, though it was by no means brought to a standstill.

The Government meanwhile had already taken steps to deal with a situation for which it had long been preparing. In accordance with the scheme made public in the previous October, the country was divided into a number of areas, each of which was put in charge of a Commissioner armed with special powers for ensuring the maintenance of the food supply and of essential public services. The strike leaders had disclaimed any intention of interfering with these requirements, but the Government did not trust them. In order to replace the labour which had been withdrawn by the strike, it opened offices for the enrolment of volunteer workers, and these immediately came forward in large numbers. Hundreds of thousands of special constables were also enrolled to assist the police. Before the first day of the strike was over a huge army of volunteers was engaged in transporting food supplies by motor, running trains and buses, and other services, and the public was

not so terribly incommoded by the situation as to be unable to relish its
novelty. . . .

Thus ended the first attempt in the history of England to use the
weapon of a general strike. The attempt was so disastrous to those who
made it that the moral drawn generally by responsible leaders of labour was
"never again." The trade unions came out of the struggle impoverished and
humiliated, doubtful whether they would much longer be able to maintain
their exceptional privileges against a Government attack. They consoled
themselves with the thought that they had given a wonderful demonstration
of working class solidarity, but this did not save them from being bitterly
reproached by the miners for leaving them in the lurch. The organisers of
the strike were undoubtedly quite sincere when they disclaimed any intention of acting unconstitutionally or illegally seizing power. But this very attitude doomed them to failure, since, as was generally recognized on the Continent, a general strike was useless unless it had a definitely political object.
The attempt, in fact, while regarded by the rank and file as a general strike
intended to coerce the Government, was conducted by the leaders as a purely
sympathetic strike in aid of the miners on the part of certain classes of workers. It thus fell between two stools, and wasted the resources of the workers
without securing them any advantage. . . .

350. NATIONALIZATION OF THE COAL INDUSTRY (1946)

Under the Labour Ministry of 1945–1951, many industries and services were
taken over by the government. The Bank of England, the coal industry, and
the gas, electrical, and transport services (including railways, busses, docks,
harbors, telephones, and telegraph) were all nationalized. The nationalization statutes differed individually in accordance with the peculiarities of
each industry or service, but the Act to nationalize the coal industry, excerpts of which follow, may be taken as typical.

Be it enacted . . . as follows:—

The National Coal Board.

1.—(1) There shall be a National Coal Board which shall, on and
after the primary vesting date, be charged with the duties of—

   (a) working and getting the coal in Great Britain, to the exclusion
       (save as in this Act provided) of any other person;

   (b) securing the efficient development of the coal-mining industry;
       and

(*c*) making supplies of coal available, of such qualities and sizes, in such quantities and at such prices, as may seem to them best calculated to further the public interest in all respects, including the avoidance of any undue or unreasonable preference or advantage.

(2) The functions of the National Coal Board (in this Act referred to as "the Board") shall include the carrying on of all such activities as it may appear to the Board to be requisite, advantageous or convenient for them to carry on for or in connection with the discharge of their duties under the preceding subsection, and in particular, but without prejudice to the generality of this section,—

(*a*) searching and boring for coal in Great Britain, to the exclusion of any other person;

(*b*) treating, rendering saleable, supplying and selling coal;

(*c*) producing, manufacturing, treating, rendering saleable, supplying and selling products of coal;

(*d*) producing or manufacturing any good or utilities which are of a kind required by the Board for or in connection with the working and getting of coal or any other of their activities, or which can advantageously be produced or manufactured by the Board by reason of their having materials or facilities for the production or manufacture thereof in connection with the working and getting of coal or any other of their activities, and supplying and selling goods or utilities so produced or manufactured:

(*e*) any activities which can advantageously be carried on by the Board with a view to making the best use of any of the assets vested in them by this Act;

(*f*) activities conductive to advancing the skill of persons employed or to be employed for the purposes of any of the activities aforesaid, or the efficiency of equipment and methods to be used therefor, including the provision by the Board themselves, and their assisting the provision by others, of facilities for training, education and research.

(3) The Board shall have power to do any thing and to enter into any transaction . . . which in their opinion is calculated to facilitate the proper discharge of their duties under subsection (1) of this section or the carrying on by them of any such activities as aforesaid, or is incidental or conducive thereto.

(4) The policy of the Board shall be directed to securing, consistently with the proper discharge of their duties under subsection (1) of this section,—

   (*a*) the safety, health and welfare of persons in their employment;

   (*b*) the benefit of practical knowledge and experience of such persons in the organisation and conduct of the operations in which they are employed;

   (*c*) that the revenues of the Board shall not be less than sufficient for meeting all their outgoings properly chargeable to revenue account . . . on an average of good and bad years. . . .

351. BRITAIN AND THE COMMON MARKET

When the European Economic Community (Common Market) was organized in 1958, Britain did not join because it feared that the planned tariff reductions of the Community would disturb existing relationships with the Commonwealth countries. Britain also feared the implication of supranationalism in the organization of the E.E.C., and decided to wait until the Community demonstrated that it could succeed. Since its inception the Common Market has proved amazingly successful for all its members— Italy, France, West Germany, Belgium, the Netherlands and Luxembourg. As a consequence, by the early 1960's Britain had changed its mind and sought membership in the E.E.C., provided that its own arrangements with the Commonwealth and the European Free Trade Association (E.F.T.A., which Britain helped to found in 1959) were not adversely affected. Speaking for the Labour government in May, 1966, George Brown declared:

We intend, therefore, in any negotiations to interpret them [the problems affecting British entry into the Common Market] in a practical way with our minds open to new ideas in the light of the existing facts and prospects. . . . There are no inhibitions on our part, provided that the Community is willing to consider our anxieties with open minds, and to help to find ways and means of meeting the problems. . . . While it may be a mistake to expect any early or dramatic developments we intend that no opportunity should be lost for probing and determining the way in which we could move forward so that when the time came, our response could be quick and positive. We want an expanded EEC, we want to be a member of it and we want to find the basis on which this would be possible. And the Labour Government in Britain, deeply conscious of its responsibilities to Europe and of Europe's responsibilities to the world is determined to play its full part in bringing about the European unity which is so fundamental to both.

352. BRITAIN'S ECONOMIC CONDITION (1966)

That Britain's economy has been generally unhealthy since the last war is well known. While there has been full employment, and the average family has more material comforts than ever before, Britain has had an unfavorable balance of trade and has had to borrow heavily, especially from the United States. A sound and healthy economy required that Britain cut down on purchases abroad (particularly in dollar markets) and at the same time greatly increase its exports. This it has been unable to do. Various explanations, apart from those arising out of the economic dislocations of World War II, have been advanced for its economic difficulties. Speaking in Toronto on September 17, 1966, James Callahan, Chancellor of the Exchequer, declared that the situation was not critical, and answered some of what he called "myths about Britain."

The belief that Britain is strike-ridden and undisciplined.
The Facts are:

Britain's record compares favorably over the years with most other countries. In the five years 1960–64 the average days per year lost through strikes per 1,000 employed in Britain was 242 compared with 722 in the U.S.A. and 1,220 in Italy . . . .

The belief that British exports are falling back.
The Facts are:

British exports rose 7 per cent in value last year and are continuing to rise this year. Britain is the world's largest exporter of agricultural tractors, commercial road vehicles, wool textiles, radio isotopes, vacuum cleaners and washing machines, telegraph and telephone equipment. Britain has the world's second biggest aircraft industry, office machinery and oil refinery industry . . . .

The belief that productivity in British industry lags behind everybody else.
The Facts are:

Britain's growth and productivity has been roughly in line with that of the U.S.A. and Canada, although some other countries certainly grew faster.

The belief that Britain still relies on traditional products and is unable to compete with other countries in modern sophisticated products.
The Facts are:

Britain has revolutionized the character of her export industry since the war and a large part of its increase has been precisely in the new

products . . . . British exports per head today are three times as great
as those of Japan and nearly twice as much per head as in the United
States. Some of the springs of this growth were British inventiveness
that produced such items as the vertical take-off aircraft, the first hover-
craft and the first nuclear power station. On this last, Britain produces
more electrical energy from nuclear power than the rest of the world
combined.

353. THE BOER WAR (1899–1902)

Great Britain acquired the Cape Colony of South Africa in 1814. Even before that time the Boers, who were independent farmers of Dutch, German,
or French extraction, had settled the region. They resented the intrusion of
British law and customs, and in the 1830's many migrated northwards into
what became the Boer republics of the Transvaal and Orange Free State,
and into Natal and Bechuanaland. The British encroached upon Boer territory in the next half-century, and in 1880 war erupted between the British
and the Boers. This long-standing hostility became more serious when, gold
having been discovered in the Transvaal in 1886, prospectors, company officials, opportunists, and the like poured into Boer territory. The intruders,
who soon outnumbered the Boers two to one, were called "Uitlanders" and
were discriminated against even though they paid a large part of the taxes
and helped to develop the territories. Meanwhile Cecil Rhodes, governor of
the Cape Colony and a wealthy mine owner, sought to extend British
dominion over the territories northwest of the Cape. The Boers, now almost
surrounded by British territory and in danger of being swallowed up in the
onrush of British imperialism, declared war. Ably led by superb generals
and expert in guerrilla warfare, they were at first victorious. Eventually,
however, Lord Kitchener, the commander-in-chief of the British forces, resorted to a policy of confining Boer families in "concentration" camps. They
were badly managed, disease was rampant, and the mortality among
women and children reached shocking proportions. This policy stirred deep
resentment in much of the world, including England. Whereas many Englishmen in 1899 had blithely sent off troops to the tune of "Goodbye Dolly
Gray," they now began to criticize the harsh policy toward the Boers, whose
army, numbering only 40,000 men, waged a heroic struggle against nearly
350,000 British and Imperial troops. Campbell-Bannerman reflected the opposition to the war in this excerpt from one of his finest speeches:

Where are the elements to be found for a settlement in the conditions to
which you have now reduced South Africa? The whole country in the two
belligerent States outside the mining towns is a howling wilderness. The
farms are burned, the country is wasted. The flocks and the herds are either

butchered or driven off; the mills are destroyed, furniture and implements of agriculture are smashed. These things are what I have termed methods of barbarism. I adhere to the phrase. I cannot improve upon it. If these are not the methods of barbarism what methods did barbarism employ? No, sir. Of course, in particular cases, where some offence has been committed against right dealing, let punishment be enforced, and in time of war things are not done in a rosewater way; but the universal treatment of a whole country in this way, and the sweeping of women and children into camps, is a process for which I venture to say nothing can furnish justification.

In the first half of the twentieth century Britain has participated in two devastating World Wars. The first of these wars (1914–1918) had no single cause. It arose largely over Austro-Russian competition in the Balkans, Franco-German rivalry in western Europe and Africa, and Anglo-German naval and trade rivalry. All the Great Powers after 1871 increased their military establishments and formed alliances and alignments which divided Europe into two opposing armed camps. Germany had allied with Austria and Italy in the Triple Alliance (1882). France and Russia had allied in 1894 in the Dual Alliance. Between 1902, when it had formed an alliance with Japan, and 1914, Britain had not signed any binding defensive or offensive alliances. In 1907, it had negotiated a treaty with Russia that had settled their grievances over Tibet, Afghanistan, and Turkey, and arranged a partition of Persia's oil fields. And, three years earlier, Britain had come to an understanding (the *Entente Cordiale*) with France whereby their outstanding colonial differences in Africa had been settled.

Germany's decision to embark on a large naval building program greatly disturbed Britain, and led it to draw closer its ties with France. In addition, Germany's greatly expanded military posture in Europe threatened what many have called Britain's policy of maintaining a "balance of power" in Europe.

354. SIR EDWARD GREY ON THE "BALANCE OF POWER"

Grey, British Foreign Secretary in 1905–1916, explained what he thought about the "Balance of Power" concept in these words:

I have never, so far as I recollect, used the phrase "Balance of Power." I have often deliberately avoided the use of it, and I have never consciously set it before me as something to be pursued, attained, and preserved. I am not, therefore, qualified to explain or define what it is. I imagine it to mean that when one Power or group of Powers is the strongest "bloc" in Europe, our policy has been, or should be, that of creating, or siding with, some other combination of Powers, in order to make a counterpoise to the strongest

Power or Group and so to preserve equilibrium in Europe. Now the Triple Alliance in 1886 and the following years, when Lord Salisbury and Lord Rosebery were Prime Ministers, was indisputably the strongest political combination, the most powerful thing in Europe. Nevertheless, the policy of friendship with it was followed by the British Government even before the Franco-Russian Alliance had come into existence as a counterpoise; and this policy was continued for many years, while the Triple Alliance continued, in spite of the Franco-Russian Alliance, to be the dominant factor in European diplomacy. During this period, therefore, Great Britain did not attempt to create any counterpoise to the strongest group; on the contrary, the British Government sided with that group. I do not affirm that this, when closely examined, disproves the theory that the tendency of British policy has been to preserve a balance of power; but there is sufficient apparent inconsistency with the theory to make it necessary to examine what may be called the Triple Alliance policy of the British Government from 1886 to the end of the century and to ask why it was followed.

I suppose that in this, as in most investigations of British foreign policy, the true reason is not to be found in far-sighted views or large conceptions or great schemes. A Minister beset with the administrative work of a great Office must often be astounded to read of the carefully laid plans, the deep, unrevealed motives that critics or admirers attribute to him. Onlookers free from responsibility have time to invent, and they attribute to Ministers many things that Ministers have no time to invent for themselves, even if they are clever enough to be able to do it. If all secrets were known it would probably be found that British Foreign Ministers have been guided by what seemed to them to be the immediate interest of this country without making elaborate calculations for the future. Their best qualities have been negative rather than positive. They would not execute sharp turns or quick changes of front; they were not disposed to make mischief or stir up strife amongst other nations, or to fish in troubled waters; for their instinct was that peace and stability in Europe were the conditions best suited to British trade; and they have generally shrunk from committing themselves for future contingencies, from creating expectations that they might not be able to fulfil, and from saying at any time more than they really meant. On the whole, the British Empire has been well served by these methods. It has, at any rate, been saved from capital and disastrous mistakes; such mistakes as are made by a great thinker, calculating far ahead, who thinks or calculates wrongly. It has also been saved from the disaster of seeing a policy that needs for success the continuous supervision of a great man break down and be wrecked when its great author has been succeeded by inferior men. . . .

355. THE OFFICIAL SECRETS ACT (1911)

The state of international affairs was such in the decade preceding the outbreak of World War I that Parliament passed the following Act as a precautionary measure against the possibility of "leakage" of vital information to the Central Powers:

1.—(1) If any person for any purpose prejudicial to the safety or interests of the State—

(*a*) approaches or is in the neighborhood of, or enters any prohibited place within the meaning of this Act; or

(*b*) makes any sketch, plan, model, or note which is calculated to be or might be or is intended to be directly or indirectly useful to an enemy; or

(*c*) obtains or communicates to any other person any sketch, plan, model, article, or note, or other document or information . . . useful to an enemy;

he shall be guilty of felony, and shall be liable to penal servitude for any term not less than three years and not exceeding seven years. . . .

2.—(1) If any person having in his possession or control any sketch, plan, model, article, note, document, or information which relates to or is used in a prohibited place or anything in such a place, or which has been made or obtained . . . or which has been entrusted in confidence to him by any person holding office under His Majesty or which he has obtained owing to his position as a person who holds or has held a contract made on behalf of His Majesty, or as a person who is or has been employed under a person who holds or has held such an office or contract,—

(*a*) communicates the sketch, plan, model, article, note, document, or information to any person, other than a person to whom he is authorised to communicate it, or a person to whom it is in the interest of the State his duty to communicate it, or

(*b*) retains the sketch, plan, model, article, note, or document in his possession or control when he has no right to retain it or when it is contrary to his duty to retain it:

that person shall be guilty of a misdemeanour.

(2) If any person receives any sketch, plan, model, article, note, document, or information, knowing, or having reasonable ground to believe, at the time when he receives it, that the sketch, plan, model, article, note, document, or information is communicated to him in contravention of this Act, he shall be guilty of a misdemeanour, unless he proves that the commu-

nication to him of the sketch, plan, model, article, note, document, or information was contrary to his desire.

(3) A person guilty of a misdemeanour under this section shall be liable to imprisonment with or without hard labour for a term not exceeding two years, or to a fine, or to both imprisonment and a fine.

3. For the purposes of this Act, the expression "prohibited place" means—

(*a*) any work of defence, arsenal, factory, dockyard, camp, ship, telegraph or signal station, or office belonging to His Majesty, and any other place belonging to His Majesty used for the purpose of building, repairing, making, or storing any ship, arms, or other materials or instruments of use in time of war, or any plans or documents relating thereto; and

(*b*) any place not belonging to His Majesty where any ship, arms, or other materials or instruments of use in time of war, or any plans or documents relating thereto, are being made, repaired, or stored under contract with, or with any person on behalf of, His Majesty, or otherwise on behalf of His Majesty; and

(*c*) any place belonging to His Majesty which is for the time being declared by a Secretary of State to be a prohibited place for the purposes of this section on the ground that information with respect thereto, or damaged thereto, would be useful to an enemy; and

(*d*) any railway, road, way, or channel, or other means of communication by land or water (including any works or structures being part thereof or connected therewith), or any place used for gas, water, or electricity works or other works for purposes of a public character, or any place, where any ship, arms, or other materials or instruments of use in time of war, or any plans or documents relating thereto, are being made, repaired, or stored otherwise than on behalf of His Majesty, which is for the time being declared by a Secretary of State to be a prohibited place for the purposes of this section, on the ground that information with respect thereto, or the destruction or obstruction thereof, or interference therewith, would be useful to an enemy.

7. If any person knowingly harbours any person whom he knows, or has reasonable grounds for supposing, to be a person who is about to commit or who has committed an offence under this Act . . . he shall be guilty of a misdemeanour and liable to imprisonment with or without hard labour for a term not exceeding one year, or to a fine, or to both imprisonment and a fine.

356. TRADING WITH THE ENEMY ACT (1914)

Be it enacted by the King's most Excellent Majesty, by and with the advice and consent of the Lords Spiritual and Temporal, and Commons, in this present Parliament assembled, and by the authority of the same, as follows:

1.—(1) Any person who during the present war trades or has, since the fourth day of August nineteen hundred and fourteen, traded with the enemy within the meaning of this Act shall be guilty of a misdemeanour, and shall—

(a) on conviction under the Summary Jurisdiction Acts, be liable to imprisonment with or without hard labour for a term not exceeding twelve months, or to a fine not exceeding five hundred pounds, or to both such imprisonment and fine; or

(b) on conviction on indictment, be liable to penal servitude for a term not exceeding seven or less than three years or to imprisonment with or without hard labour for a term not exceeding two years, or to a fine, or to both such penal servitude or imprisonment and fine;

and the court may in any case order that any goods or money, in respect of which the offence has been committed, be forfeited.

(2) For the purposes of this Act a person shall be deemed to have traded with the enemy if he has entered into any transaction or done any act which was, at the time of such transaction or act, prohibited by or under any proclamation issued by His Majesty dealing with trading with the enemy for the time being in force, or which at common law or by statute constitutes an offence of trading with the enemy. . . .

357. SIR EDWARD GREY ON REASONS FOR ENGLAND'S GOING TO WAR AGAINST GERMANY (1914)

The French and British military and naval leaders engaged in "conversations" in 1905–1906, 1911, and 1913 on the disposition of their forces in the event of a German attack on France through Belgium. The decisions reached were dependent for their implementation on the approval of the two governments. While no written pledges were made, the French concluded that the mere holding of the discussions amounted to a moral obli-

gation on the British to come to their aid. Foreign Secretary Sir Edward
Grey (later Viscount Grey of Fallodon) neglected to inform the Cabinet of
this inference, and consequently some historians have since held him
culpable for not doing so.

When England declared war on Germany, Grey had to make explanations to Parliament. He made a very able speech which he later summarized
in his book, *Twenty-Five Years 1892–1916*.

The real reason for going into the war was that, if we did not stand by
France and stand up for Belgium against this aggression, we should be iso-
lated, discredited, and hated; and there would be before us nothing but a
miserable and ignoble future. The speech was directed to presenting this
consideration in the way that would convince and make the strongest appeal
to the House, and which was, in fact, the way this issue presented itself from
the first to some of us, and in the end to all the Cabinet, except the two, John
Morley and John Burns, who resigned. I never fully understood the reason
of these resignations, and will therefore say only this about them—that we
felt sure they were based on deep and sincere conviction, not on any
pusillanimity or opportunism; and we respected them accordingly.

One other point about the speech. It was felt to be essential to make
clear to the House that its liberty of decision was not hampered by any engagements entered into previously without its knowledge. Whatever obligation there was to France arose from what those must feel who had wel-
comed, approved, sustained the Anglo-French friendship, that was open and
known to all. In this connexion there was nothing to disclose except the engagement about the north and west coasts of France taken a few hours before, and the letters exchanged with Cambon in 1912, the letter that expressly
stipulated that there was no engagement. It was not till 1923, nine years
later, that a charge of having omitted the last sentence of that letter was
brought to my notice. My first impulse was to deny the thing as impossible;
but it is so: the last sentence of the letter does not appear in the report of the
speech.

358. THE STATUTE OF WESTMINSTER (1931)

The British dominions and colonies had made a monumental contribution
in men, money, and materials toward the defeat of the Central Powers in
World War I. After the war the dominion prime ministers participated in
the Paris Peace Conference and signed the Treaty of Versailles along with
the other Allied and Associated Powers. The dominions were also admitted
to the League of Nations. Such actions, which recognized *de facto* the inde-

pendent judgment of the dominions to regulate their foreign affairs, was not legally recognizable under the existing constitutional structure of the British Empire, for, technically, Britain still controlled the foreign policy of its dominions and colonies. It is quite clear, however, that the dominions wished to regulate their own foreign affairs without the need of consulting Britain. In 1923, for instance, Canada signed a treaty respecting fishing rights with the United States without reference to Britain, and three years later appointed a minister to Washington. It was clearly time to re-define the relationship between Britain and its territories. Consequently, at an Imperial Conference held in 1926, a committee was appointed to formulate the actual relations among the far-flung parts of the Empire. The result was the famous Statute of Westminster, which formalized the existence of the Commonwealth, bound its members together under the British crown, granted the dominion governments full sovereignty in the conduct of their foreign affairs, and denied the Imperial Parliament at Westminster the right to rescind any law passed by a Dominion Parliament or to pass Acts binding in the dominions.

Whereas the delegates of His Majesty's Governments in the United Kingdom, the Dominion of Canada, the Commonwealth of Australia, the Dominion of New Zealand, the Union of South Africa, the Irish Free State and Newfoundland, at Imperial Conferences holden at Westminster in the years of our Lord nineteen hundred and twenty-six and nineteen hundred and thirty did concur in making the declarations and resolutions set forth in the Reports of the said Conferences:

And whereas it is meet and proper to set out by way of preamble to this Act that, inasmuch as the Crown is the symbol of the free association of the members of the British Commonwealth of Nations, and as they are united by a common allegiance to the Crown, it would be in accord with the established constitutional position of all the members of the Commonwealth in relation to one another that any alteration in the law touching the Succession to the Throne or the Royal Style and Titles shall hereafter require the assent as well of the Parliaments of all the Dominions as of the Parliament of the United Kingdom:

And . . . no law hereafter made by the Parliament of the United Kingdom shall extend to any of the said Dominions . . . otherwise than at the request and with the consent of that Dominion . . . :

3. It is hereby declared and enacted that the Parliament of a Dominion has full power to make laws having extra-territorial operation.

4. No Act of Parliament of the United Kingdom passed after the commencement of this Act shall extend, or be deemed to extend, to a Dominion

as part of the law of that Dominion, unless it is expressly declared in that Act that that Dominion has requested, and consented to, the enactment thereof. . . .

11. Notwithstanding anything in the Interpretation Act, 1889, the expression "Colony" shall not, in any Act of Parliament of the United Kingdom passed after the commencement of this Act, include a Dominion or any Province or State forming part of a Dominion.

359. ADVICE TO AGGRESSORS (1938)

The world-wide depression beginning in 1929 was a principal cause of World War II. Each of the major powers sought on individual terms the best means of overcoming the grave economic problems that the depression had caused, and in doing so, brought to an abrupt halt the international efforts to achieve collective security that had been undertaken in the decade after World War I. Without fear of reprisals, and in some cases in violation of the peace treaties of 1919–1920, countries like Germany, Italy, and Japan began to rearm and to implement nationalistic and imperialistic goals at the expense of weaker nations. Such actions ied inevitably to international tensions, and ultimately to war. Japan attacked Manchuria in 1931–1932, and in doing so began a Far Eastern war that merged with World War II in 1939. Germany withdrew from the League of Nations in 1933, remilitarized the Rhineland in 1936, and in 1938 invaded Austria and gained the Sudetenland of Czechoslovakia at the Munich Conference. Italy invaded and conquered Ethiopia in 1934–1935 and signed a treaty with Germany, forming the Axis Alliance. In each case the League of Nations was unable to prevent such aggression.

During these eventful years Britain steadily pursued a policy called "appeasement" by its critics. Prime Ministers Stanley Baldwin (1935–1937) and Neville Chamberlain (1937–1940), realizing that Britain could not afford a vast armament program, and deeply committed to peace, thought it better to appease the dictators than to resort to force. There is little question that most of their countrymen agreed with this policy. But, to some, such as Anthony Eden, who resigned as Foreign Minister in February, 1938, appeasement meant paying blackmail or trying to placate an enemy by giving him territory and privileges that were not Britain's to give nor his to take, and as such was cowardly and immoral. They were therefore incensed at Britain's agreeing in 1935 to permit Germany to build a navy up to 35 per cent of the strength of the British fleet, thereby being a party to the violation of the Treaty of Versailles. In the Spanish Civil War, begun in 1936 by the "Rightists" led by General Franco, Benito Mussolini and Adolf Hitler sent aid to Franco. According to international law, the Loyalist government of Spain should have been able to purchase war materials in neutral countries. But widespread fear of communism and the friendship of Russia for the Spanish Loyalist government led the Conservative party in Britain to refuse to allow the shipment of weapons and supplies to Loyalist Spain and hence doomed the Spanish Republic. And, in the Ethiopian War, Sir Samuel Hoare, British Foreign Secretary, and Pierre Laval, French Prime Minister, proposed that Haile Selassie, the Ethiopian Emperor, should abandon a large part of his dominions to Italy and give it broad economic concessions. When Hitler demanded the acquisition of the Sudetenland, Britain sent Lord Runciman to Prague to try to arrange a settlement that Germany would accept. This attempt having failed, Chamberlain personally sought to appease Hitler. This, too, failed and at Munich in September, 1938, France and Britain agreed not to oppose Hitler's annexation of the Sudetenland.

The reaction on the part of those who detested appeasement was succinctly put in a few lines of poetry entitled "Advice to Aggressors" written by an anonymous author calling himself "Sagittarius."

> Meine Herren and Signori,
> Clients of the British Tory,
> Kindly note that Number 10
> Requests your patronage again.
> Opening, as from to-day,
> As Chamberlain et Daladier,
> Messrs. Hoare, Laval, successors,
> For doing business with aggressors.
>
> Frontiers promptly liquidated,
> Coups d'état consolidated,
> Pledges taken and exchanged,
> Acquisitions rearranged,
> Loans on Fascist risks advanced,
> Nazi enterprise financed,
> European intervention
> Given personal attention.
> Have you problems of Partition?
> Let us send a British Mission.
>
> Breaking with Geneva's firms,
> We offer Nazis favoured terms.
> Let us lend to back your claim

England's honourable name.
For dirty deals both great and small
Our representative will call.
Orders carried out with speed,
Satisfaction guaranteed.
We obsequiously remain,
Daladier et Chamberlain.

Daladier became the French Prime Minister in April, 1938.

360. THE FAILURE OF A PEACE MISSION (1939)

No sooner had Hitler obtained his demands on Czechoslovakia than he began to make similar demands on Poland. In the hope of peaceful settlement
of this crisis, Chamberlain directed the British ambassador at Berlin
(Neville Henderson) to hold discussions with Hitler, who was incensed by
Britain's pledge of aid to Poland should Germany attack it. In his *Failure of
a Mission,* Henderson writes of his August 25th meeting with Hitler:

Briefly put, Hitler's proposals therein dealt with two groups of questions: (a) the immediate necessity of a settlement of the dispute between
Germany and Poland, and (b) an eventual offer of friendship or alliance
between Germany and Great Britain. My interview with Hitler, at which
Herr von Ribbentrop and Dr. Schmidt were also present, lasted on this occasion over an hour. The Chancellor spoke with calm and apparent sincerity.
He described his proposals as a last effort, for conscience' sake, to secure
good relations with Great Britain; and he suggested that I should fly to
London myself with them. I told His Excellency that, while I was fully prepared to consider this course, I felt it my duty to tell him quite clearly that
my country could not possibly go back on its word to Poland and that, however anxious we were for a better understanding with Germany, we could
never reach one except on the basis of a negotiated settlement with Poland.

Within a week Germany attacked Poland and World War II had begun in
Europe.

361. WINSTON CHURCHILL'S SPEECH ON BECOMING
PRIME MINISTER (MAY 13, 1940)

Chamberlain's failures in both domestic and foreign affairs, together with
an unbroken succession of German military victories over Poland, Den-

mark, and Norway, forced his resignation. King George VI at once summoned Churchill to form a coalition government. His explanation to the House of Commons was brief and to the point:

On Friday evening last I received His Majesty's Commission to form a new Administration. It was the evident wish and will of Parliament and the nation that this should be conceived on the broadest possible basis and that it should include all parties, both those who supported the late Government and also the parties of the Opposition. I have completed the most important part of this task. A War Cabinet has been formed of five Members, representing, with the Opposition Liberals, the unity of the nation. The three party Leaders have agreed to serve, either in the War Cabinet or in high executive office. The three Fighting Services have been filled. . . .

To form an Administration of this scale and complexity is a serious undertaking in itself, but it must be remembered that we are in the preliminary stage of one of the greatest battles in history, that we are in action at many other points in Norway and in Holland, that we have to be prepared in the Mediterranean, that the air battle is continuous and that many preparations, such as have been indicated by my hon. Friend below the Gangway, have to be made here at home. In this crisis I hope I may be pardoned if I do not address the House at any length to-day. I hope that any of my friends and colleagues, or former colleagues, who are affected by the political reconstruction, will make allowance, all allowance, for any lack of ceremony with which it has been necessary to act. I would say to the House, as I said to those who have joined this Government: "I have nothing to offer but blood, toil, tears and sweat."

We have before us an ordeal of the most grievous kind. We have before us many, many long months of struggle and of suffering. You ask, what is our policy? I will say: It is to wage war, by sea, land and air, with all our might and with all the strength that God can give us; to wage war against a monstrous tyranny, never surpassed in the dark, lamentable catalogue of human crime. That is our policy. You ask, what is our aim? I can answer in one word: It is victory, victory at all costs, victory in spite of all terror, victory, however long and hard the road may be; for without victory, there is no survival. Let that be realised; no survival for the British Empire, no survival for all that the British Empire has stood for, no survival for the urge and impulse of the ages, that mankind will move forward towards its goal. But I take up my task with buoyancy and hope. I feel sure that our cause will not be suffered to fail among men. At this time I feel entitled to claim the aid of all, and I say, "Come then, let us go forward together with our united strength."

362. CHURCHILL'S SPEECH ON THE "BATTLE OF BRITAIN" (JUNE 18, 1940)

The fall of France in June, 1940, left Britain alone in Europe to face the menace of Nazi Germany. This grave situation worried Parliament and led to a long debate in the Commons on the war situation. Churchill, characteristically direct and courageous in the face of peril, delivered one of his greatest speeches, which he concluded with these oft-repeated words:

What General Weygand called the "Battle of France" is over. I expect that the battle of Britain is about to begin. Upon this battle depends the survival of Christian civilization. Upon it depends our own British life and the long continuity of our institutions and our Empire. The whole fury and might of the enemy must very soon be turned on us. Hitler knows that he will have to break us in this island or lose the war. If we can stand up to him all Europe may be free, and the life of the world may move forward into broad, sunlit uplands; but if we fail then the whole world, including the United States, and all that we have known and cared for, will sink into the abyss of a new dark age made more sinister, and perhaps more prolonged, by the lights of perverted science. Let us therefore brace ourselves to our duty and so bear ourselves that if the British Commonwealth and Empire lasts for a thousand years men will say, "This was their finest hour."

363. THE IRISH REBELLION OF 1916

While Britain was waging war, struggling with economic problems, and consolidating and redefining its Imperial relationships, it also had grave problems with Ireland in the twentieth century. Earlier in this book we have given examples of problems that arose in Ireland since the seventeenth century. The death of Charles Stewart Parnell in 1891 temporarily retarded the Irish Home-Rule movement, and Ireland was more or less quiescent until 1912, when the Liberals, who needed Irish Nationalist support to remain in power, agreed to introduce another Home Rule Bill. It was passed in 1914 over the opposition of the House of Lords when the Commons passed it in three successive sessions over two years under the provisions of the Parliament Act of 1911. Because of the outbreak of war in 1914, implementation of the Act was postponed. The Irish Nationalist party supported the war and many Irishmen had enlisted and were fighting with the British forces. The Sinn Fein Society ("Ourselves Alone"), however, would have nothing to do with assisting the British, and, perpetrating numerous acts of violence, sought the aid of Germany to gain an independent Irish republic. On April 24, 1916, the Sinn Feiners rebelled in Dublin against the British authorities, resulting in five days of heavy fighting. The rising was suppressed and many of the leaders were court-martialed and executed. The following is an account of this Easter Rebellion that appeared in the *Annual Register:*

We have now to deal with by far the most important and most disagreeable incident which occurred in English history in the course of the year. As early as March 4 *The Times* had published an article drawing attention to the growth of the Sinn-Fein movement in Ireland and commenting on the neglect of the Government to take strong measures for suppressing the disaffection which appeared to be brewing in that country. At length on the Tuesday after Easter the Secretary of the Admiralty announced that during the night of April 20 an attempt had been made to land arms and ammunition in Ireland by a vessel disguised as a neutral merchant ship, but in reality a German auxiliary, in conjunction with a German submarine. The auxiliary was sunk and a number of prisoners were made, among whom was Sir Roger Casement, who had already acquired an unenviable notoriety since the outbreak of the war owing to his endeavour to seduce Irish prisoners in Germany from their loyalty to the British Crown. The attempt to land arms in Ireland was evidently a preconcerted signal for a general rising, and on April 24 serious disturbances broke out in Dublin. A large body of men identified with the Sinn-Feiners, mostly armed, occupied Stephen's Green, and took forcible possession of the Post Office, where they cut the telegraphic and telephonic wires. Houses were also occupied in Stephen's Green, Sackville Street, Abbey Street, and along the quays. In the course of the day soldiers arrived from the Curragh, and fighting immediately began. The rebels made a half-hearted attack on Dublin Castle which, however, was not pressed through. They held up troops on their way from barracks, and fired on them from the windows of houses; but by the following day they had been driven out of Stephen's Green with a number of casualties, although they were still in occupation of various important buildings, including the Post Office, the City Hall, and the Law Courts. Reinforcements speedily arrived from Belfast and from England, and established a cordon round the centre of the town on the north bank of the river, entirely enclosing the area of the rebellion. By April 26 Liberty Hall, the head-quarters of the citizen army and formerly of Mr. Larkin, had been wholly or partially destroyed and occupied by the military. By this time the troops had suffered casualties to the extent of about 19 killed and 27 wounded.

Meanwhile, risings, although of a far less serious character, had taken place in other parts of Ireland, notably at Ardee in County Louth, and at Swords and Lusk, near Dublin. Moreover, on April 25 German warships once again succeeded in getting across the North Sea and bombarding Lowestoft and Yarmouth for about half an hour, doing, however, very little damage. The purpose of this useless raid was, no doubt, to cause the British Government to hesitate before sending large numbers of troops over to Ireland. On April 27 the situation seemed sufficiently serious to justify the Irish Executive in proclaiming martial law over the whole of Ireland, and Sir John Maxwell left London on that date with plenary powers over the whole country, the Irish Executive having placed themselves at his disposal to carry out his instructions. . . .

At midnight on April 28–29 an official communiqué was issued describing the progress of the operations for the suppression of the rebellion. By that time the organised forces of the rebels in Dublin were confined to a few localities, the principal one being the Sackville Street district where they had established their head-quarters in the General Post Office. The cordon of troops surrounding this district was gradually drawn closer, although outside the cordon there was not infrequent sniping from houses in which small parties of the rebels had established themselves in various parts of the city. During the last two days of April the back of the revolt was gradually broken. Large numbers of rebels surrendered in Dublin and more than 700 prisoners, including the Countess Markievicz, were captured. The Post Office was destroyed by the fire of the British guns and the leaders of the revolt sent orders to their adherents in Galway and other parts of the country to abandon their attempt and give themselves up to the military. On the evening of May 1 the Commander-in-Chief of the Home Forces was able to announce that all the rebels in Dublin had surrendered, and that the city was now quite safe. The rebels in the country districts were following suit, and gradually surrendering to the mobile columns which were sent in pursuit of them. At Enniscorthy the rebels during the night of April 30 offered to surrender their leaders and arms, on condition that the rank and file were allowed to return to their homes. This condition, of course, was not accepted, and on being informed that the only terms which could be entertained were unconditional, the rebels surrendered at 6 o'clock in the morning of May 1. The suppression in Dublin was not achieved without an immense destruction of property. It was believed that the number of rebels in action from start to finish was about 5,000, and the fighting resulted in the outbreak of fires in many parts of the city. At least twenty great business establishments, three branch banks, and dozens of smaller offices and shops were burnt to the ground, as well as the General Post Office already mentioned. The total number of buildings involved in the fires was stated to be 179 and the value of the buildings and their contents was estimated, roughly, at nearly 2,000,-000*l*. The area affected on the east side of Sackville Street comprised 27,000 square yards, and that on the west side 34,000 square yards. Outside this district the only important building lost was the Old Linenhall barracks which was fired by bombs thrown by the rebels. . . .

364. THE IRISH FREE STATE (AGREEMENT) ACT (1922)

1. Ireland shall have the same constitutional status in the Community of Nations known as the British Empire as the Dominion of Canada, the Commonwealth of Australia, the Dominion of New Zealand, and the Union of South Africa, with a Parliament having powers to make laws for the peace order and good government of Ireland and an Executive responsible to that Parliament, and shall be styled and known as the Irish Free State.

2. Subject to the provisions hereinafter set out the position of the Irish Free State in relation to the Imperial Parliament and Government and otherwise shall be that of the Dominion of Canada, and the law, practice and constitutional usage governing the relationship of the Crown or the representative of the Crown and of the Imperial Parliament to the Dominion of Canada shall govern their relationship to the Irish Free State.

3. The representative of the Crown in Ireland shall be appointed in like manner as the Governor-General of Canada, and in accordance with the practice observed in the making of such appointments.

4. The oath to be taken by Members of the Parliament of the Irish Free State shall be in the following form:—

> I . . . do solemnly swear true faith and allegiance to the Constitution of the Irish Free State as by law established and that I will be faithful to H.M. King George V., his heirs and successors by law in virtue of the common citizenship of Ireland with Great Britain and her adherence to and membership of the group of nations forming the British Commonwealth of Nations.

5. The Irish Free State shall assume liability for the service of the Public Debt of the United Kingdom as existing at the date hereof and towards the payment of war pensions as existing at that date in such proportion as may

be fair and equitable, having regard to any just claims on the part of Ireland by way of set off or counterclaim, the amount of such sums being determined in default of agreement by the arbitration of one or more independent persons being citizens of the British Empire.

6. Until an arrangement has been made between the British and Irish Governments whereby the Irish Free State undertakes her own coastal defence, the defence by sea of Great Britain and Ireland shall be undertaken by His Majesty's Imperial Forces, but this shall not prevent the construction or maintenance by the Government of the Irish Free State of such vessels as are necessary for the protection of the Revenue or the Fisheries. . . .

7. The Government of the Irish Free State shall afford to His Majesty's Imperial Forces:—

> (a) In time of peace such harbour and other facilities as are indicated . . . or such other facilities as may from time to time be agreed between the British Government and the Government of the Irish Free State; and
>
> (b) In time of war or of strained relations with a Foreign Power such harbour and other facilities as the British Government may require for the purposes of such defence as aforesaid. . . .

9. The ports of Great Britain and the Irish Free State shall be freely open to the ships of the other country on payment of the customary port and other dues. . . .

Since World War II there has been constant turmoil all over the world. Dozens of new states have emerged in Asia and Africa on the ruins of old colonial empires, and the resulting racial disturbances have bedeviled the world. Since 1945 Britain has been involved in two wars—one in Korea in 1950 and another in Egypt in 1956—and discord in the Far East, Middle East, Africa, and the Western Hemisphere has meant that Britain has had to develop foreign policies quite different from those of preceding decades. The subject of British foreign policy is so vast and complex that only an indication of its role in international relations can be suggested in the next three selections.

365. THE PACIFIC CHARTER (1954)

Desiring to establish a firm and lasting basis for common action to maintain peace and security in South-East Asia and the South-West Pacific, Australia, France, New Zealand, Pakistan, the Philippines, Thailand, the United Kingdom of Great Britain and Northern Ireland, and the United States agreed, in the Pacific Charter, to proclaim:

First, in accordance with the provisions of the United Nations Charter, they uphold the principle of equal rights and self-determination of peoples and they will earnestly strive by ever peaceful means to promote self-government and secure the independence of all countries whose people desire it and are able to undertake its responsibilities;

Second, they are prepared to continue taking effective practical measures to ensure conditions favourable to the orderly achievement of the foregoing purposes in accordance with their constitutional processes;

Third, they will continue to cooperate in the economic, social and cultural fields in order to promote higher living standards, economic progress and social well-being in this region;

Fourth, as declared in the South-East Asia Collective Defence Treaty, they are determined to prevent or counter by appropriate means any attempt in the treaty area to subvert their freedom or to destroy their sovereignty or territorial integrity.

366. THE GENEVA CONVENTION FOR THE AMELIORATION OF THE CONDITION OF THE WOUNDED AND SICK IN ARMED FORCES IN THE FIELD (1957)

The horror of war in the present century has repeatedly brought to mind the necessity of caring for the sick and wounded in the field. It is paradoxical that, on the one hand, man has contrived deadlier weapons of destruction, and, on the other hand, has sought ways to help those who have suffered because of them. The following document, a revision of the original Geneva Convention of 1929, has been of great assistance to the victims of declared war and other armed conflicts involving the signatories. It has also been referred to repeatedly in connection with the Vietnam war, the Congo, and other trouble spots in Africa and Asia.

The Convention shall . . . apply to all cases of partial or total occupation of the territory of a High Contracting Party, even if the said occupation meets with no armed resistance.

Although one of the Powers in conflict may not be a party to the present Convention, the Powers who are parties thereto shall remain bound by it in their mutual relations. They shall furthermore be bound by the Convention in relation to the said Power, if the latter accepts and applies the provisions thereof.

ARTICLE 3

In the case of armed conflict not of an international character occurring in the territory of one of the High Contracting Parties, each Party to the conflict shall be bound to apply, as a minimum, the following provisions:

(1) Persons taking no active part in the hostilities, including members of armed forces who have laid down their arms and those placed *hors de combat* by sickness, wounds, detention, or any other cause, shall in all circumstances be treated humanely, without any adverse distinction founded on race, colour, religion or faith, sex, birth or wealth, or any other similar criteria.

To this end, the following acts are and shall remain prohibited at any time and in any place whatsoever with respect to the above-mentioned persons:

(*a*) violence to life and person, in particular, murder of all kinds, mutilation, cruel treatment and torture;

(*b*) taking of hostages;

(*c*) outrages upon personal dignity, in particular, humiliating and degrading treatment;

(*d*) the passing of sentences and the carrying out of executions without previous judgment pronounced by a regularly constituted court, affording all the judicial guarantees which are recognised as indispensable by civilised peoples.

(2) The wounded and sick shall be collected and cared for. . . .

ARTICLE 12

Members of the armed forces and other persons mentioned in the following Article who are wounded or sick, shall be respected and protected in all circumstances.

They shall be treated humanely and cared for by the Party to the conflict in whose power they may be, without any adverse distinction founded on sex, race, nationality, religion, political opinions, or any other similar criteria. Any attempts upon their lives, or violence to their persons, shall be strictly prohibited; in particular, they shall not be murdered or exterminated, subjected to torture or to biological experiments; they shall not wilfully be left without medical assistance and care, nor shall conditions exposing them to contagion or infection be created.

Only urgent medical reasons will authorise priority in order of treatment to be administered.

Women shall be treated with all consideration due to their sex.

The Party to the conflict which is compelled to abandon wounded or sick to the enemy shall, as far as military considerations permit, leave with them a part of its medical personnel and material to assist in their care. . . .

ARTICLE 15

At all times, and particularly after an engagement, Parties to the conflict shall, without delay, take all possible measures to search for and collect the wounded and sick, to protect them against pillage and ill-treatment, to ensure their adequate care, and to search for the dead and prevent their being despoiled. . . .

ARTICLE 16

Parties to the conflict shall record as soon as possible, in respect of each wounded, sick or dead person of the adverse Party falling into their hands, any particulars which may assist in his identification.

These records should if possible include:

(a) designation of the Power on which he depends;

(b) army, regimental, personal or serial number;

(c) surname;

(d) first name or names;

(e) date of birth;

(f) any other particulars shown on his identity card or disc;

(g) date and place of capture or death;

(h) particulars concerning wounds or illness, or cause of death. . . .

ARTICLE 17

Parties to the conflict shall ensure that burial or cremation of the dead, carried out individually as far as circumstances permit, is preceded by a careful examination and if possible by a medical examination, of the bodies, with a view to confirming death, establishing identity and enabling a report to be made. One half of the double identity disc, or the identity disc itself if it is a single disc, should remain on the body.

Bodies shall not be cremated except for imperative reasons of hygiene or for motives based on the religion of the deceased. In case of cremation the circumstances and reasons for cremation shall be stated in detail in the death certificate or on the authenticated list of the dead.

They shall further ensure that the dead are honourably interred, if possible according to the rites of the religion to which they belonged, that their graves are respected, grouped if possible according to the nationality of the deceased, properly maintained and marked so that they may always be found. . . .

CHAPTER III.—MEDICAL UNITS AND ESTABLISHMENTS

ARTICLE 19

Fixed establishments and mobile medical units of the Medical Service may in no circumstances be attacked, but shall at all times be respected and protected by the Parties to the conflict. Should they fall into the hands of the adverse Party, their personnel shall be free to pursue their duties, as long as the capturing Power has not itself ensured the necessary care of the wounded and sick found in such establishments and units. . . .

ARTICLE 20

Hospital ships entitled to the protection of the Geneva Convention of 12th August, 1949, for the Amelioration of the Condition of Wounded, Sick and Shipwrecked Members of Armed Forces at Sea, shall not be attacked from the land. . . .

CHAPTER IV.—PERSONNEL

ARTICLE 24

Medical personnel exclusively engaged in the search for, or the collection, transport or treatment of the wounded or sick, or in the prevention of disease, staff exclusively engaged in the administration of medical units and establishments, as well as chaplains attached to the armed forces, shall be respected and protected in all circumstances.

ARTICLE 25

Members of the armed forces specially trained for employment, should the need arise, as hospital orderlies, nurses or auxiliary stretcher-bearers, in the search for or the collection, transport or treatment of the wounded and sick shall likewise be respected and protected if they are carrying out these duties at the time when they come into contact with the enemy or fall into his hands. . . .

ARTICLE 28

Personnel designated in Articles 24 and 26 who fall into the hands of the adverse Party, shall be retained only in so far as the state of health, the spiritual needs and the number of prisoners of war require.

Personnel thus retained shall not be deemed prisoners of war. Nevertheless they shall at least benefit by all the provisions of the Geneva Convention of 12th August, 1949, relative to the Treatment of Prisoners of War. Within the framework of the military laws and regulations of the Detaining Power, and under the authority of its competent service, they shall continue to carry out, in accordance with their professional ethics, their medical and spiritual duties on behalf of prisoners of war, preferably those of the armed forces to which they themselves belong. They shall further enjoy the following facilities for carrying out their medical or spiritual duties:

(a) They shall be authorised to visit periodically the prisoners of war in labour units or hospitals outside the camp. The Detaining Power shall put at their disposal the means of transport required. . . .

CHAPTER VI.—MEDICAL TRANSPORTS

Article 35

Transports of wounded and sick or of medical equipment shall be respected and protected in the same way as mobile medical units.

Should such transports or vehicles fall into the hands of the adverse Party, they shall be subject to the laws of war, on condition that the Party to the conflict who captures them shall in all cases ensure the care of the wounded and sick they contain. . . .

Article 36

Medical aircraft, that is to say, aircraft exclusively employed for the removal of wounded and sick and for the transport of medical personnel and equipment, shall not be attacked, but shall be respected by the belligerents, while flying at heights, times and on routes specifically agreed upon between the belligerents concerned. . . .

Unless agreed otherwise, flights over enemy or enemy-occupied territory are prohibited. . . .

In the event of an involuntary landing in enemy or enemy-occupied territory, the wounded and sick, as well as the crew of the aircraft shall be prisoners of war. The medical personnel shall be treated according to Article 24 . . . .

367. BRITAIN AND FOREIGN AFFAIRS (1964)

On December 16, 1964, Prime Minister Harold Wilson, speaking at length on the subject of foreign affairs, said:

It is clear to everybody that the problems that we are facing to-day and are likely to face in the future, as compared with those of 15 years ago, or 10 or even five years ago, or perhaps, even compared with a year ago, have changed in their nature, intensity and, not least of all, in their geographical location. There has been an evolution in Soviet thinking on war and co-existence, which we have debated in past decades. The Chinese have exploded a nuclear device. The United Nations has more than doubled in size as the Colonial empires have passed into history. We now have a situation in which Africa has more votes in the General Assembly than any other Continent.

These are the basic facts that we are facing in the world. But there is more to it than that. Since none of the traditional spoils of war . . . are obtainable with nuclear weapons, it is legitimate to hope that the nuclear bomb may have eliminated the likelihood of war between nuclear powers. . . .

Again, the political emancipation of Colonial Territories, while inevitable and desirable . . . has highlighted the fact that political freedom in their eyes is only a beginning, and, as I remember quoting in a little book that I wrote called *War on Want,* 11 years ago:

"Democracy is a word that rumbles meaninglessly in empty bellies"

a factor which has a growing emphasis in many of these countries in their attitude to world problems. . . . I think that the objectives for which we are all working in world affairs are clear. . . . We have to find means of strengthening our relations with our Allies and with our Commonwealth partners. . . . In doing this we have not only to avoid measures which lead to the spread of nuclear weapons, whether within or outside the Alliance; we must frame our policies in such a way as to provide copper-bottomed guarantees against such proliferation.

In our policies within the Alliance [NATO] and outside it we must do everything in our power to enable us to take advantage of the opportunities which I believe now present themselves for reducing tension between East and West. In particular, we must be on the watch for any opportunity for a new breakthrough in disarmament . . . .

We must ensure that the most effective machinery is created for stopping small wars from escalating into big ones, for quarantining small outbreaks of militarism or subversion, and we must be prepared to bring new thinking to the strengthening of the United Nations peace-keeping machinery. Because of Britain's world role we have to examine and, wherever necessary, strengthen our own ability to contribute to this task . . . . We have in addition to deal swiftly and effectively with the problem of providing some international safeguards to non-nuclear Powers against the danger which results from new nations developing nuclear power . . . .

The problem we are facing derives from the fact that alone in the world—apart from the United States and the U.S.S.R.—we are trying to maintain three roles. There is the strategic nuclear role. There is our conventional role within N.A.T.O., our commitment to the defence of Europe, to which we are committed by interest and by treaty. And there is our world role, one which no one in this House or indeed in the country, will wish us to give up or call in question . . . .

368. DISESTABLISHMENT OF THE CHURCH OF ENGLAND IN WALES (1914)

Both world wars in this century resulted partly in a social revolution in Britain that has largely eliminated class distinctions based on birth, titles and pronounced differences in personal wealth. At the same time, the egalitarianism that has characterized the rise of the common man has afforded mankind opportunities for better education, better health care, and greater freedom of thought than ever before. The remainder of the readings in this book deal with aspects of religion, education, and social welfare in Britain since the death of Queen Victoria.

In 1869 the Church of Ireland had been disestablished. Thereafter the Liberal party became increasingly the agent of Nonconformist interests, and, therefore, it advocated the disestablishment of the Church of England in Wales. Since the Welsh were mostly Liberals and Methodists, and were intensely nationalistic, their demands for complete religious freedom became a national and political as well as a religious issue. This statute, passed in 1914, disestablished the state church in Wales.

1. On the day after the expiration of six months, or such extended period as His Majesty may fix by Order in Council, . . . the Church of England, so far as it extends to and exists in Wales and Monmouthshire (in this Act referred to as the Church in Wales), shall cease to be established by law, and, . . . no person shall, after the passing of this Act, be appointed or nominated . . . by virtue of any existing right of patronage, to any ecclesiastical office in the Church in Wales.

2.—(1) On the date of disestablishment every cathedral and ecclesiastical corporation in the Church in Wales, whether sole or aggregate, shall be dissolved . . . .

3.—(1) As from the date of disestablishment ecclesiastical courts and persons in Wales and Monmouthshire shall cease to exercise any jurisdiction, and the ecclesiastical law of the Church in Wales shall cease to exist as law . . . .

369. HARROW PUBLIC SCHOOL

By the beginning of this century, a great variety of schools existed in England. There were the traditional "public schools" like Harrow, Eton, and Rugby; "voluntary" schools (usually Anglican) supported by Church funds and state grants; "board schools" established by the Forster Education Act of 1870, financed by local rates, and controlled by elected school boards which were largely dominated by Nonconformists; and a few technical schools founded by the new county councils. These several types of schools generally suffered from a lack of uniformity in standards, poor administration, and inadequate financing. The situation in the public school at Harrow in the late 1880's was cleverly described by Winston Churchill, and what he said of Harrow would have been equally true a generation later. Having attended two small schools at St. James and Brighton, he entered Harrow, of which he writes:

I had scarcely passed my twelfth birthday when I entered the inhospitable regions of examinations, through which for the next seven years I was destined to journey. These examinations were a great trial to me. The subjects which were dearest to the examiners were almost invariably those I fancied least. I would have liked to have been examined in history, poetry and writing essays. The examiners, on the other hand, were partial to Latin and mathematics. And their will prevailed. Moreover, the questions which they asked on both these subjects were almost invariably those to which I was unable to suggest a satisfactory answer. I should have liked to be asked to say what I knew. They always tried to ask what I did not know. When I would have willingly displayed my knowledge, they sought to expose my ignorance. This sort of treatment had only one result: I did not do well in examinations.

This was especially true of my Entrance Examination to Harrow. The Headmaster, Dr. Welldon, however, took a broad-minded view of my Latin prose: he showed discernment in judging my general ability. This was the more remarkable, because I was found unable to answer a single question in the Latin paper. I wrote my name at the top of the page. I wrote down the number of the question 'I'. After much reflection I put a bracket round it thus '(I)'. But thereafter I could not think of anything connected with it that

was either relevant or true. Incidentally there arrived from nowhere in particular a blot and several smudges. I gazed for two whole hours at this sad
spectacle: and then merciful ushers collected my piece of foolscap with all
the others and carried it up to the Headmaster's table. It was from these
slender indications of scholarship that Dr. Welldon drew the conclusion that
I was worthy to pass into Harrow. It is very much to his credit. It showed
that he was a man capable of looking beneath the surface of things: a man
not dependent upon paper manifestations. I have always had the greatest regard for him.

In consequence of his decision, I was in due course placed in the third,
or lowest, division of the Fourth, or bottom, Form. The names of the new
boys were printed in the School List in alphabetical order; and as my correct
name, Spencer-Churchill, began with an 'S,' I gained no more advantage
from the alphabet than from the wider sphere of letters. I was in fact only
two from the bottom of the whole school; and these two, I regret to say,
disappeared almost immediately through illness or some other cause . . . .

370. THE EDUCATION ACT OF 1902

By 1902 legislation in education was imperative because court decisions had
jeopardized the continuance of the secondary schools which the secular
school boards had been establishing extra-legally.

The Education Act of 1902, the chief provisions of which are given
below, provided a solution to this and other problems.

PART I.

LOCAL EDUCATION AUTHORITY.

1. For the purposes of this Act, the council of every county and of every
county borough shall be the local education authority:

Provided that the council of a borough with a population of over ten
thousand or of an urban district with a population of over twenty thousand
shall, as respects that borough or district, be the local education authority for
the purpose of Part III of this Act . . . .

PART II.

HIGHER EDUCATION.

2.—(1) The local education authority shall consider the educational
needs of their area and take such steps as seem to them desirable, after consultation with the Board of Education, to supply or aid the supply of educa-

tion other than elementary, and to promote the general co-ordination of all forms of education . . . .

4.—(1) A council, in the application of money under this Part of this Act, shall not require that any particular form of religious instruction or worship or any religious catechism or formulary which is distinctive of any particular denomination shall or shall not be taught, used or practised in any school, college or hostel aided but not provided by the council, and no pupil shall, on the ground of religious belief, be excluded from or placed in an inferior position in any school, college or hostel provided by the council, and no catechism or formulary distinctive of any particular religious denomination shall be taught in any school, college or hostel so provided . . . .

PART III.

ELEMENTARY EDUCATION.

5. The local education authority shall, throughout their area, have the powers and duties of a school board and school attendance committee under the Elementary Education Acts, 1870 to 1900, and any other Acts, including local Acts, and shall also be responsible for and have the control of all secular instruction in public elementary schools not provided by them; and school boards and school attendance committees shall be abolished . . . .

7.—(1) The local education authority shall maintain and keep efficient all public elementary schools within their area which are necessary, and have the control of all expenditure required for that purpose . . . .

371. THE EDUCATION ACT OF 1944

The Act of 1902 had abolished the special school boards and made the county councils and county borough councils responsible for all elementary and secondary education in all types of schools. Professor A. F. Havighurst rightly observes that the Act was "extraordinarily successful, made elementary education a right and not a charity, and made possible a systematic development of secondary education." The chief criticism of the Act was that it appeared to give Anglican religious instruction at public expense. Efforts were made in 1906 and in 1908 to reconcile Anglican, Nonconformist, and Catholic views, but they failed, as did another attempt in 1930. Increasing interest in improving educational opportunities for all resulted in the passage of the Education Act of 1944, the most important domestic legislation of the war years. As can be seen from the excerpts below, it reconstructed the primary and secondary educational systems of England and Wales, raised the age for leaving school from fourteen to sixteen by 1947, gave to all children over eleven free secondary education, and provided free lunches to all children in public primary and secondary schools.

PART I.

CENTRAL ADMINISTRATION.

1.—(1) It shall be lawful for His Majesty to appoint a Minister (hereinafter referred to as "the Minister"), whose duty it shall be to promote the education of the people of England and Wales and the progressive development of institutions devoted to that purpose, and to secure the effective execution by local authorities, under his control and direction, of the national policy for providing a varied and comprehensive educational service in every area. . . .

4.—(1) There shall be two Central Advisory Councils for Education, one for England and the other for Wales and Monmouthshire, and it shall be the duty of those Councils to advise the Minister upon such matters connected with educational theory and practice as they think fit, and upon any questions referred to them by him. . . .

PART II.

THE STATUTORY SYSTEM OF EDUCATION.

6.—(1) . . . the local education authority for each county shall be the council of the county, and the local education authority for each county borough shall be the council of the county borough. . . .

7. The statutory system of public education shall be organized in three progressive stages to be known as primary education, secondary education, and further education; and it shall be the duty of the local education authority for every area, so far as their powers extend, to contribute towards the spiritual, moral, mental, and physical development of the community by securing that efficient education throughout those stages shall be available to meet the needs of the population of their area.

PRIMARY AND SECONDARY EDUCATION.

8.—(1) It shall be the duty of every local education authority to secure that there shall be available for their area sufficient schools—

   (a) for providing primary education, that is to say, full-time education suitable to the requirements of junior pupils; and

   (b) for providing secondary education, that is to say, full-time education suitable to the requirements of senior pupils other than such full-time education as may be provided for senior pupils in pursuance of a scheme made under the provisions of this Act relating to further education;

and the schools available for an area shall not be deemed to be sufficient unless they are sufficient in number, character, and equipment to afford for all pupils opportunities for education offering such variety of instruction and training as may be desirable in view of their different ages, abilities, and aptitudes, and of the different periods for which they may be expected to remain at school, including practical instruction and training appropriate to their respective needs.

(2) In fulfilling their duties under this section, a local education authority shall, in particular, have regard—

(a) to the need for securing that primary and secondary education are provided in separate schools;

(b) to the need for securing that provision is made for pupils who have not attained the age of five years by the provision of nursery schools or, where the authority consider the provision of such schools to be inexpedient, by the provision of nursery classes in other schools;

(c) to the need for securing that provision is made for pupils who suffer from any disability of mind or body by providing, either in special schools or otherwise, special educational treatment, that is to say, education by special methods appropriate for persons suffering from that disability; and

(d) to secure the expediency of securing the provision of boarding accommodation, either in boarding schools or otherwise, for pupils for whom education as boarders is considered by their parents and by the authority to be desirable. . . .

9.—(2) Primary and secondary schools maintained by a local education authority, not being nursery schools or special schools, shall, if established by a local education authority or by a former authority, be known as county schools and, if established otherwise than by such an authority, be known as voluntary schools . . . .

(4) Primary schools which are used mainly for the purpose of providing education for children who have attained the age of two years but have not attained the age of five years shall be known as nursery schools.

(5) Schools which are especially organized for the purpose of providing special educational treatment for pupils requiring such treatment and are approved by the Minister for that purpose shall be known as special schools . . . .

10.—(1) The Minister shall make regulations prescribing the standards to which the premises of schools maintained by local education authorities are to conform . . . .

23.—(1) In every county school and . . . in every voluntary school except an aided secondary school, the secular instruction to be given to the pupils shall . . . be under the control of the local education authority . . . .

24.—(1) In every county school . . . and in every controlled school and special agreement school, the appointment of teachers shall . . . be under the control of the local education authority, and no teacher shall be dismissed except by that authority. . . .

(3) No woman shall be disqualified for employment as a teacher in any county or voluntary school, or be dismissed from such employment by reason only of marriage.

25.—(1) Subject to the provisions of this section, the school day in every county school and in every voluntary school shall begin with collective worship on the part of all pupils in attendance at the school, and the arrangements made therefore shall provide for a single act of worship attended by all such pupils unless, in the opinion of the local education authority or, in the case of a voluntary school, of the managers or governors thereof, the school premises are such as to make it impracticable to assemble them for that purpose. . . .

(4) If the parent . . . requests that he [the pupil] be wholly or partly excused from attendance at religious worship in the school, or from attendance at religious instruction in the school . . . then, until the request is withdrawn, the pupil shall be excused from such attendance accordingly. . . .

26. . . . the collective worship required by subsection (1) of the last foregoing section shall not, in any county school, be distinctive of any particular religious denomination. . . .

35. In this Act the expression "compulsory school age" means any age between five years and fifteen years. . . .

41. Subject as hereinafter provided, it shall be the duty of every local education authority to secure the provision for their area of adequate facilities for further education, that is to say:—

  (a) full-time and part-time education for persons over compulsory school age; and

  (b) leisure-time occupation, in such organized cultural training and recreative activities as are suited to their requirements. . . .

43.—(1) On and after such date as His Majesty may by Order in Council determine, not later than three years after the date of the commencement of this Part of this Act, it shall be the duty of every local education authority to establish and maintain county colleges, that is to say, centres approved by the Minister for providing for young persons who are not in full-time attendance at any school or other educational institution such further education, including physical and vocational training, as will enable them to develop their various aptitudes and capacities. . . .

48.—(1) It shall be the duty of every local education authority to provide for the medical inspection, at appropriate intervals, of pupils in attendance at any school or county college . . . .

49. Regulations made by the Minister shall impose upon local education authorities the duty of providing milk, meals and other refreshment for pupils . . . .

> Sections 50 through 55 provided for board and room for some pupils, clothing for those unable to afford it, recreational facilities, and cleanliness among students.

372. NATIONAL HEALTH INSURANCE

> The government gathered much evidence that the general health of the population was far from satisfactory. It was learned in 1935, for instance, that 62 per cent of the army recruits examined for induction could not pass the physical examination. This only pointed up the fact that the nation's health was not an individual, but a national problem. In 1911 Parliament had passed a law to provide insurance against loss of health and for the prevention and cure of sickness; ten years later it created a Ministry of Health. Agitation for more adequate health legislation steadily increased in the 1930's, and in 1942 the Beveridge Committee issued its *Report*, recommending, in part, the institution of a national health service. Within a year of the end of World War II, Parliament, controlled by the Labour government of Clement Attlee, passed the National Health Insurance Act, effective in 1948.

A. *The National Health Insurance Act* (1946)

> This is a long and complicated law running to eighty-four pages of close print. Its chief provisions have been summarized very well in a digest made by *Keesing's Contemporary Archives*.

Scope: The proposed main services are:

(1) Hospital and specialist services (i.e., all forms of general and special hospital supervision, including mental hospitals, together with sanatoria, maternity accommodation, treatment during convalescence, medical rehabilitation, and other institutional treatment), covering in- and out-patient

services, the latter including clinics and dispensaries operated as part of any specialist service. Specialist advice also to be made available, if necessary, at Health Centres and in the patient's home.

(2) Health Centers and general practitioner services (i.e., general personal health care by doctors and dentists of the patient's choice) to be available both from new publicly equipped Health Centres and from practitioners' surgeries [offices].

(3) Various supplementary services, including midwifery, maternity and child welfare, health visiting, home-nursing, a priority dental service for children and expectant and nursing mothers, domestic help (where needed on health grounds), vaccination, after-care of the sick, ambulance services, and blood transfusion and laboratory services.

(4) Provision of spectacles, dentures, etc., as well as drugs and medicines, at hospitals, Health Centres, clinics, pharmacies, and elsewhere.

Availability: All the service, or any part if it, to be available without any limitation to everyone in England and Wales . . . from a date to be declared by Order in Council; it is hoped that this will be at the beginning of 1948. . . .

I. *Hospital and Specialist Services*

Existing premises and equipment of voluntary and public hospitals, including mental hospitals and mental deficiency institutions, to be transferred to the Minister of Health, who is empowered also (a) to purchase . . . other hospitals and their equipment if required, (b) to except from transfer any particular hospital if not considered necessary for the service, with that institution's concurrence. . . .

Hospital Administration: Regional hospital boards will be set up for hospital service regions . . . . They will be composed of persons appointed by the Minister for their individual suitability, subject to consultation with university medical schools, the medical profession, local health authorities, and, initially, those with experience of the voluntary system . . . .

Each board will appoint local hospital management committees, one for each large hospital or related group of hospitals forming a . . . hospital service unit . . . .

II. *General Practitioner Services*

Health Centers: A main feature of the personal practitioner services, Health Centres will afford facilities for the general medical and dental services, many local authority clinic services, and for out-post clinics of the hospital and specialist services; they will also serve as bases for various health education activities . . . .

Family Doctor Service: All doctors will be entitled to take part in the new arrangements in the areas where they are already practising when the scheme begins, and will not be thereby debarred from continuing to treat private patients provided that the latter are not on their lists as public patients or on the lists of their partners in a Health Centre. People will be free to choose their own doctor subject to the doctor consenting and being in a position to undertake their care.

All doctors participating will be in contract with the Executive Council for their area: the Council will publish lists of all general practitioners wishing to participate. People will then choose their doctor and each doctor will have his list of patients whom he has agreed to attend; persons wishing to take advantage of the service who have not chosen a doctor, or who have been refused by the doctor they have chosen, will be allocated among the doctors in the area . . . .

Drugs, Medicines, and Appliances: Those using the general practitioner service will be entitled to the free supply of necessary drugs, medicines, and appliances. All qualified pharmacists will have the right to join the new service; the Executive Council in each area will publish a list of such pharmacists, and patients may obtain their supplies on the prescription of their doctor either from a pharmacy or from any Health Centre where dispensing services are provided. Drugs, medicines, and appliances required for hospital purposes will be supplied as part of the hospital service.

Dental Service: Priority will be given to expectant mothers and young people, through the local health authority's maternity and child welfare service . . . and through the school health services under the Education Act, 1944. Outside these arrangements, there will be a general dental service, but there will at first be no guarantee that all persons will be able to obtain full dental care without waiting. Any dentist will have the right to participate in the general dental service . . . .

Eye Services: The object is to secure that the care of the eyes, as well as sight-testing and the supply of spectacles, is carried out in special ophthalmic departments and clinics . . . of the hospital and specialist service. . . .

Efficient Service: A special tribunal will be set up to investigate cases where it is claimed . . . that the continued inclusion of any doctor, pharmacist, dentist, or optician in the lists . . . would prejudice the efficiency of the service. . . . If satisfied that the representations are justified, it will direct the Executive Council to remove from the list of his area the name of the doctor, dentist, pharmacist, or optician, who is given the right to appeal to the Minister. Where the tribunal so decides a similar direction can be applied to all lists in all areas, with the same right of appeal . . . .

Central Health Services Council: This will consist of 41 members of whom 6 will be the persons for the time being holding the offices of the President of the Royal College of Physicians of London, the President of the Royal College of Surgeons of England, the President of the Royal College of Obstetricians and Gynaecologists, the Chairman of the Council of the British Medical Association, the President of the General Medical Council, and the Chairman of the Council of the Society of Medical Officers of Health, ex officio; the remaining 35 members, to be appointed by the Minister, will include 15 medical practitioners (2 being mental specialists), 5 persons with experience in hospital management, 5 with experience in local government, 3 dental practitioners, 2 persons with experience in mental health services, 2 registered nurses, 1 certified midwife, and 2 registered pharmacists . . . .

The Financial Memorandum accompanying the Bill estimated the cost of the scheme in the early years at £152,000,000 a year, of which £95,000,000 will come from the Exchequer, £32,000,000 from National Insurance, and £25,000,000 from local rates. The Government will bear the full cost of the hospital and specialist services (estimated at £87,000,000) and of the family doctor, dentist, and pharmaceutical service (estimated at £45,000,000), as well as about half of the cost of the local health authority services (estimated at £6,000,000); the latter will be on a "weighted" 50 per cent basis, with no authority receiving more than 75 per cent or less than 37½ per cent of their expenditure . . . .

B. *General Acceptance of the N. H. I. Act*

The Act aroused either praise or denunciation for approximately two years after its passage. By 1948, however, the main provisions were generally recognized by both the public and the medical profession as being beneficial for all concerned. In its issue for November 16, 1948, the (London) *Evening Standard* cautioned physicians against continued capricious opposition.

Certainly the National Health Service Act is open to question in indi vidual details. Certainly there are dangers to be sedulously guarded against, of clogging medicine with the bureaucratic apparatus of departmental control. Yet the broad principles on which the Service is to be based command general assent and are for the general welfare. Moreover the measure has now become law, enacted by the elected legislature of the British people. The

supremacy of Parliament is not open to the challenge of the doctors . . . .
Effective government in a democratic country must be entirely dependent on
the loyalty with which the minority carry out the decisions of the majority.
The British Medical Association's leaders have had ample opportunity to
state their case . . . . Now they should have the honesty to acknowledge
that the fight is over. By persisting in stubborn faction they will forfeit the
sympathy and respect of the people.

C. *"The Economist" on the N. H. I. Act*

Once the decision to have a free national health service was taken, it
would be wrong to start any cheeseparing economies which would merely
exasperate doctors and patients. It would introduce a utility medical service
that would have an inferior status in the eyes of the general public who,
judged by the statistics, are at present prepared to regard the service favour-
ably. Nevertheless, its cost, both in money and manpower, should be carefully watched. If, as now seems likely, the estimates will be far exceeded,
people should be warned what the consequences of abusing the service may
be—that they may have to choose between better education for their children
and better medical treatment for themselves.

SOURCE REFERENCES   Chapter Eight

334. Fallodon, Viscount Grey of, *Twenty-Five Years 1892–1916,* I, 198–200. New York:
     Frederick A. Stokes, 1925.
335. *Parliamentary Debates* (Commons), vol. 318, pp. 2175–2176.
336. *Public General Acts,* 9 and 10 George V, CAP. 71.
337. *Public General Acts,* 1 and 2 George V, CAP. 13.
338. Woodward, E. L., *Short Journey,* pp. 115–116. New York: Oxford University Press,
     1946.
339. *British Record. Political and Economic Notes* (Supplement to No. 12), September
     14, 1964. Issued by British Information Services.
340. Fremantle, Anne, *This Little Band of Prophets. The British Fabians,* Appendix A,
     pp. 263–264. New York: New American Library, 1960.
341. Spender, *Life of Campbell-Bannerman,* II, 123.
342. *Public General Acts,* 6 Edward VII, CAP. 47.
343. *Public General Acts,* 6 Edward VII, CAP. 58.
344. *Public General Acts,* 8 Edward VII, CAP. 40.
345. *Public General Acts,* 8 Edward VII, CAP. 57.
346. *Public General Acts,* 1 and 2 George V, CAP. 50.
347. *Public General Acts,* 9 Edward VII, CAP. 7.
348. *Public General Acts,* 10 Edward VII, CAP. 8.

349. *Annual Register* (1926), pp. 49–55.

350. *Public General Acts*, 9 and 10 George VI, CAP. 59.

351. *British Record. Political and Economic Notes* (No. 9), May 10, 1966. Issued by British Information Services.

352. *British Record. Political and Economic Notes* (No. 15), September 26, 1966. Issued by British Information Services.

353. Spender, *Life of Campbell-Bannerman*, II, 8–9.

354. Grey of Fallodon, *Twenty-Five Years 1892–1916*, I, 5–7.

355. *Public General Acts*, 1 and 2 George V, CAP. 28.

356. *Public General Acts*, 4 and 5 George V, CAP. 87.

357. Grey of Fallodon, *Twenty-Five Years 1892–1916*, II, 15–16.

358. *Public General Acts*, 22 George V, CAP. 4.

359. *The New Statesman and Nation*, September 4, 1938, p. 450.

360. Henderson, Sir Neville, *Failure of a Mission, Berlin 1937–1939*, p. 272. New York: G. P. Putnam's Sons, 1940.

361. *Parliamentary Debates* (Commons), vol. 360, pp. 1501–1502.

362. *Parliamentary Debates* (Commons), vol. 362, pp. 60–61.

363. *Annual Register* (1916), pp. 118–120.

364. *British and Foreign State Papers*, CXVI, 87–89.

365. *British and Foreign State Papers*, CLXI, 371.

366. *Public General Acts*, 5 and 6 Elizabeth II, CAP. 52.

367. *Parliamentary Debates* (Commons), vol. 704, p. 415ff.

368. *Public General Acts*, 4 and 5 George V, CAP. 91.

369. Churchill, Winston S., *My Early Life: A Roving Commission*, pp. 15–16. New York: Charles Scribner's Sons, 1930.

370. *Public General Acts*, 2 Edward VII, CAP. 42.

371. *Public General Acts*, 7 and 8 George VI, CAP. 31.

372. A. *Keesing's Contemporary Archives*, April 27–May 4, 1946, pp. 7859–7861.
  B. *Evening Standard* (London), November 16, 1948.
  C. *The Economist*, September 4, 1948, p. 369.

Glossary

The following list of words and phrases found in the readings are those which will be unfamiliar to most students. In general, these items have been included because they cannot be found in an ordinary unabridged dictionary. Words whose meaning can be determined by pronunciation are not included even though their spellings are different from present usage.

apertlie openly
apostemations purulent tumors, abscesses
barm foamy yeast produced by fermenting malt liquors
bedels servitors, servants in a university
Berwick upon Tweed a town at the mouth of the Tweed River originally fortified as a bastion against the Scots, and, as such, organized as an extra-territorial community with a government of its own
bordar cotter who held a cottage at his liege lord's pleasure and rendered minimal service in return
bot compensation for an injury or wrong
braser one who works in brass
burh town
ceorl a freeman of the lowest class, above a slave and below a thane
channerin grumbler
chanons canons
churl villain, rude fellow
cimeter sword
clancular not regulated by authority
compertes facts, details
conies rabbits, skins or fur of rabbits
connigries rabbit runs
contumax contumacious
cornetcy of horse rank of the lowest cavalry officer
couchers slackers, registers or breviaries
covin secret agreement to defraud or injure
delyvyrit delivered
disherison act of cutting off from inheritance
duch duke

els others

essoine excuse for not appearing in court at an appointed time

eyre court held by an itinerant judge

feoffors those who invest others with fiefs (land)

fremd alien

gafol-land land that is let, leased, or rented

Grailes the Gradual, an antiphon sung between the Epistle and the Gospel

granges farms belonging to monasteries

groat coin of small value worth about four pence in 1351

halbergets weapons having battle-axes and pikes at the end of long staffs

harepipes traps for catching hares

haulte haughty, arrogant

he com nowdyr non sent dedyr nowt zyt he came not here nor was sent here at any time

higler seller of provisions from door to door or one who buys livestock and fattens it for the market

holpyn helped

horse-courser a jobbing dealer in horses

Jurats magistrates or jurors

kailes game of ninepins

kyen cows

kyt cut

lastage toll paid by traders attending fairs and markets

liesings freemen

logge lodge

maingierres managers

mainprize to procure the release of a prisoner by becoming "surety" for his appearance at a specified time

master hine master of servants, domestics, or laborers

meres small lakes, ponds, or sheets of standing water

m'oney (moneywort) a European creeping plant with yellow flowers

moral Coventry ("go to Coventry") ostracism

mortlings wool plucked from a dead sheep

morphew an eruptive cutaneous disease marked by toughened, pigmented areas and scales

morth-workers murderers

nowdyr *See* **he com** . . .

noysyd nothing to do with

obits burial services

oyer and determiner commissions to magistrates to hear and determine cases in court

paneles caked variety of brown sugar

pantiles roofing tiles

paxes crusty pieces of bread, or unleavened bread used in Communion

phthisic respiratory ailment akin to asthma

pies ordinals

pillor plunderer

Pinaces small light vessels

pixes sacred vessels in which Communion hosts are preserved

pontage bridge toll or tax, or a tax assessed for repairing a bridge

portuasses portable breviaries

praepostor monitor

prestis handy, quick, fast

pulters dealers in fowl ready for cooking

queckboard board placed on the neck of a goose to make him quack

reaver freebooter

reeveship office of a chief magistrate in a town or district appointed to keep the
peace and to hold the local court or folkmoot

relyqwis relics

reprizes blame, reproaches

rereward rear of forces in battle formation

sarpler coarse sacking cloth

saucelin swelling of the face accompanied by inflammation.

servi servants, slaves

shorling pelt of sheep shorn while alive

simnel a brittle cake

socowryd succoured, helped

stallage tax or toll levied for the right to keep a stall at a fair or market

staminium thread hanging from the distaff, which is the staff from which flax is
drawn in spinning

stapela post, stake

staith wharf

syke ditch, trench

teagle lift

tenure in capite the mode by which a man holds an estate in land directly of the
crown, whether by knight's service or socage

thilke that

tilers layers of tile, tillers of soil

toc hoys took his

todyr other

trough truth

uncomes an ulcerous swelling

unqueraunce inquiry

wapentakes divisions of the shire in northern England synonymous with the hundred
in the rest of Engand

weche to save, to be sure

wether castrated ram

white-tawers tanners

wite punishment, penalty or fine imposed as punishment for a crime

wyrd fate, destiny

zyt unless, time